WHAT · E'ER · THOU · ART
ACT · WELL · THY · PART

David O. McKay

WHAT · E'ER · THOU · ART
ACT · WELL · THY · PART

The Missionary Diaries
of
DAVID O. McKAY

Edited by
Stan Larson
and
Patricia Larson

With Essays by
Marion D. Hanks
Leonard J. Arrington
and
Eugene England

Blue Ribbon Books
Salt Lake City

∞ *What E'er Thou Art, Act Well Thy Part: The Missionary Diaries of David O. McKay* was printed on acid-free paper, and meets the permanence of paper requirements of the American National Standard for Information Sciences. This book was printed in the United States of America.

04 03 02 01 00 99   6 5 4 3 2 1

LIBRARY OF CONGRESS CATALOGING-IN-PUBLICATION DATA

McKay, David Oman, 1873-1970.
 What e'er thou art act well thy part : the missionary diaries of David O. McKay / edited by Stan Larson and Patricia Larson.
   p. cm.
 Includes bibliographical references and index.
 ISBN 0-9634732-9-8 (alk. paper)
 ISBN 1-890686-01-8 (leather)
 1. McKay, David Oman, 1873-1970--Diaries. 2. Missionaries--Scotland--Diaries.   3. Missionaries--United States--Diaries.   4. Mormons--Scotland--Diaries.   5. Scotland--Church history--19th century--Sources. 6. Church of Jesus Christ of Latter-day Saints--Scotland--History--Sources. 7. Mormon Church--Scotland--History--Sources. I. Larson, Stan. II. Larson, Patricia, 1948-. III. Title.
BX8693.M3 1999
266' .93' 092--dc21   98-11619
 [B]   CIP

www.freethinkerpress.com

WHAT · E'ER · THOU · ART
ACT · WELL · THY · PART

Inscription over the Door of a Home in Stirling, Scotland, in 1898

This Book is Dedicated to

F. NEPHI GRIGG

who was President of the LDS Scotland Mission
when the original stone with the inscription
"What E'er Thou Art Act Well Thy Part"
was moved from the mission home
in Edinburgh to its present
home in Salt Lake City
in mid-1970.

TABLE OF CONTENTS

ILLUSTRATIONS

THE SOUL OF A PROPHET[1]

Marion D. Hanks

IT IS SAID that a great man is "one of those rare souls who sees sermons in stones and books in brooks and the bright light of God over everything. Across a reverently gentle lifetime he has had eyes to see and ears to hear music which most of us miss." It could be as well said, and maybe better said, of President David O. McKay as of any other man

In the clarity of his vision, the keenness of his intellect, the scope of his knowledge, the depth of his wisdom, David O. McKay stands a paragon. Poets, philosophers, prophets, all are within his ken—their thoughts stored in his memory through hours invested and hard labors performed. His perceptive mind, his noble character, his generous nature have translated, refined, applied, made wisdom the amalgam of his learning and his love. To him the words of a friend seem particularly appropriate: "I gave it and gave it and gave it until it was mine."

What to President McKay has mattered most? Wherein has been the emphasis? Recall the teachings of his great ministry, his instructions to his people. These few I note: faith in God and Christ; a Christ-like character; living outside one's self in love; a life worthy of trust, a clean and wholesome life; nobility of soul; education, discipline of the mind; cultivation of the beautiful and the uplifting; wise courtship, good marriage, family unity, family prayer; the sanctity of the home; honoring womanhood and motherhood; exemplary manhood; honoring parents and heritage; courtesy, good manners, gentility; hard work, service above self; true patriotism, love of country; every member a missionary; teaching that which has come to him from God.

How well President McKay has applied his ideals, fleshed in their skele-

---

[1]This essay is reprinted from Marion D. Hanks, "The Soul of a Prophet," *The Improvement Era* 71 (September 1968): 3-5, with the permission of the Church of Jesus Christ of Latter-day Saints.

ton, breathed into them the spirit of life! Rather than describe, let me illustrate with these incidents from my own experience.

One morning in the temple as President McKay addressed all the brethren who had come, fasting and praying, to prepare for a general conference, he calmly appraised them and then said something so simple that any one of us might have thought of it, yet none likely would have. He did, and I have not forgotten the feeling as I looked at him and heard him say (and I must paraphrase for want of specific words, but I think I have not forgotten), "We have met this morning with our bodies cleansed and clothed in clean linen, our minds prepared, our spirits subdued, to await the direction of the Lord." Would this be a good pattern for living every day for every man?

His consideration is unfailing, his courtesy also. Recently I talked with him in his office, entering to find him seated as usual behind his desk. He had not been feeling well; he was not strong. To another person in such circumstances, it possibly would not have occurred to try to rise to greet a visitor, but I had to all but restrain President McKay as he fought to get to his feet to bid me welcome. That sweet experience brought a tear to my eye.

It led me to remember another day during the first months of my ministry when I had been asked to speak at a Primary general conference. Thinking myself to be free on the appointed day, I had accepted an invitation to address the opening meeting and was distressed then to receive an invitation to attend at the same hour the regular pre-conference meeting of the brethren in the temple, which was called a little earlier than usual. When the ladies learned of this conflict, they were, of course, concerned, their program having been prepared and printed and therefore difficult to change.

I asked the counsel of several other good men, President McKay being away for the moment, and was assured by each that it was my responsibility to be at the meeting in the temple, notwithstanding my commitment to the Primary people, and I sorrowfully prepared to do that.

When President McKay returned, I had occasion to mention the dilemma to him. His immediate answer was to reassure me that I must be at the meeting to which I had committed myself and that I should so inform the ladies.

In the temple on the appointed day President McKay arose and announced to all the brethren in the beginning that I had been committed to a Primary appointment, and then he rearranged that whole meeting in order that I, the least of them, and certainly the least important, might be in attendance for the sacred purposes that had brought us together. And then I was excused to fulfill my commitment. It seemed a small thing, but not to me; and I wondered, I confess, what other man would have been so gracious and so considerate under those circumstances.

To some, on occasions, an interview may seem like an interrogation or even an inquisition. Occasionally honest persons are alienated because they resent the nature of the questions asked, or the attitude of the interviewer.

One of the sweet aspects of an interview with President McKay, as anyone knows who has had the experience, is that while one is with him he has the full attention—the eyes, the ears, the interested heart—of a great man. I shall never forget an important interview I had with the President of the Church. I have never seen fit to discuss it in detail in public, and I do not intend to do so now, but I would simply like to note the nature of his questions and the spirit of the man who asked them. It was a forthright and intensive interview, but it was an exchange, and the questions that brought from me what he wanted to hear were questions like this (not the nature of his asking): "Are you fully loyal to your family?" "Are there any improper involvements or alliances outside your home?" "Are there any unresolved problems in your life?" Who could resent or who could answer falsely such gracious and gentle and courteous questions?

Two other incidents bespeak clearly the wholeness, the wholesomeness, and the inspiration with which God has blessed this great man.

I was leaving for Vietnam shortly before the Christmas season. I had a brief interview with President McKay to receive a message he wanted carried to our men in the bush and the rice paddy. He kept me longer than I had intended, anxious to hear, apparently, my plans and prospects for this mission. Interestingly, he did not commiserate with me or sympathize a bit when he learned that the projected absence might involve the holiday season away from my family. What he said was, "What a wonderful privilege for you to be going!"

When we were through, that great hand reached out and touched me lightly on the knee, and he said something that seemed to me to summarize the glory of his ministry and a noble lifetime. "Tell them of this exchange of love," he said. "Tell them of this exchange of love." It was not the words of love to which he was referring, but the sweetness and beauty of the feeling in his heart, which I am sure he knew was reciprocated in my own. I wonder if that is not really what life is all about—to have the capacity to feel and the strength to communicate—to exchange love.

An appropriate estimate of President David O. McKay was given by a prominent labor leader [Walter Reuther] whom I was privileged to escort to an interview with him, together with the man's wife and two daughters. It was a remarkable experience—there was laughter, good humor, sometimes conversation that seemed a little light, sometimes very serious, in this half hour or so. All of us enjoyed the interview; there was no posturing, no posing, no declaiming—just the simple, warm, generous, inspired friendliness exuding and expressing itself.

When we left the room, the man and his family were all in tears, and I listened to this internationally famous man say these interesting words: "I have enjoyed the experience of meeting with kings and rulers, and I have seen leaders of many kinds in many lands, but I have never met a man like that. I don't believe our generation will ever produce a man like that." Later he repeated this statement to a group of university professors in the city, complimenting them on the blessing of living in an area near the available influence of the greatest man he had ever met.

It was said of prophets long ago, and it can be said with equal validity of David O. McKay:

> And . . . [he] did walk in the ways of the Lord, and he did keep his commandments, and he did judge righteous judgments . . . (Mosiah 29:43).
> And they did wax strong in love toward [him]; yea, they did esteem him more than any other man . . . (Mosiah 29:40).
> . . . and this was [his] faith . . . , and his heart did glory in it; . . . in doing good, in preserving his people, yea, in keeping the commandments of God, yea, and resisting iniquity. Yea, verily, verily I say unto you, if all men had been, and were, and ever would be, like unto [this man], behold, the very powers of hell would have been shaken forever; yea, the devil would never have power over the hearts of the children of men (Alma 48:16-17).

AN APPRECIATION OF DAVID O. MCKAY[1]

Leonard J. Arrington

FROM 1951 TO 1970 the president of the LDS Church was David O. McKay. A native of Huntsville, Utah, a lover of horses and fast-driving cars, McKay had been sustained to the Quorum of Twelve Apostles in 1906 and served until 1934 when he became a member of the First Presidency. He remained as a counselor in that body until 1951, when he was sustained as president. Tall, dignified, with wavy white hair and penetrating, smiling, brown eyes, he looked and acted like a prophet. I very much admired him. He was an effective speaker, and I heard him in stake conferences, at college commencements, and at other special occasions. When McKay was of advanced age, the Church leased a spacious apartment on the southeast corner of the eighth floor of the Hotel Utah as a home for the McKays. One morning McKay, returning from a meeting in the temple, stepped into the elevator, and just after him went a man with his young son. Delighted to see the president, the man said, 'James, this is President David O. McKay, our beloved prophet. This may be your last chance to meet him; he's a very old man." (The president was 94.) President McKay grinned and said, "Don't be alarmed at my future, son. Very few men die at age 94."[2]

McKay, a strong believer in education, refused to sanction Joseph Fielding Smith's extreme anti-evolution views, expressed admiration for liberal-thinking Mormon philosophers William H. Chamberlain and Sterling McMurrin, thought science blended beautifully with Mormonism, and encouraged freedom of opinion and speech. Although, as one of his sons

---

[1]This essay is reprinted from Leonard J. Arrington, *Adventures of a Church Historian* (Urbana: University of Illinois Press, 1998), 41-42, with the permission of the University of Illinois Press.

[2]Leonard J. Arrington and Heidi S. Swinton, *The Hotel: Salt Lake's Classy Lady, The Hotel Utah, 1911-1986* (Salt Lake City: Westin Hotel Utah, 1986), 56.

told me, he was sometimes "arrogant" and subject to "toadyism," we always saw him with a big smile and a saving sense of humor; he had a benevolent spirit and a tolerant attitude toward creative Mormon intellectuals. Some of his sermons and personal declarations acknowledged and affirmed intellectual diversity. A good friend related an experience with McKay at a reception. In a moment of courage, the hostess served rum cake. All the guests hesitated, watching to see what McKay would do. He smacked his lips and began to eat. One guest gushed, "But President McKay, don't you know that is rum cake?" McKay smiled and reminded the guest that the Word of Wisdom forbade drinking alcohol, not eating it.

I listened carefully to his sermons and believed him to be an excellent role model—a splendid exemplar of the teaching that "the glory of God is intelligence" (D&C 93:36), a motto especially popular during his presidency. Above all, his talks were well-organized, impressively delivered, full of substance, and resonant with sound advice and gems of inspiration. McKay represented, for me, the "voice of gladness" spoken of in the Doctrine and Covenants—a "voice of mercy from heaven; and a voice of truth out of the earth" (D&C 128:19). He was a true prophet. When he talked, as Laurel Thatcher Ulrich has written, there was "an infusion of the Spirit, a kind of Pentecost that for a moment dissolved the boundaries between heaven and earth and between present and past . . . a re-experiencing of the events [that happened to] the early Saints."[3]

---

[3]Laurel Thatcher Ulrich, "Lusterware," in *A Thoughtful Faith: Essays on Belief by Mormon Scholars*, ed. Philip L. Barlow (Centerville, UT: Canon Press, 1986), 203.

THE PLACE OF DAVID O. McKAY IN MORMON CULTURE

Eugene England

W HEN MY WIFE Charlotte and I were called as missionaries to Samoa in the spring of 1954, we had no specific sense of the important changes David O. McKay was already making in the LDS Church or of the unique cultural legacy he would create. But when he visited Samoa in January 1955 as part of his third major tour abroad since becoming president in 1951, we met him for the first time and got a direct exposure to his charismatic style and its unusual combination of qualities. Right away we saw that he remembered Samoan phrases and protocol from his first visit thirty-four years before. Then we watched him participate with impressive self-assurance and graciousness in the *fesilafa'iga fa'atupu*, a formal "kava" ceremony originally designed for visiting kings, at which he was welcomed by Samoan royalty and church leaders, Methodist and Catholic as well as Mormon.

The Samoa *kava* ceremony is both stately and sacred, a combination of parliamentary welcome and high mass, with long, poetic orations by "talking chiefs"—orators appointed and trained in the traditional mythic allusions and "respect language" of formal diplomacy—followed by the highly ritualistic drinking of a tangy, slightly anesthetic potion made from the root of the *'ava* plant. Eighty-one-year-old President McKay sat cross-legged for hours on woven mats in the magnificently decorated open-sided chiefs' *fale* near the mission home, as this ceremony unfolded, with us missionaries gathered around the outside, listening raptly. He responded to the speeches by admiring the chiefs' ornate costumes and praising their traditions, including the stylized speeches reflecting their royal rank, and then reminded them that there was one thing greater—their shared Christian faith and various callings in that faith. When the *kava* cup was passed to him, he deftly performed the ceremonial flourish of dribbling a few drops on the ground first and drank the mouth-numbing drink right down. We missionaries were mildly shocked, but impressed, by that and also when he drank the Samoan "cocoa" at the feast given him later. Both of these were liquids we had told each other, even though we drank them to be polite, might violate the church's Word of Wisdom regarding alcohol and caffeine-laden "hot drinks"—and would be avoided by the prophet.

During the next three days of conferences and testimony meetings President and Sister McKay often strolled around the grounds of the mission home, talking with the saints and with missionaries. At one point he took Charlotte and me aside and asked us very pointed questions about our experiences and our opinions concerning how the work was going, how Samoans were responding and were being treated. Then at the huge farewell gift-giving ceremony President McKay spontaneously displayed the combination of charismatic and humane, traditional and innovative, qualities that are his unique legacy. He and Sister McKay sat with the mission president and Samoan church leaders while the members of each church congregation paraded across a large lawn their variety of gifts, most prominently the huge, precious, finely woven and decorated mats called 'ietoga and bolts of colorfully dyed bark cloth, and then piled them at his feet before breaking into a farewell song.

When all had come forward and were gathered in a huge group seated on the ground before him, President McKay arose and picked up two of the gifts, a carved six-foot staff and a large fly whisk, woven of coconut husk string, both of which he had seen the orators use as they spoke in the *kava* ceremony. He stood forth, taller than the staff and with those waves of white hair curling back above his ears and shining in the tropical sun, held the staff before him, and swung the whisk over his left shoulder in the precise ceremonial fashion. Then he proceeded to bless the people and prophesy their future, including a temple to be built near them. A new place was carved out in my soul by that combination of generous respect for the Samoans' traditions and devout attention to the orthodox ideas and experiences that would bring them salvation.

Nearly fourteen years later, when he was ninety-five, President McKay touched me with that same combination of generous spiritual charisma and openness with orthodox confession and insight I had seen in Samoa. In a speech at the October 1968 general conference read by his son David Lawrence, he told how he had struggled in vain all through his teenage years to get God to declare to him the truth of his revelation to Joseph Smith. He had ridden his horse out into the sagebrush hills around Huntsville, got on his knees, and prayed, "fervently and sincerely," but had to admit always that "no spiritual manifestation had come to me." The admission was somewhat surprising—but also reassuring—to the many of us who had been conditioned to expect that anyone who asks sincerely will be able to receive a divine confirmation of truth and yet knew in our hearts that it was not always that easy.

President McKay told how he continued to seek truth and to serve

others in the Church, going on a mission to Scotland mainly because he
trusted his parents that it would be a good thing to do. There, late in his
mission, he received the witness he had sought, and in his description and
analysis of the experience, which is much more full than you will find in his
modest journal entry for 29 May 1899, he notes that it came indirectly,
through being in the right place, humbly serving, rather than through direct
pleading with God:

> The spiritual manifestation for which I had prayed as a boy in my
> teens came as a natural sequence to the performance of duty. For, as the
> apostle John declared, "If any man will do his will, he shall know of the
> doctrine, whether it be of God, or whether I speak of myself" (John
> 7:17).
>   Following a series of meetings at the conference held in Glasgow,
> Scotland, was a most remarkable priesthood meeting. I remember, as if
> it were yesterday, the intensity of the inspiration of that occasion. Every-
> body felt the rich outpouring of the Spirit of the Lord. All present were
> truly of one heart and one mind. Never before had I experienced such an
> emotion. It was a manifestation for which as a doubting youth I had
> secretly prayed most earnestly. . . .
>   During the progress of the meeting, an elder on his own initiative
> arose and said, "Brethren, there are angels in this room." Strange as it
> may seem, the announcement was not startling; indeed, it seemed wholly
> proper, though it had not occurred to me [that] there were divine beings
> present. I only knew that I was overflowing with gratitude for the pres-
> ence of the Holy Spirit.[1]

This "confession" by President McKay, which I later learned he had expressed before but at that time struck me as a crucial testament at the end
of his life, profoundly influenced the development of my testimony. I
realized that my own spiritual manifestations had come, not by direct seeking, but indeed "as a natural sequence to the performance of duty." I was
reassured that such divine affirmations were possible though they might be
seldom and slow in coming—and that they would most likely come as a by-
product of my efforts to serve, to know, even to love, very different people
from myself. I was beginning to understand why the Church, through the
context it provided of learning to love unconditionally through lay service,
was as true as the gospel.

McKay Both Conservative and Liberal

The place of David O. McKay in Mormon culture can be measured by
the unprecedented growth in both size and positive reputation of the
Church during his nearly twenty years as president. From 1951 to 1970
members increased from 900,000 to nearly three million, but even more

---

[1]*The Improvement Era* 71 (December 1968): 85. Note that with characteristic restraint
he does not, in the diary entry or the later elaboration, claim to have seen the guardian angels
himself—only that he felt the Holy Spirit in a way that finally met his need for confirmation.

dramatic was the change in the public perception of Mormonism—from a small, "peculiar," and somewhat paranoid Utah sect to a respected, genuinely Christian worldwide religion, with temples reaching out to New Zealand and Switzerland and dominating the skyline of Los Angeles and Oakland, with a world-traveling president who was praised and sought out for counsel by people as diverse as Dale Carnegie, Cecil B. DeMille, Walter Reuther, and Lyndon B. Johnson.

President McKay embodied that new image in his own person—caught perfectly in the portrait of him by Alvin L. Gittins, at ease in formal evening wear but still very much the prophet with his flowing mane of white hair and gracious, penetrating eyes. He was very tall, even imposing, known to be a rugged outdoorsman who continued while president to work on his family ranch in Huntsville and to ride his beloved horse Sonny Boy into his nineties—and to enjoy tooling around the Wasatch front in his big Cadillac. He was witty and literate and urbane, the most directly attractive Mormon prophet since Joseph Smith. By 1968 he was voted in a Gallup Poll as second only to Cardinal Cushing among the world's "most admired men" in the field of religion.

In order to explore this important change in image and its legacy in Mormon culture, I will look inward, into my heart and those of people like me who grew up in the 1950s and 1960s and still consider David O. McKay "our" president, into the Church I am devoutly part of and the culture I love and criticize—and also into his Scottish missionary diaries which are here published for the first time and which reveal with remarkable clarity the developing qualities of an extraordinary young man. I will explore what in that missionary experience shapes and reveals the future prophet and what he continues to mean to us.

My central and crucial purpose is that "conservative," "moderate," even "liberal," be seen as good words to describe the great range of his ideas and the unique qualities of his character, not as limiting labels. Certainly President McKay was a conservative. He was, in terms of Webster's definitions, "disposed to maintain existing views, conditions, or institutions" and inclined to "traditional norms of taste, elegance, style, and manners." He was also a classical liberal—and clearly the most liberal of any Mormon Prophet in the twentieth century. Yet his brand of liberality contradicts the current derogatory definition of "liberal" (as dangerously unorthodox, even immoral) that has made the term one of the unfortunate casualties in the culture wars of the past fifteen years—in both American and Mormon culture. President McKay was a "liberal" because (again using Webster's definitions) he was both "marked by generosity and openhandedness" and inclined toward "belief in progress, the essential goodness of man, and the autonomy of the individual [and] protection of political and civil liberties." At the same time his teachings focused (as all of his collections of sermons and writings amply show) on the core of the Mormon orthodoxy established by Joseph Smith and Brigham Young: the literal, physical existence of a God in whose image all humans are made and whose essential qualities all humans can emulate; a divine Savior, Jesus Christ, who both lived for our example the ideal life and suffered and died to provide means that we can overcome sin and live eternally; the family as the model for earthly happiness and literal heavenly existence; and the responsibility of all Mormons to share with their neighbors these divine and essential truths. Phrases he used that express such central orthodox ideas have become Mormon adages, such as "What e'er thou art, act well thy part," "No other success can compensate for failure in the home," and "Every member a missionary."

In the past ten years in America, both "conservatives" and "liberals" have misused those terms to attack each other rather than merely to describe tendencies or approaches in our political and cultural life—different approaches that, traditionally, through dialogue and compromise, have helped our system be progressive and yet stable. Liberals have used "conservative" to imply racist, sexist, and ignorant. Conservatives have used "liberal" to mean thoughtless revolutionaries bent on destroying morality and government responsibility—and such demonizing has crept over into Mormon culture, where both groups have let "conservative" mean devout (even self-righteous) and "liberal" mean rebellious (even libertine). President McKay's unique place in twentieth-century Mormon culture was to demonstrate, especially during his nineteen-year presidency, that a person could be both conservative and liberal—and all the while entirely faithful and orthodox. His greatest legacy could be to help us return to that traditional understanding and end the culture wars in a genuinely united and diverse Mormonism, made stronger by an inclusive interaction between believing, equally orthodox and mutually accepting, liberals and conservatives.

Conservative is the right word to describe President McKay's emphasis on the forty-year-old doctrine that converts, rather than "gathering to Zion" in Utah, should stay in their home countries and "build Zion" in the growing new stakes there. Liberal describes how he reinvigorated that traditional emphasis not only by telling the Saints to remain at home but by building and dedicating, on his world tours, fine new chapels throughout Europe and Asia, beginning, appropriately, with the one in Glasgow, Scotland, where he had served in 1897-1899. Liberal is also the right word for his less obvious influence, on church actions and statements throughout his presidency, that prepared Mormons to accept civil rights for all and eventually equal religious rights for Blacks and that allowed Mormons to see sexuality as contributing positively to marriage, beyond having children, and even to practice birth control. Conservative is the best word for his constant emphasis on a stable, self-sacrificing marriage and self-disciplined personal morality as the foundation of a good society, liberal for his remarkable resistance to dogmatism about such things as evolution and his willingness to break a rule rather than break a heart.

President McKay was identified from the first by non-Mormons as representing a change from the more "conservative," even "dogmatic" image of the Church and its leadership. *Newsweek* on his appointment in April 1951 noted that some expected he would "keep the church clear of politics, gradually withdraw it from the business field, and concentrate on converts."[2]   Catholic sociologist Thomas O'Dea wrote in his book *The Mormons* in 1957 that "while a man genuinely respected by all groups within the church, [he] is not unfriendly to the liberals . . . [and seems] to have introduced a degree of flexibility in religious thought into the sphere of official acceptability."[3] In 1970, at his death, *Time* noted his "gentleness and good humor . . . an affable new image of Mormonism. . . . He was perhaps the first Mormon president to treat non-Mormons as generously as members of his own faith."[4]

However, Richard N. Armstrong argues that the dramatic growth in numbers and favorable public image of Mormonism in the 1950s and 1960s was a direct result of President McKay's personal charisma and the powerful influence of his effectively expressed ideas *upon Mormons themselves*, rather than upon others. In his book, *The Rhetoric of David O. McKay*, Armstrong claims this influence "resulted in his own followers becoming more committed to the Church and, therefore, more willing to share their faith with nonmember friends."[5]

Armstrong shows convincingly that both the ideas and the elements of that charismatic influence were highly orthodox. Through an analysis of the 107 general conference talks President McKay delivered, Armstrong demonstrates what his central themes were. Armstrong also reminds us that the rhetorical force of these ideas derived from their being ideas that were already believed firmly by Mormons and also shared by many other Christians.

Finally Armstrong argues that President McKay's remarkable impact was enhanced by the unique power of his calm, literate, but very personal, even homespun, style and especially the accumulating charisma of both folklore about him and of his own modestly described but clearly divine experiences. These included his being told on his mission that someday he would "sit in the leading councils of the Church,"[6] his bringing a dead boy to life on his first visit to Samoa in 1921, his "prayer under a pepper tree" in Hawaii on that same trip that produced dramatic spiritual manifestations

---

[2]*Newsweek* 37 (16 April 1951): 92.

[3]Thomas F. O'Dea, *The Mormons* (Chicago: University of Chicago Press, 1957), 231.

[4]*Time* 95 (2 February 1970): 49-50.

[5]Richard N. Armstrong, *The Rhetoric of David O. McKay, Mormon Prophet* (New York: Peter Lang, 1993), 2.

[6]*The Deseret News*, Church Section, 27 October 1934, quoted in *Cherished Experiences from the Writings of President David O. McKay*, comp. by Clare Middlemiss (Salt Lake City: Deseret Book Co., 1955), 14.

for others,[7] and his direct witness in 1968 that "my testimony of the risen Lord is just as real as Thomas'. . . . I have heard his voice, and I have received his guidance in matters pertaining to his kingdom here on earth."[8]

Insights from McKay's Missionary Diaries

The missionary diaries give us a concentrated look at the young man who left his rural home in 1897 without the testimony he had yearned for, still quite rough in his manners and provincial in his attitudes, and returned two years later to move adeptly into challenging leadership callings in the Weber Stake, then in 1902 became principal of Weber Stake Academy (the future Weber State University) and in 1906, only seven years after his mission, an apostle. There are both surprises and satisfactions for us from the actions and reflections of this young elder in a less rule-bound mission culture than we know today—some of which contradict the folklore about him. For instance, the famous story of his spending an afternoon exploring Stirling Castle. On the way back he came across the inscription over a doorway, "What E'er Thou Art, Act Well Thy Part" (which is not mentioned in the diary but was recalled a year later), was moved to regret the time spent away from his missionary duties, and vowed to do better.[9] That story has always suggested to me he did not ever again go sight-seeing or indulge in mere recreation. But he did. He took companions—and mission leaders—back to Stirling Castle (see the wonderful account on 30 May 1899) and to other places of note, especially the birthplace of Robert Burns and other monuments to him.

In fact, especially after being chosen to preside over the Scottish Conference in June 1898 and permanently settling in Glasgow, he often went to the theatre. This, too, brought some moments of doubt: "I enjoyed the play while it lasted; but somehow there is something that seems to prick one's conscience after having attended a theatre, when perhaps he could have been doing missionary work—the feeling experienced after the play is over is not the one, by any means, that follows the performance of *duty*; and yet should not a missionary *not* participate in such recreation?" (10 October 1898). We know that Elder McKay's answer to his own question was "yes," because he went the very next Friday (14 October) with a visiting missionary to Shakespeare's *Merchant of Venice*, with "Sir Henry Irving as Shylock and Miss Ellen Terry as Portia. . . . Irving did not appear. . . . It was all very good, but we were a little disappointed." He even becomes something of

---

[7]See Lavina Fielding Anderson, "Prayer under a Pepper Tree: Sixteen Accounts of a Spiritual Manifestation," *BYU Studies* 33, no. 1 (1993): 55-78.

[8]Armstrong, *Rhetoric of David O. McKay*, 114-15.

[9]See Francis M. Gibbons, *David O. McKay: Apostle to the World, Prophet of God* (Salt Lake City: Deseret Book Co., 1986), 44-45.

a (rather liberal) theatre critic: "Brother Eccles and I . . . went to the Royalty Theatre to see Mr. Wilson Barrett in *The Manxman*. It was excellent. The play teaches moral lessons and right conduct by showing the opposite of these" (6 May 1899).

What Elder McKay's missionary journal documents, much like that of Lowell Bennion in Germany thirty years later, is the steady maturation of a very bright, observant, devout and intellectually expansive, witty young man. The maturation is evident in his critical appreciation of world culture in general, his love of a specific place and people, his liberal understanding and clear testimony of the gospel, and his increasingly intelligent, pragmatic, and able leadership in the Church. He goes to musicals and operas as well as plays; reads and comments on the newspaper (such as accounts of the outbreak of the Spanish American War in April 1898); visits and comments on social conditions in the almshouses, mines, asylums, and red-light districts; and describes, records, and makes clever (never condescending) comments on Scottish customs and rhetoric. He is obviously a tender and poetic young man: After visiting Alva Glen, he and a companion become convinced "that beautiful scenes are found *outside* of Utah. [We] went near the top, covered with misty clouds, and there sang hymns" (10 May 1898). After reporting his interview with a young man who "has transgressed and . . . burdened himself for life" and "made another unhappy, also," he writes a little poem in his journal about the man (27 December 1898).

The young missionary must also deal increasingly with difficult, even tragic, situations. On 18 October 1898 he gets word that a new missionary, David M. Muir, is very sick, and two days later receives a telegram that he has died. He arranges with the mission president to send temple clothes and come for a funeral, helps dress the body and stays overnight with it, and conducts the funeral and burial, all the while grieving ("the saddest affair that ever I have experienced"). Over three months later, 30 January 1899, he gets word that the new president of the Church, Lorenzo Snow, wants the missionary's body exhumed and taken home ("a task I almost dread"). He seeks legal counsel and finds this will be "a difficult, as well as an expensive, undertaking," and so it turns out to be, taking much of his time and ingenuity and emotional energy for two months—at the end of which he must actually open the coffin to confirm the identity ("a ghastly sight! I shall not attempt to describe it," 1 April 1899).

A constant trial—and test of his maturing skills as an administrator and a spiritual counselor—is the constant bickering over position in the local Glasgow branch. He works ferociously, for months, with two brethren who seem particularly proud and intractable and confides his impatience only to his journal: "O, it is disgusting; they act like children! And yet they mean to do what is right" (18 March 1899). Finally he has to release them both and take over as branch president himself—but only after the young elder has a heated meeting with them, spends a sleepless night, and holds a special priesthood meeting the next day where finally a "good spirit" is manifest and all sustained ("The hand-dealing of the Lord was manifested in this action and even in the disturbance last night," 18 June 1899).

But we see as well the unique and irrepressible spirit of a young man preparing to be an unusually liberal apostle and church president. He can laugh at himself: "Open-air meeting at night on Cathedral Square.... Our singing (?) failed to bring anyone around; in fact, it drove them away.... [We] had two men, a lamppost, and the wind as an audience!" (23 September 1898). He can take the counselor in the mission presidency and companions on a sight-seeing trip through Stirling and then on a twenty-mile hike along the shores of Loch Vennacher and Loch Katrine, trading his shoes for the president's tight-fitting ones and getting severe blisters, and then write a long, wittily nationalistic mock heroic poem to "Scots in spirit and endurance," memorializing the trip (8-12 June 1899). He can tell of going for a walk with that president while waiting for a train and being greatly moved as the president, in tears, tells of meeting and marrying his wife and the guidance of God in his life (23 May 1899).

As Elder McKay's mission comes to an end, he has the remarkable spiritual experience he retold in general conference in 1968, where he finally received divine confirmation of the truth of the gospel "as a natural sequence to the performance of duty." It seems to me characteristic of this man, who only gradually came to understand and be able to articulate the full import of his missionary experiences as their consequences worked themselves out in his life, that he does not mention in his diary the experience at the end of that conference that later became very famous in the Church. That was when he was told by his beloved President McMurrin, "Satan has desired you that he may sift you as wheat, but God is mindful of you, and if you will keep the faith, you will yet sit in the leading councils of the Church." When he first related that story in 1934, his focus was on it being "more of a caution" than a prediction of glory: "At that moment there flashed into my mind temptations that had beset my path, ... with the resolve then and there to keep the faith, there was born a desire to be of service to my fellowmen."[10]

McKay's Influence on McMurrin and Bennion

David O. McKay's careful honesty and his liberal openness about struggles and complexity and consequent respect for diversity is clear increasingly in his diaries and throughout his life. However, though I believe those qualities profoundly affected many Mormons indirectly, they were perhaps not as obvious in his public statements and actions as in private in-

---

[10]Quoted in Gibbons, *David O. McKay*, 50.

terviews and behind the scenes. Two persons who were privileged to see clearly, even experience directly, those less obvious qualities were themselves the two most well-known and influential twentieth century Mormon liberals outside the church hierarchy, Sterling M. McMurrin and Lowell L. Bennion. Both became acquainted with President McKay, who knew their fathers well, when they were young men (he performed each of their marriages in the Salt Lake Temple). They continued that friendship as they developed careers as teachers (both at first for the LDS Institute system and eventually at the University of Utah) and as writers of some of the most profound and enduring books on Mormon thought.

McMurrin lost his faith in the divine claims of the Church and left the Church Education System to become a professor of philosophy and dean of the Graduate School at the University of Utah and eventually U.S. Commissioner of Education under John F. Kennedy. But he remained fully identified with his Mormon people and in his increasingly prominent public life was often a loyal and articulate defender of the Church and its leaders. He arranged for the famous visit of the distinguished labor leader Walter Reuther in 1955 with President McKay, of which Reuther said both privately to McMurrin and then in public addresses, "I have met with major leaders all over the world, including kings and presidents; but I have never in my life met a person who made such an impression on me as this man has."[11] In 1958, McMurrin was asked by the Church to be its representative to speak at a special conference at Ohio State University and presented the material that became his landmark book, *The Philosophical Foundations of the Mormon Religion.*[12] In the early 1960s he became a liaison between the Church and the NAACP when it was pressuring the Church to more actively pursue the cause of civil rights in Utah, and as a result he wrote a statement strongly affirming civil rights for all, which was approved by President McKay and read by President Brown in the October 1964 general conference.[13]

McMurrin continued to attend Church in the 1940s and early 50s and was given occasional teaching assignments and asked to give talks at Church on special occasions. But in 1954 a new bishop in his ward told him, "I'm supposed to investigate you to see if you should be put on trial." McMurrin, in his account, speculates that word of this got to President McKay through Obert C. Tanner, his office mate at the University of Utah, who was a good friend of Apostle Adam S. Bennion. A few days later he got a call from President McKay, who insisted on seeing him at once, drove to the univer-

---

[11]Sterling M. McMurrin and L. Jackson Newell, *Matters of Conscience: Conversations with Sterling M. McMurrin on Philosophy, Education, and Religion* (Salt Lake City: Signature Books, 1996), 86.

[12]Ibid., 206.

[13]Ibid., 200-201.

sity, and spent the afternoon with him. McMurrin reports three statements from that conversation that may be somewhat surprising but are consistent with President McKay's actions and other conversations. He asked McMurrin, "Just what is it that a person is not permitted to believe without being asked to leave this Church? . . . Is it evolution? I hope not, because I believe in evolution."[14] When McMurrin suggested he may have brought on his trouble himself, by saying in his Sunday School class that he did not believe the teacher's claim that "Negroes are under a divine curse," President McKay said, "I'm glad you said that because I don't believe it either. As far as I'm concerned, it is not now nor has it ever been a doctrine of this Church that the Negroes are under a divine curse. . . . withholding the priesthood from Negroes. . . . is not a matter of doctrine. It is simply a practice and it is going to change."[15]

About the threatened trial McMurrin reports that President McKay was very angry and said, "They can't do this to you. . . . They *cannot* do this to you!" and after a pause added, "All I will say is that if they put you on trial for excommunication, I will be there as the first witness in your behalf." McMurrin says he had never felt such "warm support," and the trial never occurred.

Lowell L. Bennion remained an active and devoutly believing member all his life. Despite being denigrated as "unorthodox" and a "liberal" by some Mormons, he also felt personally the warm support of President McKay. This was apparent from the time President McKay called Bennion in for an interview at the start of his career in church education in 1935 and continued through a number of conversations about difficult issues that arose as he tried to teach students with both faith and honesty. That support was manifest publicly when Bennion was asked by President McKay to speak twice in General Conferences (1958 and 1968), the only lay member so honored, and called by him as a member of the Church Correlation Committee for Youth, where Bennion served from 1962 to 1972.

Bennion remembers that first meeting in 1935 with President McKay, then second counselor to President Heber J. Grant, as crucial to his self-confidence and direction as a beginning teacher of religion and as "a guide throughout his career." He reports that President McKay sounded him out on a number of difficult issues and then offered only this advice: "I don't care what you do or what you draw upon, but be true to yourself and loyal to the cause."[16] Later, when Bennion arranged interviews with President McKay on controversial questions like evolution and family planning, asking what he should teach in those areas, he was again invited to express his

---

[14]Ibid., 198.

[15]Ibid., 198-200.

[16]Mary Lythgoe Bradford, *Lowell L. Bennion: Teacher, Counselor, Humanitarian* (Salt Lake City: Dialogue Foundation, 1995), 65.

own ideas and beliefs, which the prophet "supported and amplified. . . . He gave me the feeling that we were thinking together, that he was incorporating my reflections into his own."[17] Bennion was particularly impressed by their discussion of *Man: His Origin and Destiny*, the book by Joseph Fielding Smith, president of the Quorum of the Twelve, which was being pushed by some as the church's official position on evolution and the age of the earth but which Bennion's students had raised questions about. President McKay made clear both his gracious respect for and his emphatic disagreement with President Smith's views. He said, "The Church has taken no official stand on this question. Each one of us gives his own opinion and my friend has a right to his even as you and I have a right to our own." Again, in a meeting with Bennion and other institute teachers in November 1953 he was "very understanding" of President Smith but stated that he himself "felt that the earth is very old and evolutionary ideas have much to commend them." As for President Smith's book, he said "very emphatically" that it had not been "authorized or approved" and "did not represent the position of the Church."[18]

Perhaps the most surprising and impressive evidence of President McKay's generous elevation of people above rules came in response to a plea from Bennion concerning a freshman student who had come to him in tears about his continuing yearning to pass the sacrament—he had been denied the priesthood because people in his Utah town believed his grandmother was Black—and then later reported to Bennion that his sister was being denied the privilege of being married in the Salt Lake Temple. Bennion went to President Hugh B. Brown, who set up a meeting with President McKay. After hearing Bennion out, he mused, "When problems like this come to me, I say to myself, 'Sometime I shall meet my Father in Heaven, and what will he say?'" Bennion responded, "He'll forgive you if you err on the side of mercy," and President McKay smiled and said, "Leave it to me." A few days later Bennion heard from the student that his sister would have a temple marriage—and a few months later the student asked him to ordain him an elder in preparation for a mission call.[19]

The Blacks and the Priesthood

David O. McKay made a number of such quiet but crucial decisions in preparation for Blacks receiving the priesthood. Given the importance of that finally successful change in 1978 to the achievement of the church's status as a mature world religion, those quiet decisions may turn out to be

---

[17]Ibid., 92.
[18]Ibid., 136.
[19]Ibid., 165-66.

the most important element in his liberal legacy. In 1954 he discontinued the practice of requiring converts in South Africa and South America to trace their genealogy back to Europe to prove their non-Black "purity" before receiving the priesthood. The practical consequence was that a number of people throughout the world who actually had Black ancestry were given the priesthood or temple blessings. If, as sometimes happened, people doing genealogy discovered Black ancestry, their priesthood or temple ordinances were not revoked; they were simply asked not to use the priesthood or go to the temple for the time being. In 1963, clearly with his support, his even more liberal counselor, Hugh B. Brown, was close to arranging the change of policy he believed was all that was necessary for Blacks to receive the priesthood, but at the last moment at least one apostle objected and the plan failed.[20] He approved the strong statement on civil rights written by McMurrin and read by President Brown in the October 1964 general conference. Finally, he approved, though he did not write, the official church statement on Blacks and the priesthood issued in 1969 that reaffirmed the policy but jettisoned all the folklore of doctrinal justifications (the reasons are "known only to God") and included the remarkable statement, "We join with those throughout the world who pray that all of the blessings of the gospel of Jesus Christ may in due time of the Lord become available to men of faith everywhere"[21]—which could be read as a plea for Mormons to pray for Blacks to receive the priesthood.

Some have wondered if it may have been President McKay's very conviction that Blacks receiving the priesthood was not a matter of doctrine, of basic beliefs about the nature of Blacks, that kept the change from being implemented during his presidency. Because he believed it only required an administrative decision to change the policy, he did not seek or receive the revelation that was apparently necessary to convince some of the Twelve. President Kimball did seek such a revelation, received it in June 1978, and shared it with the Twelve in a remarkable spiritual experience that convinced them the change was the Lord's will.[22] But I think McMurrin is right that President McKay's liberal spirit, his generous decisions and expressions, prepared the ground for the general church's acceptance of that revelation: "Without [him] in leadership over a long period of time, the change of poli-

[20]See "Mormons Weigh Stand on Negro," *New York Times*, 7 June 1963, and Armand Mauss' account of First Presidency meetings at the time, from notes taken by Eugene Campbell, in Lester E. Bush, Jr., and Armand L. Mauss, eds., *Neither White Nor Black: Mormon Scholars Confront the Race Issue in a Universal Church* (Midvale, UT: Signature Books, 1984), 156. For a description of President Brown's efforts, see the "Afterword" by Edwin B. Firmage to his grandfather's *An Abundant Life: The Memoirs of Hugh B. Brown* (Salt Lake City: Signature Books, 1988), 142.

[21]First Presidency Statement, 15 December 1969; reprinted in *Dialogue* 4 (Winter 1969): 102-103.

[22]See Bruce R. McConkie, "All Are Alike unto God," speech delivered 18 August 1978, published in *Charge to Religious Educators*, 2d ed. (Salt Lake City: The Church of Jesus Christ of Latter-day Saints, 1982), 152.

cy that came under President Kimball could not have had the immediate transforming effect which it had on the Mormon people."[23]

Concluding Observations

As I read the final entries in President McKay's missionary diaries, I thought of that remarkable legacy that combined conservative devotion, orthodox spirituality, and liberal perspective and courage. He has the remarkable spiritual experience where he finally received confirmation of the truth of the gospel "as a natural sequence to the performance of duty." He celebrates the Fourth of July in Edinburgh, noting the irony that the city is festooned with red, white, and blue bunting and full of patriotic songs— not "to celebrate America's natal day" but for a visit of the Prince of Wales, about whom he quotes Carlyle's claim that "society is founded on hero worship" and quotes a local newspaper account that the prince has no claim on society's adulation except that "he is the son of his mother!" (6 July 1899). He is sent as church representative to Cardiff for the Welsh National Eisteddfod, the world-class musical competition, meets and is hosted by the presiding officer, Dr. Joseph Parry, through a letter of introduction from Evan Stephens, and with what he considers providential help finds his mother's birthplace and some relatives at nearby Merthyr Tydfil (18-20 July 1899). Finally he leaves for home on 26 August 1899—and five days out experiences a collision with an iceberg that could well have ended like that of the *Titanic* thirteen years later save for the prompt action of the captain in reversing engines just before the collision ("It is at such critical moments as these that one fully appreciates the comforting prophetic assurance, 'You shall go in peace, and return in safety,' spoken by a servant of God [in my setting apart]").

The final entries reveal both the increased devotion and widening perspective that two years of missionary service have brought. It is not hard to imagine David O. McKay's returning home to revolutionize the training of Sunday School teachers in the Weber Stake as a member of the superintendency, to expand the physical facilities by leading the faculty in raising $40,000 for a new building and the public outreach with a distinguished lecture series as the new principal of Weber Stake Academy, and then to be called as an apostle at the age of thirty-two. A century later we can enjoy this remarkably full and frank account of a complex and attractive young man coming of age, but we can also reflect on the unique combination of his experience and his maturing response to it that went into the making of the most liberal and influential Mormon prophet of that 100 years and try to imagine how we can continue that legacy in our own mature response to it.

---

[23]McMurrin, *Matters of Conscience*, 202.

EDITORS' INTRODUCTION

THESE FORTHRIGHT diaries provide insights into a sheltered young man from Huntsville growing into a responsible adult. From our present vantage point we can look back at the life of a proselyting missionary over a century ago and learn how David O. McKay grew through the experiences of his mission. McKay wrote in a straightforward and honest manner, frankly expressing his feelings and describing his actions. The reader can feel as he felt, grow as he grew. Though times have changed and mission rules have increased, missionaries today face similar challenges.

The uniqueness of this opportunity to see through the eyes of David O. McKay is enhanced when it is realized that this is the first time that missionary diaries have been published of someone who at the time was not a general authority but who later became a president of the LDS Church. By definition, Joseph Smith was leader of the Church from 1830 and his diaries in various editions have been published. Brigham Young, after his conversion and before becoming one of the first apostles in 1835, kept diaries of his proselyting activities. Also, in the 1850s young Joseph F. Smith recorded his experiences during a mission to the Hawaiian Islands. The diaries of these latter two are in the LDS Church Archives but have never been published.

As it turns out, the McKay diaries are a real gem—informative in his detailed entries, insightful about Scottish society, descriptive of the beautiful Scottish countryside, and faith-promoting to modern readers. While on his mission McKay named babies, blessed the sick, preached in open-air meetings and rented halls, tracted in the rain, baptized converts, performed marriages, conducted funerals, wrote poems, consoled widows, nursed sick companions, counseled members concerning their problems, witnessed spousal abuse, scheduled lectures, visited historic sites, attended plays, saw drunkenness and immorality, arranged transportation for emigrants, and served as mission president over all of Scotland. These diaries provide an intimate glimpse into the feelings and actions of McKay as an LDS missionary and help us understand what made him one of the most beloved presidents of the Mormon Church.

Fig. 1 *David McKay holds David O. McKay and Jennette McKay holds Tommy. Elena (left) and Margaret (right) died in a diphtheria epidemic.*

McKay's Early Life

David Oman McKay was born in Huntsville, Utah, on 8 September 1873, the oldest son of David McKay and Jennette Eveline Evans (Fig. 1).[1] In 1885 he was ordained a deacon.[2] In July 1887 Patriarch John Smith promised the young McKay in his patriarchal blessing: "For the eye of the Lord is upon thee. He has a work for thee to do, in which thou shalt see much of the world. . . . It shall be thy lot to sit in counsel with thy brethren and to preside among the people and exhort the saints to faithfulness."[3] After the blessing the patriarch told him: "My boy, you have something to do besides playing marbles." The thirteen-year-old McKay went to his mother in the kitchen and told her: "If he thinks I am going to stop playing marbles, he is mistaken." His mother then patiently explained to him what the patriarch had meant.[4]

McKay attended the University of Utah, where he was a good student,

---

[1]For good biographies of McKay, see Francis M. Gibbons, *David O. McKay: Apostle to the World, Prophet of God* (Salt Lake City: Deseret Book Co., 1986) and David Lawrence McKay, *My Father, David O. McKay*, ed. Lavina Fielding Anderson (Salt Lake City: Deseret Book Co., 1989).

[2]Emerson Roy West, *Latter-Day Prophets: Their Lives, Teachings, and Testimonies* (American Fork, UT: Covenant Communications, Inc., 1997), 63, indicates that McKay "was the first Church President to have been a deacon because few boys received the Aaronic Priesthood before the 1870s."

[3]See Appendix A, pp. 269-70, below, for the complete text of the patriarchal blessing and compare Jeanette McKay Morrell, *Highlights in the Life of President David O. McKay* (Salt Lake City: Deseret Book Co., 1966), 38.

[4]"Inspirational Stories from the Life of David O. McKay," *The Improvement Era* 69 (September 1966): 769.

engaged in social activities, and played on the football team. He graduated in June 1897 (Fig. 2). McKay served as president of his class and also delivered the valedictory speech, in which he stated that "an unsatisfied appetite for knowledge means progress and is the state of a normal mind."[5]

The "What Ee'er Thou Art, Act Well Thy Part" Stone

David O. McKay's LDS mission covered the two-year period from August 1897 to August 1899. He arrived in Liverpool, England, on 25 August 1897 and was assigned to the Scottish Conference two days later. Most of his mission was spent in Scotland, though he did make trips to Ireland, England, and Wales. During this time period the active membership of the Church throughout Scotland was only about 150.[6] The presentation of the text of McKay's missionary diaries is, of course, the purpose of this volume. However, there are two experiences during McKay's mission that have often been told and retold in Mormon lore and require some detailed scrutiny here.

The first is McKay's inspirational story of seeing the inscription "What E'er Thou Art, Act Well Thy Part" and his resulting determination to do his duty as an LDS missionary. This particular episode is actually *not* recorded in McKay's diary, but one can pinpoint the precise day when it occurred. The evening of 25 March 1898 McKay and his companion, Peter G. Johnston, left Glasgow for their new assignment in Stirling. They stayed the night at Whitehead's Temperance Hotel, with McKay noting in his diary that he was feeling "somewhat gloomy." The next morning they got cleaned up, ate their breakfast, and went searching for a place to rent. They found a nice apartment with the Sharp family. That afternoon they spent several hours sight-seeing various places in and around historic Stirling, including Stirling Castle, the Statue of King Robert the Bruce, the Ladies' Rock, the Battlefield of Bannockburn, the Public Green, the King's Tournament, the "Fatal Mound," William Wallace's Monument, the Abbey of Cambuskenneth, and the Queens' Stand.

After spending the entire afternoon seeing these interesting places for the first time and while they were walking back to the apartment which they had rented in the morning, David O. McKay noticed a large and unusual stone above the lintel on the side of a house then being built. On closer examination he discovered that this stone was inscribed with the stirring

---

[5]Preston Nibley, *The Presidents of the Church*, 13th ed. rev. and enl. (Salt Lake City: Deseret Book Co., 1977), 312.

[6]Frederick S. Buchanan, "The Ebb and Flow of the Church in Scotland," in *Truth Will Prevail: The Rise of the Church of Jesus Christ of Latter-day Saints in the British Isles, 1837-1987*, ed. V. Ben Bloxham, James R. Moss, and Larry C. Porter (Solihull, England: The Church of Jesus Christ of Latter-day Saints, 1987), 296.

Fig. 2   *David O. McKay and Jeanette McKay*
at University of Utah Graduation.

words "What e'er thou art, act well thy part,"[7] which inscription was placed above a group of nine geometric shapes forming a magic square.[8]

The following is McKay's account, given at the October 1954 general conference:

> I was homesick, and we walked around the Stirling Castle, really not doing our duty, and as we reentered the town I saw a building, half-finished, and to my surprise, from the sidewalk I saw an inscription over the lintel of the front door, carved in stone. I said to Brother Johnston, "I want to go over and see what that is." I was not more than half way up the pathway leading to it, when that message struck me, carved there: "What e'er thou art, act well thy part."[9]

After seeing this inscription McKay made an internal determination to be a better missionary, but he did not write anything about the stone or the inscription in his diary. However, there is important, contemporary confirmation of this episode. A little over a year later, McKay revisited on 14 April 1899 all the sites in Stirling with John T. Edward, who was leaving early due to illness. Then, in a letter to Emma Ray Riggs on 25 April 1899, McKay reviewed this visit, quoted her own counsel to him, and wrote:

> The usual meetings of the branch here were attended on Sunday [23 April 1899], and conference duties have kept me busy since. The open-air meeting tonight was an excellent one so I feel like *chatting* to you with a cheerful heart.
> As I again read your letter now before me, a warm feeling of appreciation of your encouraging words comes over me; and your advice—"Do your work well"—will ever be remembered, though perhaps not *heeded* as it should be. It reminds me of a beautiful inscription carved over the door of one of the cottages in the east part of Stirling: "What e'er thou art, act well thy part." If one only chooses the good part and does his work *well*, success and happiness will certainly be his.[10]

In another account of this episode McKay mentioned additional details and drew the following moral instruction:

> As I rejoined my companion and told him what I had read [in the inscription], there came into my memory the custodian at the university from which I had just graduated. I realized then that I had just as great a respect for that man as I had for any professor in whose class I had sat. He

---

[7]Alexander Pope (1688-1744), who was very popular during the nineteenth century, expressed the following sentiment in his well-known *Essay on Man*: "Act well your part, there all the honour lies." See Pat Rogers, ed., *Alexander Pope*, the Oxford Authors (Oxford: Oxford University Press, 1993), 194.

[8]This magic square has a combination of the smallest whole numbers in which the sum of each of the three horizontal rows, the three vertical columns, and the two diagonals is the same even number—eighteen. The shapes and Roman numerals in the compartments of the stone convert to the numbers on the right:

5	10	3
4	6	8
9	2	7

[9]*Conference Report*, October 1954, 83.

[10]David O. McKay, Letter to "My Dear Friend, Ray," 25 April 1899, located in the David Oman McKay Collection, Manuscript 668, Box 1, Manuscripts Division, J. Willard Marriott Library, University of Utah, Salt Lake City, quoted in D. L. McKay, *My Father*, 24.

acted well his part. I recalled how he helped us with the football suits, how he helped us with some of our lessons. He was unassuming, unostentatious, but did his duty well. To this day I hold respect for him.

Decide what your duty is, ever remembering that the greatest battle of life is fought within the silent chambers of your own soul. Life is a battle for each person every day. Fight this battle with yourself and decide upon your course of action regarding what your duty is to your family and to your fellow men. Then set out from this to go beyond it. "What e'er thou art, act well thy part."[11]

McKay told and retold this story about the stone during his lifetime.[12]

Luckily, in 1965 Richard D. Brammer and David E. Goff, the two Stirling missionaries, were teaching a young family named the McArthurs, who lived near Stirling Castle on Back o' Hill Road in the block of apartments known as Albany Crescent—in fact in the very upstairs apartment whose living-room window was right next to the "What E'er Thou Art, Act Well Thy Part" Stone (see Figs. 22-23, pp. 80-81, below). These investigators told the missionaries that they were moving since the entire row of apartments would be demolished. Brammer and Goff passed this information on to their mission president, Phil D. Jensen. He drove to Stirling, bought the stone with its inscription for £30, had it moved to Edinburgh, and placed it outside the headquarters of the North Scottish Mission (Fig. 3).[13]

A few months after David O. McKay had passed away in 1970, Apostle Mark E. Petersen (through John E. Carr, director of the church's translation services) made an urgent request to F. Nephi Grigg, who was the president of what was then known as the Scotland Mission. Petersen wanted Grigg to release the rescued stone from its location on the grounds of the mission headquarters in Edinburgh so that it could be moved to a permanent home in Salt Lake City. It was first taken to 33 Richards Street (where the McKay family saw it), then to a local storage unit, then to the Church Office Building, and finally to its present location at the Museum of Church History and Art.[14] A full-size, stone replica is on display at the Missionary Training Center in Provo, Utah, and a full-size, fiberglass copy has been placed inside the Edinburgh mission home.

The message on this stone changed McKay, and it became an important guideline throughout his life. Today it remains a reminder to missionaries —and for that matter, anyone—of the importance of their chosen work.

---

[11]David O. McKay, *Secrets of a Happy Life*, comp. Llewelyn R. McKay (Englewood Cliffs, NJ: Prentice-Hall, Inc., 1960), 145.

[12]See Appendix C, pp. 273-75, below, for the complete text of one of McKay's accounts of the "What E'er Thou Art, Act Well Thy Part" Stone.

[13]Phil D. Jensen, Letter to Stan Larson, 17 April 1999, including a copy of his diary for 12 March 1965; and David E. Goff, Letter to Stan Larson, 2 June 1999. After the stone was set up on the grounds of the Scottish Mission Home, A. Hamer Reiser, "Sunday School Pioneer," *The Instructor* 101 (September 1966): 334, re-told the story, including a photo of the stone.

[14]For an account of Mark E. Petersen's 1970 assignment to move this stone to Salt Lake City, see John E. Carr Collection, Accession 1747, Manuscripts Division, J. Willard Marriott Library, University of Utah, Salt Lake City.

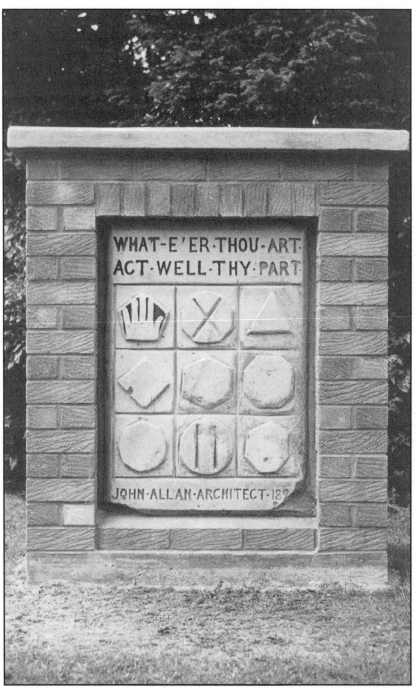

Fig. 3 *The "What E'er Thou Art, Act Well Thy Part" Stone, Edinburgh.*

The Vision of Guardian Angels

The second mission experience frequently retold in Mormon lore is the vision of guardian angels during a priesthood meeting on 29 May 1899. We are very fortunate in having numerous accounts of this meeting, each adding certain details. There are the following ten sources: a reminiscence given a half century later by a local member, William Cooke[15]; the published summary of the meeting in the *Millennial Star*[16]; the official handwritten minutes in the LDS Archives,[17] parts of which are quoted in two sources[18]; the contemporary diaries kept by seven missionaries in attendance that day—William S. Gould, Thomas A. Kerr, David O. McKay, Joseph H. Mitchell, William P. Nisbet, Henry B. Thompson, and John B. Young.[19]

Since one of the guardian angels seen that day belonged to John B. Young, it seems appropriate to quote the account from his diary:

> While I was speaking, the room was filled with the spirit of the Lord. Pres. Woolfenden saw two holy angels, one of them he said was my guardian angel. From the feeling that was in the room, I am sure that the room was full of holy beings. The most of the elders wept with joy. President McKay stated that to show our appreciation of the glorious manifestation of the presence of holy angels he would offer a prayer unto the Lord. President McMurrin thanked the Lord for his goodness towards us. He stated how he had been acquainted with me and how faithful a young man I was. The other angel that Pres. Woolfenden witnessed Pres. McMurrin said was the guardian angel of Bro. Eccles. Pres. Woolfenden stated that it was, it had been made known unto him. President Allen said that it was revealed unto him that before the meeting commenced that such would take place in the meeting; stated where it would be seen, that is in what part of the room it would be seen. President Naisbitt addressed the elders. Told of the experience[s] he had passed through. This was one of the grandest meetings that ever I had [the] pleasure of attending. The spirit of the Lord filled the room. Most of the elders wept with joy."[20]

In a sense McKay's own account of this meeting is contained in two sources —his contemporary diary and his first public recital of the episode in 1934, thirty-five years after the event. Later recountings follow that reminiscence,

---

[15]James S. Campbell, *Biography of George Gordon Campbell* (n.p., 1957), 9, located in the George Gordon Campbell Collection, Accession 851, Box 2, Manuscripts Division, J. Willard Marriott Library, University of Utah, Salt Lake City.

[16]William Leggat, "Scottish Conference," *The Latter-day Saints' Millennial Star* 61 (1 June 1899): 342.

[17]Scottish Conference Records, the British Mission, LR17716, ser. 11, located in the LDS Church Archives, Historical Department, The Church of Jesus Christ of Latter-day Saints, Salt Lake City.

[18]See Gibbons, *David O. McKay*, 49-50, and Campbell, *Biography of George Gordon Campbell*, 7-9.

[19]For McKay's full diary entry for this day's meeting as well as quotations from each of these sources, see 29 May 1899, pp. 239-41, below.

[20]John B. Young, Diary, Accession 1738, 29 May 1899, located in the Manuscripts Division, J. Willard Marriott Library, University of Utah, Salt Lake City.

with varying introductions and conclusions. All of them by McKay are essentially the same as the account in his contemporary diary. One detail not in McKay's diary is the remark made by James L. McMurrin, counselor in the mission presidency. McKay reported the following:

> When he [McMurrin] turned to me and gave what I thought then was more of a caution than a promise, his words made an indelible impression upon me. Paraphrasing the words of the Savior to Peter, he said, "Let me say to you, Brother David, Satan hath desired [to have] you that he may sift you as wheat [Luke 22:31], but God is mindful of you." Then he added, "If you will keep the faith, you will yet sit in the leading councils of the Church." At that moment there flashed into my mind temptations that had beset my path, and I realized even better than President McMurrin, or any other man, how truly he had spoken. With the resolve then and there to keep the faith, there was born a desire to be of service to my fellow men.[21]

This experience, too, had a permanent effect on McKay's life and in later years he often recounted this episode.

End of His Mission and Return Home

A most valuable insight into McKay's work as a missionary is now available. Platte De Alton Lyman, president of the European Mission, filled in the following report concerning David O. McKay's activities as an LDS missionary in Scotland:

Name of elder: David Oman McKay.
Residence: Huntsville.
Age: 25.
Office: Seventy.
Name of mission: British Mission.
President: Platte D. Lyman.
Date of arrival: 25 August 1897.
Date of departure: 26 August 1899.
As a speaker: Good.
As a writer: Good.
As a presiding officer: Very good.
Has he a good knowledge of the gospel? Yes.
Has he been energetic? Very.
Is he healthy? Yes.
Is he married? No.
How many missions has he filled? One.
What is his education? Good.
Is he discreet and does he carry a good influence? Yes, sir.
Does he speak more than one language? If so, what? No.
Remarks by Pres. Platte D. Lyman: "No better in the mission."[22]

---

[21]David O. McKay, "Two Significant Statements," *The Deseret News*, Church Section, 27 October 1934, 1, 8, with the spelling "counsels," quoted in David O. McKay, *Cherished Experiences from the Writings of President David O. McKay*, comp. Clare Middlemiss (Salt Lake City: Deseret Book Co., 1955), 14.

[22]"Report given by President Platte D. Lyman, President of the European Mission, con-

McKay left Glasgow on 26 August 1899 on the S.S. *City of Rome*. This ship collided with an iceberg and McKay's account is transcribed in the "Concluding Note" at the end of his diaries (see p. 268, below). Orson F. Whitney, in his account of Elizabeth Ann Claridge McCune, who was a fellow-passenger with McKay on the ship, said the following:

> On the evening of Thursday, August 31, off Cape Race, in latitude 48:30 and longitude 48:44, the steamship *City of Rome*, on which she was a passenger, crashed into an immense iceberg, undiscernible till then on account of a dense fog. But for the prompt action of the captain and crew in stopping the engines and reversing the vessel's course, it would have been wrecked, with nearly thirteen hundred souls on board."[23]

Another passenger on that ship was a returning lady missionary, Lettie Dewey Campbell, who in a later reminiscence provided the following account of that dramatic collision:

> The morning of the fifth day I was standing on deck and admiring the beautiful ocean and the sun apparently coming up right out of the water. Everybody seemed happy and jovial and were so kind to me, and someone constantly had the baby as she was good-natured and the only infant on board.[24] The ship sailed on. In the early afternoon fog appeared as we were near the banks or coast of Newfoundland, and the foghorn began to blow. Oh, that terrible, terrible sound. I shall never forget it.
> Dinner was being served at 5:30 P.M. The first table had just finished when all of a sudden the foghorn gave an extra hard blast and the old ship gave a lurch on one side and to all appearance she must go over.
> It was a fearful sensation and the surrounding scene was terrible. Women were fainting, children screaming, men with white faces, the sea was looking angry, as if it would gladly destroy all of the living freight on board and give all, even the proud old ship, a watery grave. I seemed fairly petrified. In fear that I may be trodden under foot in the terrible panic, I rushed to a seat and hugged my darling babe to my breast and prayed God to save us.[25]

The slightly damaged ship landed at New York on 4 September 1899, and McKay arrived home in Salt Lake City six days later.

David O. McKay married Emma Ray Riggs on 2 January 1901 at the Salt Lake Temple, the first couple married in that temple in the twentieth century.[26] They had seven children: David Lawrence, Llewelyn Riggs,

---

cerning President McKay's activities in the British Mission from 1897 to 1899," typescript located at the end of the 1898-1899 diary in the David O. McKay Collection, Box 3.

[23]Orson F. Whitney, *History of Utah* (Salt Lake City: George Q. Cannon and Sons Co., 1904), 4:610.

[24]She married Chester F. Campbell on 12 April 1898 and they both were called as full-time, proselyting missionaries, arriving in England in July of that year. Their first child, Lettie Victoria Campbell, was born in June of 1899, and they then decided that the mother should return to Utah with the baby.

[25]Lettie Dewey Campbell, "An Encounter with an Iceberg," in the Lettie Dewey Campbell Collection, Accession 1724, Manuscripts Division, J. Willard Marriott Library, University of Utah, Salt Lake City.

[26]James B. Allen, "David O. McKay," in *The Presidents of the Church: Biographical Essays*, ed. Leonard J. Arrington (Salt Lake City: Deseret Book, 1986), 285.

Louise Jeanette, Royal Riggs, Emma Rae, Edward Riggs, and Robert Riggs. Five years after being married, McKay was ordained an apostle. In October 1934 he was made a counselor in the First Presidency. In April 1951 he was sustained as president of the Church of Jesus Christ of Latter-day Saints, serving in this position until his death in January 1970. His sixty-four years as an LDS general authority is longer than any other person.

The Editing of McKay's Missionary Diaries

There are three Scottish missionary diaries, and they are preserved in the Manuscripts Division of the J. Willard Marriott Library at the University of Utah in Salt Lake City. Diary One measures 3¼" x 5" and covers the period from 30 July 1897 through 2 December 1897. Diary Two measures 3⅛" x 5⅛" and covers from 3 December 1897 through 17 January 1898. Diary Three is two inches thick and measures 6¼" x 7¾." It covers the period from 1 January 1898 through 20 July 1899, with the first seventeen days of January being recopied from the second diary. McKay gave to this diary the title of "A Few Happenings of My Daily Life."

Most entries appear to have been written at the end of each day, sometimes so late that it was technically the next day. For example, on 6 March 1899 McKay pointed out that he wrote the entry at 1:00 A.M. There are a few instances where the entries are retrospective. For example, the entries from 30 August to 7 September 1898 were written on the last date; on 10 March 1899 he "wrote diary to date"; the entries for 17-20 March 1898 were written on the last date; also, the very last diary entries covering his visit to Wales during 18-20 July 1899 were actually written on 9 August 1899, when he had returned to Glasgow.

All dates for diary entries have been standardized to the form: "Monday, 3 January 1898," and (when McKay added it) the town where he was at the time. The text of McKay's diaries is presented in modern dress. The spelling has been corrected, the capitalization has been updated, punctuation added, paragraphing rearranged, quoted titles have been italicized, and minor grammatical corrections made. Words McKay underlined for emphasis are printed in italics All exclamation marks and ironic questions within parentheses—(?)—are McKay's. Quotation marks have been added to direct quotes. When a scriptural passage is quoted without a reference to its location, this is added in square brackets. Most abbreviations are spelled out, except in direct quotations. The ampersand "&" is printed as "and." These things were done to make reading easier and in line with modern style. The few instances of bad grammar are silently corrected. Minor rearrangements of words have sometimes also been done. For example, McKay's "Leggat (Wm)" is recast as "William Leggat." Square brackets enclose all editorial additions. The same policies apply to the quotations in the footnotes from the diaries of other LDS missionaries.

An attempt has been made to provide the full names of proselyting missionaries, local members, and nonmembers mentioned by McKay. Sometimes such information has been unavailable. Also, a short synopsis is provided in the footnotes for (1) McKay's fellow missionaries in the Scottish Conference, (2) presidents of other conferences in the British Mission, and (3) other important individuals. The entire text of McKay's three missionary diaries is here presented, with the exception of two short statements (indicated by ellipses) that did not seem relevant; suggestions on this matter were made by the McKay family, but we take full responsibility for these two deletions.

Acknowledgments

Appreciation must first and foremost be expressed to the living children of David O. McKay—Lou Jean, Emma Rae, Ed, and Bob—who were gracious, encouraging, and helpful throughout this entire project. Marion D. Hanks, the late Leonard J. Arrington, and Eugene England provided insightful essays about McKay for this volume. The following individuals helped financially during the research, writing, and editing of this volume: Midene McKay Anderson, Alan C. Ashton, Conway and Emma Rae Ashton, Clifford Cutler, Una Loy Clark Farrer, Addie C. Grigg, Delbert V. Groberg, Catherine Iba, Phil D. Jensen, Nina Johnston, Garth N. Jones, Natalie C. McMurrin, Marie Barker Nelson, Teddy Lynn Parmley, Waldo C. Perkins, Roy W. Simmons, Richard P. Smoot, Martha Stewart, Betty C. Stokes, Marian Robertson Wilson, and Ned Winder. A percentage of the revenues from this book goes to the David O. McKay Foundation to assist in the preservation of the family home in Huntsville, Utah.

Lavina Fielding Anderson, after assisting David Lawrence McKay in writing his memoirs about David O. McKay, provided helpful leads that eventually led to the original McKay diaries being donated by Joyce McKay Bennett and Midene McKay Anderson to the J. Willard Marriott Library at the University of Utah. Gregory C. Thompson, assistant director for Special Collections, gave permission for the publication of these diaries. Permission to reprint the text of David O. McKay's essay "What E'er Thou Art, Act Well Thy Part" and Marion D. Hanks's essay "The Soul of a Prophet" was given by Intellectual Reserve, Inc., of the Church of Jesus Christ of Latter-day Saints and to reprint the text of Arrington's essay was given by the University of Illinois Press. Permission to reproduce the images in this book was received from the following institution and individuals: the Utah State Historical Society, Frontispiece; Emma Rae McKay Ashton, Figs. 1, 2, 4, 60, and 61; Phil D. Jensen, Figs. 3, 22, 23, and 37; and Midene McKay Anderson, Fig. 48. Linda L. Burns of the Marriott Interlibrary Loan Department acquired numerous volumes not available in Utah. Frederick S. Buchanan interpreted the meaning of several unusual Scottish expressions. Using the consumer price index, Peter L. Kraus calculated the relative monetary values of items during the late 1890s and the present. Robert Ian Williams, Alma Carter, and Dafydd Ifans of Wales sent valuable information about the Welsh National Eisteddfod. George M. McCune provided references to Elizabeth Ann Claridge McCune, who was on the S.S. *City of Rome* with McKay when it struck an iceberg. David J. Whittaker answered several questions about nineteenth-century missionary tracts and pamphlets. Robert R. McKay provided a copy of his father's patriarchal blessing, which is printed in Appendix A, pp. 269-70, below.

Originals or photocopies of the diaries of the following contemporary missionaries were donated to the Marriott Library: Archibald R. Anderson by Vivian McKay; Hyrum B. Calder by Larry C. Stratford; John T. Edward by John E. Carr; Alexander Faddies by Carolynn Craner Slater, James L. Craner, and Linda F. Landon; William S. Gould by Detta M. Dabling; Thomas A. Kerr by Thomas B. Kerr; Thomas A. Leishman by Barbara Manfull; Joseph H. Mitchell by Alice M. Lillywhite; William P. Nisbet by Noni Eggertz; Henry B. Thompson by Shirley Watkins; and John B. Young by John D. Young. The reference staff in the following libraries and archives provided valuable assistance: the LDS Archives, Historical Department, The Church of Jesus Christ of Latter-day Saints, Salt Lake City; Special Collections, J. Willard Marriott Library, Salt Lake City; Special Collections and Manuscripts, Harold B. Lee Library, Brigham Young University, Provo, Utah; the library of the Utah State Historical Society, Salt Lake City; the British Library, London; the Mitchell Reference Library, Glasgow; and the University of Glasgow Library, Glasgow.

Angie Larson, our daughter-in-law, typed the text into the computer, and since we had not yet read McKay's diaries, reported each night the interesting accounts she had typed that day. Lavina Fielding Anderson, Carolyn P. Bennion, Martha S. Bradley, Frederick S. Buchanan, Karen L. Carver, Connie Disney, and Ann Reichman read a draft of the manuscript and offered many valuable suggestions. James Larson and Dan Larson assisted in all computer aspects of getting this book published. Tania A. Tully drew the map of Scotland. Ron Stucki and Connie Disney designed the dust jacket, and Robert T. Barrett painted the illustration for the front panel of the jacket. Barry and Glenda Smith extended their hospitality to us during a research trip to England and Scotland. Beverly Alker helped locate rare Edwardian postcards for some of the illustrations. Though these old cards show signs of their use during the intervening period, we hope that illustrations drawn from near the time of the diaries will help the reader gain a greater feeling for life during McKay's mission.

As can be clearly seen, we are indebted to many people for many things in many ways. It has truly been an exciting project to bring David O. McKay's words into print.

MAP OF SCOTLAND

CHRONOLOGY OF DAVID O. McKAY

1873   Born in Huntsville, Utah, the son of David McKay and Jennette Evans

1881   Baptized by Peter Geertsen at Huntsville

1885   Ordained a deacon by C. F. Schade

1887   Received his patriarchal blessing from John Smith

1891   Ordained a teacher

1893   Ordained a priest

        Served as principal of the Huntsville District School

1894   Entered the University of Utah Normal School

1897   Graduated from the University of Utah; president and valedictorian of his class

        Called on a mission to Great Britain, ordained a seventy, and assigned to the Scottish Conference

1898   Saw the words "What e'er thou art, act well thy part" inscribed on a stone over the lintel of a home being constructed in Stirling, Scotland

        Chosen to preside over the Scottish Conference of the British Mission

1899   Released from mission

        Began to teach in Weber Stake Academy in Ogden, Utah

1900   Appointed to Weber Stake Sunday School Board

1901   Married Emma Ray Riggs in the Salt Lake Temple

        Birth of David Lawrence McKay

1902   Appointed principal of Weber Stake Academy

1904   Birth of Llewelyn Riggs McKay

1906	Ordained an apostle in the Quorum of the Twelve by President Joseph F. Smith
	Sustained as second assistant general superintendent of the Deseret Sunday School Union
	Birth of Louise Jennette McKay
1908	President of General Priesthood Committee
1909	Birth of Royal Riggs McKay
	Sustained as first assistant general superintendent of the Deseret Sunday School Union
1912	Death of Royal Riggs McKay
1913	Birth of Emma Rae McKay
1914	President of the Ogden Betterment League
1915	Birth of Edward Riggs McKay
	Laid the cornerstone of the Alberta Temple at Cardston
1918	Appointed General Superintendent of the Deseret Sunday School Union
	Published book, *Ancient Apostles*
1919-1921	Served as Church Commissioner of Education
1920	Birth of Robert Riggs McKay
1920-1921	Made a world tour of the missions of the Church, visiting all fields outside the United States except South Africa and traveling 62,500 miles
1921	At Peking dedicated the land of China for the preaching of the gospel
1921-1922	Member of the board of regents of the University of Utah
1922	Received the only honorary Master of Arts degree ever bestowed by Brigham Young University
1922-1924	Presided over the European Mission
1932	Elected chairman for Utah Council for Child Health and Protection at its organization, following the White House Conference on Child Welfare
1934	Sustained and set apart as second counselor to President Heber J. Grant

1938-1947	Chairman of the Utah State Centennial Commission
1940	Named to the board of trustees of Utah State Agricultural College
	Laid the cornerstone of the Idaho Falls Temple
1942	Chairman of the Utah State Advisory Committee of the American Red Cross
1945	Sustained and set apart as second counselor to President George Albert Smith
1948	Toured the Mexican Mission
1950	Sustained and set apart as president of the Quorum of the Twelve Apostles
1951	Sustained and set apart as president of the Church of Jesus Christ of Latter-day Saints
	Named Stephen L. Richards as first counselor and J. Reuben Clark, Jr., as second counselor in the First Presidency
	Became senior editor of *The Improvement Era*
	Attended the Hill Cumorah Pageant
	Dedicated the site of the Los Angeles Temple
1952	Toured missions in Europe
1953	Dedicated the Mormon Pioneer Memorial Bridge near Omaha, Nebraska
	Awarded the Boy Scouts' highest honor, "The Silver Buffalo"
	Dedicated the site of the temple at Berne, Switzerland
	Dedicated the site of the temple at New Chapel, south of London
1954	Toured missions in South Africa and Latin America
1955	Visited Europe with the Tabernacle Choir
	Toured missions in the Pacific
	Dedicated the Swiss Temple
1956	Dedicated new Relief Society Building
	Dedicated the Los Angeles Temple
1958	Dedicated the New Zealand Temple

	Dedicated the London Temple

Dedicated the London Temple

Dedicated the Church College of Hawaii

1959   Named J. Reuben Clark, Jr., as first counselor in the First Presidency

Named Henry D. Moyle as second counselor in the First Presidency

1960   Dedicated East Bay Inter-Stake Center

1961   Dedicated Palmyra Branch Chapel, New York

Dedicated Hyde Park Chapel in London and organized London Stake

Announced that members of the First Council of the Seventy would be high priests

Named Henry D. Moyle as first counselor in the First Presidency

Named Hugh B. Brown as an additional counselor and later as second counselor in the First Presidency

1962   Dedicated site for Oakland Temple

1963   Named Hugh B. Brown as first counselor in the First Presidency

Named N. Eldon Tanner as second counselor in the First Presidency

1964   Dedicated the Oakland Temple

1965   Named Joseph Fielding Smith and Thorpe B. Isaacson as additional counselors in the First Presidency

1968   Named Alvin R. Dyer as an additional counselor in the First Presidency

1970   Died in Salt Lake City, Utah

The Missionary Diaries
of
DAVID O. McKAY

DAVID O. McKAY
MISSIONARY DIARY ONE

Friday, 30 July 1897

W ENT TO OGDEN to meet Mrs. White and Miss Riggs.[1] They arrived in Ogden at 1:30 P.M. All went up to Josie Chambers. At six o'clock we started for home; Josie went with us. Farewell party at night; many friends present. Had a delightful time.

Saturday, 31 July 1897

Spent day at home. In the afternoon took ice cream with Mrs. Anna Plater, Mrs. White, Ray, Tillie, and Miss Dalquist. Theona, Amelia, Lizzie,[2] Nettie,[3] D. R. Alma, Christian [Mortensen] were there.

Sunday, 1 August 1897

Attended Sunday School and meeting. In the evening took a ride over on south hills. Saw purple mountains at sunset—very beautiful. Sunday evening went strolling with Ray. Told each other secrets. A memorable night!

---

[1]Emma Ray Riggs McKay (1877-1970) was the daughter of Obadiah H. and Emma Robbins Riggs. After McKay's return, they got engaged and were married by Apostle John Henry Smith in January 1901 in the Salt Lake Temple, being the first couple married in that temple in the twentieth century. They had seven children: David Lawrence, Llewelyn, Louise Jennette, Royal, Emma Rae, Edward, and Robert. For a survey of her life, see John J. Stewart, *Remembering the McKays: A Biographical Sketch with Pictures of David O. and Emma Ray McKay* (Salt Lake City: Deseret Book Co., 1970).

[2]Elizabeth ("Lizzie") Odette McKay (1884-1971), David O. McKay's sister, was born in Huntsville on 30 October 1884. She married George R. Hill in 1914.

[3]Jeanette ("Nettie") Isabella McKay (1879-1971), David O. McKay's sister, graduated with him from the University of Utah in 1897. She married Joseph R. Morrell in 1907. Jeanette McKay Morrell published *Highlights in the Life of President David O. McKay* (Salt Lake City: Deseret Book Co., 1966).

Monday, 2 August 1897

Mrs. White, Ray, and Josie went home. Cut hay in afternoon. At night George Ferrin, Mr. and Mrs. [Andrew P.] Renstrom, Tillie, and the Misses Dalquist spent the time with us.

Tuesday, 3 August 1897

At home. Wrote in the forenoon and raked hay in afternoon. In the evening, according to appointment, went to Eden to see Minnie. Nettie, Tillie, Lizzie Langlois, and the Misses Dalquist went with me.

Wednesday, 4 August 1897

Made final preparation for mission. Spent a few hours with John and Amelia Grow.[4] At Mrs. Renstrom's early in evening. Later relatives and friends spent evening at our house.

Thursday, 5 August 1897

The saddest morning ever spent in Huntsville or anywhere else! At eleven o'clock bid my home (Fig. 4), dear ones, relatives, and friends good-bye. Sobbed. In Ogden attended Uncle Howell's[5] funeral at 6:35. Took train for Salt Lake City. Secured a room at the White House [Hotel], then spent the evening with Ray.

Friday, 6 August 1897

Went through the [Salt Lake] Temple.[6] Called on Mr. and Miss Moody. Ate dinner at 6 P.M. with Mrs. White. Later called to see Claire [Whitehead]. My last night. Bid her good-bye for two years. She and Winnifred [Whitehead] presented to me a beautiful Baxter Bible.

Saturday, 7 August 1897

Bid Ray good-bye and left for Ogden at 8 A.M. Spent day in that city, and at 6:35, after bidding good-bye to relatives and friends, left for the East. Josie and Clara Chambers gave me an excellent pocket book. The train was crowded; four of us gave up our seats to ladies and went into "smoker.". . . Could not stand such company, so hired a berth in a sleeper. Met Mr. and Mrs. Marriott. Made me happy. While going through a sleeper, stumbled over a footstool, throwing one satchel in a man's shoulder and the other in a lady's lap. With a quick "Excuse me! I beg your pardon," I gathered myself and left.

---

[4]John M. Grow (1874-1932), McKay's cousin, married Amelia Bergitta Wangsgard in 1895.

[5]Howell Evans (1848-1897) was born in Clwyd Faguyr, Glamorganshire, Wales, and married Annie Browning in 1873.

[6]McKay was also ordained a seventy and set apart for his mission by Seymour B. Young on this day.

Fig. 4 *The McKay Family Home, Huntsville.*

Sunday, 8 August 1897
In train, spent the morning hours with Mr. and Mrs. Marriott and Mrs. Gabby. Passed through the Royal Gorge or the Grand Canyon of the Arkansas.[7] Mr. and Mrs Marriott bid me good-bye at Colorado Springs.

Monday, 9 August 1897
In Burlington and Missouri [River] Railroad. Passed through Lincoln and Omaha, Nebraska. Large cornfields. Wrote to Tommy.[8] Changed at Omaha [to] Chicago, Burlington, and Quincy [Railroad].

Tuesday, 10 August 1897
At 8 A.M. arrived in Chicago, visited Lake Michigan, Statue of John A. Logan,[9] then took elevator to the auditorium tower. Left at 10:25.

Wednesday, 11 August 1897
Arrived in Washington at 11:55. Wrote to Claire. Visited capitol, a

---

[7]McKay incorrectly wrote: "The Royal Gorge of the Gr. Canyon of the Arkansas."

[8]Thomas E. ("Tommy") McKay (1875-1958) was David O. McKay's younger brother. On 10 August 1900 he was set apart as a missionary to the European Mission, serving in Germany, and returned in September 1903. He served as a missionary in the Swiss-German Mission from 1909 to 1911 and as mission president in the same mission beginning in July 1937. Thomas was called as a general authority and served as Assistant to the Quorum of the Twelve Apostles from April 1941 until January 1958.

[9]John A. Logan (1826-1886) was an American general and politician, who helped organize the Grand Army of the Republic.

beautiful building 751 feet long, covering an area of 8½ acres. Saw beautiful paintings: "Washington and Lafayette," "Washington at Yorktown," "Entrance to Golden Gate," "Perry's Victory, September 10, 1813," "First Fight of Ironclads," etc. Echo Room, President's Room, very beautiful. One painting looks to be in same position from four corners. Rotunda is 181 feet high. Heard the Marine Band, one of the best in the U.S. They played "Home Sweet Home" for our benefit I suppose?

Thursday, 12 August 1897
In Washington. Visited [the] Bureau of Painting and Engraving. Thirty days to print one sheet of four bills. Fifty-two people print and issue between ten million and twelve million stamps daily. Bills counted fifty-two times.

Washington Monument. 554 feet high. From east loop hole one can see Smithsonian Institute, Agricultural Building, Medical Institute, National Institute, Capitol and Library, South Potomac River.

White House. On wall were pictures of Washington, Jefferson, and Lincoln, also Mrs. [Lucy Webb] Hayes.

State, War, and Navy Building. Old Negro who waited upon Jefferson Davis, Grant, and others, oldest official—forty years—Wilson. Relics: Benjamin Franklin's cane, Washington's eyeglasses given him by Lafayette, Washington's sword, whale's tooth used as a treaty with Fiji Islands, Jefferson's desk, hand-writing, Union flags, etc. Sat in chair of Secretary of State! Passed under a piece of verd antique, excavated from Temple of Jupiter in Pompeii, 1848. I shall never be burned!

Smithsonian Institute and National Museum. Historical and personal relics of George Washington. Field glass, sleeping tent, etc. His suit worn when he resigned commission—buckskin color, brass buttons. Also saw Lincoln's coat and vest worn as office suit up to day of his death. Oldest complete locomotive in America.

Left Washington at 3 P.M. Went to New York over Baltimore and Ohio [Railroad]. Arrived at 8 P.M. Lone boy in a great city! Took elevated railroad to East 135 Street. Found Will and Josie Simms.

Friday, 13 August 1897
Left Josie. Crossed Brooklyn Bridge, Statue of Liberty in the distance. River full of all kinds of boats. Visited aquarium, very interesting. Blackfish, carp, mudfish, sturgeon, whitefish, eel, catfish, harbor seals, shark, striped bass (pretty), West Indian seals, etc., etc. Left New York at 4:40; arrived in Philadelphia two hours later. Stopped at Green Hotel; met all the missionaries (twenty-one).

Wrote to Mamma[10] and Miss Riggs.

---

[10]Jennette Eveline Evans McKay (1850-1905), David O. McKay's mother, was born in

Saturday, 14 August 1897

Sailed at 11 A.M. for Liverpool in S.S. *Belgenland*. While going down Delaware River, wrote to Claire, David R., and my sister Annie.[11] Pilot left us near Cape Henlopen. At night all felt happy. Met Miss Appleton.

Sunday, 15 August 1897

Arose about six o'clock. Felt well. At ten o'clock held services in the dining room. Colored people sang sectarian hymns and David Haigh and I spoke. Our first experience—poor attempt—at a religious sermon. Charles Stevenson sang "O My Father" and Brother Holt[12] dismissed. Gave passengers something to talk about. Attacked by a woman! Found out I knew nothing about the Bible. Had the "blues." Sailed 197.3 miles.

Monday, 16 August 1897

After a good night's rest, arose about six o'clock. Saw a steamer. Played shuffleboard. During the day saw four ships. Toward night the sea became rough. Sailed 281.3 miles.

Tuesday, 17 August 1897

Ship rolling from side to side—*so were we!* Arose about six o'clock but lay down again. Felt a little better and went up on deck. Laughed at Paul [J. Kammeyer] and the others who were sick. Went down to breakfast but did not eat. Sick all day. Sailed 238 miles. 48° north latitude.

Wednesday, 18 August 1897

Felt better. Took a drink of lemonade and ate a light breakfast. Weather cloudy; had a little rain. Saw porpoises. At twelve entered a dense fog. Passed a sailing vessel. At 5:30 entered another fog, which we were still in when I retired about nine o'clock. While in this fog, the number of watchmen was doubled, the whistle blew every minute, and every precaution was taken to avoid a collision. 289 miles.

Thursday, 19 August 1897

Fog has disappeared; the sea is calm, and it seems we shall have a

---

Cefn Coed, Glamorganshire, Wales, and was the daughter of Thomas and Margaret Powell Evans. She married David McKay on 9 April 1867 and they had ten children: Margaret, Elena, David O., Thomas, Jeanette, Ann, Elizabeth, William, Kathrine, and Morgan.

[11]Ann ("Annie") Powell McKay (1881-1967), David O. McKay's sister, was born in Huntsville on 29 April 1881. She married Thomas Bramley Underwood Farr in 1905.

[12]Samuel Holt (1835-1909) of Millville, Cache Co., Utah, was set apart for a mission in Great Britain on 6 August 1897, arriving in Liverpool on 25 August 1897. Since he came to England to do genealogical research and proselyte his friends and relatives in Birmingham, he was assigned to the Birmingham Conference. Fourteen weeks later he was honorably released from this mission and sailed on the S.S. *Furnessia* at the end of December 1897. It was customary in the nineteenth century for persons traveling to a foreign country to conduct genealogical research to be set apart as missionaries.

beautiful day. Contributed $1.00 to a purse of $17.50 for the benefit of Paul Kammeyer, a fellow missionary who would otherwise have landed in Amsterdam without a cent. 280.2 miles. 78.4° north latitude.

Friday, 20 August 1897

The most pleasant morning that we have had; the wind is somewhat chilly, yet the sea is calm and beautiful; the horizon seems to be more extended. Can see a steamship. Loudin's Original Fisk Jubilee Singers will give a concert tonight. At five o'clock passed very close to sister steamer *Rhynland*. At sunset, while sitting on south side of deck, saw a most beautiful scene. Ocean, a dark blue and billowy, while the horizon was filled with pale blue or light-colored clouds tipped with sunlight. Saw porpoises. Heard Paul's love story; all about his courtship. The concert was good. Some of our boys[13] are disgracing themselves and bringing reproach upon us all. About ten o'clock, stood on the stern, and looking back in the track of the ship, saw a white streak in the midst of the dark blue expanse. This streak was brilliantly dotted with phosphorescent lights, sparkling like diamonds. Beautiful! 209.4 miles.

Saturday, 21 August 1897

Last night the ship tossed from side to side. The sea is still swelling and the same motion continues. It is a common sight to see persons reel from side to side as though intoxicated. Birds and porpoises are still seen. Ship rolled all day; not seasick but sick of the sea! Ocean is beautiful as it heaves and swells. It looks like a long stretch of rolling hills and intervening valleys. Listened to Mr. Early's description of Texas—very amusing. Said he would not eat porcupine meat. "Them *things* might come out through your sides!" Sailed 289.7 miles.

Sunday, 22 August 1897

Stormy. The wind is blowing from the south, beating the rain against the south deck. Very cold. At ten o'clock held services in saloon. Captain presiding. Mr. Arrison read text: Eph. 3. Gospel: Matt. 22. The meeting was strictly sectarian. After noon saw many porpoises; seagulls and small birds are still seen. Read the *Four Men*.[14] I. "The man the world sees"; II. "The man as seen by his best friend"; III. "The man as seen by himself"; IV. "The man God sees." At night the Jubilee Singers sang sacred songs.

> If you want to know a Christian,
> Just watch his acts and walks;
> If you want to know a Christian,
> Just listen how he talks.

---

[13]Here the word *boys* means LDS missionaries.

[14]Rev. James Stalker, *The Four Men, Delivered to the Students of Yale University* (New York: Fleming H. Revell Co., 1891).

Fig. 5 *The Fastnet Lighthouse, Ireland.*

Sailed 282 miles.

Monday, 23 August 1897

Pleasant morning; sun shines brightly. Wrote a letter to Nettie. About 1:30, while standing on the deck, saw one of the grandest scenes of the voyage. The sun shone brightly, although dark clouds hung around the horizon. The sea was a dark blue; the wind strong enough to throw the waves high as the ship. One moment we would be on the crest of a billowy wave, then sink to the surface of a watery valley, while behind us would rise another mighty heave tipped with ocean foam! All around us the waves are rising high in the air. Luckily the wind is in our favor; as it is two have already washed the lower deck. The steerage[15] passengers are not to be seen! Another steamer. Sailed 294.2 miles.

Tuesday, 24 August 1897

Last night was rough. This morning the sun is shining brightly, although the wind is cold. The steerage passengers had trouble with a crazy man. He was held by six or eight men and put in a "straight jacket" and his feet chained. At twelve o'clock we are 107 miles from Queenstown, Ireland. At one o'clock saw land—a welcome sight! At the same time, in fact while looking at the distant mountains, we saw a huge light-brown monster near the prow of the ship. It proved to be a whale. Saw it twice afterwards. The fast S.S. *Teutonic* passed us. At 3:30 finished reading *New Witness for God*.[16] At four o'clock passed close to the southwestern coast of Ireland—quite rugged. Lighthouses all along the coast. One on a solitary cliff southeast from us is the Fastnet (Fig. 5), revolving flash-light. Saw ruins of old

---

[15]The *steerage* is the part of the ship allotted to the passengers who travel at the cheapest rate.

[16]B. H. Roberts, *A New Witness for God* (Salt Lake City: George Q. Cannon and Sons, 1895).

castles. At 5:30 ship stopped, boats were lowered, and the rudder examined. Fishing smacks all around us; seagulls flying everywhere. Posted Nettie's letter at 6:30. Singing at eight by Jubilee Singers.

Selections

"O Father, Protect Us."

Trio, Misses [blank] and Miss Wilson.

Chorus, "Jordan River," and others. All good.

Arrived at Queenstown at 10 P.M. The "tender"[17] came alongside of our ship and carried those bound for that city to shore. We then sailed for Liverpool.

Wednesday, 25 August 1897

Beautiful morning; sailing northeast up St. George Channel. The shore of Wales is dimly seen in the distance. Sea calm and beautiful. At 12:30 passed Holyhead Lighthouse, seventy miles east from Dublin. The lighthouse cliff is separated from mainland by a chasm over which extends a bridge. Holyhead Church is seen in the distance. At 1:15 passed Skerries Lighthouse. A steamer wrecked on these rocks was lying on its side floundered. Mr. Arrison of Philadelphia invited me to be sure to call on him when I returned. At 6:20 sailed up the Mersey River and looked for the first time at the smoky city of Liverpool. A tugboat pulled us into port. Felt gloomy until we met missionaries, Brothers [Joseph S.] Broadbent and [George W.] Barnes. Going up the street, the little ragged urchins crying out, "Paper, paper, sir," "Matches," "Give me ha'e penny!" "See the Yanks from Philadelphia," "Needle points!" etc. At 42 Islington [Street] received three letters: one from Thomas [McKay], another from George Morris,[18] and one from Joseph L. Peterson. I felt quite happy.

Thursday, 26 August 1897

Received a letter from Claire and another from Tommy. Visited the Free Public Museum. Condor Vulture. The natural arrangement of the home of the birds was a striking feature. The family of flycatchers was interesting. Some had a feather in the shape of a fan just over the bill; the feather was yellow with black tips. The birds of paradise, with their extraordinary plumage, tufts of delicate bright-colored feathers springing from each side of body beneath the wings, with the feathers of the tail elongated

---

[17]The term *tender* refers to a small vessel employed to convey passengers or supplies to and from a large ship anchored in the deeper water.

[18]George Q. Morris (1874-1962) was the son of Elias and Mary L. Walker Morris. From 1899 to 1902 he served a mission to Great Britain, being assigned to the Welsh Conference and then transferred and appointed president of the London Conference in October 1900. Later he served as a bishop for ten years and as president of the Eastern States Mission from 1948 to 1951. In October 1951 he was sustained as Assistant to the Quorum of the Twelve, and then in April 1954 he was ordained an apostle by McKay. He served in this position until his death in April 1962.

into wires twisted into fantastic shapes, were very beautiful. They live on fruits and insects. Besides these there were parrots, toucans, cuckoos, group of tigers, etc., etc.

Wrote to George Morris.

Went into wrong lodging house and asked for my satchel before noticing my mistake! Later, got locked out of office, climbed over wall, borrowed a hat from Mrs. Stewart, inquired the way to Pleasant Street, and joined the elders in meeting. Spoke. After meeting went back to office and met Mr. Parry,[19] counselor to Brother Wells.[20]

Friday, 27 August 1897

Clear morning. Received my appointment to labor in Scottish mission. Bid good-bye to the other boys and started with Brothers Mitchell[21] and Edward[22] for Glasgow [by the] London and North Western Railroad. Arrived in Glasgow at 6 P.M. and took a cab[23] to 130 Barrack Street, the headquarters of the mission. A gloomy-looking place and I was a *gloomy-feeling* boy. Wrote to Claire and Tommy.

Saturday, 28 August 1897

Spent a few hours looking at the city. The people, many of them, are in a deplorable condition. Some of the women are bare-headed and barefooted, ragged and dirty; and such women are raising children! It is a common sight to see women *reeling* along the street. It is enough to make a

---

[19]Edwin F. Parry (1860-1935) served as second counselor to Rulon S. Wells in the presidency of the European Mission from March 1896 to July 1898. During this same period he worked as assistant editor of the *Millennial Star*. Parry wrote *Sketches of Missionary Life* (Salt Lake City: G. Q. Cannon and Sons, 1899), *Joseph Smith's Teachings* (Salt Lake City: Deseret News, 1912), *The Way of Eternal Life* (Salt Lake City: Deseret News, 1917), and *Stories about Joseph Smith, the Prophet* (Salt Lake City: Deseret News, 1934).

[20]Rulon S. Wells (1854-1941) was the son of Daniel H. and Louisa Free Wells. He was sustained as one of the First Seven Presidents of Seventy in 1893 and served as president of the European Mission from June 1896 to December 1898. See his "Greeting," *The Latter-day Saints' Millennial Star* 58 (30 July 1896): 488-89. He then became the Salt Lake manager of the Mutual Life Company of New York.

[21]Joseph H. Mitchell (1860-1944) was baptized in 1882 at the age of twenty-two in Kilwinning, Ayrshire, Scotland, and then emigrated to Utah. When he arrived in Ogden, he was invited to eat at the home of David O. McKay's grandfather, William McKay. Mitchell was set apart as a missionary to Great Britain on 6 August 1897, arriving in Liverpool on 25 August 1897. Within the Scottish Conference Mitchell labored in the areas of Airdrie, Ayr, Burnbank, Glasgow, Lanark, and Newarthill. He was released in July 1899, arriving home later that month. See the Joseph H. Mitchell Collection, Accession 1770, located in the Manuscripts Division, J. Willard Marriott Library, University of Utah, Salt Lake City, with the original diaries being at the LDS Church Archives.

[22]John T. Edward (1867-1959) married Mary Elizabeth Thomas in 1891, and they had a daughter but she died six weeks later. He was set apart as a missionary to Great Britain on 3 August 1897, arriving in Liverpool on 25 August 1897. Within the Scottish Conference he worked in the areas of Ayrshire, Glasgow, and Edinburgh. He was released from his mission early due to ill health, leaving Scotland in April 1899. After his return to Salt Lake City, he continued his profession as a butcher. See the John T. Edward Diaries, Accession 1710, located in the Manuscripts Division, J. Willard Marriott Library, University of Utah, Salt Lake City.

[23]A *cab* or *cabriolet* was a carriage with either two or four wheels, drawn by one horse.

person sick. *Utah* is *dearer* than *ever*. At night took an hour's stroll through the streets. During that time, I saw one fight, four women quarreling and swearing, twenty drunks—half women and as many more doubtfuls! Truly Glasgow is a rocky city—*rock* houses, *rocky* streets, and on Saturday night, *rocky* people.

Sunday, 29 August 1897

Stormy. At eleven o'clock went to Sunday School on Oxford Street. The actions of one of the teachers were such as would drive the members away. After Sunday School took a stroll with Brother George Campbell. At two o'clock attended meeting, after which went to Sister Neilson's where we spent a very pleasant afternoon. She prepared an excellent dinner and made us so welcome that I felt quite at home. I made a mistake in calling her *dessert* (cornstarch pudding) mush. Changed it as a joke!

At 6:30 another meeting. Had to preach. At eight o'clock we held the first open-air meeting that I ever attended. The girls of the branch were with us. Two speakers. Had a good meeting. Bid acquaintances good-bye. Miss Neilson invited me to call during the week. Received appointment to labor in Lanark.

Monday, 30 August 1897

Spent the morning at conference house,[24] studying the Bible. At 5:15 left Glasgow for Lanark, where I arrived about one hour and a half later. We were met by Brothers Pender,[25] Johnston,[26] and Jones.[27]

Wrote a letter to the folks at home.

---

[24]The mission headquarters (at 130 Barrack Street) was known as the *conference house*. The Scottish Conference included both the proselyting missionaries and the local members in the branches throughout all of Scotland.

[25]William Pender (1844-1902) was born at Glasgow, Lanarkshire, Scotland. In Salt Lake City he was set apart for a mission to Great Britain on 23 April 1897, arriving at Liverpool on 12 May 1897. Within the Scottish Conference Pender labored in the areas of Airdrie, Glasgow, and Stirling. He returned to Utah in September 1898 due to sickness.

[26]Peter G. Johnston (1864-1931) had married Alice Duckworth in 1893, and they already had one son and another on the way when he was set apart for a mission to Great Britain on 15 November 1896, arriving in Liverpool on 10 December 1896. In the Scottish Conference he labored in the areas of Motherwell, Stirling, and Wishaw. In May 1898 Johnston was transferred from the Scottish Conference to the Irish Conference. Johnston was released five months later, arriving home in November 1898. He and his wife had a third son in 1901. Johnston served as bishop of the Blackfoot Ward, Blackfoot Stake, from 1904 to 1905. Complications of childbirth caused the death of both his wife and daughter in 1910. Four years later he married Flora Harding. He was called to Oregon to preside over the Union Stake from June 1917 to March 1918, being set apart to this position by Apostle David O. McKay. Johnston also served eight terms as a member of the Idaho State Legislature. See the Peter G. Johnston Collection, Accession 1755, located in the Manuscripts Division, J. Willard Marriott Library, University of Utah, Salt Lake City.

[27]Thomas W. Jones (1863-1902) was set apart for a mission to Great Britain on 28 February 1896, arriving in Liverpool on 18 March 1896. In the Scottish Conference he labored in the areas of Airdrie, Lanark, and Wishaw. In December 1897 Jones was transferred to the Welsh Conference, and in March 1898 he left to return to his home in Idaho.

Tuesday, 31 August 1897

Distributed one hundred and fifty tracts—seventy-five double ones.[28] This was my first experience, and although the people treated me courteously and with a few exceptions accepted the tracts, yet I never felt so gloomy in my life.[29] I have heaved a *thousand* sighs! I expect to heave a thousand more before our meeting is over.

At 2 P.M. visited the beautiful Falls of the Clyde, Wallace's[30] Leap, Wallace's Cave, and Bonnington Falls. I will enjoy the memory perhaps more than the reality—I was so "blue."

Meeting at 7:30 in Mrs. Brown's house,[31] Bannatyne Street. The house was full, and Brother John Robertson[32] spoke to them for about an hour and ten minutes. The order was good.

Wednesday, 1 September 1897

Took a stroll around suburbs of Lanark. Crossed one of the old Saxon bridges, built 1200 A.D. At 10:30 stood on a long rock bridge spanning[33] the Mouse River,[34] from which place I had a good view of the Cartland Crags.[35] The luxuriant growth of forest trees on either bank and totally covering the entire hillside made the scene truly picturesque. Descended to the river and looked at the bridge from below. It is a beautiful stone structure, built seventy-five years ago, and is 145 feet high. Walked around the old hiding places of Wallace.

---

[28]The primary method to find potential converts was door-to-door tracting. The number of tracts successfully distributed was seen as an index of the missionary's skill, and on one day in April 1898 McKay distributed 240 tracts. McKay, in a 9 September 1897 letter to Emma Ray Riggs, expressed his dislike of tracting: "The distributing of tracts, too, is unpleasant for me. When I first started, I could do nothing but heave sighs. I sighed as I knocked at the door, breathed heavily as I gave the tract, and sighed again as I walked away. This was repeated about seventy-five times in three hours. If I had continued, I would have sighed myself away!"

[29]Concerning this first experience in tracting McKay stated at the end of his mission that he "was quite discouraged and downhearted. These feelings were removed by humble prayer." See minutes of meeting, 7 August 1899, the Scottish Conference Records, British Mission, LR17716, ser. 11, located in the LDS Church Archives, Historical Department, The Church of Jesus Christ of Latter-day Saints, Salt Lake City.

[30]Sir William Wallace (ca. 1270-1305) was a Scottish patriot who led a revolt against King Edward I of England, defeating the English in the Battle of Stirling Bridge in 1297. In 1305 Wallace was captured, taken to London, condemned as a traiter, hanged, disemboweled, beheaded, and quartered.

[31]McKay incorrectly wrote "hall."

[32]John W. Robertson (1851-1906) was born in Glasgow, Lanarkshire, Scotland. He was set apart for a mission to Great Britain on 3 April 1896, arriving in Liverpool on 22 April 1896. In the Scottish Conference Robertson served in Airdrie, Glasgow, and Paisley. In September 1897 Robertson was transferred and made president of the Irish Conference. He returned in May 1898. Robertson served another mission to Great Britain from 1903 to 1905.

[33]McKay incorrectly wrote "expanding."

[34]What McKay calls the *Mouse River* is technically known as the Mouse Water. In Scottish, *water* refers to a stream or brook. The Mouse Water starts at an altitude of 1,100 ft. in northeastern Lanarkshire, winds sixteen miles to the southwest, and falls into the Clyde near Lanark Bridge.

[35]McKay incorrectly wrote "Getting Crags."

Fig. 6 *Municipal Building, Glasgow.*

Thursday, 2 September 1897

Left Lanark at 8:45 for Wishaw. Walked about three miles and met the family of Brother [Robert] Orr. He went with us to Newarthill, where we held a meeting at the home of Sister [Nellie] Jack, a newly confirmed member. Brother McMillan[36] met with us. We had an excellent time; Sister Jack's daughters could not do too much for our entertainment and comfort. From here we walked to Brother Orr's. Although we had eaten heartily at Mrs. Jack's, we ate another dinner here, after which we walked to Motherwell and called on Brothers Cameron[37] and Montgomery[38] (missionaries). From Motherwell we went to Glasgow where we held an open-air meeting at Bridgeton Cross. Retired about eleven.

Friday, 3 September 1897

In Glasgow. At 11 A.M. took a bath. I was surprised to see how inferior their bath-rooms and plunge are to the Salt Lake Sanitarium. Visited the Municipal Building (Fig. 6), a magnificent stone building erected at the cost

[36]William McMillan (1849-1904) was set apart for a mission to Great Britain on 14 August 1896. He was assigned to the Scottish Conference, working in the areas of Glasgow and Wishaw. In September 1897 he was appointed president of the Scottish Conference and was released the following March.

[37]Robert Cameron (1869-1957) was born at Paisley, Renfrewshire, Scotland. He was set apart for a mission to Great Britain on 24 April 1896, arriving in Liverpool on 14 May 1896. Within the Scottish Conference he labored in the areas of Glasgow, Motherwell, and Wishaw. Cameron was released in May 1898, arriving home the next month.

[38]Alma Montgomery (1852-1921) was set apart for a mission to Great Britain on 1 May 1896, arriving in Liverpool on 20 May 1896. Within the Scottish Conference he labored in Ayrshire, Dunfermline, Glasgow, and Motherwell. Montgomery was released in May 1898.

of 750,000 pounds. As it is not yet completed, it will cost much more. The banquet room is very beautiful, being eighty-four feet long and forty-four feet wide and having 210 combined electric and gas lights. West of this building stand many monuments, the central one being Sir Walter Scott's,[39] [which] towers above all the rest.

Received two letters: from Father[40] and Claire.

Saturday, 4 September 1897

In Glasgow. Spent the day in reading and writing. Mailed a letter to Claire. At 8:55 P.M. left Glasgow in company with Sister Jack and family, also Brothers Johnston and Orr, and went by train to Omoa. Stayed with Brother Orr; treated very cordially.

Sunday, 5 September 1897

Fast Day. At 12 M. [meridian] went to Newarthill with Brothers Orr and Johnston and held an open-air meeting. The people stood in their doorways to listen. Some stood in the street one block away. Here, standing in the middle of the street on both sides of which was a long row of whitewashed houses about six feet to the square, I made my first open-air speech. I shall never forget it. The day was cold and cloudy (I had been wishing that it would rain), and the street was dismal and uninviting. Perhaps there were about thirty eager-looking eyes staring wonderingly in mine. My remarks were brief and made in fear and trembling!!! A Brother Duncan was with us.

At two o'clock we held another meeting at Mr. Orr's house. Made a few remarks here. At 6:30 P.M. held another meeting in the same place. Was unexpectedly called upon to speak here also. Spent a very pleasant evening with Mrs. Orr and Miss Jack and others and retired about 10 P.M.

Monday, 6 September 1897

At 11 A.M. left Brother Orr's and walked to Wishaw. Visited Mr. and Mrs. Gardner, friends of Brother Johnston, who insisted on our spending the afternoon with them. They had an organ and a piano in the house. Had a pleasant time and were warmly invited to call again. Left Wishaw for Lanark at 4:20.

Mrs. Wylie told us how the people had expressed themselves about our meeting (Tuesday last). "The preachin' was good," says one, "but you should come and hear their singing: it's terrible!" Another said, "Ah, it was

---

[39]Sir Walter Scott (1771-1832), Scottish poet and romantic writer, published many historical novels, including *Waverley, Old Mortality, Rob Roy, The Heart of Midlothian, Ivanhoe*, and *The Talisman.*

[40]David McKay (1844-1917), David O. McKay's father, was born in Geise, near Janetstown, Caithness, Scotland. He was set apart on 7 April 1881 as a missionary to Great Britain, serving in Scotland and returning two years later. Also, he served as bishop of the Huntsville Ward from 1885 to 1905.

sad!" etc., etc. It was sad, for we sang "Farewell, All Earthly Honors." One woman said she wants to hear us preach tomorrow night, but she is going out when we sing!!

Tuesday, 7 September 1897

At Lanark. I stayed in the room nearly all day reading. At 7:30 went to the hall in company with Brothers Pender and Johnston and held a meeting. Johnston occupied most of the time. Brother Pender and I made a few closing remarks. There were only about twelve attentive listeners: the others came for curiosity—maybe to hear us sing? After meeting I received a long, interesting letter from Ray. Retired about 11 P.M.

Wednesday, 8 September 1897

Twenty-fourth birthday! I am beginning to feel my age! Wrote a letter to Mamma and one to Joseph Burrows. At 4:15 left Lanark for Glasgow to attend a farewell party given to President Williams.[41] The evening was spent in singing and speaking. Some of the young saints have excellent voices. Maggie Gain sang, "Till the Roses Come Again," very beautifully. I had a very pleasant time. Slept that night at the hotel.

Thursday, 9 September 1897

In Glasgow. Went down to the Anchor Line wharf to see Brother Williams sail away. To see him go made me homesick, and thoughts that I would have to stay here two years longer made me sad. At 8:30 testimony meeting in conference house. Wrote to Ray. As the conference house was crowded, Brother Johnston and I went to the hotel—Craig's Temperance Hotel[42] on Candleriggs Street.

Friday, 10 September 1897

At 10:30 went down to the docks to see the Duke and Duchess of York[43] land. We waited for three hours; at length the prow of his ship was dimly seen through the fog. The boat was beautifully decorated with the national colors, and as she came slowly up the Clyde, the cheers from the crown welcomed the royal party. The Duke, dressed in a Prince Albert suit,[44] stood on the *bridge* tipping his hat to us, I believe, for we were standing on boxes above the others. The Duchess stood by her husband's side.

---

[41]Milford Williams (1865-1933) was set apart for a mission to Great Britain on 25 October 1895, arriving in Liverpool on 13 November 1895. He was assigned to work in the Liverpool Conference and in May 1896 he was transferred and appointed president of the Scottish Conference. Williams was released in September 1897.

[42]A *temperance hotel* provided guests with lodging and meals but not alcoholic beverages.

[43]George, Duke of York (1865-1936) was the second son of Edward, Prince of Wales (later Edward VII). In 1892 George was made Duke of York and the next year he married Princess Mary of Teck. In 1910 he became King George V.

[44]A *Prince Albert suit* was a double-breasted coat with the upper part fitted to the body.

Fig. 7 *West End Park, Glasgow.*

She was dressed in a violet-colored dress with a light-grey cape over her shoulders, while her hat was trimmed with light-colored feathers, matching her dress very tastefully. The streets through which they passed were gayly decorated. As the procession moved along, it was cheered by hundreds of thousands of people. All this and much more just because he held the title of "Duke"!! He came to lay the cornerstone to the art gallery near the West End Park (Fig. 7).

In the afternoon wrote to Christian Mortensen. Received an interesting letter from Annie [McKay].

Visited the Necropolis (Fig. 8) and viewed the tombs of "unnumbered dead." Stood at foot of the John Knox[45] Monument.

> At night I was homesick, miserable, and sad.
> If I had made a discovery, I am sure I had been mad!
> Do you ask what made me so sick at my heart?
> I itched, and felt sure that I had a "start"!!

Saturday, 11 September 1897

Spent the day at the conference house. Read the Acts of the Apostles. Went to the [public] bath-rooms and searched for "travelers,"[46] but found none. In the evening strolled through some of the streets with Brother Mitchell. Drunken men and women staggered through the principal thoroughfares as usual. Saw a fight in which the participants' wives were trying to separate the drunken beasts.

Sunday, 12 September 1897

Took cab for Blantyre, in company with Brother Johnston. Met in a

---

[45]John Knox (ca. 1514-1572) was the leader of the Scottish Reformation and set the austere moral tone of the Church of Scotland.

[46]In the Scottish dialect, *travelers* were head lice.

Fig. 8 *Glasgow Cathedral and Necropolis, Glasgow.*

meeting capacity with the members of the branch there. Preached about fifteen minutes. After meeting spent the afternoon with Brother Irvine's family, Mr. [Thomas] Halliday being present also. Had a good time. At six o'clock went to Brother [John] Cook's and from there to Brother [Samuel] Steven's, where we were treated to our *fourth* meal.

Accepted Mr. Halliday's invitation to stay with him all night.[47] He lives at 12 Bothwell Street, Hamilton. His house is very comfortable, and he and all his folks—parents and two brothers—treated us very courteously. Soon after we were seated in the parlor, he sat down to the organ, saying, "I'll sing you my favorite hymn." He is not a Mormon, so I expected a sectarian hymn, of course. Imagine my surprise and delight when he began to sing that inspired song, "O My Father." He sang every verse from memory. Time passed pleasantly; and it was not until [the] clock said "midnight" that we bid goodnight to our genial host and retired.

Monday, 13 September 1897

Spent the morning in the parlor. Mr. Halliday sang and Brother Johnston played the violin; so we had quite a concert among ourselves. After breakfast, we walked to Blantyre and spent a few minutes with Brother and Sister Irvine, after which we boarded the train for Glasgow. Met Miss Birchell. Open-air meeting at Bridgeton Cross.[48]

Brother [John H.] Bailey came to conference house.

---

[47]Since most elders during this time period lived in rather spartan apartments, they welcomed the opportunity to visit, eat, and sleep overnight with members—and even non-members.

[48]Archibald R. Anderson, Diary, 13 September 1897, added that David O. McKay offered the opening prayer at the open-air meeting. See Archibald J. Anderson, "A Brief History," 11, in the Archibald R. Anderson Collection, Accession 1735, located in the Manuscripts Division, J. Willard Marriott Library, University of Utah, Salt Lake City.

Tuesday, 14 September 1897

Stayed in conference house and wrote three letters—one to Annie, one to Mr. Moody, and still another to John Hall.

While writing, a man stood in the middle of the street and began to sing. Moved by curiosity, I stepped to the window and listened to his pitiful story, a wife and children starving, out of work, soon [to] be driven from home; all clothes pawned. "You see my condition," said he, as he unbuttoned his coat exposing his nakedness! Threw him some money. Mrs. Noble gave him a vest and some food. We found out afterward that we had been duped by a professional beggar.

At night went to a minstrel concert with Brothers Pender, McMillan, and Anderson.[49] It was a "fake." I think I got my shilling's worth in experience.

Miss Birchell left that night for Preston.

Wednesday, 15 September 1897

Spent most of the day at the conference house. After buying some clothing including an overcoat, I left Glasgow, in company with Brothers Johnston and Mitchell, for Lanark.

We found all things right at Mrs. Wylie's and, after reading awhile, went to bed to enjoy a good night's rest.

Thursday, 16 September 1897

Spent the day studying and writing.

Wrote to May and Angus [W. McKay].[50] Received a letter from Claire.

Friday, 17 September 1897

A beautiful day. The sky is clear and the sun rays are warm and pleasant —something unusual in Lanark for this time of the year.

Answered Claire's letter.

The three of us—Brother Johnston and Brother Mitchell—visited Mrs. McMannis, an old member of the Church, also a Brother Nebeker and wife, who were once members. All were pleased to see us.

Visited an old weaver, who was sitting at his loom throwing the shuttle back and forth making a bolt of gingham. He weaved about seven yards in a day and received for his monotonous toil about 2/9[51] or 66¢! This is nearly

---

[49]Archibald R. Anderson (1868-1948) was set apart as a missionary to Great Britain on 25 October 1895 and when he arrived in Liverpool was assigned to the Scottish Conference. He labored in the areas of Aberdeen, Burnbank, Edinburgh, and Glasgow, returning in December 1897. He was a woolgrower and banker in Fairview, Utah, and served in the North Sanpete Stake High Council for twenty-one years.

[50]Angus W. McKay (1872-1956), David O. McKay's cousin, was the son of Angus and Williamena McKay. He was set apart for a mission to the Southern States on 16 June 1897 and returned in November 1899.

[51]In the British monetary system there were twelve pence in a shilling and twenty shillings

Fig. 9 *The Old Roman Bridge, Lanark.*

twice as much as some earn.

Visited again the Cartland Bridge, also the old Roman Bridge (Fig. 9) over the River Mouse. Crossed the Clyde to Kirkfieldbank. Returned to lodgings in evening.

Saturday, 18 September 1897

Spent the forenoon studying the New Testament. After dinner visited St. Mary's Roman Catholic Church. From here we went to the Church of St. Kentigern, built about the middle of the twelfth century. Nothing remains now but the crumbling walls of a once-magnificent church, now visited by all tourists. It was here that Sir William Wallace first saw his wife.

> On from the kirk that was without the toun. . . .
> Upon a day to ye kirk as she went,
> Wallace hyr saw, as his eyne can cast
> (Blind Harry's "Wallace").[52]

In the churchyard are many ancient graves, as the following inscription, taken from a tombstone lying a few steps south of the Lee Aisle will show:

Heir lyes Wiliam Hervi who sufered at the cros of Lanerk the 2 of March 1682 age 38 for his adhering to the word of God and Scotlands covenanted work of Reformation.

Another interesting tombstone is one bearing an inscription chiseled by

---

in a pound. In 1897 each shilling was equal to twenty-four American cents. In this case the notation "2/9" refers to two shillings and nine pence and the sixty-six cents that this amount was worth in 1897 would be equivalent to $5.36 today (based on a calculation using the consumer price index).

[52]Cf. Matthew P. McDiarmid, ed., *Hary's Wallace: (Vita Nobilissimi Defensoris Scotie Wilelmi Wallace Militis)* (Edinburgh: William Blackwood and Sons, 1968), 1: 91, ll. 604-605. Henry, the minstrel (ca. 1440-1492), flourished from A.D. 1470-1492, and the poem about Wallace was composed about 1477.

Scott's Old Mortality[53] in memory of one James Buchanan. Style: "In Memory of" etc. The Lee Aisle is the place of interment of many of the Lockhart family. While we were there, the old sexton laid another being in his last resting place, yet the graves are so close together now that one walks over them as he reads the ancient inscriptions on the tombstones.

From here we took Brother Mitchell to see the Falls of the Clyde, Wallace's Leap, etc. I enjoyed this visit much more than I did the other one. Johnston grew quite poetic as we viewed the Corra Linn Falls (Fig. 10). Hear him:

> See the dashing roaring torrent,
>   Leaping from rock to rock,
> Encased by rage majestic,
>   Making your head swim at the top!

and

> It's like ten thousand devils,
> Dashing headlong to —
>   To h--l knows where!!

We wandered through the wood and along the river's bank until nearly dark. We returned to our lodgings about 7:15. After eating a good supper, we retired to dream of home and happy days gone by: such has been my experience nearly every night since coming here; but with the morning comes disappointment and loneliness.

Sunday, 19 September 1897

At 12:15 went to the town hall and listened to Mr. Blair's sermon. He is known here as the "town preacher" and is one of the leading ones in opposing us. I have never before heard a sermon which made me such a strong Latter-day Saint. His subject was "The Atonement," and he tried to show that Christ did it all. We have nothing to do. After dinner studied passages showing that Christ redeemed us from the bonds of death, but we must work out our own salvation.

About five o'clock we took a stroll along the banks of the Mouse River. For two hours we walked through one of the most beautiful woods that I have ever seen. On each side of the path the sturdy oak and beech grew strong and stately, forming an archway overhead with their intertwining branches. Sometimes we could stand on the brink of a precipice and look at the river beneath or cast our eyes down along its densely wooded banks. The sun, just sinking behind the horizon, painting the sky with varied hues, and sending his faint rays through the gently stirring leaves, lent his aid to make the scene more enchanting. Saw a hedgehog.

---

[53]Sir Walter Scott, *Tales of My Landlord*, 4 vols. (Edinburgh: William Blackwood, 1816). Vols. 2-4 contained *The Old Mortality*. The character known as "Old Mortality" is said to be Robert Paterson.

Monday, 20 September 1897
    Walked six miles to the town of Carluke. Tried in vain to get a hall in
which to preach. Distributed 100 tracts (300 in all) and then walked back
to Lanark, where we arrived about 6:30, tired, leg-weary, and hungry. I had

Fig. 10 *Corra Linn Falls, Lanark.*

two refusals—both Catholics.

> All missionaries know this stubborn fact:
> To offer a Catholic a gospel tract,
> Is like pouring water down the small of your back.
> Such a look does he get as the door goes "smack"!

Tuesday, 21 September 1897
Stayed in the house all day. We did not go to Carluke because it looked as though it might rain.

Wednesday, 22 September 1897
After breakfast started for Carluke with 100 tracts each. Just as we entered the town, it began to rain and continued all day.[54] With our waterproofs on and umbrellas up, we went from house to house. My district was somewhat scattered, so I had much walking to do. Before I got through I was nearly tired out; and then I had five miles to walk (the other boys had gone ahead of me, thinking I might overtake them). As I trudged along through the pouring rain, I thought of home and particularly of the horses. Before I reached my lodgings, I was not only tired but sick. That night I had a burning fever; my head ached and my brain seemed to be on fire. Towards morning the fever left me.

Thursday, 23 September 1897
Cold and stormy. Stayed in the house, studying and writing.
Received a long letter from home. Answered it and wrote another to Joseph L. Peterson.

Friday, 24 September 1897
Storming. Another day in house. Copied a part of an old record of the Orkney Branch for Brother Johnston.[55]

Saturday, 25 September 1897
Walked to Carluke and distributed 111 tracts. One old lady, who had heard of the "Mormonites" and who "didna' like the creed," said to me, "Ah, my young man, search yer ane heart for I think yer creed is wrong." She was a very pleasant old lady; and the short conversation we had made me feel encouraged. After trying to get the schoolhouse in Braidwood,[56] Brother

---

[54]Joseph Mitchell, Diary, 22 September 1897, explained about McKay's persistence: "Bro. McKay felt that we should give out our tracts, and after we had worked for a while, Bro. Johnston and I proposed that we should give it up and wait for better weather, but it seemed that Bro. McKay was determined to stay with it—rain or no rain. So we joined him and stayed with it until we had given out all the tracts we had."

[55]Peter G. Johnston was born in Graesay, one of the Orkney Islands, on 15 August 1864.

[56]McKay wrote "Braidshaw" instead of the correct "Braidwood," which is found in Joseph Mitchell's diary.

Mitchell and I walked home. (Brother Johnston took the train in order to fill an appointment.) At night, I was tired out. My head ached; my muscles ached; my heart ached.

Received a letter from Claire at 9:30 P.M.

Sunday, 26 September 1897

Spent most of the day in reading and writing.

Monday, 27 September 1897

Started for Lesmahagow, a town lying about seven miles southwest from Lanark, and arrived there about 2 P.M. Distributed tracts. The people were bitter. One woman tore a tract in pieces as soon as I gave it to her. Another, after finding out what it was, shut the door in my face. After tracting the town, we had a good dinner at a restaurant and started for Lanark. On our road we distributed more tracts. I met an estimable old lady who, after hearing who I was and what I was doing, became very much interested. We had a long conversation, during which she said, "Weel, I've been a long time in my church and I dinna think Christ will forsake me noo." When I went to leave, she extended her hand and with tears in her eyes said, "God bless ye, for I believe your doin' a noble work." She did me a *world* of good. Arrived in Lanark at 8:30 P.M.

Tuesday, 28 September 1897

Beautiful morning. Holiday for Lanark and vicinity—races. Wrote to Claire. Walked out around the racecourse and saw part of one race. Met Mr. Blair, the town missionary, and he and Brother Johnston had quite a controversy on authority. Brother Johnston had the better of it, so much so that Blair, looking at his watch, took an abrupt though pleasant leave. At night walked through the "show." Donkeys for hire was a unique feature.

Wednesday, 29 September 1897

Studied in morning and visited Mrs. McMannis and others in the afternoon. At night made preparations for leaving Lanark on the morning train, as we have been advised by those in authority (priesthood) to change our field of labor.

Thursday, 30 September 1897

Left Lanark on the 8:45 train. Stopped at Wishaw and walked to Newarthill, where we held a meeting in Sister Jack's house. Had an excellent time. Mrs. Jack and her daughters, especially Nellie, are faithful Latter-day Saints. Their home is neat and comfortable, which fact, with their intelligence and cordiality, makes a visit always pleasant. After meeting walked back to Wishaw (stopping a few minutes at Brother Orr's, Cleland) and took the 5:30 train to Glasgow. Testimony meeting at night. While at Sister

Jack's, Brother McMillan gave me two letters—one from Tommy and one from Joseph L. [Peterson].

Friday, 1 October 1897

At conference house. Wrote to Tommy. Had a pleasant conversation with a young lady in post office. She accepted some tracts and inquired about the time and place of meeting. At night we all went to the Royalty Theatre, where a London company played the drama written by William Gillette[57] and entitled *Secret Service*. The actors, with few exceptions, were good.

Saturday, 2 October 1897

At conference house, copying names and addresses of missionaries. At night walked through the town, saw two women fighting and another with a little babe in her arms trying to stop them. A crowd of *men* witnessed it. The drunkenness and debauchery in Glasgow [on] Saturday night is appalling.

Sunday, 3 October 1897

Clear day. Brothers Anderson and Mitchell went to Blantyre to meet a branch of the saints; Brothers McMillan and Johnston went to Newarthill to organize a branch; and Brother Pender and I met with the Glasgow Branch. We attended Sunday School at 12 M. [meridian] and testimony meeting at 2 P.M., after which I went home with John Neilson. Brother Pender went with Brother [Joseph] Leggat. I had an excellent dinner and a sociable time. At 6:30 P.M. went to meeting. Was called to speak first. Enjoyed a good spirit. Brother Pender spoke next, after which meeting dismissed. There is much ill feeling in this branch; something [is] wrong.

Monday, 4 October 1897

Letter from Claire.

Assisted in ruling and arranging conference records. Studied. Went to Newton, then back to Rutherglen in search of a Mr. Hamilton; treated courteously by strangers. At night went to the zoo; the lions were the best I have ever seen.

Tuesday, 5 October 1897

At conference house. Wrote to Ray and Claire. Met with the choir at night. Spent quite a pleasant evening. Considering the circumstances under which the members are placed, they are doing well.

---

[57]William Gillette (1853-1937), an actor and playwright, acted the part of Sherlock Holmes on the stage.

Wednesday, 6 October 1897

Copied monthly reports for President McMillan. Did some studying. In the evening young McEwan of [the] Sunday School called to see us.

Thursday, 7 October 1897

Just as I was getting out of bed, the postman came with the American mail. I received three letters: one from Nettie, one from Tommy, and one from George Morris. Answered Tommy's letter and then went down to the Anchor Line wharf to see the boat sail for America. There were twenty-six elders and about forty emigrants—all from Scandinavia. Meeting in the conference house at night.

Friday, 8 October 1897

In the morning read a letter from Claire. Spent the forenoon assisting the president in sending out monthly reports. Wrote to Nettie and in the evening sent a letter to Claire. Stormy day.

Saturday, 9 October 1897

Worked in the office, addressing wrappers for *Millennial Stars* and making out bills. In the afternoon, in company with Brothers McMillan, Pender, Johnston, and Mitchell, visited the Glasgow City Water Works. They are perhaps the best in the world. The water is taken from Loch Katrine and is held in two ponds, one covering an area of thirty-five acres and the other fifty acres. Each has an average depth of about fifty feet. The water is filtered through a brass sieve—nineteen squares to the inch. Beautiful flowers growing all around. At night read a venomous article in the *Hamilton Advertiser* from Herman Smith, Josephite,[58] in which he attempts to prove that Joseph Smith never gave a revelation on celestial marriage but that Brigham Young gave it on August 9, 1853!

Sunday, 10 October 1897

Stormy day, wind and rain. Attended Sunday School at twelve noon, meeting at 2 P.M. after which, in company with President McMillan and Brother Mitchell, I took dinner at Brother [Fletcher] McDonald's on Mansion Street, Possilpark. With Mrs. [Annabell Pauline] McDonald's kind welcome and free hospitality, and the pleasant company of Miss [Janet] Lang, her sister, and of her cheerful daughter, Mary, it is needless for me to say, I enjoyed myself, as did the others also. At 6 P.M. all except Mrs. McDonald took the car[59] for Gorbals, where meeting commenced one-half hour later.

---

[58]"Josephite" refers to a member of the Reorganized Church of Jesus Christ of Latter Day Saints, which since 1860 had been led by Joseph Smith III. See Roger D. Launius, *Joseph Smith III: Pragmatic Prophet* (Urbana: University of Illinois Press, 1988).

[59]A *car* or *carriage* was a wheeled vehicle, especially one with only two wheels.

Brothers Anderson and Leggat were the speakers. After meeting: "Good-night," "Remember," "Cured?" "Keep," etc., etc.

Monday, 11 October 1897

In the morning at conference house. After dinner President McMillan, Brother Pender, Brother Neilson, and I went to Auchinairn to administer to an unfortunate man who has lain in his bed for eight years. He was hurt in a pit. Although he is not a Mormon, still it was at his request that we went there. It is pitiful to see him, lying there helpless. After the administration, he seemed to feel easier and invited us to come again. Choir practice at night. We are loafing around the house here, waiting for our appointment.

Tuesday, 12 October 1897

Housecleaning day. Brother Johnston and I called on Mrs. Anderson. After having a short conversation with her, we went back to Argyle Street, where we met Mr. Halliday. Visited the Botanical Gardens, and then went to a Mrs. Galbraith's, Mrs. Halliday's aunt. Here we spent a very pleasant evening. Received an invitation to call again. Reached conference house at 10 P.M.

Wednesday, 13 October 1897

Received my appointment from President McMillan to labor in Glasgow and to assist him in the office. Met Mr. and Mrs. Phipps from Wales en route to Utah. They have no relatives nor acquaintances out there, yet the little woman is as full of hope and cheer as though she were going right to the bosom of her friends. I hope she is. She has the address of Elias Morris. The *address only*, not even a word of introduction. Rather cool in the elder who gave it!

Thursday, 14 October 1897

Received letters from Dr. Moody, D. R. [Alma], and Chris Mortensen. Addressed mail to the missionaries. Read one hour, then went down to the Anchor Line wharf to see the *Furnessia* sail. Here I had a pleasant talk with some of the emigrants. Gave Mr. and Mrs. Phipps a letter of introduction to George Q. Morris. They felt pleased and so did I. Kindness begets friendship. At 1:30 she sailed down the Clyde. Spent the afternoon in office reading. Testimony meeting at night.

Friday, 15 October 1897

In house all day. Wrote to George Morris and Lizzie [McKay].

Saturday, 16 October 1897

In the morning, addressed wrappers for *Millennial Stars*. Read *Star*. In afternoon visited the Glasgow Cathedral (Fig. 11), the most interesting structure of its kind in Scotland. It dates back to the year 601—not the building as it now stands, but the see[60] was established then. Modern antiquaries have added many things to it. The painting on the windows costs $90,000: one alone, donated by Raird Company, cost £2,500, $12,500. The nave is full of interest, as is also the choir. The crypts are *solemn*, though interesting. The damp, misty odor that arises, together with the tombs of departed saints (and sinners also), makes one feel as though we were about to enter the doomed cell into which Constance was thrown by the old abbot as described by Scott in *Marmion*.[61]

Finished reading *From Jest to Earnest* by Rev. E. P. Roe.[62] This book was loaned to me by Mr. Halliday's uncle. It is very interesting. The heroine is like a very dear classmate of mine.

Sunday, 17 October 1897

Went to Sunday School at twelve noon. The lesson was on the twenty-fourth chapter of Matthew. The more I studied the chapter, the more confused I became. The others, too, were confused, as was even [James] Clark himself, our teacher. One of the members opened the Pearl of Great Price and read from it Joseph Smith's interpretation [JS-M 1:1-55]. The truth flashed upon our minds as clear and distinct as the sun in the cloudless sky. Such instances as this show the divinity of Joseph Smith's mission. At meeting we had another feast. Ate dinner at Brother [William] Hamilton's. Meeting at 6:30.

Monday, 18 October 1897

Received a letter from Ray.

Spent the morning hours in study. In the afternoon in company with President McMillan and Brother Pender, I visited Mr. [Daniel] Ferguson, the old gentleman who has lain in bed for eight years. He testified that after the last administration he had no pain for four days. We administered to him again and left him feeling better than he has for many years, according to his wife's statement.

Tuesday, 19 October 1897

About eleven o'clock while we were preparing our tracts for distribution,[63] Sister Catherine Anderson entered, carrying a large bundle. After

---

[60]The see or cathedral town was the seat of a Catholic bishop's office and authority. The present building dates to the late thirteenth and early fourteenth centuries and is located on the site of a monastery founded by St. Kentigern in the late sixth century. See Nigel M. de S. Cameron, *Dictionary of Scottish Church History and Theology* (Downers Grove, IL: InterVarsity Press, 1993), 365.

[61]Sir Walter Scott, *Marmion: A Tale of Flodden Field* (Edinburgh: J. Ballantyne and Co., 1808). This book of narrative poetry includes Scott's best-known ballad, "Lochinvar."

[62]Edward P. Roe, *From Jest to Earnest* (New York: Collier, 1902).

[63]Getting tracts ready to distribute involved folding the printed sheet to make a tract and writing the time and address of their meetings. Missionaries had to buy the tracts they used.

greeting us, she opened it and presented two sheets, one pair of woolen blankets, and a beautiful coverlet, saying, "You elders have come awa' here to do us good and to call sinners to repent, and I dinna think that we who are in our ain beds should let you suffer: so I give you these to keep you

Fig. 11 *The Interior of Glasgow Cathedral, Glasgow.*

warm." Brother Pender expressed our feelings by saying, "Sister Anderson, ye've taken our breaths and we dinna ken what to say to ye." Her kind act touched the heart of everyone. It seemed impossible to express our feelings. She was truly happy, for she had done something which filled her benevolent soul with joy. When she was leaving, she said, "I leave my peace and blessing with you."

In the afternoon distributed tracts on West Graham Street. Had conversations with three women. Their different views of religion impressed me greatly. There was the woman who felt that the churches were not doing as the word of God directs and so thought the "fireside Christians were all right." Then there was the woman who "has nothing to do" [because] Christ has saved her. Another believed that the Catholics were wrong but all Protestants were preaching the gospel! She said that God would have to reveal himself but did not believe he had done so to Joseph Smith.

At night visited a sick girl, not a member of the Church. At her request we administered to her. I think she has consumption.[64] Before retiring we administered to President McMillan, who is suffering more than we know. His arm is wasting away and I believe one of his lower limbs also. He is fasting and praying for relief.

Wednesday, 20 October 1897

Fasted with Brother McMillan. Distributed fifty-two tracts. Felt gloomy and sad all day. Wrote to Joseph L. [Peterson]. Everything looks dark. Administered to Brother Mack [i.e., McMillan] at night.

Thursday, 21 October 1897

Dull, dismal morning. President McMillan, after eighty-seven-hour fast, says he feels better. We shall break our twenty-four-hour fast at 9:00. Received letters: Thomas, Nettie, and Claire. In the afternoon distributed tracts. Testimony meeting at night.

Friday, 22 October 1897

Wrote letters to Nettie, Thomas, Claire, and George E. [Ferrin]. At night, in company with Brother Johnston, visited Mr. [William] Carney.

Saturday, 23 October 1897

Went with Brothers Anderson and Mitchell to administer to Miss Good, who is still suffering with consumption. Her mind is getting weak. After we administered to her, a dead silence seemed to come over all present. As she lay there so quietly and peacefully with her pale thin face and stead-

---

[64]In the nineteenth century, *consumption* meant, in general, a gradual wasting away of the body or meant, more specifically, pulmonary tuberculosis, a disease of the lungs accompanied by fever and emaciation, often but not invariably fatal.

fast eyes, her long brown hair hanging over the edge of the pillow, we could hear the low *gurgle* in her throat accompanying every short breath. I think her mind just then wandered, for while the stillness yet continued—a stillness only broken by the monotonous ticking of the clock—she began to sing. At first we could scarcely hear her so weak and feeble was her voice, but soon we recognized the hymn she was singing. Her breath was short and difficult and the words came at intervals, but we heard distinctly the words: "Beautiful home of my Savior, bright beautiful home." That scene I shall never forget. Her white countenance depicting the suffering she has endured; her dark hair streaming in striking contrast to her death-like face; that audible gurgle in her throat; the gloomy surroundings occasioned by the dull day; the dead silence broken only by the seeming knell of the kitchen clock; her feeble plaintive tones as she sang that heavenly hymn—all made an impression on me that can never be effaced from memory.

At night saw *Hamlet* in the Royalty Theatre, played by the British tragedian, H. Beerbohm Tree.[65] He is inferior to our American stars.

Sunday, 24 October 1897

Sunday School at twelve; meeting at 2 P.M. Went with Miss McDonald to dinner. Miss Lang and Miss Gain and Brother Anderson went also. Had a pleasant time. Meeting again at 6:30. Was unexpectedly called upon to speak first. Spoke on the "Atonement," and as I led up to its universal application, I cited as my first proof the third verse of Daniel 12—I mean I started to cite it, for I could not recall a word; everything seemed dark. Suddenly Revelation 20:12-13 flashed before me and I proceeded with my speech. It was a peculiar experience.

Monday, 25 October 1897

In company with Brothers Anderson, Johnston, and Mitchell, went to Auchinairn to administer to that old man, Mr. Ferguson. Cold reception by son. In afternoon distributed tracts.

Wrote to David R.

Tuesday, 26 October 1897

Brother Anderson and I called upon a Mrs. Gray, whom I had met while tracting. At her request we went at ten o'clock. A lively discussion followed and continued for one hour and a half. I gave her two more tracts; she promised to read them and invited us to call again. We felt encouraged, even at her opposition, for she could quote the Bible.[66] Mr. Anderson introduced me to a Mr. Hay, one of his friends from Paisley. He took us through

---

[65]Herbert Beerbohm Tree (1853-1917), a British actor, became famous for his Shakespearean productions and was knighted in 1909.

[66]David O. McKay, Letter, 29 October 1897, commented that "the women here seem to know the Bible as well as I know the *Lord's Prayer*," quoted in Gibbons, *David O. McKay*, 43.

his hat-cleaning rooms. Saw how ladies' hats are made. Wrote to Mr. and Miss Moody. At night attended an interesting meeting at Brother McDonald's. This is the first of a series to be held during the winter. Meetings will be held in houses of other saints, also.

Wednesday, 27 October 1897

The morning hours spent in writing to Mr. and Miss Moody.

Distributed tracts in the afternoon, during which time I met some very intelligent people. Brother Anderson and I spent the evening in company with Miss [Martha] Officer and the Misses Neilson, and Brother and Sister [Alexander] Hoggan, a very pleasant young couple just starting out on their matrimonial voyage. We had an enjoyable time eating, talking, and having a good social time in general.

Thursday, 28 October 1897

Morning mail brought a letter from Angus [W. McKay] in the Southern States Mission. He seems to be enjoying a good spirit. At twelve o'clock, in company with President McMillan, Brothers Pender, Anderson, Johnston, and Mitchell, boarded a clutha[67] and sailed down the Clyde to Govan.

We entered the Fairfield Shipbuilding and Engineering Company's yards and at 2 P.M. saw the *Carisbrook Castle* slide boldly and gracefully into the waters of the Clyde. This vessel, built for the South African mail service, is 500 feet long and about 7,500 tons gross register. It is built to accommodate 250 first-class, 150 second-[class], and 220 third-class passengers. The launch was a complete success and, to me, a grand sight indeed. To see that massive structure, supported in the air, trembling as it were in eager anticipation of her rush into the sea, only waiting to receive her name before launching out on her watery career, filled me with awe and admiration. Soon we saw her move! Then, feeling her freedom, she started for the sea! The timbers creaked and smoked and the crowd admired and cheered as the gallant ship plunged into the bosom of the deep, where she floated as quietly and contentedly as a babe in the rocking cradle. As the broken timber began to float around her, she seemed to defy all winds and waves and to "laugh at all disaster." It was a "bonny" launch!

Friday, 29 October 1897

Wrote a letter to Aunt Mary[68] in answer to hers received the same day. It was one of the best encouraging letters I have received.

In the afternoon went in company with Brothers Anderson and Mitch-

---

[67]The term *clutha*, which is Latin for Clyde, refers to a small boat used on the Clyde River.

[68]Maria ("Mary") Stowell Evans (1859-1945) was born in Ogden, Utah. She married Evan Evans, David O. McKay's uncle, in 1878.

Fig. 12 *St. Enoch's Subway Entrance, Glasgow.*

ell to administer to Miss Good. She felt cheerful and is improving.
Received letters from May and Claire.

Saturday, 30 October 1897

Wrote to Mamma.

Addressed wrappers and mailed *Stars*. Stayed in the office until evening, except the few minutes on a bicycle. In the evening went to Partick with Brother Mitchell to attend a Halloween party. There were present, besides Mr. and Mrs. Leggat, the Misses Gains, Miss McDonald, Miss Lang, Messrs. Leggat, McDonald, McEwan, Murray, Cooke, McQueen, and others —sixteen in all. The room was small, but, considering the circumstances, we had a very pleasant time. Took *subway*[69] home—first ride (Fig. 12).

Sunday, 31 October 1897

Sunday School at twelve. Visited and administered to Miss Good. Went in company with President McMillan, Brother Pender, and Mitchell. Meeting at 2 P.M. Went to Neilson's for dinner. Was welcomed and made to feel at home. The Misses Neilson are very entertaining. Meeting again at 6:30. Brother Pender's testimony was the strongest *practical* one I have ever heard. Received another invitation to a social.

Monday, 1 November 1897

Went to Auchinairn with President McMillan and Brother Pender to visit Ferguson. Dreadful! Woman (his wife), [who was] waiting on him, was drunk. We came away as soon as possible. In our way back called to see Sister Lang in Springburn. At night Brothers Mitchell, Montgomery, and I

---

[69]A *subway* was an underground railway system, which had been extensively constructed in both Glasgow and London in the mid-nineteenth century.

visited a Brother Murray and sons in Partick. Spent a pleasant evening talking and eating cakes, apples, and nuts. He remembered seeing Father seventeen years ago.

Tuesday, 2 November 1897
Wrote to Ray.
Stayed in conference house all day, reading and writing. At night went down to Neilson's. Spent the evening in singing and eating fruit.

Wednesday, 3 November 1897
Wrote to Claire and Christian Mortensen.
Copied monthly reports. President Mack and Brother Pender have gone to Motherwell to hear a debate, "Is Baptism Essential?" Later— Debate. Dry. Decided in favor of Mormons.

Thursday, 4 November 1897
Letters from Nora and Annie.
Copied monthly reports. Thursday testimony meeting at night. "Do not condemn anything until it's proven false."

Friday, 5 November 1897
Posted personal accounts, finished financial report for month of October, and took a bicycle ride—[Alma] Montgomery's wheel. At 4:20 took train for Motherwell, in company with Brother Johnston, who has been appointed to labor there with Cameron. Left his satchel at Brother [George] Taylor's and walked to Newarthill. We spent an hour at Mrs. Jack's and then went with Nellie, her mother, and others to Sister Major's, where we held an interesting meeting. At 9 P.M., after having had a *feast* both spiritually and otherwise, bid friends goodnight and walked to Holytown, Brother Johnston and Cameron accompanying me to the station. Bid them goodbye and Ewing,[70] Anderson's relative, invited me back. Brother Anderson is about to leave.

Tuesday, 9 November 1897
Brother Anderson and I visited Mrs. Gray, an investigator; met her husband, who has been in America. Cordially received. Invited to visit again. Meeting at Brother McDonald's at night.
Wrote to Nora.

Wednesday, 10 November 1897
Stayed in the conference house, writing and studying. Elders arriving from England sail tomorrow.

---

[70]George Ewing had married Anderson's cousin, Jane Whitelaw, in June 1897.

Thursday, 11 November 1897

Morning mail brought letters from Claire and John Hall. Both very interesting.

At twelve went down to Anchor Line docks to see elders off. Met Mrs. [Mary] Davis, a lady from Salt Lake City, who came over when I did. As the boat sailed down the Clyde, I thought that:

> Men may come and men may go,
> And some from friends ne'er sever.
> But here in Glasgow I must stay.
> My mission goes on forever!

In the afternoon visited Miss Good; she was not quite so well. Testimony meeting at night.

Friday, 12 November 1897

Letters from Josie Simms and Joseph L. [Peterson].

Stormy day, the first for several weeks. Answered letters and studied. At night went to the Royalty Theatre to see Henry Irving[71] and Miss Terry[72] in *Madame Sans Gêne*. Excellent.

Wrote to Claire.

Saturday, 13 November 1897

Addressed wrappers for *Stars*. President Mack and Brother Pender went to Dunfermline and Alloa; will not return until Monday.

Brother Anderson and I went to Shettleston to go down a coal mine. Met Mr. Ewing at his home, and after exchanging our stiff hats and coats for caps and jackets more suitable, we proceeded a short distance to the mine. There we were met by Mr. Kerr, the under-manager, who, after preparing lamps for us and showing us the pumping engine, conducted us to the head of the shaft. Then down we went hundreds of feet into, it seemed to me, a dark chasm. I was alive with interest: the ponies, the loaded cars, the long low tunnel, the "cousies,"[73] "levels," "faces," the working of safety lamp, the petrified trees, some twisted with a storm of past ages, the imprints of fern leaves, etc., all tended to heighten my interest and make our visit a profitable one. Mr. Kerr treated us very kindly.

Sunday, 14 November 1897

Brother McKinnon[74] and I walked in the rain eight miles to Blantyre to

---

[71]Sir Henry Irving (1838-1905) was an English actor and in 1895 became the first actor to be knighted.

[72]Ellen Terry (1847-1928), an English actress born in a theatrical family, played at the side of Irving for twenty-one years.

[73]A *cousie* was a self-acting incline on which one or more filled, descending coal-boxes pull up a corresponding number of empty boxes.

[74]Malcolm McKinnon (1869-1947) was set apart for a mission to Great Britain on 5 June

meet with the saints at that place. Held a good meeting, after which we went to Sister Irvine's for dinner. Mr. [Thomas] Halliday, now a member of the Church, was with us. Towards evening went to Burnbank. Had "tea"[75] at Brother Steven's. Spent the evening hours in singing, eating, and talking. Went to Hamilton with Mr. Halliday. Retired at 2 A.M.

Monday, 15 November 1897
After a good, warm breakfast, bid our kind host and his parents goodbye and came to Glasgow. McKinnon went to Baillieston. Spent the rest of the day in writing and visiting the Cooke family, in company with Brother Anderson. President Mack and Brother Pender returned from their visit at 10:30 P.M.

Tuesday, 16 November 1897
Studied. Visited Miss Good. She has taken a relapse. When we entered, she was so weak she could hardly speak; but after the administration, she entered upon quite a brisk, lively conversation. She felt quite encouraged again. Choir practice at night.

Wednesday, 17 November 1897
Ruled a record for the Newarthill Branch. Did some office work and studied. At night attended a farewell party given in honor of the release of Brother Anderson. It was held in Neilson's house. We had a real Utah picnic consisting of cakes, apples, oranges, figs, candy, etc., etc. Spent a very enjoyable evening. When we returned to the conference house, found three welcome letters: Nettie's, Tommy's, and Claire's.

Thursday, 18 November 1897
At conference house. Spent the day with returning missionaries. Took a bicycle ride. Testimony meeting at night.

Friday, 19 November 1897
Received a comforting letter from Mamma—just what I have been looking for. Answered it and wrote to Claire.
Spent the afternoon with missionaries. In the evening visited Miss Good; she has suffered a relapse. Found Jens Nielsen at the Argyle Hotel; he is on his way home from Denmark. We had much to say to each other. I had the pleasure of meeting President Wells. Twenty-five missionaries returning.

1896, arriving in Liverpool on 24 June 1896. In the Scottish Conference he served in the areas of Edinburgh and Glasgow. He served as president of the Scottish Conference from February to June 1898, sailing from Glasgow the next month.

[75]McKay added quotes around the term *tea* because here (and often) it refers to a meal of refreshments in the late afternoon or evening.

Saturday, 20 November 1897
Letter from Claire.

Mailed *Stars* to saints and missionaries. At four o'clock sailed down the Clyde to Stobcross Quay to see the *Furnessia* sail. Bid Brother Nielsen good-bye and returned to conference house. President McMillan [and] Brother Pender, accompanied by President Wells, left Glasgow for Edinburgh. Brothers Mack and Pender will spend the week visiting the saints.

Sunday, 21 November 1897
Sunday School at twelve, meeting at two and 6:30 P.M. Dinner at Sister [Elizabeth] Neilson's. Visited Miss Good; found her much better. After meeting, walked home with Miss Rennie. She seemed to be more impressed[76] with our belief than she was at the last meeting. Had a very pleasant conversation and an agreeable walk.

Monday, 22 November 1897
At conference house writing, studying, and arranging books.

Tuesday, 23 November 1897
Paid gas and water rates for conference house. Met Mr. [David H.] Christensen at Argyle Hotel. Wrote to Tommy. Visited Miss Good. Studied in the evening.

Wednesday, 24 November 1897
Wrote to Nettie and Claire. In the office most of the day. In the evening went to the Empire Theatre in company with Johnston, Anderson, and McKinnon. *Variety*, good acting, good singing. The comedies were ridiculous.

Thursday, 25 November 1897
Hunted for more rooms more suitable for the headquarters of the mission; was not very successful. Testimony meeting at night.

Friday, 26 November 1897
Johnston and McKinnon left conference house for Newarthill, their field of labor. I remained in office. Answered correspondence and studied. In the afternoon visited Miss Good and found her to be much improved again; she having been out of bed for a few minutes during the day. She was very much encouraged and so were we (Brother Anderson and I). (*My Vow.*)

---

[76]Originally, McKay wrote that Miss Rennie was "more pleased with our belief," then the word "pleased" was crossed out and "impressed" written above it.

Saturday, 27 November 1897

Went down to Anchor Line office to learn how soon luggage can be placed on the boat, which sails December 2nd. Returned and sent information to some English emigrants. Sent *Stars* to missionaries and saints. Secured the option on three rooms and kitchen until Tuesday when President McMillan will decide whether or not they are suitable. Studied in the evening. Montgomery and Mitchell called later at night.

Sunday, 28 November 1897

Raining and blowing. Brother Anderson and I started to Blantyre, but the storm drove us back. After drying our wet clothing, or making the necessary changes, and the storm having abated its fury somewhat, we determined to accomplish our object. However, it was too stormy to walk, so paid for a ride in the "bus" or "brake."[77] Held a good meeting with the little branch of saints, after which we spent the afternoon and evening at Irvine's. Sister Irvine is a very good cook, jolly, hospitable, and kind. Mr. Halliday was with us.

After "tea" we bid them good-night and returned to Glasgow, Mr. Halliday and Thomas Irvine accompanying us about two miles on our way. The storm had ceased, although the wind was still strong. The sky was clear; the crescent moon shone brightly; the [Big] Dipper and North Star, so often looked at when strolling with *pleasant* company at home; the neat, comfortable dwellings so much more homelike than the crowded tenant houses of crowded Glasgow; the lads and lasses taking their Sunday evening's walk and enjoying the same, no doubt, in spite of the wind; all seemed to fill my mind with thoughts of home; however, I enjoyed our eight-mile walk for there was something about the *unusual* clear sky that pleased us both.

Then the crossing of the Clyde at night on a foot bridge and the beautiful scenes around it were enough to make us feel delightful, to say the least. Mrs. Noble had a bright warm fire in our room; so, seating ourselves around its glowing heat, we spent a few minutes in rehearsing the events of the day; after which I penned these few notes just for a reminiscence in years to come, and then—well, now I am going to bed, thinking of home and friends. See?

Monday, 29 November 1897

At conference house in the morning, writing and studying. In the afternoon walked to Partick Hill to look at some houses: decided they were too far out. President McMillan returned from the north. Reported everything prospering. Said that one of the elder's actions was disgusting—always com-

---

[77]A *bus* (i.e., *omnibus*) or *brake* was a public street-carriage, which was a long-bodied, four-wheeled vehicle for carrying passengers, generally between two fixed stations, the seats being arranged lengthwise, with the entrance at the rear.

Fig. 13 *St. Enoch's Station, Glasgow.*

plaining, whining, and begging. The storm of yesterday raged in the North. Ships wrecked and lives lost.

Tuesday, 30 November 1897

Arose at 6:30 and went to St. Enoch's Station (Fig. 13) to meet returning missionaries from England. Answered some correspondence and then took a stroll with Brother Pender. Had an interesting debate. Question— "If these 'saved' men receive the power which they claim to receive to overcome their evil habits,[78] does it come from God or Satan?" "Does the false assurance that belief alone is sufficient benefit or injure a man?" If he is sincere, I believe it will be a benefit. Visited an evening class in mathematics. Met a Mr. Smith, Brother Mitchell's friend.

Wednesday, 1 December 1897

House full of returning missionaries. Posted accounts for month of November. At night strolled through the city with Mr. [David H.] Christensen, former superintendent of Utah County schools, and Mr. [Almon D.] Robison, returning missionary. Saw the usual amount of drunkenness and sin. Women with bleeding faces reeling through the streets, sometimes carrying an innocent babe, whose face is also besmeared with the vile blood of its besotted mother! Young women lifting up drunken boys; little children running around barefooted at eleven o'clock at night; fights right under policemen's nose[s]; men wheeled away in a wheelbarrow—are a few of the disgusting scenes on the Trongate (Fig. 14) in the city of Glasgow.

---

[78]McKay originally wrote "their bad habits."

Thursday, 2 December 1897

Long letter from Father, encouraging and full of wisdom and good advice. Took passengers down to the docks. Bid Brother Anderson good-bye. Made me feel "blue."

About 4:30, just as the boat was about to leave, a woman's scream struck terror through the crowd. I rushed around to the edge of the dock and peering down into the Clyde between the ship and wharf saw a woman struggling for life! A man leaped from the ship and swam to her assistance. Soon ropes were lowered and three more sailors were lowered to the rescue. Two "life buoys" were thrown down to them and to one of these the moaning woman was tied. The first man now began to cry for help. He had seized a rope when the other men took the woman and, being thus relieved of his burden, he began to realize his own position. The plunge into the cold water had chilled him and now he began to feel benumbed. In vain he called to them to pull him up, but it seemed those at the rope did not understand him. His face turned deathly pale, and it was evident he was losing strength. Some of the crowd were speechless, while others yelled with frenzy. The three men who had gone down on ropes had by this time secured the woman by tying her to one of the strongest among them. The "derrick" hook was lowered and the man and woman hoisted in the air and landed safely on the platform. In the meantime a rope ladder had been lowered to rescue the drowning man. He was so near "frozen" that he could not draw his limbs out of the water. He was carried or rather dragged to the deck of the ship, the other two men were hoisted and all saved from a watery grave. It was one of the most exciting scenes I have ever witnessed. Women screamed, men yelled, and sailors swore. The woman moaned and the drowning man cried for help. I became almost as excited as any. Testimony meeting at night.

Fig. 14 *Trongate, Glasgow.*

DAVID O. McKAY
MISSIONARY DIARY TWO

Friday, 3 December 1897

$\mathbf{M}$ADE OUT FINANCIAL and traveling elders' reports for the month of November. Finished them about 10 P.M. and after a short discussion on the reason of Christ's baptism—baptism for the remission of sins—I retired.

Saturday, 4 December 1897

Letters from Claire, Uncle Evan,[79] and David R.

Ruled cash account, answered office correspondence, and spent the rest of the day studying and talking with elders.

Sunday, 5 December 1897

Priesthood meeting at 11 A.M., Sunday School at 12:30, and meeting at 2 P.M. Broke fast at 4:30 at Brother Leggat's house. Treated very cordially. He related circumstances and incidents which happened when Father was here sixteen years ago.

Before the evening meeting we visited Miss Good. She felt discouraged, and for the first time since I have known her she broke down and the poor girl sobbed as though her heart would break. It was a touching scene, for her mother, too, gave way to tears. She felt better before we left. As it was a stormy night, the hall was not crowded, although we had a good meeting, with the exception of Neilson's blunders: "Previous day—the day after." Discussed the parable of the Ten Virgins, as recorded in Matthew 25, and then went to bed.

---

[79]Evan Evans (1844-1926) was born in Dan Choy Fag Wyn, Merthyr Tydfil, South Wales. He married Maria Stowell in 1878.

Monday, 6 December 1897
Sent notices of conference to the several branches. Ruled blank reports. Wrote letters home.

Tuesday, 7 December 1897
At conference house arranging reports for conference. Choir practice at night.

Wednesday, 8 December 1897
At conference house arranging accounts and studying a little.

Thursday, 9 December 1897
Letters from Aunt Mary and Annie. Sent letters to presidents of branches. The weather is dark and stormy. Lamps are lighted at 3:30 P.M. Testimony meeting at night.

Friday, 10 December 1897
Around Glasgow in the morning. Studied some in afternoon. Elders are coming in from fields of labor to conference.

Saturday, 11 December 1897
Secured rooms in hotel for elders and saints during conference. Spent the day in making other arrangements. There were twenty-two in conference house for supper, and only two small rooms and a bedroom containing two beds! There was scarcely room to turn around. Besides meeting the saints from Edinburgh and other branches, all of whom were pleasant and sociable, met Miss Snedden, a charming young woman from Dunfermline. She is intelligent and pretty, too.

Sunday, 12 December 1897
Conference day. At 10:30 o'clock met at 11 Oxford Street in Breadalbane Hall. Besides the traveling elders[80] and local priesthood, there were present many saints from surrounding districts. President [Rulon S.] Wells and Counselor McMurrin[81] were on the stand with President McMillan and

---

[80]The term *traveling elders* refers to full-time proselyting missionaries (almost all of which were from America). The terms *local elders* or *home elders* indicate native Scottish men holding the priesthood and living in the local branches.

[81]Joseph W. McMurrin (1858-1932) was called on 24 June 1896 as first counselor to Rulon S. Wells in the presidency of the European Mission, arriving in July 1896, being released in October 1898, and leaving December 1898. McMurrin was sustained as one of the First Seven Presidents of Seventies on 5 October 1897 and was set apart to that position by Anthon H. Lund at Liverpool on 21 January 1898. Because Lund used the words "set apart" instead of "ordain," there was some controversy about the validity of the ordination. However, on 13 April 1899 the First Presidency and Twelve Apostles unanimously supported Lund's ordination of McMurrin. See Stan Larson, ed., *A Ministry of Meetings: The Apostolic Diaries of Rudger Clawson* (Salt Lake City: Signature Books, 1993), 46.

a few elders. The speakers in the morning were John Robertson,[82] J. E. Hoggan,[83] George Allen,[84] and D. Archibald.[85] After singing and prayer, all retired to another room where was prepared a good lunch for all. At 2:30 meeting was again called. Four or five elders occupied the time. Lunch again at 5 P.M.

The evening meeting was crowded; many strangers[86] being present [were] given something to think about. It is pronounced to be one of the best conferences ever held in Glasgow. One feature about it though was rather annoying and to strangers perhaps sacrilegious; between meetings the saints were too noisy and boisterous, although it was all done in the spirit of goodwill and sociability. Nevertheless, I think it caused a bad impression.

Brother McMurrin occupied most of the time. He is an eloquent speaker and explains the principles of the gospel in a clear and comprehensive manner. He was followed by President Wells, who confined his remarks chiefly to "Blood Atonement."[87] He was very logical and concise in his remarks. Everyone present seemed to enjoy the meeting immensely, and those not of our faith were [satisfied].[88] After the evening meeting, there was a regular siege of handshaking. The good-byes [being] over, all left for their several abiding places, feeling happy and fully satisfied with the day's proceedings.

Monday, 13 December 1897

Priesthood meeting at ten o'clock. Sat just four hours, listening to elders' reports. Busy the rest of the day making up expenses and settling with elders.

---

[82]McKay wrote "John Robinson," but the editors have corrected this to "John Robertson," just as McKay correctly wrote this name at the entries for 31 August and 15 December 1897.

[83]James E. Hoggan (1840-1919) was born in Dunfermline, Fife, Scotland. He was set apart for his mission to Great Britain on 8 May 1896, arriving in Liverpool on 27 May 1896. Hoggan was assigned to the Scottish Conference, working in the areas of Alloa, Dunfermline, and Edinburgh. He was released in May 1898.

[84]George Allen (1863-1942) was born in Clackmannan, Clackmannanshire, Scotland. He was set apart for a mission to Great Britain on 17 January 1896, arriving in Liverpool on 6 February 1896. Within the Scottish Conference he worked in the areas of Alloa, Edinburgh, and Tillicoultry. Allen was released in January 1898 and returned to Utah the next month.

[85]David Archibald (1849-1931) was born in Dalry, Ayrshire, Scotland. He was set apart for a mission to Great Britain on 23 October 1896, arriving on 13 November 1896. In the Scottish Conference Archibald labored in the areas of Aberdeen, Burnbank, and New Pitsligo. He returned to Utah in September 1898.

[86]The term *strangers* is often used in late nineteenth-century Mormon writing in referring to nonmember visitors or investigators at a meeting.

[87]For discussions of the early Mormon doctrine of blood atonement, see Charles W. Penrose, *Blood Atonement, as Taught by Leading Elders of the Church of Jesus Christ of Latter-day Saints* (Salt Lake City: Juvenile Instructor Office, 1884) and Joseph Fielding Smith, *Blood Atonement and the Origin of Plural Marriage: A Discussion* (Salt Lake City: The Deseret News, 1905).

[88]McKay did not finish this sentence, which is at the end of a diary page, so the editors have supplied an ending.

Tuesday, 14 December 1897

Settled hotel bill and, after returning to the office, was kept busy all day with elders' *Star* and book accounts. Many have gone back to their assigned fields, while some will remain until tomorrow. Choir practice at night.

Wednesday, 15 December 1897

Settling accounts. Copied general church authorities for John Robertson, to be presented before the Irish Conference, Sunday, 19th December. Several of the boys are going over. President Wells has been in the office with us all day. Visited Miss Good. She is improving and is now on a sure road to recovery. Brother McMurrin returned from a visit to Airdrie.

Thursday, 16 December 1897

Received letters from Father and Claire.

At ten o'clock took train for Cambuslang, where I visited a Mrs. Crosby, whose husband joined the Church several years ago and emigrated to Utah. She is antagonistic towards the doctrine of the Latter-day Saints. She is "saved," having been "washed in the blood of the Lamb" [cf. Rev. 7:14]. We had quite a debate on religion—quite a friendly one. Before leaving her, she prepared a lunch for me, had me read some of her letters, and, in fact, treated me as courteously as she could—considering her ill feeling toward our religion. She invited me to call again, but I thought she rather regretted it afterward.

In the afternoon settled accounts. Testimony meeting at night. Brother McMurrin spoke on duties of members, mentioned tithing, and was openly opposed by Brother [illegible], the latter taking the stand that members need not pay tithing until they gather with the body of the Church. His stand was an absurd one. President Wells and Brother McMurrin[89] left for Ireland at 11 P.M.

Friday, 17 December 1897

In the morning around town buying a few necessary articles. At four o'clock Brother Johnston and I went to Newarthill. Spent an hour and a half at Mrs. Jack's. Nellie [Jack] made me a present of a neat little birthday autograph album; she gave it in such a good spirit that I felt very grateful. At seven o'clock we walked over to Sister Major's and held a cottage meeting. I spoke upon the subject of authority and felt better and spoke longer than I have ever done before.

---

[89]For McMurrin's account of his visit to Scotland from 10-16 December 1897, see the Joseph W. McMurrin Collection, Accession 1029, located in the Manuscripts Division, J. Willard Marriott Library, University of Utah, Salt Lake City.

Saturday, 18 December 1897

Wrote a letter to Annie and sent away New Year cards.[90] Mailed *Stars* to missionaries and saints. At the books in the evening.

Later, while making up the week's board bill, we were all surprised at its being so much for each of us. Brother Pender was chosen to investigate; and he, before mentioning the amount, began to state little things which have happened and which appear to throw suspicion. I do not know all that passed between them (Mrs. Noble and him), but when I went in, they had decided that Mrs. Noble was to leave the following Monday, and she and Aggie were sobbing as though their hearts would break. It arose from a mistake in the account and, as no one was to blame for it, restitution was made and all things went on again as usual.

Sunday, 19 December 1897

Meetings as usual. There is enmity existing among the presiding local elders.

Monday, 20 December 1897

Wrote letters to all the elders, asking them at the request of President McMillan to observe next Wednesday as a Fast Day to be observed in behalf of Mary Good. Wrote a letter to Tommy and Father.

Tuesday, 21 December 1897

In the office all day, writing, studying, etc. Priesthood meeting at night.

Wednesday, 22 December 1897

The boys returned from Ireland. Reported fine weather in Belfast, while here in Glasgow the lamps must be lit in order to dispel the darkness. It is now 2 P.M. and it is so dark and misty that one cannot see but a few yards ahead of him. At four o'clock, in company with President McMillan, Brothers Pender, Mitchell, Montgomery, and Edward, administered to Miss Good. Just at the same time all the elders in the Scottish Conference were praying in her behalf. Letters had been sent out Monday, asking them to thus unite with those administering. The result was a blessing to Mary; for notwithstanding the smoke and fog—enough to make strong healthy men's lungs burn—she sat up in bed after we left and talked and chatted with her mother and sisters for quite a length of time. Her case is a singular one.

---

[90]In McKay's letter accompanying the card to Emma Ray Riggs, he presented this poetic thought:

> Accept this simple Christmas card,
>   As a token of friendship and *true regard;*
> It has no value—but by it I send,
>   The sincerest wishes of a *real true friend.*

There are certainly other powers (evil in nature) at work, besides that of the priesthood.

Thursday, 23 December 1897
The fog still continues. The papers report many accidents yesterday. One may get an idea of the density of this mist when he learns that two men returning from work walked into the Clyde and were drowned!! It is complete darkness in Glasgow, while two miles out the sun is shining bright and clear.

Received twenty dollars from home as a Christmas present from Mamma, also a beautiful silk muffler from Claire. Both came as complete surprises; and I think I have never before appreciated anything so dearly as these two tokens of love and friendship. Such expressions as these to one another are the flowers that strew the pathway of life.

Friday, 24 December 1897
At conference house. In afternoon went to bookbinders, stationers, and to several other places. At night went to Neilson's to spend Xmas eve. Brother Pender and I were the only ones in the conference house. The others (except President McMillan and Hogg,[91] who were in Newarthill) having gone to Dunfermline to a party. The Neilson folks were disappointed, but we had a very pleasant time anyway.

Saturday, 25 December 1897, Christmas Day
Received a Xmas card from a cousin in the North, Bella McKay, another from Miss Rennie. Sent *Stars* to elders and saints. Mrs. Noble prepared us a fine plum pudding for dinner; Brother Pender's niece sent him a large fruit cake and these, with a few oranges and apples and *an occasional look at the almanac*, helped to remind us that it was Xmas, Merry Xmas. The plum duff and cake were fine, but I felt homesick.

> I pictured home and all its joys,
> The merry girls and happy boys,
> The private party and social dance,
> All seemed my longing to enhance.

Visited Mary and found her and her mother both quite sick. She (Mary) began to sob when we entered—not particularly because of her own weakness or discouragement but more because of pity for her mother. As I shook her hand and heard her whisper between the sobs, "I wish you a Merry Xmas," I was touched to the *quick*. I could not under the circumstances return the good wish, so with a "Thank you, Mary, God bless you,"

---

[91]Robert Hogg, Jr. (1840-1914) was born in Channelkirk, Berwickshire, Scotland. He was set apart for a mission to Great Britain on 15 January 1897, arriving in Liverpool on 3 February 1897. Within the Scottish Conference he labored in the areas of Berwick, Burnbank, Glasgow, and Newarthill. Hogg was released in June 1898 due to ill health.

I turned away. We tried to cheer them up and left our blessings with them. At night I wrote to Mamma.

Sunday, 26 December 1897
Sunday School at twelve. In the absence of the teacher, I was called to take charge of theological class. I felt my weakness in the presence of nine other traveling elders and several local elders. The lesson was on the parable of the Ten Virgins, Matthew 25, and the previous discussion on this had been made warm by the opposition of Brother Leggat to the regular teacher. Later the teacher (Clark) came in but insisted on my continuing. The discussion was rather heated, but all the members, except Leggat, accepted explanation of the teacher.
Meeting at 2 P.M. Dinner at Neilson's. Evening meeting at 6:30. After meeting walked home with Miss Rennie and took this opportunity of ascertaining her opinion of the gospel. She is quite favorable [and] acknowledged that they are in perfect accord with the teachings of our Savior.

Monday, 27 December 1897
Ordered suit of clothes. Answered letters and studied. In the evening went to the pantomime, *Blue Beard*, in the Metropole. Attractive features were beautiful scenery, elegant costumes, good dancing, fair singing, and pretty girls. Some of the actresses were stiff and ugly, but most of them were all right.

Tuesday, 28 December 1897
Spent several hours looking for a trunk suitable for traveling. Choir practice at night.

Wednesday, 29 December 1897
Arose at six o'clock and went to Central Station to meet a returning missionary and emigrants. Very wet morning. Later wrote to Claire and then studied.

Thursday, 30 December 1897
6:45 A.M. at Central Station to meet Brother [Samuel] Holt and others, who sail today in S.S. *Furnessia*. In forenoon posted accounts. At 2 P.M. went down to docks with returning missionaries and emigrants.
Visited Mary [Good] in the evening and found her and her mother both sick, downcast—yes, heartbroken. Mary could not speak; the pitiful, pleading expression on her face as she tried to bid us good-bye will never be forgotten. It was a sad scene to see the daughter, young and beautiful, lying so near *death*, and the mother in the same room, sick and discouraged, weeping for her child, yet unable to give her any assistance. The other daughter is compelled to work or lose her position, and this would shut out half their sustenance—in fact all when the son is out of work. I felt very gloomy and

sad when we came away, as well as while we were there.

Testimony meeting at night.

Friday, 31 December 1897

The last day in the year spent in making out *Star* and book accounts and sending bills to subscribers. In the evening all the elders, except me, went to theatre. I mailed letters and *Stars* and am now enjoying a few moments of quietness. At this moment [of] twelve o'clock the old year, 1897, passes away. The new year is being ushered in by the blowing of whistles, ringing of bells, singing, and rejoicing. President McMillan and Brother Pender have retired; Brother Johnston's letting down the folding bed, Brother Cameron [is] fixing a button on his shirt, Brother Adamson[92] is sitting by the fire, and I am writing this as a reference for New Years yet to come. "Ring out the old; ring in the new." Weather clear and mild. "Ring out the false; ring in the true."

---

[92]Alexander G. Adamson (1841-1902) was born in Arbuckle, Lanarkshire, Scotland. He was set apart for a mission to Great Britain on 7 April 1896, arriving in Liverpool on 6 May 1896. He was assigned to the Scottish Conference and worked in Ayrshire. Adamson was released in May 1898, returning the next month.

DAVID O. McKAY
MISSIONARY DIARY THREE
"A FEW HAPPENINGS OF
MY DAILY LIFE"

Saturday, 1 January 1898

SPENT THE MORNING hours in office, 130 Barrack Street, Glasgow. This was my first New Year's day ever spent away from home. At 3 P.M., in company with Brothers Johnston, Cameron, and Mitchell, boarded the train at Central Station for Blantyre for the purpose of attending a New Year soirée[93] given by the branch. As we entered the hall, which was well-lighted and decorated, we were greeted by members of the branch and outside friends.

At 4:15 the exercises began. A short program consisting of songs and recitations was rendered. Mr. Thomas Halliday's reciting was very commendable, especially the "Fishing Scene" from *The Starling* by Rev. Macleod[94]; his rendition of "[blank] Piano Playing" was not so good; it was too *heavy* for him. After the program, the room was cleared and the children turned loose—oh, the noise! One would think he was in Pandemonium! Then the older ones took a hand and were very successful in making more noise than the children. The dance was noisy and boisterous; however, I succeeded in getting two or three good waltzes. One feature was commendable—the early commencement and seasonable closing, an example worthy of imitation. Stayed that night with Mr. Halliday in Hamilton (Johnston and I).

---

[93]A *soirée* was an evening party or reception.

[94]Norman Macleod (1812-1872) published his novel, *The Starling: A Scotch Story*, in London in 1867.

Fig. 15 *A Street in Hamilton, Lanarkshire.*

Sunday, 2 January 1898

After singing a few hymns and enjoying some instrumental music, we walked from Hamilton (Fig. 15) to Blantyre and attended meeting. Had an interesting and instructive time, after which we were invited to partake of Brother and Sister Irvine's kind hospitality.

After dinner visited the birthplace of Dr. David Livingstone;[95] entered the house in which he was born (could not see the room); also saw the old mill in which he worked with his Latin book before him. Both are situated on the banks of the Clyde just below Blantyre.

Meeting at Brother Steven's at 6:30 P.M. Back to Hamilton at night. Sat in the parlor, singing and reciting until 12:30 A.M.

Monday, 3 January 1898

Arose at seven. After a light breakfast, which Willie insisted on preparing, we boarded the train for Glasgow, leaving Hamilton at 8:25.

Prepared a report of traveling elders and sent it to Liverpool. At about noon the saints and elders from surrounding districts began to come in for the evening soirée. At six o'clock the rooms were full.

At seven all went to the Breadalbane Hall, S[outh] S[ide], and were assigned seats at the tables. Bags of cakes, fruit, and "sweeties" were given to each one present. There were present about 300 or more persons—members and nonmembers. After lunch a lengthy program was rendered. I was unexpectedly called upon here, as in Burnbank, to give a reading. After the concert, the violin began to tune; "A" was struck on the piano, but amid the noise and confusion the violinist failed to strike the right key. But really if

---

[95]David Livingstone (1813-1873), a Scottish missionary and explorer in Africa, was born in Blantyre, Lanarkshire, Scotland, and received a medical degree from the University of Glasgow. He was sent by the London Missionary Society to practice medicine and be a Christian missionary in Africa.

the violin had been correctly tuned, it would have been out of harmony with the *discord* which then prevailed! Some of the young folks were waltzing; the older ones talking and laughing; and the children, dodging around the others, were skating across the floor! While this disorder still continued, the president requested me to assume control during the rest of the night. It was a herculean task but I did my best, although it seemed almost impossible to keep good order. I had several good dances, yet I cannot say I enjoyed the evening as a whole—I felt worried. The dance, interspersed with songs and whatnot, continued until three o'clock in the morning!

After dismissal I went to Possilpark, 2½ miles, assisting Mrs. McDonald and Mrs. Cairney home with their eight little ones. Janet Lang and Mary McDonald were along also. Walked home with Janet, who lives in Springburn, then down to conference house, where I arrived at six o'clock, Tuesday morning! "Elder's hours"!!!

Tuesday, 4 January 1898
In office until evening and then accompanied Brother Pender in visiting a family who attended the soirée and requested an interview. The man, Mr. Thompson, was not in—he evidently having repented of asking us—but the women in the house, the mistress and two visitors, treated us cordially and requested us to call again.

Wednesday, 5 January 1898
Made out bills and examined old accounts. At night went to the Royalty but were too late to get in! Every seat was taken three-fourths hour before play commenced.

Thursday, 6 January 1898
Made out financial report for December. At night Brother Johnston and I went again to the Royalty, determined to see *La Poupée*, if possible. We were nearly an hour early, yet we had to take our places in the crowd for the gallery. It was an eager, anxious crowd, the most genteel one I was ever in. The opera was excellent.

Letters from George Morris, Claire, and T. Allen.

Friday, 7 January 1898
President McMillan entered the Western Infirmary (Fig. 16) to see if anything can be done to check the progress of the disease that seems to be literally eating away his muscles. Stayed in office, answering correspondence and studying. In the evening visited Brother McDonald and family, also Brother Mills and family.

Saturday, 8 January 1898
Wrote to Tommy and Claire.

Sent *Stars* to elders and saints and commenced yearly financial report.

Fig. 16 *Western Infirmary, Glasgow.*

Brother Pender and I were alone in conference house—something unusual. Had a warm argument on the deceit and trickery of American officials—he has no love for *America*.[96]

Retired at 1 A.M. We had scarcely fallen asleep before we were aroused by a knock at the hall door. I answered it and received the dreadful news from Brother [David] Cairney that Brother McDonald was dead. He passed away suddenly at his home on Mansion Street. Died in his wife's arms. We hurriedly dressed ourselves and accompanied them (Brother Cairney and little Fletcher) to the stricken family. A touching scene followed our entrance into the room. The bereaved wife was sick and almost heartbroken. We stayed with them until morning.

Sunday, 9 January 1898

Took a few hours sleep.

After dinner I went to the infirmary to visit Brother Mack. He is feeling quite cheerful and contented. The infirmary is a beautiful and comfortable place, situated on the banks of the Kelvin River near the Glasgow University (Fig. 17). The grounds are well-kept and everything presents an attractive appearance. Attended meeting at night.

Monday, 10 January 1898

Worked all day at financial report: found the accounts have been poorly kept.

At night sat up with Brother McDonald's family. Met Mr. Lang, Janet Lang's brother. Janet has shown her noble nature in this hour of trial for her sister, Sister McDonald.

Tuesday, 11 January 1898

Slept about two hours and then prepared to attend funeral services. As we were going to Possilpark, saw the funeral procession of the four firemen

---

[96]John T. Edward, Diary, 13 April 1898, added his insight concerning the value of Brother Pender being Scottish: "Bro. Pender is the proper man to go visiting the people of Scotland with, being a Scotch man himself, they will pay more attention to him than they will to an American."

Fig. 17 *University of Glasgow, Glasgow.*

who were killed at the great fire on Renfield Street last Thursday night. The procession was indeed a very impressive one and was viewed by thousands of people who thronged the streets for miles to see the biers as they passed. All seemed to unite as one in expressing their sympathy.

The services at Brother McDonald's were short, yet comforting to his family. He is buried in Sitehill Cemetery.

Received letters from Father and John Hall. Answered Father's.

Wednesday, 12 January 1898

Finished financial report for 1897 and sent out statistical blanks to all the branches. Visited the Neilson family. Brother Pender administered to Brother Neilson, who has been ailing for some time.

We then visited Mary Good; she is very low, unable to speak. She recognized us and then seemed to sink into a stupor. Hearing us say that we did not think we would administer to her, she opened her eyes and beckoned with her frail wasted hands, making signs expressing her desire to be administered to, even at the last moment. We complied with her request. At the conclusion of the ordinance, she said distinctly "Amen" and seemed to feel contented. It is a pity to see her thus wasting away, but it seems to be impossible to hold her here.[97]

Mr. Halliday called in the evening. I was alone at the time. Had several hours conversation. He left for Hamilton at 11:05.

Thursday, 13 January 1898

Made out statistical report for 1897. Testimony meeting at night.

---

[97]McKay's small pocket diary, known as "Diary Two," begins with 3 December 1897 and continues through 17 January 1898. Then McKay purchased a larger, much thicker diary and recopied the January entries so that "Diary Three" begins at 1 January 1898. The "but" clause of this sentence appears in the earlier Diary Two as: "but it seems to be God's will that it should be so."

Friday, 14 January 1898
   Worked in office all day, excepting a few hours walking out to a friend's.

Saturday, 15 January 1898
   Sent letter and reports to Liverpool, mailed *Stars* to saints and elders, and after dinner visited Brother McMillan in the infirmary. Had an interesting talk with him; left him feeling quite cheerful; in fact, he is a man that does not get gloomy. Why goodness! His affliction would make me worry my life away. (I made a blunder in going into the ladies' ward.)

Sunday, 16 January 1898
   Sunday School and meetings as usual. Miss Rennie was again at the evening meeting. As we were walking home, she questioned me about polygamy.[98] Her questions were intelligent ones, yet quite amusing. She had an abhorrence of the principle. I told her the true condition of things; after hearing which, she said, "Well, there's one mystery cleared away."
   Brother Pender and I spent several hours in a confidential talk.

> Sitting around the smouldering embers,
>   when the day is past and done
> Is a time when secrets whisper,
>   and our hearts are often won.
>
> We talked of many subjects:
>   of *love, religion, fun.*
> These, he said, were needful,
>   but goodness! *politics* shun.

   "In the name of goodness, David, don't be a politician."

Monday, 17 January 1898
   This morning is somewhat stormy. For nearly four weeks now we have had very mild, pleasant days—quite unseasonable in fact—more like spring than winter. Letter came from "42" [Islington Street] asking for "list of tithe payers." I hurriedly wrote one and sent it and Relief Society report to Liverpool. Later discovered that the amounts each had paid during the year were required, so the day was spent in ruling and summing up accounts. In the afternoon went to Maryhill to see branch record kept by Willie Cooke. Succeeding in obtaining the necessary information, I arose to go, but Mrs. Cooke and Agnes said, "Na, Na! You must stop and have 'tea.'" Mr. and Mrs. Beattie came in, the latter making us jolly with her glee; she can talk "like a Tartar."

---

[98]For two modern discussions of Mormon polygamy, see B. Carmon Hardy, *Solemn Covenant: The Mormon Polygamous Passage* (Urbana, IL: University of Illinois Press, 1992) and Richard S. Van Wagoner, *Mormon Polygamy: A History*, 3d ed. (Salt Lake City: Signature Books, 1992).

Tuesday, 18 January 1898

Sent correct tithing list to Liverpool. The bookbinders are out on a strike. At one o'clock, as one of the men who will not join them in it was coming home to lunch, he was hooted and jeered at by the rabble. Hundreds thronged Duke and Barrack Streets to witness the scene when he came out to go back to his work; but three policemen came and protected him, so serious trouble was averted.

At 3:40 P.M. Mary Good passed away to another sphere, after having lain in her bed with only an occasional respite for about eight months. The last time we visited her, she whispered for us to pray that God would relieve her by taking her away. She was a lovely maiden, full of faith and patience. She was only twenty-three years of age, still in the bloom of youth, but the cruel frost has killed the bud and the flower in all its beauty (wasted away) will in this life never be seen.

Wednesday, 19 January 1898

Wrote to Ray and William Wallace. Visited Mrs. Thompson, a fine young wife and mother favorable to our faith. Her husband was not in, so we did not stay long. At her earnest request we promised to call again soon. She is anxious that Mr. Thompson should join. Brother Pender and I had another evening talk.

Thursday, 20 January 1898

Letters from Claire and Josie. Readdressed letters to elders.

At two o'clock attended Mary's funeral services. My first attempt at a funeral sermon. The services were short but impressive. All the elders, with her friends and relatives in Glasgow, accompanied the remains to their last resting place in Lambhill Cemetery.

She was laid to rest in silence,
As the sun was sinking low;
It seemed his golden wreathlets
In her grave he wished to throw.

The western sky was crimson,
The hilltop brightly shone
So did the soul of Mary
As it neared the great white throne.

No tombstone grand or costly
Is erected o'er her grave;
But her noble soul has won her
The memory of the brave.

Sleep in peace, kind Mary,
You suffered many a pain;
But we know you will be happy,
And a righteous crown you'll gain.

Friday, 21 January 1898

Visited President McMillan in infirmary. He says they are treating him well. The attendants (all women) are very thoughtful and attentive.

Kind act of a fallen woman: gave a starving man money to buy food. "In the name of God, get something to eat!" The scene was witnessed by Brother Pender, who afterward accosted the man and asked if the woman had helped him. "I'm starving," he said. "She's an angel." (Here is food for thought.)

Another illustration of the true character of these poor women! One carried home beastly intoxicated; the man trusted her next day, leaving her in sole charge of his house. When he returned, the whiskey he had left her was untouched [and] the house neat and comfortable. Within two weeks he married her and she proved to be a true wife and mother.

Saturday, 22 January 1898

A beautiful morning. A few gleams of sunshine are seen dancing on the window sill. Letters to Nettie and Claire. Addressed wrappers and mailed 122 *Stars* to elders and saints. Missionaries from Par[tick], Govan, and Springburn called in the afternoon. Answered correspondence, did some studying, and arranged books. Gave my last shilling to a poor woman. I hope a letter from home comes Monday morning or I'll be "in it." The woman told me about her drunken son. If what she said be true, he ought to be prosecuted. She wished he were dead! I believe she is a respectable, hard-working woman.

Had a short conversation with a clerk who has traveled extensively in India, Australia, and America. He does not like the Americans, says they are not so hospitable as the people in the colonies.

Sunday, 23 January 1898

Weather still fine. Sunday School and meeting as usual. Took dinner at conference house. Brother Leggat, who is at present feeling miserable over some of the acts of his brethren, walked up with us. His remarks showed that the branch is in a very precarious condition. Envy and strife, suspicion and jealousy are causing any amount of trouble. Had an excellent meeting at night. Had a pleasant walk and conversation with Miss Rennie. I do not know whether she is a real *investigato*r or not.

Monday, 24 January 1898

Alone in the conference house. Brother Pender has gone up to Dunfermline to arrange matters there. Wrote to Cousin Bella. Posted accounts. Letter from Father. Welcome.

Tuesday, 25 January 1898

Somewhat windy; streets dry and dusty. Wrote letters to returned missionaries to see if they will do anything toward helping Sister McDonald.

Fig. 18 *The Art Gallery, Glasgow.*

In the afternoon visited President McMillan; he was outside walking around. Called on Mrs. Anderson. As I came from the infirmary, I stood on the Kelvin Bridge just as the sun was setting. The entire side of the hill in front of and around the university and infirmary was as green as lawn in June. The trees along the banks of the Kelvin were budding; the sun, coming out from behind a cloud seemingly to smile at the tender buds, reflected his golden light from the university windows and added a tone to the surrounding scene that seemed inspiring.

At night met Brigham T. Cannon, just returning from a three-year mission in Germany.

Wednesday, 26 January 1898

Acted as guide around the city. Brothers Cannon, [Thomas J.] Webster, and I visited the Art Gallery (Fig. 18) on Sauchiehall Street; the Cathedral on High [Street]; the People's Palace on Glasgow Green; the Botanical Gardens on Kelvinside; and the Western Infirmary. "The Boar Hunt" by Van Dyck;[99] "Burns in Edinburgh," C. Martin Hardie;[100] "The Dog in the Manger," Hunt;[101] "Faith and Reason," Sir Joseph Noel Paton;[102] "Love at First Sight"; and "Burns and Highland Mary" were all very striking paintings. We spent a real day at sight-seeing. Went to the Royalty at night to see *The Circus Girl.* It was a splendid burlesque, plenty of hearty laughing. Yet, after all, it was very silly.

---

[99]Sir Anthony Van Dyck (1599-1641), a Flemish portrait artist, was one of the leading painters of the Baroque period, and in 1632 King Charles I appointed him court painter and knighted him.

[100]C. Martin Hardie (1858-1916), a Scottish painter born in East Linton, East Lothian, Scotland, was famous for his portrait, landscape, and genre paintings.

[101]W. Holman Hunt (1827-1910), a Pre-Raphaelite painter, was born in London and studied in the British Museum and the National Gallery before entering the Royal Academy Schools in 1844.

[102]Sir Joseph Noel Paton (1821-1901), a Scottish painter, was born in Dunfermline, Fifeshire, Scotland, and was knighted in 1866.

Thursday, 27 January 1898

Letter from Claire. In the morning wrote a few letters to some of Brother McDonald's [friends] in Utah, notifying them of his death and of the needy condition of his family.

Brothers Cannon and Webster came up and the former and I took a stroll around the cattle market and slaughter yards. The method here of killing hogs is very primitive as compared with the method in Chicago. Here it is all done by hand, taking six or seven men about twenty minutes to kill and dress seven hogs. In Chicago one hog is dressed and on ice in thirty-eight seconds after he made his last grunt!! After seeing seven shoats[103] *stabbed, dragged, scalded, scraped,* and *hung up,* we started to the *cattle* house to see the method of murder there; but just as we neared the door, a man stopped us and asked our business. We told him; whereupon he called our attention to the notice at the entrance, "No admittance except on business." We told him that we had not seen it, as we came in another way. "You will have to see the proprietor before going further," said he. We did so, were granted permission as "American tourists," and saw blood flow to our hearts' *disgust.* Cattle's skull smashed; blood saved for puddings![104]

At 3:20 the *Anchoria* with the three elders on board left the Stobcross Quay for New York. Man fell in the Clyde but was rescued with less trouble than the woman, referred to in December, was. Testimony meeting at night.

Friday, 28 January 1898

Worked in the office all day. In the evening wrote to Claire and Lizzie.

Saturday, 29 January 1898

Wrote to Willie and Fay and mailed one dozen letters to Brother McDonald's friends. Addressed *Stars* to elders and saints. Brother Edward is lying sick.

In the afternoon the elders from Motherwell came in. Signed a petition to the First Presidency of the Church of Jesus Christ of Latter-day Saints, setting forth the needs and desires of the saints and missionaries in Europe, especially in Great Britain. The petition was voted upon at a recent congress of the presidency of the mission and presidents of conferences. I signed it, of course, for President McMillan, who is still in the infirmary. "Siberia" in Hengler's Circus.

---

[103]A *shoat* is a hog, usually less than one year old.

[104]*Blood pudding* or black pudding was a kind of sausage made of a large proportion of blood and suet, seasoned with salt, pepper, onions, etc., and sometimes with the addition of a little oatmeal.

Sunday, 30 January 1898

Stormy day. Priesthood meeting at 11 A.M., Sunday School at 12:30, meeting at 2 and 6:30 P.M. Had an excellent time at all the meetings. Each was well attended and a good feeling prevailed. I now really enjoy speaking, especially if I feel I have the support of the audience.

Monday, 31 January 1898

Attended to office correspondence. Visited President McMillan in infirmary. Later Brother Pender and I went to Springburn to administer to Brother Mitchell, who came from Blantyre sick; he had gone there to preach on Sunday.

In the evening we visited Mrs. Robertson and her brother [Duncan Thomson] and wife on Comelypark Street. Mr. [Thomas] Thomson and wife from Shettleston were there. She, Mrs. Thomson, did not want anything to do with Mormonism, because all who joined it "were expected to go to Utah," and she could not "see why God wouldn't save the people of Glasgow just as well as those in Utah."[105] "Why don't you build churches and get large congregations?" she pertinently asked. Brother Pender did most of the talking. We had a fine time and were invited back.

Letters from Mamma and Mosiah Hall,[106] also a present of 8/2 [eight shillings and two pence] from the latter.

Tuesday, 1 February 1898

Posted accounts and made out financial report for January. The weather is stormy; the wind is blowing fiercely. The warm weather of January made the trees bud, but it seems that February will nip them. The farmers have begun to plow the ground and set out plants! Word from Utah says that it is twenty degrees below zero!

Wednesday, 2 February 1898

Wrote letters to Mosiah Hall and May, expressing my sympathy for the latter in her bereavement—the sad death of her father. Brother Neilson called in the afternoon and spent several hours "cracking."[107] Mr. Halliday called at night. News of the disastrous snow storm in America has just reached us. Messages from New York to Boston must go by way of London

---

[105]Frederick S. Buchanan, "The Ebb and Flow of Mormonism in Scotland, 1840-1900," *Brigham Young University Studies* 27 (Spring 1987): 35, 51n32, stated that the policy encouraging members to gather to Zion changed in August 1899.

[106]Mosiah Hall (1862-1949) was a prominent Utah educator and one of McKay's teachers. In 1894 Hall was made superintendent of Weber County Schools and in 1898 became professor of the science and art of education at Brigham Young College in Logan. Becoming an authority on sociology and child training, he wrote *Practical Sociology* and *Parent and Child*. See John G. Church, "The Life and Educational Contributions of Mosiah Hall" (M.A. thesis, University of Utah, 1950).

[107]The Scottish term *cracking* means chatting or engaging in light conversation.

on account of demolished wires! The gale here has ceased, and tonight the sky is clear and the moon shining in all her splendor! A moonlight night is a strange sight in Glasgow!

Thursday, 3 February 1898

Raining again this morning. Letters from Claire and Amelia Peterson. Both very interesting and encouraging. Spent several hours arranging books and papers in conference house, answered mission correspondence, went over to the tailor's, ruled a page in the record book, and—it was supper time! So time flies! It sometimes seems, though, that it has a wing broken! After supper Brother Pender and I visited Mrs. Robertson[108] in the hopes of finding her brother at home, but he is working at night.

Returned to testimony meeting. The *Record* announced today that England has met a diplomatic defeat! Russia it seems has gained her point on the Eastern question. There is an American boycott in Glasgow—butchers refusing America's meat! I do not know the reason, evidently through the actions of one man. Received an excellent pamphlet from A. P. Renstrom—*Are We of Israel?*[109]

Friday, 4 February 1898

Attended to sundry duties in office. Visited Brother [James] Clark and wife. Made out financial and statistical reports for January. Wrote T. Allen.

Saturday, 5 February 1898

Letters from Annie and Mr. and Mrs. Marriott.

Answered conference correspondence, addressed wrappers, and mailed *Stars* to elders and saints. While posting some papers, a gentleman recognized me as coming "from Salt Lake." He was an entire stranger to me and my curiosity was much aroused to know how he knew I was a Mormon. "O, when you've traveled," he said, "you can tell people wherever you see them." We had a short conversation, during which he inquired about our place of meeting, etc. He accepted my card and "Art[icles] of Faith" and parted in a very friendly manner.

At night in company with Brother Edward visited his father's cousin [Mary McMinn] and her family. Spent a delightful evening. The family consists of the mother, two sons, and four daughters, three of whom are young women. A Mr. Black and one Miss Hall were also present. Singing was an important part of the evening's entertainment. Mrs. McMinn made us very welcome and all expressed their desire for us to call again. Such pleasant evenings and agreeable company make life in Glasgow more cheerful.

---

[108]McKay incorrectly wrote "Mrs. Robinson."
[109]George Reynolds, *Are We of Israel?* (Salt Lake City: J. H. Parry, 1883).

Sunday, 6 February 1898

When I awoke, I thought we were going to have a beautiful day; but now at 11 A.M., it seems different. One hour ago the sun shone brightly and the "salvationists"[110] were singing "hallelujah!" just beneath our window. Now the wind is beating the rain and sleet against the window pane! The weather is very changeable.

Sunday School at twelve noon, after which Brother Pender called President Neilson's attention to the bad habit the latter has of speaking and often chastising the saints at the close of all the meetings. He has been a "preaching bishop" in its fullest sense! The correction was a severe blow to him. The testimony meeting at 2 P.M. was good. Brother Neilson said no impressions!! Nothing!! Wonderful!! Meeting at 6:30 P.M. Mrs. Noble is doing her best to make us feel comfortable and happy at the conference house. She is a fine woman.

Monday, 7 February 1898

General office work. In the afternoon visited President McMillan. The doctor is not doing him much good. Brothers [John W.] Grace and [John W.] Crawford, returning missionaries, arrived from England.

Tuesday, 8 February 1898

Attended to correspondence, accompanied missionaries through the Municipal Building and other places of interest, and in the evening wrote letters to M.I.A. Huntsville,[111] David R., Claire, and Aunt Mary [Evans]! The missionaries went to see the *Merchant of Venice*.

Wednesday, 9 February 1898

Time occupied in meeting missionaries and emigrants and attending to general duties. The weather is fine. There are six emigrants and nine returning elders. Among the company are four young ladies, viz., Anna Snedden, twenty-three; Edith Ellerby;[112] Anna B. Carrington, twenty-six; and Ettie Langstaff. At night all gathered in the Nelson Hotel on Ingram Street and spent several hours in singing. Miss Ellerby is a good pianist and an excel-

---

[110]"Salvationists" are followers of William Booth (1829-1912), who in 1865 resigned his Methodist ministry and began to evangelize the poor. In 1878 Booth established the Salvation Army, which is an evangelistic and charitable organization based on military principles.

[111]In this letter to the young men of Huntsville, whom he addressed as his "brethren and playmates," McKay gave the following recommendation: "Do you intend to accept the call to go on a mission? If so, do not do as I did—let the study of the tenets of our belief be a minor consideration—but prepare now, while you have the comforts and convenience of home." See the David O. McKay Collection, Manuscript 668, Box 1, Manuscripts Division, J. Willard Marriott Library, University of Utah, Salt Lake City.

[112]Edith Maud Ellerby Langlois (1874-1970) was born in Bradford, Yorkshire, England. She joined the Church in 1895 and on 8 February 1898 she married David Richard Langlois of Huntsville, who was McKay's friend at Huntsville and the University of Utah. Two days later they sailed for America. They had eight children.

Fig. 19 *A Horse-Drawn Lorry, Glasgow.*

lent singer. Miss Snedden is also a good singer; she has an excellent voice. Both are pretty, Miss Langstaff, especially. Her "Beautiful Star" and "Farewell, Mother, Kiss Your Darling" were sung exceedingly well. She was assisted by her father.

Miss Ellerby's "Mary of Argyle" and "Annie Laurie"—in fact all she sang—were excellent and showed taste and culture. She is leaving home against the wishes of her parents; they would not even bid her good-bye. Think of a young lady leaving father, mother, brothers, and sisters and all that is near and dear to her for the sake of her religion! There is certainly a feeling of carrying conviction of the truth to the heart and filling her soul with hope of realized joy and love, if not in this life, in the one to come.

Thursday, 10 February 1898

Mild weather continues. At ten o'clock hired a lorry[113] (Fig. 19) and gathered up the luggage—some here at the conference house, some at the hotel, Queen Street Station, St. Enoch's, and the Central. This method is chosen for cheapness. At twelve o'clock all luggage was at the Queen's docks. A few minutes later the elders and saints came down.

Miss Ellerby's father [Alfred Ellerby] and chapel minister were at the docks for the purpose of preventing her from sailing! They came from England at midnight last night. The father was almost mad! And he accused his daughter of insanity—religious mania! "If I had a pistol," said he, "I would rather shoot you than see you go out there!" The minister said her leaving would cause the death of her mother! In vain were their threats! She heeded not their pleadings, although thoughts of her mother nearly broke her heart. She reminded them of the treatment she had received at home

---

[113]A *lorry* was a long, horse-drawn wagon consisting of a nearly flat platform set on four wheels, which are either entirely under the platform or do not rise above it.

since her acceptance of the Latter-day Saints' belief and assured them that her leaving was not due to any persuasion from anyone; it was her own feelings and determination. She was left to her fate. The minister bid her good-bye, but the father's heart was stone!

I had a long talk with Edith after this interview. She is a noble, sympathetic, true-hearted young woman! Her last regret, or the only one she mentioned, was expressed for her mother! I shall never forget her last look as she said good-bye!

Friday, 11 February 1898

My attention was called to an article in the *Springburn Express* under the heading of "Mormon Leaflets in Springburn," in which the writer maliciously attacked our religion, calling us followers of "adulterous Joseph Smith," "Latter-day devils," etc. He signed himself "Truth," but I believe no one could possibly be further from the truth! "Liar" would have been a more appropriate signature! Brother Mitchell and I spent the afternoon in writing a reply.[114]

At night wrote a letter to Father and Mother. I have never before done so much writing, yet my penmanship is getting illegible! Since President McMillan went to the infirmary, it seems that it is *write, write,* write! "Old Time is fast a flying!"

Saturday, 12 February 1898

Copied in ink the reply to *Express*. Addressed wrappers and mailed *Stars* to elders and saints. Sent letters to Wood[115] and Liverpool. Paid gas rates 16/1 per quarter.

Sunday, 13 February 1898

Brother Pender is unwell and unable to attend the meetings. Sunday School and meetings as usual. There is a better spirit manifest in the branch. Brother Leggat, one who has always felt imposed upon, is feeling fine! Brother Edward and I occupied the time at the evening meeting, after which Brother Leggat came to me and putting his arm in mine said, "I want to have a 'crack' with you." He accompanied us nearly home, telling all about former and present existing conditions. Wrote this and retired!

---

[114]Joseph H. Mitchell, Diary, 11 February 1898, said: "Asked Bro. McKay to assist me with my letter, which he cheerfully did, and my letter was greatly improved by the many valuable suggestions he offered."

[115]George C. Wood (1854-1923) had married Adelaide Ridges in 1879 and Juliett Howard in 1886, and was for that reason charged, convicted, and imprisoned for polygamy and unlawful cohabitation from May 1886 to November 1889. See Stan Larson, ed., *Prisoner for Polygamy: The Memoirs and Letters of Rudger Clawson at the Utah Territorial Penitentiary, 1884-87* (Urbana, IL: University of Illinois, 1993), 30, 92, 107, 132, 135, 152, 165, 231, 234. After his release from prison, Wood was set apart on 21 February 1896 for a mission to Great Britain, arriving in Liverpool on 12 March 1896. In the Scottish Conference he labored in the areas of Cairneyhill, Dunfermline, and New Pitsligo. He returned to Utah in February 1898.

Monday, 14 February 1898

Attended to usual office duties, correspondence, addressing mail, etc. George S. Taylor spent several hours in office. In the afternoon visited President McMillan. Found him still well and apparently happy. Had an evening's walk and talk with Miss Rennie. She does not seem to be very much interested in the gospel; thinks it is all right and lets it go at that. Gave her the Book of Mormon to read.[116]

Letter from Claire.

Tuesday, 15 February 1898

Letter from Liverpool, stating that a boat will leave on the twenty-fourth instant, as the company will be too large to sail on the tenth [of] March as intended. Notified by letter the three released elders of the change and then visited Mr. [Thomas] Beggs, the house-factor,[117] to see about getting this room re-papered. The weather is very stormy; a fierce gale is blowing.

Wrote to Annie and Claire.

Wednesday, 16 February 1898

Storm raged all night and the wind is still strong. At eleven o'clock left Central Station for Newarthill, where two meetings were to be held. On account of Brother Pender's illness, I was compelled to go alone. The nearest station is Holytown, which is about two miles from Newarthill. The meeting in Mrs. Jack's was very "slim," but we nevertheless enjoyed it—two nonmembers were present. Brother Cameron from Motherwell presided. After meeting we visited Mrs. Major and Robert Orr and family.

At 6:30 we held meeting in Mrs. Major's house, at which a good spirit prevailed. A Mr. McKay—no relation to me, at least so far as we know—said he and his wife are ready for baptism. After the meeting we enjoyed a good meal, a pleasant talk, and then bid each other good-night. Brother Cameron went to Motherwell and I to Holytown, thence to Glasgow, where I arrived about 10:15 P.M.

Arriving at the conference house, had a pleasant surprise in the form of two letters—one from Father and another from Nettie. I felt grieved as I read about Mamma's sickness as described by Father, but her speedy recovery even before the letter was written brought comfort. The words "she is now looking over my shoulder, etc." seemed perfect music. Nettie's was affectionate and encouraging.

---

[116]John T. Edward, Diary, 8 December 1898, indicated that a copy of the Book of Mormon cost 6/9.

[117]A *house-factor* was a person employed in the sale, renting, and care of houses and, in this case, a manager of an apartment house.

Thursday, 17 February 1898

Visited Brother Clark and wife, and also President McMillan. Met John Crosby from Lesmahagow. He is the only Mormon there and stands all the ridicule his neighbors—yes, even his wife—can heap upon him. He is a staunch man. Mr. [Samuel R.] McCall, clothier and drapier, manifested his kind and obliging nature in furnishing me with a suit, trousers, and a trunk. He is really an obliging man. So are his clerks, *especially the ladies.* Testimony meeting at night.

Friday, 18 February 1898

At 11 A.M., according to previous appointment, met Mr. McCall, who went to Queen Street with me to select a trunk. After finding what I wanted, he kindly showed me through the immense establishment of Arthur and Co., Limited. It is a wholesale department, carrying everything "from a coal scuttle to a steam engine." Mr. Arthur, the founder, was born in Paisley in ordinary circumstances; but, through his own efforts and financial ability, established this, one of the largest business houses in Glasgow. Later in life he began to drink and such a slave did he become to intoxicants, that nearly every night he was hauled home beastly drunk. He died at about the age of sixty. McCall [said], "Whiskey hastened his death about fifteen years!" In the evening Brother Edward and I visited D[avid] Cairney and A[lexander] Hoggan; Mrs. Hoggan was very entertaining, as all were. The weather was clear and bracing, much more pleasant than the usually stormy days of Glasgow.

Saturday, 19 February 1898

Wrote to Thomas.

Then addressed *Stars* and mailed them and orders for books and tracts to elders and saints. These duties occupied my time until well on [into] the afternoon. Brother Edward and I then went on Sauchiehall Street to get some articles to send home. In the evening we went to the Royalty Theatre to see the Royal Carl Rosa Opera Company[118] in *Il Trovatore.* All the leading characters are *artists.* Lenora and the Mother were indeed excellent; the tenor was also. We felt well-paid for going. Brother Wood came in.

Sunday, 20 February 1898

Sunday School and meetings as usual. Brother Wood spoke in the afternoon and Brother Pender and I at night. Home with Miss R[ennie].

---

[118]The Royal Carl Rosa Opera Company was founded by German violinist Karl August Nicolaus Rose and was dedicated to performing opera in English. Queen Victoria conferred the "Royal" title on it in 1893.

Monday, 21 February 1898

After attending to office duties (correspondence, etc.), spent an hour or so in correcting a mistake occurring in Brother Wood's account in June 1897. He proved himself to be a person of mercenary propensities. His actions shattered my faith in his object (as he had hitherto expressed [it]) of *trying* to travel without purse or scrip.[119] It is right to be saving but utterly wrong to be *miserly*.

Visited Brother McMillan. Brother Pender decided to go and stay a week or two at his niece's home on Cedar Street, as this house is so *drafty* that he cannot throw off his cold. He has a very severe attack of catarrh and influenza. President McMillan's and his absence will throw a greater responsibility upon Brother Edward and me.

Tuesday, 22 February 1898

The forenoon was spent in searching for a suitable house. Found one on Patterson Street—not what is wanted exactly but one much better and more convenient than this one. Studied during the afternoon and at night, in company with Brother Wood and two returning elders from Scandinavia, went to Springburn to attend a meeting, previously announced to be held in the Argyle Hall. The saints of Glasgow were well-represented, many of them being there in time to assist in the singing at an open-air meeting, held simply to announce the one in the hall. Besides the elders and local saints, there were present at the regular meeting about twelve or fifteen *unbelievers*. Brothers Mitchell and Montgomery occupied the time. At the close of the services, two or three came to the front and asked about "pre-existence" and "polygamy." One became very abusive in his language, saying that "the old prophets who had more wives than one sinned against God, and so do the Mormons." "If you believe it to be a true principle, you are cowards for discontinuing its practice!" When I heard this, I thought of an old saying quoted by Father: "We'll be damned if we do and we'll be damned if we don't!" The man's arguments were as weak and fallacious as his accusations were false and calumnious. I believe he is the author of the article in the *Express* signed "Truth." I think more of the Glasgow saints than ever; they showed their true colors.

Wednesday, 23 February 1898

Visited Brother Pender. Greeted cordially by Mrs. Harrison. President McMillan received his release and Malcolm McKinnon[120] his appointment to

---

[119]The phrase "without purse and scrip," which is found in Luke 22:35, means literally "without money-bag and traveler's bag" and refers to missionaries traveling without money and living on the hospitality of others. See Louis F. Moench, "Preaching the Gospel without Purse or Scrip," *The Latter-day Saints' Millennial Star* 49 (24 January 1887): 49-52, and Richard L. Jensen, "Without Purse or Scrip? Financing Latter-day Saint Missionary Work in Europe in the Nineteenth Century," *Journal of Mormon History* 12 (1985): 3-14.

[120]Malcolm McKinnon (1869-1947) was set apart for a mission to Great Britain on 5 June

succeed Brother McMillan as president of the Scottish Conference. This change will probably necessitate more changes in the near future. Met returning elders from England. S.S. *Ethiopia* sails tomorrow.

Thursday, 24 February 1898

Conference house full of missionaries and two emigrants—sixteen in all. Took their tickets to the Anchor Line office and made the necessary changes from steerage to second cabin. Brother Edward took charge of luggage. After all arrangements were made, directed them to the quay. Went on board with him. Met Mr. Aitchison, Henderson Brothers' agent. The *Ethiopia* is not a comfortable boat. Bid the elders good-bye and returned to conference house tired and hungry, though glad that all the responsibility of this company at least was off our shoulders.

Testimony meeting at night.

Friday, 25 February 1898

Six months ago today since the old S.S. *Belgenland* landed us safely in Liverpool! As I look back, the time seems very short, but looking ahead, it seems a *lifetime* before two years shall have passed. So it will be when this life draws to a close. The past will seem but as a span, with the centuries of eternity still before us. Letter from Claire. Received [news]papers from home and the first four numbers of the *Era*.[121]

At 2:24 Brother Edward and I took low-level train[122] to Cambuslang, where we went to visit a Brother [James] Robertson and wife. They made us very welcome.[123] Their daughter-in-law, not a member of the Church, brought her little baby girl for us to bless and name. I was mouth in giving the blessing. This is the first child I have ever blessed.[124] She was named

---

1896, arriving in Liverpool on 24 June 1896. In the Scottish Conference he labored in the areas of Berwick, Edinburgh, and Glasgow. In February 1898 McKinnon was appointed as president of the Scottish Conference. Four months later he was released, arriving back in Utah in July 1898.

[121]Three months after McKay left for his mission the Church's Mutual Improvement Association began publishing the *Improvement Era*, with Joseph F. Smith and B. H. Roberts as the first editors. It ceased publication at the end of 1970, being replaced by the *Ensign*.

[122]The *low-level train* was an underground train that serviced the towns around Glasgow.

[123]John T. Edward, Diary, 25 February 1898, added: "They said that they had been in the Church since 1849. They also said that they had met Pres. [Brigham] Young and most all the early apostles."

[124]The blessing of this baby appears to be the stimulus for McKay's writing of the following 1898 poem, which is printed in Llewelyn R. McKay, *Home Memories of President David O. McKay* (Salt Lake City: Deseret Book Co., 1956), 132-33:

"To a Baby Dressed in White"

Sweet, innocent, heavenly treasure,
    Spirit offspring of God from above,
Gift of an All-Wise Creator,
    Expression of heavenly love!

Christina Cowan Robertson, born December 30th, 1897, in Clydeford Terrace, Cambuslang. After another hour's chat, we bid them good-night, and walked to Rutherglen, where we called upon Mr. Taylor and family. (He is in the Church but his wife is not.) Administered to their son Allan, who has been troubled with weak eyes. The administration was effective. Mrs. Taylor's last words, as we said good-night, were: "Haste ye back again."

Walked to Glasgow in the storm. At the conference house we found President McMillan, who had left the infirmary, as it has done him no good.

Letter from Father.

Saturday, 26 February 1898

Wrote to Nettie.

Addressed *Stars* to elders and saints. Brother McKinnon has come in to take charge of the mission according to his appointment. In the afternoon Brother Edward and I visited Brother Pender and found him very downhearted, indeed. He sobbed for a while, as though his heart were flooded with grief and loneliness! We remained with him all the afternoon. As we came to our lodging, a feeling of homesickness came over me and is still over me now as I write this (9:30 P.M.). Everything seems gloomy. Mrs. Noble feels the same way.

Thou stirrest my soul with emotion,
   I feel nearer God and the right;
For nothing is half so inspiring,
   As a baby dressed in white.

When you left the bright regions of glory
   And your spirit playmates so fair,
Did you realize what would await you,
   As a mortal surrounded by care?
Did you know that your mem'ry of heaven,
   Would vanish as morning's light dew?
To environment you would be subject,
   Dependent on circumstance, too?

Did the heavenly choirs sing praises,
   As earthward you vanished from sight?
Did you know what kind parents would rear you,
   Love you, and dress you in white?
Only a smile is my answer,
   Yet radiant with heaven's pure light;
Eternal thou art and e'er shall be,
   Sweet baby, now dressed in white!

Daisies adorn the fresh meadow,
   Lilies gladden the field;
Roses make bright every wayside;
   Each twig hath some beauty to yield—
All are expressions of goodness,
   And praises to God invite;
But the glory of all creation,
   Is a *baby dressed in white*.

Sunday, 27 February 1898

At nine o'clock Brother Edward and I started on foot for Blantyre, for the purpose of meeting with the branch at that place. The sun was shining brightly when we began our journey, but within an hour it was raining. Alternate sunshine and showers continued all day. We reached the meeting hall about thirty minutes before time. Greeted the saints as they came in. There were quite a number present and all seemed attentive and interested in what was said. Ate dinner at Sister Irvine's and tea at Sister Sneddon's (sister to Jean Russell, the carnival queen).

At 6:30 held a cottage meeting in Brother Steven's house. Two strangers were present, besides a houseful of saints. After the meeting was over, Mr. Halliday quite insisted on our staying with him as usual; but we had determined to go back to Glasgow. Several of the saints earnestly invited us to stay; but we bid them good-night and, accompanied with several of the brethren who walked a good way with us, we started on our eight-mile walk. (The trains do not run on Sunday, and the last *bus* had gone.)

Brother Edward had just recently recovered from an illness and, consequently, could not stand much exertion. His shoulders began to ache [and] his neck would grow quite rigid, so that ever and anon he was compelled to grasp the top of a fence or the limb of a tree and stretch his spinal column! About the time we reached Cambuslang, he was nearly tired out; and I, too —though much stronger than he—began to feel "leg-weary." We had four miles yet to go! It was raining, and the wind blew the *torrents* directly in our faces, which were partly shielded by our umbrellas! On we trudged, swinging our feet as a "knock-kneed" horse, and stopping ever once in a while for Brother Edward to stretch the *padding* between his vertebrae and to work his neck slowly to make sure that it still worked on a pivot! While he was going through these maneuvers-of-relief, I was stretching my sartorius muscles with my toes pointing towards the laughing moon, just peeping from behind a rain-driven cloud to see the fun. We could not help but laugh, though our tones were somewhat whining! We reached "130" [Barrack Street] at 11:30 P.M., after having walked twenty miles and held two meetings! As we threw ourselves on the bed, Brother Edward remarked, "I wouldn't do that again for my grandmother!"

Monday, 28 February 1898

When I awoke, I found myself so hoarse I could hardly speak. The cold with which I have been provoked during the last three days was aggravated by my tramp through the wet yesterday. Brother McMillan returned from Dumbarton. He wants me to go to Ireland with him. Visited Brother Pender and found him better.

Spent the afternoon posting accounts and making out financial report for February. At night bathed my feet and took hot drinks to see if I could break up my cold.

Tuesday, 1 March 1898

Felt a little better; cold somewhat relieved. In the forenoon I was busy arranging the conference records and making out monthly financial reports and a statement of cash on hand, preparatory to transferring all records to Brother McKinnon. In the afternoon, in company with Brother McMillan, visited Brother Neilson and family, Sister Anderson, Brother Pender (who we found much better), and a Mr. Smith on Cedar Street. Mr. Smith is a friend of Brother McMillan. He treated us very courteously and invited us back.

It was eight-thirty before we reached the conference house, so necessarily had to make haste to finish preparations for our trip to Ireland. We decided to take the eleven o'clock train from Central Station to Ardrossan, thence by boat to Belfast. At the Central we heard a very appropriate farewell song, rendered near the car in which was a young man evidently bound for London. His friends gathered around him and sang "God Be with You Till We Meet Again." It was very beautiful.

An hour's swift run brought us to Ardrossan where, as we stepped out of the station, we got a good moonlight view of the harbor. A cold wind was blowing. It was our intention to stay on deck and enjoy a moonlight sail; but the gale grew stronger and the sea rougher. After two waves washed part of the deck and water dashed around us, we concluded to "go below." Soon that peculiar sensation—that *miserable, indescribable* sensation —called "seasickness" came upon me! O what misery! I dreaded the humiliating thought of being the first in the room to run; but, thanks to some *weaker* stomach and more *dizzy* head, I was not the first—just the *third!* I ran upstairs and —! —! —! —! —! Well, I was sick and did not care who knew it! Sick all the way! Turned almost inside out!! Lost all hope—all energy— all gallantry, if I ever had any. I finally stretched out on a bench and ever and anon made *strenuous* efforts to place my internal organs in the right place or *on the floor*—I did not care much which!

Just before we arrived in Belfast, I fell asleep and found a few minutes rest in dreamland. We reached Belfast at 6 A.M., *tired, sleepy, lank*, and *limpy*.

Wednesday, 2 March 1898

Immediately upon our arrival, we went to 84 Mount Street and sought comfort with the elders. After breakfast (?), visited the art gallery and one or two public buildings but found them rather devoid of interest on account of (1) drowsiness on my part and (2) inferior pictures and statues on exhibition. Strolled back to Mount Street, wrote to my parents, and then took a short nap. Awoke—or rather was awakened—at 7:15 P.M. Meeting at night. "Elders from Glasgow" occupied the time. Many inquired about

Uncle Hugh McKay.[125] The saints in Belfast are not very *numerous* and many who belong to the Church are not Latter-day Saints.

Thursday, 3 March 1898
After a good night's rest, felt refreshed. Visited the Belfast Ropework Company factory and saw the raw hemp changed into twine-lines, yarn, and ropes of all sizes from the small clothes-line to a rope twenty inches in circumference! The chief fibers used are Russian and Italian hemp, Manila hemp, sisal, New Zealand fibre, and coir. The window sash cords are made in a very ingenious manner. The *holders* revolve around a common center in a zig-zag, "grand-right-and-left" way, wrapping the bobbins as they go around. There are about 2,000 persons employed, 200 of whom are working in the netting room making fishing nets, etc. Our visit here was very interesting.

At 12:05 P.M. we left Belfast for Ballycastle, where Brother McMillan intended to get some names for genealogical purposes. We passed through Antrim and Ballymena to Ballymoney. The ride was a very pleasant one, and we had a good view of the surrounding country as the weather was clear. The farmers were plowing. Passed several peat bogs. At Ballymoney we stopped one hour and, as it happened to be the March Market Day, we found it very interesting. Saw the Irish country folk at their best on Market Day. On account of the crowded cars, we secured a first-class ticket from here to Ballycastle but found the accommodation not much better than the third[-class ticket] in England. Every time the engine would start, my head would jerk back against the car side; then I would have to restore my equilibrium and scramble to keep my hat off the floor! The distance is sixteen miles. The train runs this in one hour and a half "when she's pushed"!!!

At Ballycastle we secured lodging in a cosy little room in a temperance hotel, kept by a Mrs. Cameron. Called on "Father" Conway to get permission to search records but found none. Walked around the coast just west from Fair Head. The sea was quite rough, and as the waves dashed wildly against the shore, I felt to say, "Break, break, break on thy cold, gray shores, O sea!" The scene was very pleasing and inspiring to a mountain lad unaccustomed to such sights. After supper, wrote to Josie and retired.

Friday, 4 March 1898
Beautiful morning. Walked about two miles to "Father" McDonald's. I would judge him to be a very careless, slovenly man. I was not at all favorably impressed with him. No records. From here we went to the ancient

---

[125]Hugh McKay (b. 1843), the son of William and Barbara McKay, was born in Strathy, Sutherlandshire, Scotland. He was set apart for a mission to Great Britain on 18 November 1892, arriving in Liverpool on 6 December 1892. Hugh McKay was assigned to labor in the Irish Conference and in October 1893 was appointed as president of that conference. He returned to Utah in November 1894.

abbey of Bonamargy; here we found "McCay" and "McMullan" on some tombstones.

At 2:30 left Ballycastle in an "Irish jaunting car"[126] and rode over whin-covered braes[127] around the rugged coast to the Giant's Causeway. Saw the Carrick-a-rede, a small island or rather a large rock, separated from the mainland by a deep chasm, sixty feet in width. A rope bridge connects it with the mainland. Some lives have been lost in the attempt to cross it. Our driver was a typical Irishman and talked glibly all the way. Showed us the ponds in which flax is soaked and decomposed. In commenting upon the northwest wind that was blowing, he said characteristically: "The north wind is cold whatever direction it comes from!" Referred to an old-fashioned house by saying: "The front of it's in the back."

At Kane's Hotel we secured a guide and were shown the wonderful basaltic formation known as the Causeway. The many thousand pillars forming this crystalized phenomenon are all different—some pentagons, some heptagons and hexagons. Two diamond figures are also found. One pillar thirty feet high is composed of thirty-nine separate and distinct blocks. The Causeway is divided into three divisions, known respectively as the Small, the Middle, and the Grand Causeway. The Middle is also called the Honeycomb. Interesting figures are the Keystone, the Lady's Fan, and the Wishing Chair. My wish: — (relating to future happiness). The Grant's Spring is quite a curiosity. Wrote to Tommy. (Lighthouse in distance.)

Saturday, 5 March 1898

In the morning secured some views of the Causeway, paid our bill (a good round sum, 9/9), and, taking our seats in a "jaunting car," left for Coleraine, where Brother Mack's grandmother was born. The ride through the country was quite a pleasant one. At Coleraine visited "Father" Mon-Holland, who treated us cordially and told us that in his opinion we could find no Catholic records in Ireland antedating the year 1825, as previous to that time the Catholics were compelled to hold their services in secret places on account of the Protestants' persecutions. He was very sociable and asked many questions about Utah and her people; he has been in Ogden.

Failing in our efforts to find any trace of Brother McMillan's ancestors in the Catholic records, we went to the Protestants. Visited Reverend Giles, Reverend Dudley, and the "Curator." The first [Rev. Giles] took us to his church, a neat, clean edifice, and brought out his records, but no births were recorded. It was in this church that I first played on a pipe organ. It was at the minister's request. First selection "We Thank Thee, O God, for a Prophet," followed by "O My Father" and "Nearer My God to Thee." He

---

[126]An *Irish jaunting car* was a light, two-wheeled, horse-drawn vehicle, having two seats extended back to back over the low wheels for the accommodation of passengers, a compartment for luggage, and a perch in front for the driver.

[127]*Braes* are hillsides.

seemed quite pleased that I know what "grace" is and that I attended church!
We then told him who we are—Latter-day Saints. He felt a little agitated
but continued to be very civil. I have noticed that nearly every intelligent
sectarian will treat us with the same respect with which we treat them.

Reverend Dudley promised to search his records and send names if he
found any. We left Coleraine at 3:30 and arrived in Belfast at 5:40. Priesthood meeting at night.

Sunday, 6 March 1898

Fast Day. Met with the saints of Belfast. Attended the evening meeting. Felt free in speaking—subject, "The Gospel." After services went to
Brother Lindley's and partook of refreshments.

Monday, 7 March 1898

Received letter from Claire; made a reply.

We strolled around the docks and had a look at the *Queen of the Sea*,
the largest ship ever built; it is now in [the] course of construction. After
dinner went to Robinson and Cleaver's establishment and got a good view
of the city of Belfast from the top of their magnificent building. One of the
managers seemed pleased to entertain us as Americans. Signed our names
in "Visitors Book."

From here Mr. [Frederick J. A.] Jaques and I visited the anatomical
rooms. O, what a ghastly sight! Nude bodies of human beings lying all
around us! Some of them cut and slashed in the most inhuman manner con-
ceivable!! Our guide would pick up a heart, or a lung, or some other vital
organ, or perhaps a limb, and throw it around as carelessly and thoughtlessly
as though he were handling a piece of molded clay! O, it was horrible!! I
was soon out of there!

At 7:30 Brother McMillan left for Dublin, and two hours later I took
the boat for Glasgow. Mr. [Walter J.] Knell and Mr. Jaques were very kind
and entertaining. Went with me to the docks. The voyage was a pleasant
one, the sea being as calm as Salt Lake when the wind is not blowing. There
was no "rocking" at all.

Tuesday, 8 March 1898

Arrived at Central from Ardrossan, where I landed at 5 A.M. Arriving
at conference house, found letters from John McKay, Archibald Anderson,
P. G. Johnston, and paper from home. Took a three-hour sleep. Spent the
day arranging accounts and sending out reports. Very foggy.

Wednesday, 9 March 1898

Went to Queen Street Station to meet George Shorten, returning elder
from London. The rest of the day and part of the night was spent in
meeting and directing returning elders and emigrants. There is a company

of thirty-one sailing tomorrow. Brothers Pender and Edward are both ill and Brother McKinnon has just assumed control, so I shall be kept busy.

Thursday, 10 March 1898

Arose at 6 A.M. and went to Central Station. Forwarded [William] Crane's trunk to Liverpool. Went over to St. Enoch's and met an elder and nine emigrants; Miss Price and Miss Waur were among the number. Securing their tickets and providing for their comfort as best I could, I returned to conference house and satisfied my craving. The lorry then arrived; so the next three hours were occupied in gathering up luggage. The boat sailed at 1:45 with all on board. Everything went along all right, with the exception of a few *hitches* with Brother McKinnon.

Letter from Tommy. Testimony meeting at night.

Friday, 11 March 1898

Hunted for a suitable conference house. Found one on Dumbarton Road, but Brother McKinnon seemed afraid to close the bargain. It is a fine, three-roomed house with a good kitchen, presses,[128] bath, and a large lobby beside. I am afraid he will procrastinate and lose it. If he does, I shall not care to look for any more. It is not a very pleasant job, but I do want to get out [of] this *dingy street*. Wrote to A. P. R[enstrom], Fay, and Morgan.

Saturday, 12 March 1898

Addressed wrappers and attended to the usual Saturday morning duties.

After dinner Brother Pender and I, by request, went to Partick to administer to a sick woman. Imagine our surprise when we found her all alone! She was lying in a dirty bed in a—what seemed to me—a very uncomfortable position. She was in intense agony and seemed at times to be hardly able to speak. At her breast was a newly born infant, while behind her lay another little one about eighteen months old!! Her husband was at work—compelled to go or lose his job! We did all we could for her relief and then notified the right authorities of her condition. Later I learned that she had the proper attendance. A missionary sees all kinds of sights.

Quite tired at night.

Sunday, 13 March 1898

Sunday School meeting at 2 and at 6:30 P.M. Brother Pender and I spoke in the afternoon and Brothers Edward, Mitchell, and Montgomery in the evening.

---

[128] A *press* was an upright case or cupboard in which clothes, books, china, or other articles were kept.

Monday, 14 March 1898
Letters from Ray and [David R.] Alma.

Attended to some office work, went to the bookbinders on Ingram Street after dinner, arranged—or tried to arrange—the accounts in the new books adopted by Professor Paul.[129] I am afraid his system will not prove a success.

Tuesday, 15 March 1898
Wrote to George E. Ferrin and Professor Paul, asking the latter some questions about his books.

In the afternoon accompanied Brother Edward to the Western Infirmary, where he went to consult a doctor about a continued pain in his side; he is very unwell and has been ever since our long walk to and from Burnbank. The infirmary is a great boon to the poor people of this large city. They get consultation and prescriptions free by appearing before a class.[130]

Choir practice at night.

Wednesday, 16 March 1898
Word came from Liverpool to secure a good house while we are at it. Brother McKinnon and Brother Pender looked at one on Holmhead Street and finding it suitable secured it. So now on the 28th of May we "flit."[131] The house on Dumbarton Road was lost through procrastination. When he went to get it, it was gone; but perhaps it is a good thing as this one seems to be cheaper and better and much more convenient. Wrote to Tommy and studied for the first time in two weeks.

In the evening, in company with Brother Pender, visited Mr. Anderson and wife. He is not in the Church but has been favorable to our religion for many years; he still holds to his own creed, however. Evidently, he looks upon all religions as being the same.

Letter from T. Allen.

Thursday, 17 March 1898
Letter from Claire.

Weather very stormy. Brother McMillan returned from England. Spent

---

[129]Joshua H. Paul (1863-1939) was president of Utah State Agricultural College from 1894 to 1896. He was set apart for a mission to Great Britain on 29 August 1896, arriving in Liverpool on 24 September 1896. In the Scottish Conference he labored in Edinburgh and then was appointed to preside over the Birmingham Conference in June 1897. When he returned to Utah in October 1898, he served as president of the Latter-day Saints University in Salt Lake City for nine years. Then he was made professor at the University of Utah until his retirement in 1928. See the Joshua H. Paul Collection, Accession 864, located in the Manuscripts Division, J. Willard Marriott Library, University of Utah, Salt Lake City.

[130]In order for a poor person to receive medical attention at no cost, it was required that he be examined in the presence of a group of physicians to determine his inability to pay and the nature of his illness.

[131]In Scottish, *flit* means to move from one home to another.

the day in attending to sundry duties, particularly transferring accounts to *Star* book. Testimony meeting at night.

Friday, 18 March 1898
A very dull day. I felt as though I could give up everything! In transferring accounts, I became tired and wearied and discontented. After taking a refreshing walk, felt better. Nothing worth recording happened.
Wrote to Claire.

Saturday, 19 March 1898
Wrote to Miss [Florence] Dye about "Class Day."
Addressed *Stars* and attended to usual duties. At 7 P.M. eight baptisms took place at the bath. In the evening, in company with Brother McMillan, visited Mr. Smith, 4 Myrtle Street, and a Mr. Donald, 145 Springburn Road. Treated well and welcomed at both places. Good conversations on Utah and the gospel. Earnestly requested to come back. "We are not Mormons, you know, but we are far enough along that we can *now* associate with them— something we couldn't think of doing awhile back," said Mr. Donald, as he bid us good-night, after having walked about half a mile with us on our way home. As several of the elders came in to the conference house, Brother Johnston and I went to the hotel.

Sunday, 20 March 1898
Arose about nine o'clock. Breakfast at the conference house. Sunday School as usual and meetings at 2 and 6:30 P.M. "Mizpah"[132] from Maggie [Gain]. The evening meeting was crowded and an excellent spirit prevailed. It was a beautiful night and I had a pleasant walk and conversation with Miss Rennie. At ten o'clock went to hotel. Wrote diary from March 17th to *here* and retired.

Monday, 21 March 1898
Received an appointment to labor in Stirling with Brother P. G. Johnston as companion. This means real practical missionary work. I look forward to our coming experience with a feeling of eagerness, seasoned with a little dread. I am sorry to part from Brother Pender. He and I have worked together now for nearly six months, and I now feel that I am losing an excellent companion and adviser.

Tuesday, 22 March 1898
A beautiful morning for Glasgow. The sun is shining brightly. Spent

---

[132]In Scottish custom, a *mizpah* was a short expression of faith in the watchful care of the Lord, placed at the end of a letter. It is a Hebrew word meaning "the lookout point" and refers to the passage in Gen. 31:49, which states: "The Lord watch between me and thee, when we are absent one from another."

most of the day arranging accounts in new *Star* book. Brothers McMillan, McKinnon, and Johnston have gone to Newarthill. Brother McMillan's last visit. Wrote to Mamma. Returning elders from Wales.

Wednesday, 23 March 1898

The sun is shining brightly, although the air is keen and bracing. Completed the transferring of accounts into the new "cash and day" book. At night attended the farewell social given by the Glasgow Branch in honor of Brother McMillan. Called upon to recite. Songs, recitations, and speeches were the order of the evening. The branch presented Brother McMillan with a valuable Bible and a muffler. The evening was a very pleasant one.

Thursday, 24 March 1898

Went to St. Enoch's Station to meet a Miss Scofield; she did not come at the time stated. Concluded that she had come earlier and had become lost or misdirected. Telegraphed to Manchester. At 3 P.M. received an answer that she would be here at 7:45 P.M. This settled a great deal of trouble and worry. Visited Mrs. [Duncan] Thomson on Comelypark Street. Sister Robertson and her sister-in-law [Mrs. Thomas Thomson] were in the room. Spent a pleasant hour. "Be a good boy while you're in Stirling." At 7:45 met Miss Scofield and Mrs. Gadhill. Took them to the hotel and then came up to testimony meeting. Retired about 11:45 P.M.—"Elder's hour."

Friday, 25 March 1898

Gathered up passengers' luggage, calling for that purpose at St. Enoch's and Central Stations. Arrived at the Stobcross Quay at 11:30 A.M. Stopped until 2:10 to see the S.S. *Furnessia* with the elders and saints, including President McMillan on board, sail down the river. At the conference house made out a cash statement, gave up all office work, and made preparations for Stirling. At 5:45 P.M. bid Brother Pender good-bye. We have labored together just long enough to get well-acquainted and form an attachment to each other. I felt very sorry when I shook his hand. I did not like to leave Mrs. Noble either. She has been very kind, indeed. But missionary life is made up of changes and disappointments, mingled with seasons of true pleasure and rare enjoyment.

At 6:10 left Queen Street Station for Stirling, where we arrived about one hour later. Checking our luggage, we went to Whitehead's Temperance Hotel in the arcade and secured lodgings for the night. I felt somewhat gloomy, but Brother Johnston will not give one much time to brood over anything. Wrote to Ray.

Saturday, 26 March 1898

After the morning toilet and a good breakfast, we started out to secure lodgings. We did not walk around long before we succeeded in getting apartments at 9 Douglas Street with a family named Sharp. Our room is

Fig. 20   *Stirling Castle, Stirling.*

well-furnished—piano, easy chairs, comfortable bed, and all that, but I fear our bill at the end of the week will be a regular *purse-presser.*

During the afternoon we visited the old historic Stirling Castle (Fig. 20). The first thing which attracts one's attention as he walks up the esplanade is the Statue of King Robert the Bruce (Fig. 21).[133] Crossing the drawbridge and past the armed guard, one finds himself in the yard of this ancient fortified place, this rendezvous for so many kings! The Ladies' Rock is seen firm and steadfast, surrounded by the graves of departed heroes and residents of Stirling, and upon which Monck,[134] under Cromwell,[135] planted his cannon and battered the only weak place in the castle wall until he gained an entrance. The field of Bannockburn, where the immortal Bruce with 30,000 men defeated the English army of 80,000 men, is seen in the distance marked by a white flagpole.

Other places of interest seen from the wall are the Public Green, where once stood the Castle Park; the King's Tournament, "Where the good yeoman bent his bow and the tough wrestler foiled his foe"; the "Fatal Mound" that "oft has heard the death-axe sound, as on the noblest of the land fell the stern headsman's bloody hand";[136] Wallace's Monument, reared

---

[133]Robert the Bruce (1274-1329), king of Scotland, spent most of his life in the struggle for Scottish independence from the English. In 1306 Bruce was crowned King Robert I. In 1314 he won the decisive Battle of Bannockburn against the much larger English army under Edward II. In 1328 England recognized Scotland's independence. He died of leprosy one year later.

[134]George Monck (1608-1680), an English general and naval commander, was imprisoned by the Parliamentarians for two years in the Tower of London, but Cromwell offered to free him if he would serve in the army. He served as commander in chief of Scotland in the 1650s. Later, Monck helped restore the Stuarts to the English throne in 1660.

[135]Oliver Cromwell (1599-1658) led the armed forces of Parliament to victory in the English Civil War during the 1640s against King Charles I and ruled England, Scotland, and Ireland from 1653 to 1658 with the title of "Lord Protector."

[136]Both quotes are from Sir Walter Scott, *The Lady of the Lake*, canto V, xx, in *Scott: Poetical Works*, ed. J. Logie Robertson (London: Oxford University Press, 1971), 257.

Fig. 21 *Robert the Bruce Statue, Stirling.*

in commemoration of his worth and honor; the battlefield just below is pointed out as the place where Wallace regained the castle from the English —all these places, together with the enchantment of the scene in the sleeping valley with the winding [River] Forth almost surrounding the old Abbey of Cambuskenneth, awaken an indescribable interest in and profound respect for the heroes and gallant chiefs of bonny Scotland! Then follow the guide as he points out the "Lion's Den,"[137] the *dungeon* that held Sir Roderick Dhu,[138] the Queens' Stand, and all that and really one can hardly help but wish that those old days of bloody knighthood might return—just the pleasant part of them though!!

We returned[139] to our lodgings about five o'clock and spent the evening in our room. Miss [Annie] Sharp appears to be a very pleasant, intelligent, young woman and quite *bonnie*, too. She told us all about her experience as Madam Patti's[140] maid while in London. After hearing her description of that great singer's *makeup* (false hair, false teeth, glass eye, and foolish attention to a dog), one could hardly appreciate her magnificent voice!

---

[137]The *lion's den* was the hollow or small interior square court of the palace. McKay incorrectly wrote "lion's dens."

[138]Roderick Dhu is a fictional character in Sir Walter Scott's *Lady of the Lake.*

[139]After visiting all these historic places in and around Stirling and absorbing the rich cultural experience, David O. McKay and his companion, Peter G. Johnston, walked back to the apartment they had rented that morning. On the way McKay saw a home under construction with a large stone inscribed with the words "What e'er thou art, act well thy part" (Figs. 22-23). Francis M. Gibbons, *David O. McKay: Apostle to the World, Prophet of God* (Salt Lake City: Deseret Book Co., 1986), 46, summarized the importance of this episode to McKay: "There can be no doubt that this experience, which planted the motto in his mind under such unusual circumstances, was one of the major factors in the growth and development of David O. McKay. He referred to it often during his long and productive life." For further discussion of this inscription, see the Editors' Introduction, pp. xxxiii-xxxvi, above.

[140]Adelina Patti (1843-1919), an Italian soprano, became famous for her singing and acting in operas.

Fig. 22 *The Home with the "What E'er Thou Art" Stone (in situ), Stirling.*

Sunday, 27 March 1898

Attended services at the Free Church,[141] Rev. Angus, pastor. Long prayers and "vain repetitions" grated on my nerves. He thanked God for his *tired* and *weary heart.* I felt to thank him for my merry, lightsome heart made so by the freedom of the gospel of our Saviour as revealed in this dispensation!

Attended evening services at 6:30. A Rev. Dougal (?) conducted them. His text was the twelfth verse of the thirty-third chapter of Deuteronomy. His sermon was not a very logical one. No principle of the gospel was explained, but some good advice was given. One thing especially impressed me as being very commendable. After the last prayer had been offered, all the congregation sat down quietly and remained seated for about a minute, then arose and walked out. This is far better and shows much more respect for a house of worship than the habit some people have of rushing to the door as soon as "Amen" is said. Wrote to [David R.] Alma.

Monday, 28 March 1898

Raining. After morning toilet, we walked through the business part of Stirling, bought a few necessary articles, and then made preparations for an afternoon visit in Alva, a town seven miles distance, where Brothers Gil-

---

[141]The Free Church of Scotland was formed by evangelicals who withdrew from the Established Church in 1843. It joined with the United Presbyterian Church in 1900 to form the United Free Church.

Fig. 23 *The "What E'er Thou Art" Stone (close-up), Stirling.*

christ[142] and McKnight[143] are laboring. We walked by way of Causewayhead along the foot of the mountain. The country is beautiful! Some of the mountain dells reminded me of my own native hills around the peaceful town of my childhood! The boys secured a hall for next Thursday and advertized us as the speakers.

From Alva we went with the boys to Sauchie, where we called on a Mrs. Thompson, then to Clackmannan to see Mr. and Mrs. Snedden. Both families bid us welcome. Miss Snedden (sister to Annie) is a bonnie lass. Came to Stirling on train. Letters from Tommy, Claire, Nora, and Brother Pender. Answered Brother Pender's.

Tuesday, 29 March 1898
Still cold and stormy; the hills are bleak and covered with snow. Walked out to the field of the Battle of Bannockburn, stood in the place and saw the identical spot where Bruce planted his flagstaff. Distributed about sixty-five tracts in St. Ninian's. Oh, I do dislike tracting; there is nothing pleasant about it.[144] Brother Johnston tried every way to find an excuse to

---

[142]Thomas Gilchrist (1859-1904) was born in Armadale, Bathgate, Linlithgow, Scotland. He was set apart for a mission to Great Britain on 13 August 1897 and assigned to the Scottish Conference, working in Alva, Stirling, and Tillicoultry. Gilchrist was made president of the Newcastle Conference in August 1898. He was released in August 1899 and returned to Utah the following month. He got sick from working in the mines in Park City, Utah, and died in December 1904.

[143]Joseph H. McKnight (1880-1959) was only sixteen when called on a mission, though he had turned seventeen when he was set apart on 2 April 1897 to serve in Great Britain. He arrived in Liverpool three weeks later. Within the Scottish Conference McKnight labored in the areas of Alva, Ayrshire, Glasgow, and Stirling. He left in March 1899, arriving home the following month.

[144]Henry D. Moyle (1889-1963), a missionary in Germany in 1910 and later a counselor to McKay in the First Presidency, wrote the following sentiment in his diary: "I never saw anyone yet that did [enjoy tracting]. The only reason I do it and so much of it is that it is hard, and by doing it I overcome my dislikes and desires; then I believe good is also accomplished thereby. But you can't realize how hard it is," quoted in Richard D. Poll, *Working the Divine*

Fig. 24 *Abbey Craig Park and Wallace Monument, Stirling.*

not go out today but he failed; so, heaving a sigh, he consented to go. We both felt miserable but perhaps did some little good—it is very doubtful, though. Brother Johnston's feelings were afterwards expressed in this characteristic manner: "If anyone had crossed me when I started to tract, I would have hit him in a minute!" And I believe he would. Wrote to Joseph McFarlane[145] and Claire.

Wednesday, 30 March 1898

Fair day. Studied in the morning. Afternoon went to the arcade to secure a hall. They wanted 7/6 for two hours! Inquired about others before deciding to take this one. I think it is the best. At night went to a concert given by Loudin's Original Fisk Jubilee Singers. We crossed the Atlantic together last August. The audience was small, but the singing was nonetheless excellent. At the close I stepped to the front and shook hands with them. They seemed pleased to see me, and I am sure I was glad to see them. . . . I have a warm spot for these beautiful singers.

Thursday, 31 March 1898

A beautiful spring morning. Took a morning stroll. After dinner we started on foot for Alva where, according to previous announcement, we were to meet with Brothers Gilchrist and McKnight to hold a public meeting in the town hall. The walk by way of Abbey Craig (Fig. 24), upon which

---

Miracle: The Life of Apostle Henry D. Moyle (Salt Lake City: Signature Books, 1999), 30.

[145]Joseph C. McFarlane (1874-1934) of the Ogden Third Ward was McKay's friend. McFarlane was set apart on 10 November 1897 for a mission to Great Britain, arriving in Liverpool on 1 December 1897. He was assigned to the Norwich Conference and then in June 1898 transferred to the *Millennial Star* office. McFarlane was released in March 1900, arriving home in Ogden in May 1900. He served as second counselor in the Mt. Ogden Stake Presidency. In August 1934 McFarlane and his wife Pearl were tragically killed when their car hit a train.

towers Wallace's Monument, was indeed a delightful one! The sun shone brightly. Bright yellow flowers and the peeping daisy were basking in its warmth, while the tender grass on the peaceful hillside shot forth, as if by magic! Tender buds along the hedge rows burst forth into tiny green leaves, and the air, so exhilarating and buoyant, seemed filled with the fragrance of budding life! Quiet peaceful homes nestled against the mountain, while the contented farmhand followed in the furrow behind his fat steady horses that squirmed and twisted and stretched their necks as though they were the most imposed upon of all horses in Scotland! Yes, it was a beautiful morning, full of beautiful rural scenes!

There were not many at our meeting, but those present seemed attentive and interested. After singing a hymn, Brother McKnight offered prayer. We then sang "Do What Is Right" and D. O. [David O. McKay] was introduced by Brother Gilchrist, who presided as the first speaker. He spoke about forty minutes on the "Gospel" and was followed by Brother Johnston on the "First Principles." Brothers McKnight and Gilchrist bore their testimonies and after singing "May the Grace [of Christ, Our Savior]," etc., the meeting was dismissed by Brother Gilchrist. We chatted until the wee small hours and then retired.

Friday, 1 April 1898
After breakfast, accompanied by the brethren, we started back to Stirling. The morning was more spring-like than ever, and the hillside seemed literally clothed with its green, grassy cloak! Today the men are sowing the newly plowed land. Two men, each sowing with both hands and supplied with grain by two stout healthy women, running back and forth with their bucket of oats, are busy covering the ground with seed! Three teams are lazily dragging the harrows, covering it up! The air is more fragrant than ever! The boys walked with us about four miles, then returned.

Miss Sharp waited for us a long time last night, as we intended when we left to return the same evening. She is an ideal housekeeper and a pleasant, cheerful, intelligent young woman! Everything she does is done in a tidy orderly way, and her home is clean from "cellar to dome." She is all right! After dinner we secured the Lesser Arcade Hall for a meeting next Thursday night. Letter from David R. and papers from home. Wrote to Lizzie.

Saturday, 2 April 1898
Mrs. Sharp came home last night. Have not had the pleasure of meeting her yet. I hope she is as amiable as her daughter, for really the latter is as thoughtful and as obliging as any young lady I have met. She reminds me somewhat of _____ (a dear friend) in her manifest willingness to seek to make one comfortable. She may change in her manner when the slander and calumny of the servants of Satan ring in her ears. These may cause her to be suspicious of us, as many others are, but whatever attitude she may assume towards us in the future, I shall always remember with pleasure my first

week in Mrs. Sharp's home and the kind treatment received from *Annie, the gem of the household!*

Sunday, 3 April 1898
At 11 A.M. attended the [East] Church, frequented by Mrs. Sharp and family—Mr. Lang, minister. Text: Luke 3:6. Preached in the interest of foreign missions. Spent the afternoon in our room. It was a cold, bleak day.
Wrote to Cousin Bella.

Monday, 4 April 1898
Morning mail brought a beautiful present from May and a letter from Claire. The *photo case* from May has been delayed about two months or more. It was sent to the dead-letter office.
Went out tracting! Distributed 240 tracts, announcing at the same time the place and time of our first meeting in Stirling. Had but one or two short conversations. Put ad in the *Observer*. Studied. In the evening Miss Sharp entered into a lengthy chat with us, during which she asked some very intelligent questions about our religion. Thinking it a favorable opportunity to do so, I gave her some gospel literature. Brother Johnston gave her the "Articles of Faith." She says she is going to our meeting. Letter from Brother Pender.

Tuesday, 5 April 1898
Distributed 230 tracts, visiting about 120 houses. I am getting quite anxious about this pending war between the States and Cuba. I wonder if, in the event of a conflict, the missionaries will be called home? The papers state today that the situation is critical. I hope our country stands firm.
In the afternoon we wrote the time and place of the coming meeting on about fifty handbills, having the "Art[icles] of Faith" on opposite side. We then ordered, printed, and made arrangements for posting as many large ones. The cost of advertising alone, without the tracts, will be at least seven shillings each. In the evening spent about two hours enjoying ourselves with the piano and violin. Brother Johnston plays the *fiddle*. Prepared tracts for distribution tomorrow.

Wednesday, 6 April 1898
Wrote to Liverpool (Messrs. Staveley and Co.) about an extra 3/6 which they charged me for postage. Wrote time and place of meeting on about 300 tracts. Distributed one hundred and seventy.
The women can hardly understand me when I offer them a "gospel tract." Nearly everyone misunderstands me or asks me what I said. One woman thought I said "gas bill" and promptly answered, "No, we don't burn gas!!" Today one old haggard-looking creature took the tract, squeezed it in her hand, and with gnashing teeth yelled, as she threw the tract at me, "I'm a lost sinner, and I dinna want yer blatherin' gospel! I hate the name

o't!!" She was a terror!

The *Record* says McKinley's[146] message will mean war. I believe I would as lief *fight* as *distribute tracts*!

Thursday, 7 April 1898

Wrote a letter to Brother Pender, Glasgow. Brothers Gilchrist and Mc-Knight came from Alva at about 1 P.M. We took a stroll through and around the castle cemetery.

At 7 P.M. went to the Arcade Hall to hold a meeting. Only about eighteen persons were present; but they were mostly shrewd, intelligent-looking men, among whom was one minister. Mrs. Sharp and her daughter, Annie, were also there. Brother Johnston presided. Opened the meeting by singing "Beautiful Zion"; prayer, Brother Johnston; singing, "O My Father." I was called as the first speaker, subject "The Gospel." Brother McKnight followed with the "First Principles." After singing the Doxology in which nearly all present joined, Brother Gilchrist dismissed by prayer. A good spirit prevailed and all seemed to be favorably impressed. One woman said she could not leave the hall without speaking to us. She expressed herself as believing that what we said was true. She shook our hands warmly and asked us to visit her father and family with whom she is living.

When we got back to our room, Miss Sharp had a lunch prepared for us, after eating which we enjoyed ourselves by playing the piano and violin and in singing hymns. Retired about 1 A.M.

Friday, 8 April 1898

Walked out to the Borestone[147] on the Battlefield of Bannockburn, then back to the Stirling Castle. After dinner went up to see the old Beheading Stone and then accompanied the boys for about three miles on their way to Alva. Promised to meet them Sunday. Wrote to May.

Saturday, 9 April 1898

Wrote a letter home. Brother Johnston has gone to Glasgow. During the day had several very interesting talks with Miss Sharp, during which she often unconsciously manifested a noble character, a pleasant though quite determined disposition, a warm generous heart (toward those she respects but a cold disdainful one toward others), and a true, genuine, unselfish nature. She asked some questions about our religion, among which was one about polygamy. This principle is a stumbling block in the path of all of

---

[146]William McKinley (1843-1901) was elected president of the United States in 1896. The Spanish-American War was precipitated by the explosion in February 1898 of the battleship U.S.S. *Maine* in Havana harbor in Cuba, with war being declared in April 1898 and an armistice ending the fighting in August. McKinley was assassinated in September 1901.

[147]According to tradition, King Robert the Bruce planted the Scottish royal standard in this stone.

them. She was not, however, very antagonistic. As soon as she understands more fully the true situation, she will not be prejudiced. Brother Johnston returned at 11 P.M.

Sunday, 10 April 1898

At 11 A.M. we started for Clackmannan, where we were to attend a cottage meeting in Mr. Snedden's. We walked by way of Alloa. Met Brothers Gilchrist and McKnight just before we reached our destination. Brother McKnight presided at the meeting. Brother Johnston and I were called upon to occupy the time. After the services were over, Miss Snedden prepared "tea," after enjoying which we spent an hour or so singing hymns and "cracking" and then walked to Fairfield Sauchie and held another meeting in Mr. [Alex] Thompson's. Brother Gilchrist presided. D. O. [David O. McKay] and Brother Johnston were the speakers. We stopped all night with [the] Thompson's. All made us very welcome indeed. They are favorable to our religion; will be baptized soon.

Monday, 11 April 1898

The boys came from Alva about ten o'clock and found us in the kitchen with Mrs. Thompson and her daughters, with whom we had chatted since 8 A.M. We bid our kind hostess good-bye, promising not "to be long ere we're back again" and went to Gabusson Place, Alloa, where we visited a Mrs. Morrison. She came from Thurso and, hearing that my father was born there, had been "anxious to see me." She was very sociable, prepared a lunch for us, asked us to visit her again, and promised to give me a letter of introduction to some friends in Thurso.

From here we went to Alva, ate dinner at 2:30, and then started for Stirling. The boys walked about four miles with us. Really, we all have formed a fast friendship. At Stirling we found everything—so far as we are concerned—all right. Our room was as neat and tidy as the Queen's! It seemed as though I was stepping once more into one of Mamma's rooms! It seemed so pleasant and inviting that I could not refrain from sitting at the piano, *first thing*, to play "Home, Sweet Home"! Miss Sharp is a jewel! Just the touch of her hand puts everything in "apple-pie order" and makes it look clean and neat! If she is fortunate in getting a good husband and one worthy of her love, she will make his home an *Eden*. Shortly after we came *home* (this is the first place I have felt like calling *home*), I received a letter from Tommy and one from Claire.

Tuesday, 12 April 1898

Spent the morning hours in the house, studying and writing. In the afternoon, it being a clear day, we went to the top of the Wallace Monument, from which place an impressive view of the surrounding valley and hills was obtained. The fertile valley, dotted with thriving cities, holding in its bosom the winding [River] Forth, and bounded by green, time-leveled mountains, presents one of the most inspiring landscape scenes one can behold.

At night wrote to John.

Wednesday, 13 April 1898
Wrote to Tommy and Claire.

The weather is stormy. Rained nearly all day. During the evening learned that the woman who was so favorably impressed at our meeting is prohibited from speaking to us by her father.

Thursday, 14 April 1898
Distributed 114 tracts ("second tracting").[148] Had several interesting conversations. Nearly every one who took a tract last week seemed pleased to accept this one. Several asked when we would hold another meeting. This is the most pleasant tracting day I have experienced.

The war between America and Spain seems to be inevitable and imminent. Today's outlook is very portentous. Spent half an hour in the cattle auction market. Milch cows sold at prices ranging from twelve pounds to sixteen pounds each, and sheep from eighteen shillings to forty shillings each. Prepared tracts for distribution.

Friday, 15 April 1898
Distributed 102 tracts. Had an excellent conversation with one Mrs. Whigham. Was treated courteously by nearly every one. At 5:10 P.M. Brother Pender came from Glasgow. He is going to stay with us here in Stirling. His presence is greatly appreciated, for he will be good company, a wise counselor, and a good speaker at meetings. He reports conditions in Glasgow being very deplorable. Brother McKinnon is acting very unwisely. After supper he and I walked around the esplanade in front of the castle. Here Brother Pender, thirty years ago, marched around as a *raw* recruit! He pointed out the very room in which he slept while in Stirling. He has seen many changes since then!

Saturday, 16 April 1898
Wrote to David R. Spent the afternoon studying and strolling around to see the interesting places of Stirling. Notes: "Wedding cake from London," "Fate sealed," etc., etc. Names: J. A. and E.

Sunday, 17 April 1898
Spent the day reading scripture and talking about a little of everything.

---

[148]A *second tracting* refers to going over the same area again but distributing a different tract.

Monday, 18 April 1898
Prepared tracts for contribution [distribution]. Had a long interesting talk with Miss Sharp. She cannot understand why "men will leave their families to come over here to preach." "It's all right for you," said she, "but fancy an old man like Mr. Pender coming!" Distributed 112 tracts.
Wrote to A. R. Anderson.

Tuesday, 19 April 1898
Distributed 112 tracts. Nothing very interesting or important happened. Met some very kind, intelligent women. Nearly every house was clean and tidy, and the inmates seemed contented and happy. A long conversation with one woman showed me that many of the people are rather dissatisfied with the incompleteness of their religion, yet they doubt the divinity of Joseph Smith's mission. The truth shakes the sandy foundations of the existing, sham religions.

Wednesday, 20 April 1898
Stirling's "Spring Holiday." No tracting. Wrote to C[laire]. Received letters from Father and Claire. An interesting conversation with Miss Sharp.

Thursday, 21 April 1898
President McKinley sent his ultimatum to Spain yesterday. The *Daily Record* this morning declares that actual hostilities between America and Spain cannot be deferred longer than Saturday next! Britain's sympathy is with the U.S. and the latter nation should keep it, if possible. An alliance between these two nations, I believe, would be an excellent policy. I hope our government will act wisely on this question. England is in favor of it.
Distributed 150 tracts. I believe there will be a larger attendance at our meeting tomorrow night than there was at the last one. There is considerable talk about the "Mormon Missionaries."

Friday, 22 April 1898
Diplomatic relations between the United States and Spain are broken off and a "state of war" declared to exist. General Woodford,[149] U.S. minister to Spain, leaves Madrid at once.
Distributed 100 tracts. About 5 P.M., the brethren from Alva came in, and the rest of the afternoon was spent in social conversation, interspersed with a little music.
Our meeting commenced at 8 P.M. Only a small audience present. I was called to preside. Brother Johnston was the first speaker, followed by Brother Gilchrist, while Brother Pender made some closing remarks. A

---

[149]Stewart L. Woodford (1835-1913) was a Civil War veteran, a lieutenant governor, a congressman, and a federal district attorney before becoming U.S. ambassador to Spain in 1897.

good spirit prevailed and good instructions were given by each, especially by Brother Pender. The remarks of each were very good. All present seemed to enjoy the meeting, except one man who at the close tried to refute what had been said. His arguments, or rather accusations, were so ridiculous that even those not in sympathy with our doctrine repudiated him. One woman, hearing him accuse us of not believing in the "Blood of the Lamb," denied his accusation point blank and so quickly and completely hushed him up that he had not a word to say in his defense but sought refuge behind the calumnious wall reared by the opposers of polygamy. From here he fired two or three blank lies and retreated. The apparent sympathy and good will of all present, save this one man who became so antagonistically excited, caused Brother McKnight to quote Job: "The sons of God came to present themselves before the Lord, and Satan came also" [Job 2:1]. Mrs. and Miss Sharp were present at the meeting. A homelike scene as we entered our room! Bright fire and everything pleasant.

Fig. 25 *Cambuskenneth Abbey, Stirling.*

Saturday, 23 April 1898

U.S. warship has captured a Spanish cruiser. Cuban ports to be blockaded. Spain's tactics rather hidden. Prolonged struggle anticipated.

Brothers Pender and Johnston went to Glasgow. The rest of us visited Cambuskenneth Abbey (Fig. 25), near the old tower of which the remains of James III[150] and his queen are buried. After dinner we spent about two hours talking. They then took the train at Causewayhead for Alva. I returned from my walk with them at about 5 P.M.

After tea I spent four of the happiest hours that I have seen in Scotland, and I may say anywhere else; Miss Sharp, of course, made them so. We became mutually confidential. I explained, as best I could, the first principles of the gospel, all of which she accepted; but she could hardly understand why the subject for baptism must be immersed. After asking several questions about this ordinance, she continued: "And do you put them right under the water?" "Yes," I replied, "right under the water." "Head and all?" She was quite astonished when I gave her an affirmative answer to this; but

---

[150]James III (1452-1488), King of Scotland from 1460, was a weak monarch who faced rebellions from the nobility. In 1488 James III was defeated by rebels at the Battle of Sauchieburn, captured, and killed.

after we referred to the examples of baptism recorded in the New Testament, she quite agreed that immersion must be the proper mode. She seemed very interested in the early history of the Church in this dispensation. She is a *noble* young woman, *refined*, *attractive*, and *intelligent*. From her I learned something about the character of the man who tried to cause trouble last night. He is a Salvationist and often makes it a point to create disturbances after such meetings. At 11 P.M. Brother Johnston's footstep was heard, so she said good-night and joined her mother in the kitchen.

Sunday, 24 April 1898

Attended services in the East Church. Rev. Lang is minister. Subject, "Benefits of Confessing Christ by Partaking of 'The Holy Communion.'" Studied in the afternoon. During the evening we strolled through the King's Park. Flowers from little "Hetty," a sweet little girl who visits Miss Sharp.

Monday, 25 April 1898

In the house most of the day. Called at police headquarters and obtained permission to hold open-air meetings. Brother Pender came from Glasgow at 1 P.M. The work in Glasgow is not in a very flourishing condition. Brother John Robertson came to visit us. He will spend two or three days in Stirling.

Tuesday, 26 April 1898

Accompanied Brother Robertson through the castle and around the interesting places of Stirling. Spent the evening in social chat.

Wednesday, 27 April 1898

Visited Cambuskenneth Abbey. Had a pleasant ride in a small ferryboat across the Forth (Fig. 26). A young lady did the rowing. An excellent dinner—plum pudding—given by Brother Robertson as a farewell dinner. The three of us made him a present of some beautiful, plush views of Stirling. He was very much affected. We enjoyed an excellent afternoon and evening.

Fig. 26 *The Forth River and the Old Bridge, Stirling.*

Thursday, 28 April 1898

Brother Robertson left at 10:30. Spent the day writing and studying. There is a *lull* in the war.

Friday, 29 April 1898

At 10:30 boarded the train for Alloa, where a grand procession is to take place in commemorating the opening of the Alloa Baths, a magnificent building built as a gymnasium, reading room, etc., and donated to the city by a Mr. Patten. The procession was excellent, the most attractive features being the yarn display, the glass display, the crockery display, and the decorations and samples shown on the co-op wagons. The music of the Alloa Band was very commendable, especially the pleasing Scotch air, "Will Ye No' Come Back Again?" No yelling nor boisterous conduct was seen anywhere. The best of order was observed by all.

Meeting at 6 P.M. at Mrs. Thompson's.

Saturday, 30 April 1898

The morning hours were spent with Mrs. Thompson.

At 11 A.M. the boys came from Alva and accompanied us through the New Gymnasium and Alloa Bath Building. Everything is arranged according to modern improvements. Walked over to Clackmannan and ate dinner at Snedden's.

About 5 P.M. father Snedden and his son Peter were baptized in the Devon River. Brother Gilchrist officiated. Later they were confirmed by Brothers Pender and Johnston. Brother Johnston and I walked back to Sauchie and remained all night with Mrs. Thompson. The boys went back to Alva. Mrs. Thompson is a fine woman and does everything in her power to make us welcome.

Sunday, 1 May 1898

Spent the forenoon reading.

At 2 P.M. attended fast meeting in Snedden's. At night we held a meeting, previously announced and arranged for by Brothers Gilchrist and McKnight, in Coalsnaughton. Very few present. Several young "hoodlums," who evidently intended to disturb our meeting, were expelled from the room. After that, good order prevailed. Brother McKnight was the first speaker and D. O. [David O. McKay] the next; Brother Johnston bore his testimony; Brother Gilchrist presiding. Brother Snedden and his son David were present also. Brother Pender was unwell.

After the meeting all had to walk from four to six miles in a pouring rainstorm. We all felt well in doing so though.

Monday, 2 May 1898

Effective administration to Brother Pender. Met a Mr. Morrison, an acquaintance of Brother Gilchrist's. He showed us through the Carsebridge Brewery.[151] Very interesting, especially the process of yeast making. They make in this one place alone from 30,000 to 40,000 gallons of whiskey every week!

We next visited the Alloa Pottery. Here we learned by actual observation what "clay in the hands of the potter" [cf. Jer. 18:6] really means. The hand process of making dishes, vessels, vases, etc. is the most interesting feat I have ever seen. Lumps of clay were transformed into inkstands, cups, bowls, or vases—almost like magic! We saw how the baths are made, also.

Later we called on Mrs. Morrison and at 4:20 came to Stirling. Our visit was enjoyable throughout. Beautiful flowers in our room, [due to the] kindness of Miss Sharp.

Tuesday, 3 May 1898

At "No. 9" [Douglas Street] writing and studying. Brother Pender went to Glasgow.

In the evening attended the first of a series of addresses to be given in the Lesser Public Hall by Dr. W. T. P. Walston. His subject was "The Midnight Cry." I was very much disappointed. He is one of these *saved* men, and a worse perverter of the true gospel cannot be found among men of even ordinary intelligence. Nothing to do but to say, "I am saved." O, it is abominable! I wonder why it is that such men cannot see their error. Surely they know that they are not teaching correct doctrine. After the meeting, we overheard a man telling a minister about the doctrine the "Mormons" preach.

Wednesday, 4 May 1898

Wrote to Cousin Bella, Claire, and Alex Edward, who has made inquiry concerning his son's health. Brother Leggat called and spent several hours with us. Brother Johnston went with him to Glasgow.

The paper this morning states that the Stars and Stripes now wave over Manila. Commodore Dewey,[152] after a fierce conflict in which almost the entire Spanish fleet was destroyed, has taken possession of the Philippines. Spain is in an uproar.

Thursday, 5 May 1898

Spent the morning hours studying. After the dinner hour, Miss Sharp came in and together we enjoyed an hour or more in pleasant conversation.

---

[151]Technically, Carsebridge was a whiskey distillery, not a beer brewery.

[152]George Dewey (1837-1917), an American naval officer, became a hero due to his victory—without the loss of a single American life—at the Battle of Manila Bay.

She has evidently lost confidence in her minister and well she might for he has acted rather indiscreetly, to say the least, in his eagerness to get her to his church. She is an intelligent young lady and, I believe, anxious to do what is right. I sincerely hope and pray that she will investigate the principles of the true gospel, for she is brave and dauntless and will not hesitate in obeying what she knows to be true. We spent the evening together; and more pleasant hours, I fancy, have never passed. I shall ever remember this night as one of the sweetest of my life. I cannot say that we talked all the time about "repentance and baptism," but *sincerity* was mentioned and thought of, by me at least, quite often. And since sincerity is truth and since the gospel comprehends "all truth," we can say that it is all in the gospel plan! I trust that our associations will always be as pleasant.

Friday, 6 May 1898

Wrote a letter to class of 1897 [at the University of Utah] and one to Nettie.

Studied. Enjoyed Miss Sharp's company. I fear if some of the good (?) people of Stirling knew how sociable we are one with another, they would at once conclude that Miss Sharp will be going to Utah, but I suppose they would soon learn their mistake. Brother Johnston came from Glasgow about seven o'clock.

Saturday, 7 May 1898

A beautiful day. [I went] on Gowan Hill. Conversation with a nice old gentleman, who seemed to become all aglow as he described the Battle of Stirling Bridge[153] and pointed out to us the interesting places of Stirling. Brother Pender came home.

Sunday, 8 May 1898

The weather is still fair. The sun is shining brightly. Took our Bibles and spent the forenoon on Abbey Craig. Read during the afternoon. Nothing at night.

Monday, 9 May 1898

Distributed 100 tracts. The people were not *very* sociable but rather cold and distant. As I passed a group of gossiping women, who had evidently gathered to discuss the object of our distributing tracts, etc., I heard one say, "Well, he canna get married in this country." No doubt they had concluded that our object here is for wives. Poor deluded souls! If they could only pass through Utah and see the hundreds of pretty young women there, I think such a foolish idea would leave them. They cannot under-

---

[153]At the Battle of Stirling Bridge in 1297 William Wallace in association with Andrew Murray, defeated the English who were led by King Edward I.

stand—they will not believe that we are here on our own expense to offer them the true gospel of Jesus Christ. There are some here, however, who now know us and who are honest in their belief that the message we bear is true. May their belief soon become a knowledge.

Brother Leggat spent the evening with us.

Tuesday, 10 May 1898

At 10:30 boarded the train for Alva. Brothers Gilchrist and McKnight met us at the depot. After dinner we all went up the Alva Glen, a picturesque ravine in which the water has cut deep chasms. A fine winding walk, or path, leads all the way up, and as one nears the summit and looks down upon the beautiful valley and upon the surrounding mountains, literally covered with a carpet of green over which sheep are roving and little lambs gamboling, he becomes almost enchanted with the scene before him! He becomes convinced, too, that beautiful scenes are found *outside* of *Utah*. Brother McKnight and I went near the top, covered with misty clouds, and there sang hymns.

Came back to Stirling on the 6:30 train. At 7:30 attended another of Dr. Walston's lectures. "What's the latest news from heaven?" he asked during his remarks. I was very much tempted to cry out, "That all the churches but one are wrong," for this is the latest news. He quoted as an answer the last verse but one in the Bible, "Surely I come quickly" [Rev. 22:20]. How inconsistent! when we.[154]

Sunday, 15 May 1898

Conference day. Just as we completed our morning toilet, Mr. Jensen came into the room, evidently intent upon disproving some of the articles of our faith, which he had been reading. As he entered, he said good-morning and beckoned with his finger for Brother Johnston to move near the window. Then, after clearing his throat by a short "ahem" and spreading his feet a little apart, he began to point to the several articles, saying: "Dat is all right, so is dat von; but I don't believe dat, nor dat von neidder." He became thoroughly interested but did not consent to go with us to meetings.

At 10:30 A.M., after having shaken hands [with] President Wells, Counselor McMurrin, Elder [Herbert L.] James from Liverpool office, twenty-two elders, and many of the saints, I found myself seated with the many others preparing to sing the opening hymn, "Did You Think to Pray." The speakers were Elders Adamson, Montgomery, and Hoggan—all recently released to return home. The afternoon meeting was excellent. After a few remarks by Brother [Robert] Cameron (also released), Brother James addressed the audience. He was followed by President McMurrin, who de-

---

[154]McKay wrote the words "when we" as the last words on a page. However, at this point there are two leaves (that is, four written pages) missing from McKay's diary. The next page skips to 15 May 1898.

livered one of the best sermons I have ever heard. The hall was full, many strangers being present.

Met Mrs. Thomson of Shettleston. She is a fine woman; so is her husband a fine man. Both were deeply impressed. She and Sister Robertson came back to the evening meeting, at which Brother McQuarrie,[155] president of the Irish Conference, and President Wells spoke to the assembly. This was also an excellent meeting, made so by President Wells's remarks. The conference was a success. Called on Mrs. Good. Back to lodgings.

Monday, 16 May 1898

Another interesting conversation with Mr. Jensen. This morning he came in, feeling quite assured that he had a deadly shot to fire at Mormonism. Handing Brother Johnston the Bible, he said, "Show me where dat Book of Mormon is mentioned in de Bible." Gave him thirty-seventh of Ezekiel. He did not understand it very well and because of this changed the subject to authority and baptism. He was called to breakfast several times and ours was getting cold, but he was too interested or curious to heed either. The time for priesthood meeting drew near, so we had to go after hurriedly swallowing our porridge. When I bid our host good-bye, he expressed a hope of seeing me again. (Brother Johnston goes back tonight to stay with him.) The priesthood meeting was good, although my having to take the minutes made me a little tired before the four hours were passed.

Ate dinner at the conference house and then all went to the photographers. What happened there will be seen later. Called on Mrs. McDonald in Possilpark. At 10 P.M. Brother Pender and I bid good-bye to the brethren, who went with us to the station, and left for Stirling. As we neared our "Stirling home" the light from the window showed that our sweet hostess, Miss Sharp, had our room all prepared for us. As we entered it, the first thing that met my gaze was the beautiful bouquet of flowers in the center of the table. Their sweetness is only surpassed by the kind, loving maiden who placed them there. We are both pleased to be back again.

Tuesday, 17 May 1898

Wrote letters to Claire and Nettie and copied the minutes of priesthood meeting. Had expected President Wells, but as it is very stormy, he no doubt has concluded not to come. Raining all day.

Wednesday, 18 May 1898

At 12:30 left Stirling for Edinburgh where, according to previous ar-

---

[155]Hector A. McQuarrie (1862-1926) was set apart on 7 April 1897, arriving in Liverpool on 10 May 1897. He was assigned to labor in the Irish Conference, and in March 1898 he was appointed president of that conference. However, McQuarrie was released as president in December 1898 and appointed to labor for six months in the Scottish Conference before returning to Utah. He also served in the Southern States Mission from 1903 to 1905.

Fig. 27 *Holyrood Palace, Edinburgh.*

rangements, I shall work in the registry office in search for Brother Pender's genealogy. A homelike "good-bye' [was shouted] from the window. Crossed the noted Forth Bridge. At Edinburgh met President McMurrin and Elder James. Secured lodgings at 7 Edina Place with a Mrs. Paterson.

Through the kindness of Mrs. White, Brother James and I were escorted through the glass works. The *furnace*, the *blowing*, the skill shown in shaping the vessels, and the *engraving* especially were all interesting and instructive. At night, with Elder[s] James and Gilchrist, went to the Empire Theatre; expert cyclists were the attractive feature.[156]

Thursday, 19 May 1898

As the registry office will be closed half the day, I thought it best not to commence work but take a holiday with the rest of the people in celebrating the Queen's birthday.[157] President McMurrin, Elder James, and I went to the Holyrood Palace (Fig. 27), where the Lord High Commissioner received the dignitaries of the Church and State and declared the general assembly of the Established Church[158] to be opened. As Brother James the day before had obtained passes for us, we entered the palace with the rest of them. At 11:30 the procession began to form in front of the castle, so we went out to see it. The soldiers drawn up in front of the palace presented a fine appearance. The Scots Grays[159] were among them. I have never before seen so many carriages at one time.

---

[156]McKay recorded in a separate notebook that the ticket cost one shilling. See the David O. McKay Collection, Manuscript 668, Box 14, located in Marriott Library, University of Utah.

[157]Alexandrina Victoria (1819-1902), queen of the United Kingdom of Great Britain and Ireland and empress of India, acceded to the throne in 1837 and had the longest reign of any British monarch.

[158]The *Established Church* refers to the Church of Scotland, which was formally constituted in 1560 when the authority of the Catholic pope was rejected and the Scots Confession was adopted. However, the Church of Scotland is independent of civil authority.

[159]The *Scots Grays* was a regiment of dragoons in the British Army, mounted on gray chargers.

After the procession left, we reentered the palace and were conducted through all the apartments open to visitors. The rooms of Queen Mary[160] were very interesting, though very small as compared with the bedrooms and dressing rooms built today. Saw where Riccio[161] was murdered. Queen Mary's work box was very interesting. The visit was an enjoyable one. Later visited the castle (Fig. 28). The Crown Room and Queen Mary's bedroom in which James VI[162] of Scotland was born occupied most of our attention.

Fig. 28 *Edinburgh Castle, Edinburgh.*

Friday, 20 May 1898

In the registry office. Not very successful, owing to meager information.

Saturday, 21 May 1898

Wrote a long letter home. In the afternoon met Miss Sharp, who has come to Edinburgh to visit her cousin. I was very pleased to see her. We spent the afternoon and evening together walking around the Holyrood Palace (Fig. 29), climbing the green *slope* of the Salisbury Crags, and ascending to the top of Nelson's[163] Monument, from which we had a good view of the city of Edinburgh. Ate lunch at the hotel, and then, after a walk to Edina Place, took the car for Marchmont Road. Bid her good-night and was soon on the car for my lodgings, 10:45 P.M.

---

[160]Mary, Queen of Scots (1542-1587) was the daughter of James V and Mary of Guise, succeeding to the throne six days after her birth. She was a Roman Catholic and in 1565 married her cousin, Lord Darnley. Two years later Darnley was killed when his house was blown up by gunpowder. Three months later Mary married the Earl of Bothwell, even though he probably planned Darnley's murder. She was forced to abdicate her throne in 1567 and was kept under house arrest in England from 1568 until her execution by beheading in 1587.

[161]David Riccio (1533-1566), an Italian musician, was Queen Mary's private secretary. In 1566 he was dragged from the queen's supper room in Holyrood Palace and stabbed to death.

[162]James VI of Scotland, James I of England (1566-1625), was the son of Mary, Queen of Scots, and Lord Darnley. He was crowned King of Scotland at the age of thirteen months when his mother abdicated. In 1603 he left Edinburgh for London where he was accepted as King James I of England. James believed in the divine right of kings. He chaired a discussion between Anglican puritans and Anglican bishops at Hampton Court, and the only important result was the sponsoring of a revised English translation of the Bible that is now known as the King James Version.

[163]Horatio, Viscount Nelson (1758-1805), an English naval commander, was made famous by his victories in the battles of the Nile and Trafalgar, in the latter of which he was fatally wounded.

Fig. 29 *The Royal Chapel, Holyrood Palace, Edinburgh.*

Sunday, 22 May 1898

According to our agreement yesterday, Miss Sharp accompanied me to the branch meeting. Elders Montgomery and Gilchrist were the speakers. After the services we walked leisurely through Queen and Princes Streets, enjoying a good, pleasant chat. At 6 P.M. we were again in the little hall ready for the evening meeting. D. O. [David O. McKay] and a Brother Kenley from Aberdeen occupied the time. While walking home, we took the wrong road and strolled about a mile or two out of our course. Neither of us felt much disappointed, however, as the walk through Canaan Lane and the quiet streets leading back proved to be very pleasant indeed. The day was very pleasantly spent, and I hope it was profitable, also.

Monday, 23 May 1898

In the registry office until 4 P.M. Met Miss Sharp at 5:45 and enjoyed her company until 9:40, at which time she left for Stirling. During the time we were together, she told me many of her past experiences. The time we spent together in Edinburgh shall always be remembered as some of the happiest hours in Scotland—and, in fact, anywhere else. I felt lonesome after she left.

Tuesday, 24 May 1898

In the registry office. Better success. At night witnessed a display of fireworks near the castle. It was very good. Princes Street was one solid mass of humanity! This is the *eightieth* anniversary of the Queen's birthday. "God Save the Queen" was cheered to the echo.

Wednesday, 25 May 1898

At 10 A.M., as we were going to the registry office, we met Brother Pender and Brother Johnston, who came for a day's visit. In the office until 4 P.M. Letter from Miss Sharp. Met Mrs. Brixen from Salt Lake City. She and her husband[164] are taking a tour through Europe. She is a plucky, little woman. She attended the open-air meeting at night. Brother Pender, Brother Johnston, and I did not go as their last train left before the meeting would close. (I wanted to have a talk with them.)

Thursday, 26 May 1898
   In registry office. Quite successful. Open-air meeting at night. While Brother Montgomery was speaking, a good-natured *drunk* stood before him and said, "Stop yer blasted preaching and go to singing!" I followed and spoke really for the first time on the street. The crowd was quite attentive. (My first *attempt* was in Newarthill.)

Friday, 27 May 1898
   In the registry office. Open-air meeting at night. There were not many present. I think that the results of these outdoor meetings are of a doubtful nature.
   Letter[s] from Miss Sharp and Tommy.

Saturday, 28 May 1898
   In registry office until 1 P.M. In the afternoon I was seized with a very gloomy feeling, mixed with homesickness, lonesomeness, and a variety of other unpleasant moods—all of which combined to make me very miserable. I strolled down to the seaside to see if I could find comfort in solitude, but the restless sea offered little consolation. Spent the evening writing and reading.

Sunday, 29 May 1898
   Meetings at 2 and 6:30 P.M. Outdoor meeting at night. Very cold. At Mrs. White's until 11:30 P.M.

Monday, 30 May 1898
   Registry office. At 7 P.M. visited Mr. [William] and Mrs. [Isabella] Gracie. Both were very sociable. We enjoyed ourselves with instrumental music and by singing hymns.

Tuesday, 31 May 1898
   Registry office.
   In the letter which came from Tommy last Friday morning was this

---

[164]Andrew C. Brixen (1858-1900) was manager of the Brigham Young Trust Company and his wife Julia Matilda Gutke Brixen (1859-1948) was a general board member of the Young Women's Mutual Improvement Association.

Fig. 30 *Sir Walter Scott Monument, Edinburgh.*

P.S.: "Please find enclosed money order for $20.00. You're always in a hurry. Brother Tom." Instead of finding an order, I found one of his receipts. I was "broke," so imagine how I appreciated the *joke*. The order came today. Welcome.

Wednesday, 1 June 1898

Last day in registry office. I was surprised and pleased to meet Brothers Jacobs[165] and [James H.] Davis, both just returning home from England. Spent a very pleasant afternoon with them visiting the castle, Calton Hill, Scott's Monument (Fig. 30), and other places of interest.

At 9:05 P.M. (or rather at 9:35, as the train was late) I left Edinburgh for Stirling, where I arrived at about 10:45. Just as I was leaving the station, I was highly pleased to meet Miss Sharp. She and Jeanie had come to the station to see some lady friends off, just about the time that my train arrived, so I was fortunate enough to meet them. It seemed as we were walking from the station that I was really and truly *home*. I shall always have a cherished spot in my heart for my friends in Stirling.

Thursday, 2 June 1898

Spent the morning hours explaining and arranging Brother Pender's genealogy, as I had found it in the office. Afterward we had a nice, confidential talk. I shall always remember (and I hope with profit) the encouragement and advice which he gave me.

Last Friday I received a letter of inquiry from President Wells, in which he intimated to me that I might be called to the Liverpool office. I do not think, however, that he will appoint me there, as my reply, I think, would not merit his doing so. However, we shall not go ahead with our intended series of meetings until things become definitely settled again.

Friday, 3 June 1898

Wrote to Uncle John.[166]

Brother Pender left for Glasgow to attend the marriage ceremony of William Leggat and Miss Officer. The afternoon was spent in reading, the evening in music and social conversation with Miss Sharp and Jeanie. Sat in "the gloaming."[167]

Saturday, 4 June 1898

The morning was spent quietly, though *sweet* and peacefully. Brother Pender returned just as the dinner table was being cleared. While taking a

---

[165]This could refer to either Henry C. Jacobs or John T. Jacobs, two missionaries to Great Britain who were returning together on the S.S. *Furnessia*.

[166]John W. Grow (1848-1916) was born on 21 December 1848 at Platt, Missouri. In 1869 he married Catherine McKay, David O. McKay's aunt.

[167]The term *gloaming* refers to the period of evening twilight or dusk.

stroll in the evening, joined some men who were jumping. "Who is he?" "Who is he?" Were questions whispered after I took a "hop, step, and a jump."

Sunday, 5 June 1898

Fast Day. At 9:30 started on foot for Alva. Brother Pender, being unwell, stayed at home. Stood the walk remarkably well. Met the boys at 11:30. At 2:30 held a meeting at Mrs. Thompson's who, by the way, was baptized last Thursday. Administered the sacrament and enjoyed a spiritual feast. At 6:40 P.M. we held an open-air meeting in Sauchie. An attentive crowd listened to what we had to say.

At 8:05, after having expressed a lot of excuses—real and imaginable—for not accepting the pressing invitations to stay all night, I started for Stirling. Brothers Gilchrist and McKnight accompanied me about half the distance. As the town clock struck ten, I was just entering the outside door. The day had been a pleasant one, well-spent.

Monday and Tuesday, 6-7 June 1898

Thinking it best not to do any tracting until we learn more about the proposed change (after which we shall secure the hall and give a series of meetings), I have spent these two days in talking, walking, and studying.

Wednesday, 8 June 1898

Brother Pender has concluded to go to Glasgow and get medical advice. He is feeling very unwell. He accordingly left Stirling at 1:07. Another pleasant evening spent with Miss Sharp. During our conversation, she expressed her belief in the principle of baptism. She has read several of our works on "The First Principles."[151]

Letter from Cousin Bella.

Thursday, 9 June 1898

Letter from home.

The morning hours were spent very pleasantly. About 11:30, while walking through the town, I was accosted by a gentleman who had attended our meetings. He asked about some of our doctrine, accepted the *Voice of Warning*,[152] and said he would call on me and learn more about the *proofs* we have to offer. He gave me his name—Mr. Bundy, 13 Viewfield Place. Our

---

[151]"First Principles of the True Gospel of Christ," a four-page tract attributed to Joshua H. Paul, was often used by missionaries. Other popular tracts distributed during this time in Great Britain include: "Character of the Latter-day Saints," George Teasdale's "Glad Tidings of Great Joy," "The Only True Gospel," Charles W. Penrose's "Rays of Living Light," and "Scriptural Revelations of the Universal Apostasy."

[152]Parley P. Pratt, *Voice of Warning and Instruction to All People; or, An Introduction to the Faith and Doctrine of the Church of Jesus Christ of Latter-day Saints*, 13th ed. (Salt Lake City: George Q. Cannon and Sons Co., 1891).

meetings evidently did some good.

At 3:30 Miss Sharp handed me a "long" letter. Upon opening it I found it to be an appointment to the presidency of the Scottish Conference.[153] Realizing to some extent what a responsibility this is, I just seemed to be seized with a feeling of gloom and fear, lest in accepting this I would prove incompetent. I walked to a secret spot in the wood, just below Wallace's Monument, and there dedicating my services to the Lord, implored him for his divine assistance. Later Brother Pender came in. He was evidently very pleased and encouraged me all he could.

Letter from David R.

Friday, 10 June 1898

Stock Fair in Stirling. After attending to some correspondence, Brother Pender and I went to the King's Park and witnessed the parade of fine cattle, horses, etc. The races were very good—[especially the] hurdle.

Saturday, 11 June 1898

The morning hours were spent in visiting some acquaintances who have manifested an interest in our religion. Kindness of Mrs. McKenzie! Gratuitous act.

When I began to "pack up," I felt homesick, for it really seemed that I was again leaving home. Miss Sharp has decided to go to Innellan to see her Mamma. She will go to Glasgow on the same train as me. At 4:20 P.M., after playing my favorite *songs*, I bid good-bye to Jeanie and James and, in company with Annie, went to the station, Miss Jeanie waving to us from the window as we walked up Wallace Street.

The ride to Glasgow was pleasant. Brother Pender secured a cab and took the luggage to the conference house, while I went to Gourock with my pleasant *companion*. This was a pleasant yet somewhat *sad* evening. We parted on the boat that sailed for Innellan at 9:50 P.M. Reached the conference house at 11:30; nearly all had retired. Gloomy-looking place—unfurnished, bare rooms.

Sunday, 12 June 1898

Attended Sunday School [at noon], meeting at 2:00, open-air meeting at 5:30, and evening meeting at 6:30 P.M. Addressed the saints in the afternoon. The responsibility is weighing heavily upon me.

---

[153]In McKay's letter of acceptance to this position, he told Rulon S. Wells: "Realizing to some extent the responsibility thus placed upon me, I truly feel weak and unable to fill this position—and if I expressed my own desire, I would say, 'Choose another.' Yet I feel to say, 'Not my will, but thine be done.' And since God, through his servants, has seen fit to place this duty upon me, I shall accept it, depending upon his unerring Spirit for guidance." See the David O. McKay Collection, Manuscript 668, Box 14, located in the Manuscripts Division, J. Willard Marriott Library, University of Utah, Salt Lake City.

Monday, 13 June 1898
Received the books and accounts from Brother McKinnon. He then left for Edinburgh. Open-air meeting at night. Debate.

Tuesday, 14 June 1898
Around the town, making preparations to buy some furniture. Open-air meeting at Govan Cross. Received an encouraging letter from Brothers Gilchrist and McKnight.

Wednesday-Thursday, 15-16 June 1898
Buying linoleum, furniture, etc. A monotonous experience with a salesman! Three hours steady talking!! Brother Pender and Sister Noble were along. Brother Pender finally succumbed—gave up in despair—but Mrs. Noble stood it to the last!!

Friday, 17 June 1898
Furnished one room; it is now fit for a visitor to come into. Met Mr. [John H.] Bailey, returning elder. Open-air meeting on Cathedral Square.

Saturday, 18 June 1898
The S.S. *Anchoria* sailed at 9:30 A.M. with forty emigrants (Scandinavians) and six returning elders on board. Telegraphed to Liverpool that all were safely aboard.
Letter from Miss Sharp.

Sunday, 19 June 1898
Sunday School at twelve noon, after which Clark and Leggat had hot words. "Liar and the truth is not in you!" Leggat. "Disgrace to the branch!" etc., Clark. In settling this, there will be trouble. Open-air meeting, besides other two. The responsibility is growing heavier. God must manifest his power or I do not know what will become of some of us. Enmity.

Monday, 20 June 1898
Attended to correspondence. Brother Mitchell has been appointed to the Ayr[shire] District and Brother Edward to the Glasgow field. The day is wet and gloomy—a real Glasgow day.
Wrote to Annie.

Tuesday, 21 June 1898
Went to Anchor Line Office to see Mr. Aitchison. A company of Scandinavians has arrived (by mistake) twelve days before the next boat sails from Glasgow. Mr. Johnston asked me to do what I can to keep them contented. They are in the charge of the company. Open-air meeting at Govan Cross. Some disturbance was made by persons in the crowd, but the meet-

ing was, nevertheless, very good. Lizzie Neilson and Maggie Gain assisted with their presence and singing.

Wednesday, 22 June 1898

Attended to some office work. In the afternoon the four of us (Brothers Pender, Calder,[154] Edward, and I) went to Brother Joseph Leggat's and administered to his daughter, Katie, also to Mrs. Hamilton. Miss Jeanie Jack spent several hours in the office. She is a staunch Latter-day Saint.

Open-air meeting at Bridgeton Cross—one of the best yet held. The large crowd surrounding us were attentive and interested. At the conclusion tracts were distributed. So eager were they to get them that they literally crowded over each other reaching for them; they saw that the tracts were few and the crowd large. One man expressed himself as "having been moved" and promised to come to meeting. Another walked toward our lodgings, arguing against "works." Others manifested similar interest.

Letter from Annie.

Thursday, 23 June 1898

Visited the emigrants staying on York Street. They seem to be contented. Wrote to Annie. Letter from [my] sister Annie. Stormy day. Testimony meeting at night. Letter from William Gibbons.

Friday, 24 June 1898

Correspondence. Office duties. Rain still continues. Brother Orr came in. Letter to Liverpool. Held a short open-air meeting on Cathedral Square. Raining at the time.

Saturday, 25 June 1898

At "53" [Holmhead Street], arranging conference matters.

Sunday, 26 June 1898

Meetings as usual.

Monday-Friday, 27 June-1 July 1898

Time was spent in attending to a thousand and one little duties in the conference and branch. No time to even write in my diary. Friday night in Blantyre, attending Thomas Irvine's farewell party.

---

[154]Hyrum B. Calder (1873-1946) was set apart for a mission to Great Britain on 11 September 1896, arriving in Liverpool on 1 October 1896. He was assigned to the Scottish Conference and served in the areas of Alloa, Edinburgh, and Glasgow. Calder was released in September 1898 and returned to Salt Lake City the following month. He served as bishop of the Vernal First Ward for seventeen years and president of the Uintah Stake for thirteen years. See the Hyrum B. Calder Collection, Accession 1730, located in the Manuscripts Division, J. Willard Marriott Library, University of Utah, Salt Lake City.

Saturday, 2 July 1898

Conference house full of returning elders. President McMurrin came from Liverpool last night. A company of thirty-six saints and returning elders sail on the S.S. *Furnessia* today, leaving at 6:30 P.M. Everything arranged satisfactorily.

Sunday, 3 July 1898

Just after morning prayers Dr. James E. Talmage[155] surprised us by his unlooked-for presence. We were very pleased to welcome him. He made us merry with his rich jokes and ready wit. At 11 A.M. he and I attended services at the U. P. [United Presbyterian] Free Church.[156] We then went down to 9 Oxford Street. Testimony meeting at 2 P.M. Brother Talmage spoke. Meeting at 6:30 P.M. The Doctor [Talmage] and President McMurrin were the speakers. The meeting was fine; we had a *feast*. A pleasant evening at the conference house.

Monday, 4 July 1898

O, how different this *Independence Day* from the one last year!

> Then I was free as the air,
> Now I'm tied down with care!

Letter and money order from Tommy.

Spent the morning hours with Dr. Talmage and Brother McMurrin. Made out elders' report for June.

Tuesday, 5 July 1898

Made out statistical report of the conference for June. Open-air meeting at night. President McMurrin spoke. The audience were as attentive as though they had been in a hall. He bore a powerful testimony to the divinity of Joseph Smith's mission.

Wednesday, 6 July 1898

Office correspondence. Visited [James] Clark. Brother McMurrin, Brother [John] Houston, and Brother [Vincent R.] Pugmire have taken an excursion trip through the Trossachs.

---

[155]James E. Talmage (1862-1933) served as president of the University of Utah from 1894 to 1897. McKay had been a student at the university during this time. Talmage was ordained an apostle in 1911. He wrote *The Articles of Faith: A Series of Lectures on the Principal Doctrines of the Church of Jesus Christ of Latter-day Saints* (Salt Lake City: The Deseret News, 1899), *The Great Apostasy* (Salt Lake City: The Deseret News, 1909), *The House of the Lord: A Study of Holy Sanctuaries* (Salt Lake City: The Deseret News, 1912), and *Jesus the Christ: A Study of the Messiah and His Mission* (Salt Lake City: The Deseret News, 1915).

[156]The United Presbyterian Free Church was formed in 1847 by a union between the United Secession Church and the Relief Church. Numerous divisions and reunions followed. During the nineteenth century, Presbyterians introduced organ and instrumental music into worship services.

Thursday, 7 July 1898

An appalling disaster occurred off the coasts of Halifax last Monday morning, the particulars of which are given in this morning's papers.[157] See back of book.[158]

Brother McMurrin returned from his trip. He stayed last night at Miss Sharp's, for whom he has nothing but words of praise and commendation. Testimony meeting at night. Had an excellent time together.

Friday, 8 July 1898

Attended to various office duties. Received a telegram stating that Miss Sharp is coming to Glasgow. Met her at Buchanan Street Station at 2 P.M. Spent a very enjoyable afternoon in Kelvinside Park. Back to conference house at 6 P.M. She stopped at her cousin's, 22 Willow Bank Crescent.

At 8 P.M., according to previous appointment, the elders here met many of the saints at Bridgeton Cross, where an open-air meeting was held. It was very gratifying to see how well the young men and women came out to assist. Brother Edward presided. I was called upon first. Imagine my surprise and pleasure when, after speaking but a few minutes, I saw Miss Sharp and her young lady friend, standing in the crowd directly in front of me. They remained as long as they could, leaving at nine o'clock to catch the 10 P.M. train. Brother Calder was the second speaker. Brother Leggat bore a faithful testimony. The meeting was pronounced a grand success.

Saturday, 9 July 1898

S.S. *Ethiopia* sailed at 3 P.M. Six of our company on board. Brother McMurrin has gone to Edinburgh. At 5:30 held a council meeting with Brothers Neilson and Leggat, in which ordinations and other branch matters were considered. At 9 P.M. called on Brother Clark. At 10 P.M. in Partick at Brother Murray's. Bed at 12:30.

Sunday, 10 July 1898

Special priesthood meeting at 10:30 A.M. An excellent spirit prevailed.

---

[157]McKay placed here in his diary a newspaper clipping with the following account of the shipwreck: "One of the most terrible catastrophes that have happened for many years has occurred off the coast of Newfoundland, and . . . it is beyond doubt that something like 600 persons have been drowned. The Glasgow sailing ship *Cromartyshire* whilst proceeding on a voyage from Dunkirk to Philadelphia was collided with by the French transatlantic liner *La Bourgoyne. . . .* The great liner, which carried 714 passengers and crew, foundered soon after the collision, carrying with her by far the greater portion of her human freight. Immediately after the impact there seems to have been a terrible panic on the steamer, and if the stories of survivors are to be believed, there was a brutal struggle for the boats—a struggle in which helpless women and children were pushed aside and trampled under foot in the wild fight for life. Of 200 women and children who were aboard the ill-fated liner, only one was rescued. It is a striking comment on the conduct of the crew of the *Bourgoyne* that half of their number are among the survivors and that such a large proportion of the passengers was drowned."

[158]McKay placed at the back of his diary another newsclipping, providing additional details from survivors concerning the atrocities of the crew of *La Bourgoyne*.

Sunday School at twelve noon; meeting at 2 P.M. William Leggat and William Hamilton ordained elders; William Cooke ordained a priest; Charles Murray, a teacher; and Donald McDonald and James Neilson ordained deacons. One dissenting vote on the first two named. Meeting at 6:30 P.M.

Monday, 11 July 1898

Brother Edward and I called upon several secretaries of literary and art societies for the purpose, if possible, of getting some society to give Dr. Talmage's lecture under its auspices. As the Glasgow Fair Holidays will soon be on and so many of the people at the seaside, none of them would undertake to give it before the month of October. We shall probably take the responsibility upon ourselves. Office duties.

Tuesday, 12 July 1898

Letter from Father.

Visited Sister Robertson and Mrs. [Duncan] Thomson, Comelypark Street. Received the usual cordial welcome. Open-air meeting just below Paisley Toll Cross. Brother Clark was the first speaker, followed by Elder Calder and Brother Leggat. Brother Neilson bore his testimony to the divinity of Joseph Smith's mission. While he was doing so, a voice was heard [saying], "Where's Joseph Smith's name in the Bible?" Brother Neilson continued, not heeding the interruption. The man yelled, "It's a damn lie!" "That's adultery!" etc., etc. While he was still yelling, we began to sing "Farewell, All Earthly Honors." The meeting was dismissed quietly and without further interruption. Went to William Leggat's home and partook of his and Martha's kind hospitality.

Wednesday, 13 July 1898

Went to the Atheneum and obtained the price of hall (4½ guineas);[159] then to St. Andrew's Hall. The Berkeley Hall there without stereopticon[160] will cost £3/10/0. Mr. [Walter] Freer, the attendant, said if the meeting did not prove a success, he would give 10/0 of his own money. He was very obliging. Visited Brother Clark at night. Weather warm.

Thursday, 14 July 1898

Office duties. Called on bill posters to get prices of advertising. Brother Pender was with me. Called at news office to get cost of printing bills. The advertising alone, exclusive of the papers, will cost about £4/0/0. Visit-

---

[159] A *guinea* was twenty-one shillings. See footnote 51 on British money at 17 September 1897, p. 20, above.

[160] A *stereopticon* was a double magic lantern arranged to combine two images of the same object or scene upon a screen, in order to produce the appearance of solidarity. It is also used to cause the image of one object or scene to pass gradually into that of another with dissolving effect.

ed Sister McDonald, Brother and Sister Cairney in Springburn. Testimony meeting at night. Brother [Peter G.] Johnston came from Ireland.

Friday, 15 July 1898
After attending to the usual work pertaining to the conference, I called on Sister Gain and family. Found Lizzie ill. Spent an hour or two very pleasantly with them. This is one of the best families in the branch. At 7:30, in company with Elders Calder and Edward, Brother Neilson, and John Good, went to Rutherglen where, according to previous appointment, a meeting was held in Brother Taylor's house. An excellent spirit prevailed.

By request after the meeting we administered to Miss [Katie] Faulds, daughter of Sister Faulds, who has but recently joined the Church. The young woman was suffering from a sprained ankle. So intense was the pain that she could not step upon her foot. She seemed to manifest much faith, and I have no doubt concerning the effectiveness of the administration. Reached conference house at 11 P.M.

Saturday, 16 July 1898
Nearly every factory and shop in Glasgow is closed today. The Glasgow Fair Holidays commenced last Thursday and today thousands have gone to the seaside and other pleasure resorts. Called on Brother Clark and consulted [with] him concerning the reorganization of the Sunday School. He was very pliable—willing to do what was required.

At 7 P.M., in company with Brother Johnston and Brother McKinlay,[161] I went to Barnum and Bailey's Great American Circus. It has been in Glasgow three weeks. As this was the last performance, we thought we would see it. Some of the "freaks" were wonderful. "Sword-eater," the "midget," "chest expander," etc., etc. The performance was fair. The menagerie was excellent.

Sunday, 17 July 1898
Sunday School and meetings as usual. An excellent spirit prevailed throughout. Miss Faulds at meeting, entirely well. Walked next day after administration.

Monday, 18 July 1898
This is the day for the picnic at the seaside for the Glasgow Branch! According to arrangements, we all met at the Queen Street Station at 9:10 A.M. We were fortunate in securing first-class compartments in the train for Cardross, the place selected for the day's amusement. After a pleasant

---

[161]Robert McKinlay (1832-1900) was born in Tranent, Haddington, Scotland. He was set apart for a mission to Great Britain on 1 April 1898, arriving in Liverpool on 21 April 1898. McKinlay labored in the Scottish Conference in Dunfermline and Fifeshire, but he returned home to Idaho in October 1898 due to sickness.

hour's ride along the banks of the Clyde, we arrived at our destination. The committee had referred to "the park" whenever they mentioned the picnic. I had pictured in my mind a place where trees grew luxuriant by throwing their cooling shade over some commodious pavilion. Imagine our surprise (I say *our* because the others were of the same opinion) when, instead of going to a park, we were shown into a *pasture*, where not a tree grew and where the only accommodation for seating was a small haystack! The weather was very disagreeable. The wind was cold and the showers of rain were frequent. However, we made the best of it.

The older members surrounded the haystack and watched the others at football, rounders, pomp, double tag, etc., etc. The picnic was served in a hall on the other side of the station. In the afternoon the weather was more suitable for outdoor games. O, how we did run! Pomp, football, dancing, and rounders were the favorite games! All seemed to enjoy themselves.

Tea was served in the hall at 4:30 P.M., after which the races were run and prizes awarded to the winners. The tide was out and as the beach was not a very good one, no boat riding was indulged in. At 8 P.M. all joined in singing a hymn "Farewell, All Earthly Honors," and the day's enjoyment was concluded by prayer. Then came the question of getting back to the city. We had been promised special carriages, but there were so many people down below us that every train was packed. However, we managed to get up in two divisions, the last of which reached Queen Street at 10 P.M. All reached home in safety after a day of romp and pleasure.

Tuesday, 19 July 1898

When eight o'clock came, I could hardly get out of bed—so tired and stiff were my muscles after yesterday's running. As there will be a meeting tonight with Brothers Neilson and Leggat concerning branch matters of serious importance, I have concluded to fast that the object desired might be attained. Visited the Atheneum and Berkeley Hall to see which is more suitable for the coming lecture by Dr. Talmage. Neither is very suitable.

At 8 A.M. Brother Neilson, Brother Leggat, and I were in private conference. Brother Neilson had a bad spirit and for a time a warm discussion ensued over the appointment of a certain brother to the superintendency of the [Sunday] School. Many unpleasant things were mentioned. However, an understanding was reached, and we parted at 10:30 in peace.

Wednesday, 20 July 1898

At 8 A.M. Brother [Joseph] Leggat came in and informed us of the sad and sudden death of his daughter-in-law, Sister James Leggat.[162] She was with us at the picnic and enjoyed herself immensely. Yesterday she was

---

[162]Catherine ("Kate") Cairney Leggat (1871-1898) was baptized in 1890 and her death was caused by inflammation. See *The Latter-day Saints' Millennial Star* 60 (4 August 1898): 496.

Fig. 31 *Buchanan Street, Glasgow.*

playing and joking with her neighbors; at nine o'clock she washed her husband's jacket, and at 1:10 A.M. she was dead! Died in her husband's arms. As soon as possible, I went to Springburn and notified Sister McDonald, Sister Cairney, and Janet Lang, all of whom promised to go down and see that all needed assistance was rendered. In the afternoon Brother Calder and I went down to see Brother [James] Leggat; he feels the shock keenly. Maggie Gain, Jeanie Gain, Janet Lang, Sister McDonald, and Sister Cairney spent a few hours in the conference house during the evening.

Thursday, 21 July 1898

At 10 A.M. went to see Mr. Freer, curator for [Glasgow] City and St. Andrew's Halls. Secured the City Hall (on Albion and Candleriggs Streets) for £7/0/0. Seating capacity 3,000. If the lecture is a failure, we shall be buried so deep under the ruins of financial failure that no one can uncover us.

At 3 P.M. funeral services over the remains of Sister [Kate] Leggat were held. She is buried in the Lambhill Cemetery. Grave left open for other coffins! Nothing to mark the spot! When we reached the office at 6:30 P.M., a message was awaiting us to go to Rutherglen immediately as Sister Faulds was dangerously ill. Brother Calder, Brother Edward, and I went out. Administered to her, anointing the afflicted part of her body.[163] She was much easier when we left. Her sickness is a result of the inclemency of the weather on Monday last at the picnic.

Friday, 22 July 1898

Busy all day, arranging for advertising lecture. Decided to give the contract for printing to the *News* company. J. Muir Wood and Co., Buchanan Street (Fig. 31), will sell tickets, so also will Ewing and McIntosh, music

---

[163]Lester E. Bush, Jr., *Health and Medicine among the Latter-day Saints: Science, Sense, and Scripture* (New York: Crossroad Publishing Co., 1993), 78-81, stated that in the nineteenth century the anointing with consecrated oil was often applied on the afflicted part of the body.

sellers, Sauchiehall Street. Brother Edward and I called on Mr. Harold Ryder, organist in the Established Church, and secured his services for August 2nd for £1/1/0.

About 10 P.M. a message came from Rutherglen, requesting two elders to go out there at once to administer to Sister Faulds. Brother Edward and I hastened out. Found Sisters McDonald and Cairney attending her. After the administration she became easier, but about twelve the pain returned. We remained all night, leaving at 4 A.M., at which time she felt quite easy.

Saturday, 23 July 1898

Saw Mr. Freer about the [Glasgow] City Hall organ. Further arrangements about advertising. Boat sailed at 1 P.M., one family belonging to the Church on board. Letter from Tommy. At 7 P.M. went with Brother W[illiam] F. Olson to the Royalty to see the opera *Mikado*. It was good.

Sunday, 24 July 1898

Reorganized the Sabbath School. William Leggat, superintendent; David Cairney and William Cooke, assistants. Meeting at 2 P.M. Presented Sunday School authorities and teachers for the saints' approval. All votes unanimous. Explained nature of lecture and what means have been adopted to defray expenses. Brother Olson spoke. Meeting at 6:30. An excellent spirit was enjoyed throughout the day. After meeting Brother Pender and I went home with William Leggat and enjoyed a cup of Martha's excellent cocoa.

Monday, 25 July 1898

General office duties. Busy with arrangements for the lecture. Got plan of City Hall and arranged for reserved seats. Notified elders, etc.

Tuesday, 26 July 1898

Brother Edward, Brother Calder, and I called on Mr. Samuel M. Taylor, U.S. consul, and obtained his services to act as chairman of the meeting next Tuesday night. He treated us courteously and said he would be glad of the honor. Saw proof of posters and bills. Five hundred tickets are out. Sent seventy-five invitations to the Lord Provost and members of the town council (Glasgow). Gave each a complimentary ticket. Received a ticket from Glasgow to Stirling from Brother Olson, who wants me to come up and go from there to Edinburgh. Had to refuse on account of work. A card from President McMurrin states that the first of the Talmage lectures delivered last night in Newcastle was an "unqualified success." I hope ours will be.

Wednesday, 27 July 1898

After the usual morning duties, we took about 450 large bills announcing Dr. Talmage's lecture to the bill posters. Attended to correspondence, talked with several saints who called, and before I hardly knew what had been done, night was again upon us. Took an evening stroll up Sauchiehall Street, the fashionable street of the town!

Thursday, 28 July 1898

Called at Anchor Line S.S. office, announcing the lecture, and gave Mr. Aitchison and the Messrs. Johnston complimentary tickets. After dinner called on Sister Robertson, Comelypark Street, and after a pleasant talk went to Shettleston to visit Mr. Ewing and wife, Brother Anderson's friends. As they had moved to Baillieston, I continued my journey to that place. After inquiry, I found them and enjoyed an hour or so in pleasant talk. They seemed pleased to see me and cordially invited me to return.

At 8 P.M. was back in Glasgow attending testimony meeting—the "best ever held in Glasgow." The spirit of testimony and of prayer was upon all present. Each one present felt to bless everyone else.

Friday, 29 July 1898

Placed advertisements of the lecture in *News* and *Citizen*. Gave an order to [Robert] Beith to put out two barrows covered with large bills. At 5 P.M. boarded the train for Edinburgh, where according to previous appointment I was to meet Cousin Bella from Wick. As I was walking along Leith Walk, met Brother W. F. Olson just on his road for Glasgow. He concluded to stay until I returned with him.

We returned with the brethren (Elders Leishman[164] and Miller[165]) to their lodgings and, after a short chat, went to Sister Whyte's and secured a home for the night. She always makes the elders welcome. We then visited George White and family, Brother [William] Gracie and family, and Brother and Sister [David] Henderson. All treated us fine. Took a short walk on Princes Street (Fig. 32), one of the finest in the world. Beautiful girls were there by the scores; nearly every one of them was a dissipater.

Saturday, 30 July 1898

Visited my cousins John, Donald, and Bella [McKay]. Bella is the picture of health and is truly a bonnie Scotch lass. After dinner we all went to Albert Place and took the elders with us to visit Holyrood Palace, also St.

---

[164]Thomas A. Leishman (1843-1930) was born in Johnstone, Renfrewshire, Scotland, and emigrated to Utah in 1852. He was set apart for a mission to Great Britain on 17 February 1897, arriving in Liverpool on 10 March 1897. Leishman served in the Liverpool Conference for a year, and then in April 1898 he was transferred to the Scottish Conference, where he labored in the areas of Airdrie and Edinburgh. He was released in November 1898, returning to Utah the next month. See the Thomas A. Leishman Collection, Accession 1740, located in the Manuscripts Division, J. Willard Marriott Library, University of Utah, Salt Lake City.

[165]James K. Miller (1868-1940) was set apart for a mission to Great Britain on 18 March 1898, arriving in Liverpool on 7 April 1898. Within the Scottish Conference he labored in the areas of Edinburgh and Glasgow. In August 1899 when McKay returned home, Miller was appointed to be the next president of the Scottish Conference. He returned to Utah in June 1900.

Fig. 32 *Princes Street, Edinburgh.*

Fig. 33 *St. Giles Cathedral, Edinburgh.*

Giles Cathedral (Fig. 33). A short service was being held in the last-named place. Through the acquaintance of Bella, I met a Mrs. Andrew Mackay and family and learned to my surprise and pleasure that she remembered meeting my father sixteen years ago! We were acquainted immediately.

It was our intention to leave the city on the 6:45 train, and I had made an appointment to meet Brother Olson at the station ten minutes before that time; so bidding Mrs. Mackay and family good-bye and promising to return in the near future, I went to the station accompanied by John, Donald, Bella, and Miss McKay. Brother Olson did not get there in time, so we were left. Had fifteen minutes to catch train at other station. Bid all good-bye and hurried. Left again! Stayed until 8:20; arrived in Glasgow at 10:25!!

Sunday, 31 July 1898

Attended to the usual meetings: priesthood meeting at 11 A.M., Sunday School at twelve, meeting at 2 P.M., dinner at 4:30, and another meeting at 6:30 P.M. A pleasant day.

Monday, 1 August 1898

Arranged for the printing of 1,000 programs for tomorrow night. Wrote letters and sent complimentary tickets to the editors of the *News*, *Citizen*, and *Times*. Secured the services of six Scandinavian missionaries to help distribute handbills. Brother Edward and I had a pleasant conversation with the *News* girls in advertising department. Tomorrow night is the lecture! We are quite anxious about the result, especially about the financial outcome. Our expenses now aggregate about £18/0/0!

Tuesday, 2 August 1898

Went to Beith's with a dozen more large posters and told him to put another barrow on the principal thoroughfares. The rain was coming down in a stream, but later I saw the notice "Tonight Dr. Talmage's Lecture,"[166] etc., on the streets—rain or no rain. At 11 A.M. received a telegram from Dr. Talmage, stating that he has unavoidably missed the morning train and could not reach Glasgow until 7:35, twenty-five minutes before time of lecture!!

We had arranged for a meeting between the U.S. consul and Brother Talmage at 3 P.M. and while they were making necessary arrangements about the manner of procedure, the operator accompanying Dr. Talmage could be in the hall arranging screen, stereopticon, etc. Everything was nicely planned, but this telegram upset everything and everybody. We were disappointed, but every one of the elders, including Brother Olson, was ready to do anything and everything to make preparations. So we secured a screen, [and] the boys helped put it in the hall; a stereopticon and operator were hired and everything prepared again.

Mr. Taylor was taken to the Argyle Hotel, close to St. Enoch's Station, where (as soon as he arrived) Dr. Talmage would be taken to make any hurried changes necessary for the lecture. Leaving Brother Pender in the hotel with Mr. Taylor, I hurried over to the station where Brother Calder was waiting for the train. It was then fifteen minutes to eight o'clock. Imagine our feelings when we saw announced on the bulletin board "train from Carlisle thirty minutes late"!

The thoughts of facing an impatient Scotch audience with an excuse for tardiness are anything but pleasant, I assure you! Under the present circumstances they were torturing! And added to this was the doubt about the slides fitting the lantern! Oh, what if it (the lecture) would after all prove a failure!!!

Brother Calder stayed at the station, secured two cabs: one for the operator to hurry direct to the hall and the other for Dr. Talmage to go the hotel and meet the chairman, Mr. Taylor, and then both hurry to the meeting, while I jumped into another cab and was driven to the hall where about 1,500 people were waiting.[167] As I entered, the anxious brethren almost sank when told that the train was a half hour late. However, peals from the large pipe organ showed us that Mr. Harold Ryder, whose services had been secured, was doing his best to entertain those present with some favorite Scotch airs and other beautiful selections. At 8:15 it fell to my lot to make an explanation. The applause showed that the audience was contented to

---

[166]The series of lectures by James E. Talmage was delivered in Newcastle upon Tyne, Norwich, London, Bristol, Nottingham, Leeds, Oldham, Sheffield, Glasgow, Belfast, and Liverpool and covered the period from 25 July to 5 August 1898. Joseph H. Mitchell, Diary, 2 August 1898, gave the title of Talmage's lecture as "Utah and Its People" and said that "it was a treat and brought many familiar scenes forcibly to my mind."

[167]John T. Edward, Diary, 22 July 1898, indicated that the hall, which was rented for £7, had a seating capacity of almost 3,000 people.

wait a few more minutes. They had not long to wait, for at 8:30 the Doctor arrived![168] He and Mr. Taylor were greeted with a hearty applause.

The chairman's introductory speech was fine. Dr. Talmage commenced his lecture at 8:40 and held his audience for two hours and five minutes! It was a remarkable fact that the frequent applause given could not have been more expressive had the lecture been a popular one and delivered by a world-famed orator. It was interesting throughout. The audience was select and appreciative. Dr. Talmage's power to hold an audience is really wonderful![169]

At the close a cab was in readiness to take Mr. Taylor to the station; he stays in Helensburgh, down the Clyde. As we rode along, he expressed himself as being well-pleased, but I fancied I felt that he did not just mean all he said. After bidding him good-night, I hurried back to the hall and found Dr. Talmage all ready to go to Ireland. (We had secured rooms for him to stay until morning.) Throwing his trunk and luggage on top of the hansom,[170] out of which I had just stepped, we all three—Talmage, [Robert A.] Anderson, and I—got inside and ordered the driver to drive with all possible speed to St. Enoch's. Arriving there we learned that the train for Ardrossan leaves the Central Station at 11 P.M.; we had one minute only! We hurried over, and, thanks to a late train, were in time! Paid the cabman 2/6 and then had a five-minute talk with the brethren before the train left. Brother Talmage was highly pleased with our efforts.[171] He has lectured every night since the twenty-fifth of July! He is doing a good work. The lecture delivered here will do more toward allaying prejudice[172] than the efforts of all the elders could possibly do in two or three, yes five years, under the ordinary circumstances.[173] After the train left, I went to the hotel and told Mr. [George]

---

[168]James E. Talmage, Diary, 2 August 1898, which is located in the James E. Talmage Collection, Manuscript 229, Special Collections and Manuscripts, Harold B. Lee Library, Brigham Young University, Provo, Utah, explained the unusual method he used to wash himself while on the train heading to Glasgow: "Dusty and black from the 220-mile ride, I made use of a rain storm then in progress and 'hung myself' out of the window, catching the falling water on face and hands; that was the best available approach to a wash; then donned a dress suit and persuaded myself that I was ready."

[169]In its account of Talmage's lecture, the *Glasgow Evening Times* stated: "The doctor is worth hearing. . . . He did not preach Mormonism, but he praised the Mormons in many an eloquent sentence. . . . We were shown temples and colleges and cooperative buildings—marvelously fine structures which stand as monuments of Mormon industry and culture." See John R. Talmage, *The Talmage Story: Life of James E. Talmage—Educator, Scientist, Apostle* (Salt Lake City: Bookcraft, Inc., 1972), 148.

[170]A *hansom* cab, which consisted of a low, two-wheeled, one-horse, covered carriage, with the driver mounted back of the top, was named after Joseph A. Hansom (1803-1882), the English architect who invented the carriage.

[171]James E. Talmage, Diary, 2 August 1898, explained: "The hall was a magnificent one and all the preparations were of high order and efficiently made."

[172]Thomas A. Leishman, Diary, 2 August 1898, expressed the idea this way: "We think it [Talmage's lecture] will do a great deal of good in breaking down the superstition that exists against us."

[173]David O. McKay, "Lime-light Views: Scottish," *The Latter-day Saints' Millennial Star* 60 (11 August 1898): 509, explained: "The good effects of the lecture are already realized. Businessmen are eager to tell anyone interested in the meeting about the merits of Dr. Talmage as a lecturer. They treat us as courteously as they possibly can."

Doogan we would not want the room. He kindly relieved us of all responsibility.

When I reached the conference house, the brethren were all elated over the success. The proceeds will amount to about £14/5/0; expenses £19/10/0.[174] We thanked the Lord for blessing us in our efforts and then retired—but I could not sleep for hours. It was near morning. Truly August second will be long remembered!

Wednesday, 3 August 1898

Paid bills for printing, posting, etc., etc. Everyone we met who was present at the lecture last night expressed his satisfaction and delight over the excellent discourse of Dr. Talmage. It has produced an excellent effect. Spent the day settling up accounts and finishing odds and ends. The total expenses amount to £18/5/9, less than we anticipated; the proceeds are £14/10/0. At night took a stroll with Brother Olson.

Thursday, 4 August 1898

Went to Anchor Line office and secured saloon[175] passage for [N. S.] Christofferson and Olson. Mr. Aitchison expressed himself as being well-pleased with the lecture. At 11:30 went down to the docks. Mr. Johnston invited me (as he has done several times before) to go to Greenock on the boat and come back by train. As this was his last day here and the last chance I would get to have his company down, I concluded to go. The day was fair, and hence the sail was delightful. Ate dinner in saloon. The U.S. consul and wife were at the table.

At Greenock bid all the saints good-bye, boarded the *tender*, and went ashore. Waited fifteen minutes for train and in fifty-five minutes was in Glasgow. Testimony meeting at night.

Friday, 5 August 1898

Made out monthly reports. Meeting at night with Brothers Neilson and Leggat, appointing teacher.

Saturday, 6 August 1898

Answered Dr. Talmage's letters and sent the papers commenting upon his lecture to his address in Utah. Writing most of the day. Saw a disgusting sight on King Street!! A woman catching fleas or something worse on her breasts! Awful!

---

[174]McKay wrote "£18/8/10" underneath. Evidently, the total expenses were a little less than originally figured. The next day all expenses were carefully added and the total amount was £18/5/9.

[175]*Saloon* passengers had access to the main cabin of the steamship and paid first-class fares.

Fig. 34 *Botanical Gardens, Glasgow.*

Sunday, 7 August 1898

Sunday School as usual. Fast meeting. Blessed Sister Alex Hoggan's little baby. His name is Thomas Hoggan and was born June 25th, 1898. Lizzie Gain carried him to Church. Brother Pender and I went home with the parents to dinner. Lizzie, Maggie, and Jeanie Gain; and Bella and Lizzie Neilson were there also. An excellent dinner! Outdoor meeting at 5:30 P.M. Evening meeting at 6:30. Several strangers present.

Left Ogden one year ago!

Monday, 8 August 1898

Spent the morning hours attending to office duties. Sent book money to Liverpool. Brother [John] Good and Brother J. Leggat called. About 2 P.M. I was surprised and pleased to see Annie and Jeanie Sharp, who called at the office to see us. I spent the afternoon with them, visiting the Glasgow Cathedral and Botanical Gardens (Fig. 34). We parted at Willow Bank Crescent. I promised to return in one hour to meet her friend, Miss Lewis. At the conference house met Mr. Whyte, a young man who is investigating our religion. Sister McDonald was there also and reported fifteen shillings on hand for tickets sold. She has done well.

At 8:30 was at Mr. Lewis's and found the father and daughter very agreeable and entertaining. Spent an hour or so in the parlor playing piano and banjo—Miss Lewis at the piano and her father the banjo. Met the mother as we were coming away. Received cordial invitation to visit them again. Miss Lewis accompanied the Misses Sharp and me to Buchanan Street Station, where the train left at 10 P.M. for Stirling. I walked home again with Miss Lewis. Pleasant conversation. Promised to call on her next week.

Tuesday, 9 August 1898

Called on Mr. McColl—he was not in. While walking down Argyle Street (Fig. 35) was accosted by Sister Clark. She and her husband [James Clark] are not getting along agreeably. He drinks (a few evenings ago, he was drunk) and received a beating from his mother-in-law. He called her

Fig. 35 *Argyle and St. Vincent Streets, Glasgow.*

names. We had him up before the priesthood. As he manifested a humble spirit and asked forgiveness, he was restored to our confidence. Well, today Sister Clark told me all about her troubles. Really, it is awful to think that such conditions exist. She says, if he does not keep straight after this, she will take serious steps toward a separation. I gave her what counsel and encouragement I could and then went to Sister Gain's; she is a fine woman. The trifling troubles of the branch do not seem to worry her much. Met a Mrs. Irvine. Returned to conference house at 1:15 P.M. While Brother Calder and Brother Edward assisted some members of the branch to hold an open-air meeting, I visited a Mr. Smith and family, 4 Myrtle Street. Spent a pleasant evening. He is a miller. His employer alone receives about 1,600,000 bushels of wheat annually from America. He walked with me to Parliamentary Road, nearly to conference house. Janet Lang and Mary McDonald attended meeting and called as they were going home.

Wednesday, 10 August 1898
In the office most of the forenoon. At 5:18 Brother Edward and I boarded the train at Central Station for Newarthill, where at 6:30 we attended a meeting in Sister Major's house. An excellent spirit prevailed, as is always the case in meetings with this little branch. All made us welcome; said they had been expecting us for some time. After tea we spent a few minutes in Sister Jack's home, received some nice roses from Nellie, and bid them good-bye, returning on the 9:30 train.

Thursday, 11 August 1898
Sent statements of expenditures for the receipts from lecture to all the elders. Five shillings is required from each to clear expenses.[176] Testimony meeting at night.

---

[176]Hyrum B. Calder paid five shillings as his share of these expenses; see the entry for 8 August 1898 in the Hyrum B. Calder Collection.

Friday, 12 August 1898

Visited a Mrs. Thomson, granddaughter of Sister Niven. She was recently confined. Expressed herself as being pleased to see us. At 1:45 Brother Edward and I met Miss Thompson of Sauchie, and accompanied her to the Central Station, as she is a stranger in Glasgow. At 4:05 P.M. boarded the train for Stirling. Was met at the station by Elders Thomas Gilchrist, Joseph McKnight, and Robert Gilchrist.[177] We all walked down to 65 Wallace Street and had tea.

After an hour or two of questions and exchange of news, I went up to Mrs. Sharp's and received a hearty welcome from all. Only stayed a few minutes, as we intended to hold an open-air meeting, but before we were halfway to the selected place, the rain came down in torrents and thus compelled us to postpone our preaching; it was just as well. We went back to the boys' lodgings on Wallace Street and held a council meeting, after which we all went up to Mrs. Sharp's and spent the evening singing hymns and songs and playing the piano. Mrs. Sharp insisted on preparing lunch for all of us. Miss Sharp and Jeanie were as pleasant and charming as ever. It was a dark, stormy night outside, but within all was comfort and pleasure. I stayed all night, sleeping in the comfortable bed in the same cheerful room that seemed just as homelike as it did two months ago.

Saturday, 13 August 1898

Spent the morning hours with Mrs. and Miss Sharp in the parlor. (James and Jeanie had gone to work as usual.) At 11:30, according to promise, went over to Cambusbarron to eat dinner and spend the afternoon with Brothers [Thomas] Gilchrist and McKnight. Promised to be back to take tea with Mrs. Sharp and family. At Cambusbarron met Sister Thompson, who had come up from Sauchie. All four elders were also present. Mrs. Donovan and daughter (the hostesses) were very obliging. After dinner we went back to Stirling, walking through the King's Park. Sister Thompson and I went to Mrs. Sharp's and the brethren went to Wallace Street.

At 6 P.M. Mrs. Thompson went shopping, and I stayed and spent an hour and a half with Annie. We had a good, social, confidential talk. Bid them all good-bye, promising to visit them again as soon as possible, called on Mr. and Mrs. McKenzie, and then hastened to the station to see Mrs. Thompson off. She left for Alloa at 7:50, and I for Glasgow at 8:03. All the brethren were there to see us off.

---

[177]Robert F. Gilchrist (1875-1945) was set apart for a mission to Great Britain on 15 November 1896, arriving in Liverpool on 10 December 1896. Within the Scottish Conference Gilchrist labored in the areas of Aberdeen, Edinburgh, Hawick, and Stirling. He was released in November 1898 and spoke at the conference in Glasgow early in December 1898 before returning to America.

Arrived in Glasgow at 9:15 and found all well and a fine letter from Father, containing the good news that all at home were well and twenty dollars besides. Felt happy.

Sunday, 14 August 1898

Sunday School at twelve. The new superintendency are doing well. Pupils are taking an interest. Meeting at 2 P.M. One of the members told me, as others have done before, that there is a better feeling among the members of the branch than has been for many years. God is ready to bless them when they seek him. Open-air meeting at 5:30. I was the first and only speaker, as the rain compelled us to stop.

Meeting at 6:30 P.M. Hall full, after which the elders and William Leggat and Martha, also Brother [William] Hamilton, went to Brother Joseph Leggat's to administer to Katie. Brother Leggat is having a hard time of it, yet feels well through it all. We reached home about 10:30 P.M. Brother Neilson still manifests a disagreeable spirit.

Monday, 15 August 1898

Attended to general conference duties. Elder Wickens,[178] having just arrived from Utah, was appointed to labor in Dunfermline. I pity him, poor boy! He will have a hard struggle for a while. At 7:30 P.M. Brother Edward, Brother Calder, and I held an open-air meeting on Cathedral Square. "One of the best ever held in Glasgow," said Brother Edward. It was well-attended and the hearers paid good attention, receiving the tracts gladly after the dismissal.

Tuesday, 16 August 1898

Attended to correspondence. Visited Brother Leggat's and found his daughter a little better. Called in to see Brother and Sister Neilson. She was very sociable, so also was Lizzie. At 8 P.M. visited Mr. Lewis and his amiable daughter, 22 Willow Bank Crescent. Spent a very pleasant evening. After talking about a little of everything, we began on religion—Mr. Lewis broaching the subject first. After a "crack" on polygamy, we started in earnest about other principles, particularly salvation for the dead, which subject we were on at 10:45, when I took my leave, promising to send some of our church works and as soon as possible to come back and continue the subject. He became very interested in baptism for the dead: "I'm inclined to doubt

---

[178]James H. Wickens (1875-1944) was set apart for a mission to Great Britain on 22 July 1898, arriving in Liverpool on 11 August 1898. He was assigned to the Scottish Conference and labored in the areas of Dumbarton, Dundee, Dunfermline, Edinburgh, Fifeshire, and Glasgow. Wickens was transferred to the London Conference in June 1900, and he returned to Utah in October 1900.

it," said he. "However, we should 'prove all things and hold fast to that which is good'" [1 Thes. 5:21]. He is a well-informed, intelligent man, I believe.

Wednesday, 17 August 1898

According to appointment, Brother Halliday was at the office at 9:30 A.M. and together we went to the town to do some shopping. Purchased a bedspring (19/6), wool mattress (12/6), and bolster and two feather pillows (8/0). This now makes a fine bed for the conference house, Brother Halliday having himself donated sheets, pillow cases, one pair blankets, and a coverlid.[179] He is a willing and useful member of the Church.

Wrote to Annie.

At 4 P.M. Mrs. J. E. Cardon, Logan, Utah, came from Leeds, England, where she has been visiting relatives. It seemed so pleasant to talk with a real Utah girl again. We all enjoyed her company. At 8 P.M. Brother Edward, Brother Calder, and I were meeting with some of the saints at Anderston Cross, holding an open-air meeting. Janet Lang and Mary McDonald were there, having walked about four miles and a half. I wonder how many of our Utah girls would walk that distance to attend an open-air meeting! Maggie and Jeanie Gain were also present. Brother Calder and D. O. [David O. McKay] occupied the time. The crowd was attentive and no disturbances.

Thursday, 18 August 1898

The S.S. *Ethiopia* leaves today at 12:30 P.M. All our passengers have not arrived. Secured Mrs. Cardon's ticket. She and Elder [William M.] Gerrard go in the saloon. As all were not aboard at the time the ship left the quay, I went to Greenock. Remained there until the evening train brought the Swiss emigrants. Bid all good-bye and came to Glasgow on the express. Tried on my new clothes at the tailors. Wrote to Liverpool, wrote this and —I am done. The boys are at testimony meeting.

Friday, 19 August 1898

Spent the morning hours reading and writing. Brother Calder went to Ayr. In the afternoon Brother Edward and I went shopping. Bought a tile hat[180] and I do not like to wear it, but one's dress is not complete without it.

We called on Sister Hoggan. She and the baby are well. Met Miss Burnell, Georgina's friend. Cottage meeting at night in Brother Taylor's house, Rutherglen. Three strangers were present. Administered to the little baby. The poor little thing suffers very much. The weather was somewhat *blustery*.

---

[179]The term *coverlid* is a variant form of "coverlet," referring to a bedspread.
[180]A *tile* hat was a high silk hat.

For some time past the heat has been very oppressive; but as the rains begin to come, the air will get cooler.

Saturday, 20 August 1898
Arranged accounts. Spent an hour or so reading. At 3 P.M., in company with Brother Pender and Brother Edward, went to William Leggat's and met with the officers and teacher[s] of the Sunday School. (Brother Clark was not there; came to hear "amen" said. He and Brother Neilson are not feeling to support the present officers.) A good feeling prevailed and many good suggestions were made. With the exception of the bad feeling awakened by Clark and Neilson, all went well.

Sister Martha [Leggat] prepared tea and bade us stop. She is an excellent housekeeper. At 8 P.M. Brother Edward and I visited Sister Gain. The girls were at the theatre. Retired about 11 P.M. Gloomy!! sad!! homesick!!! discouraged!!! angry!!! sorry!!!! and whatnot!

Sunday, 21 August 1898
At 10 A.M. took the bus from Queen Street to Burnbank, where I attended Sunday School at 11:30 and meeting at 12:30 with the Burnbank saints. Ate dinner at Brother [John] Cook's. Treated well by Mrs. Cook, not a member of the Church. Met Mr. Brown of New Jersey. At 6:30 attended cottage meeting at Brother Steven's. As I had told the elders that I would be back, I declined the pressing invitations to stay all night and walked into Glasgow. The night was pleasant but somewhat oppressive with the heat. I walked rapidly and the perspiration came from every pore. Arrived at the conference house at 11:35 P.M. A very successful and pleasant day.

Monday, 22 August 1898
Spent the morning hours writing. In the afternoon visited Brother Leggat, Sister Gain, and Sister Neilson. After tea Brother Calder and I went to Rutherglen to administer again to Sister Faulds. We called to see Sister Taylor, whose little baby is very low. Thought best to dedicate it to the Lord and asked him to call it home, if it be his will. Retired about 11 P.M.

Tuesday, 23 August 1898
Brother Taylor came in and reported his baby's death—died this morning at three o'clock. Word just received that Sister McDonald has a little girl. As one is called away, another is sent in its place.

Received an answer from the editor of the *Cumnock Express*, in which he refuses to publish the article I sent him and denounces the "new doctrine" as being a "rascally lie" and "will not defile his paper by discussing it." The poor, deluded sinner! Held an open-air meeting in Springburn. An attentive crowd was present. After the meeting we spent an hour or two with Sisters McDonald, Lang, and Cairney. Conference house again at 11 P.M.

Wednesday, 24 August 1898

Wrote to Father and Mother.

Attended to conference correspondence. At 2:30 went to Rutherglen to attend to the funeral services of Brother Taylor's little one. The services were short as the undertaker had understood that he should be in readiness at the time set for the meeting.

It is surprising the way people in this country bury their dead. Their manner is cold and indifferent. After the prayer is offered, the undertaker picks up the coffin (aided by another if the corpse is a large one) and carries it carelessly down the stairs. No order is observed in following it. The men only go to the cemetery. Not even the mother nor wife, as the case might be, accompanies her loved one to the last resting place. No sister to see the body of her deceased brother or sister laid in the tomb. The men only pay the last respects. At the cemetery, if the bereaved ones have no spot of their own, the coffin is put in a grave, barely covered with a few shovelfuls of clay, and there left until other coffins are put in beside it! I attended one funeral at which the time occupied in services and all was only fifty-five minutes! The cemetery was one mile from the home, too! The cemeteries are beautiful; trees and flowers adorn each side of the well-kept walks and drives.

At night attended an open-air meeting at Anderston Cross. A noisy element was present, making it very hard to speak. There were several interruptions but not much disturbance.

Thursday, 25 August 1898

In the morning called to see a young girl, whose passage money (half of it) has been sent by her uncle in Utah. She is too old to go on half fare. Her mother is dead, her father has deserted her, her four little brothers and sisters were in the poorhouse[181] (now she does not know where they are). She has no home and few friends. It is pitiful! Her eyes filled with tears as she told about her cruel treatment at the last place where she worked. Sad!

Met Mr. [Andrew] and Mrs. [Julia] Brixen. Testimony meeting at night. Mrs. Brixen spoke about three-quarters of an hour.

Friday, 26 August 1898

Office duties. At twelve o'clock Brother Edward and I had our photograph taken. Attended to correspondence. Brother Thomas Gilchrist came in from Stirling. He is on his way to Newcastle to preside over the conference there. He is one of our ablest men and one that will be missed. It was my intention to place him over the Glasgow Branch with Brothers Neilson and Leggat [as] counselors; but now things must be changed. Brother Pender has received his release. I am sorry to see him go, but his health will not

---

[181]A *poorhouse* or almshouse was an establishment in which persons receiving public charity are lodged and cared for.

permit of his staying longer.

At night, in company with Elders Gilchrist, Calder, and Smith,[182] went to the Royalty to see Wilson Barrett[183] and his excellent company in *The Sign of the Cross*. It was fine.

Saturday, 27 August 1898

Only two passengers in our charge going on *City of Rome*.[184] Train left St. Enoch's Station for Greenock at 9 A.M. Returned and spent a few hours with Brother Gilchrist. He left at 1 P.M. Both of us were loath to part. Left Glasgow for Dunfermline at 8:15 P.M. I was sure that I was in the right train when I left Queen Street Station, so sat contentedly in my seat as the train sped along. Sometime after crossing the Forth Bridge, I became uneasy and when I looked at my watch, it was past time when the train was due at Dunfermline! At the next station I inquired of the porter "if this train would ever reach Dunfermline." "Ah," he said, "You're way past Dunfermline; you should have changed at Dalmeny before crossing the bridge." I hurried out of the carriage and tried to blame everybody or somebody in particular for this blunder, but it all fell on my own stupidity.

I was in Kirkcaldy—eighteen miles from my destination—where the brethren were waiting for me! It was then ten o'clock! What was to be done? Upon inquiry I learned that part of a relief train which *might* go to Dunfermline was due. I waited about fifteen minutes for it and then found out that it was only going five miles further on to Burntisland. I rode the five miles and, failing in my presumptuous request to have them go further, inquired about the road to Dunfermline. If ever you want to get confused, just ask a country Scotchman to direct you. Whenever they begin, it will remind you of Launcelot's directing his father, as given in *The Merchant of Venice*; after they are through, you feel to exclaim with Gobbo. "Zounds, it will be a hard way to hit." Well, on this occasion, after receiving my directions, I concluded that "it would be a hard way to hit," especially at that time of night when I would meet no one to guide me or to tell me if I was right. Then, too, the road was strange—never had been in that part before!

Just as I was about to start and risk it, the yardmaster came and offered to "smuggle me on the relief engine to Inverkeithing," where he said I could catch the branch passenger train from Aberdeen to Dunfermline. While

---

[182]John S. Smith (1869-1942) was set apart for a mission to Great Britain on 7 April 1898, arriving in Liverpool on 27 April 1898. Within the Scottish Conference he served in the areas of Aberdeen, Airdrie, Ayr, Burnbank, Edinburgh, Glasgow, and Hamilton. Smith was released in June 1900 and returned to Utah the following month.

[183]Wilson Barrett (1848-1904), an actor-manager, had few equals in British melodrama.

[184]The *City of Rome* was an iron-hulled steamship launched in 1881. She had four masts and three funnels; her tonnage was 8,453 tons gross and she was 560 feet long. For McKay returning to America on the *City of Rome* when she collided with an iceberg, see the concluding note after the entry for 20 July 1899, p. 268, below, and for a profile illustration of the S.S. *City of Rome*, see Fig. 59, same page. Three years later this ship was sold and broken up in Germany.

they were preparing this, he took me in the switch-house, where I was quite comfortable. A "goods" (freight) train was going up about the same time, and they concluded I would be more comfortable in the "van" at the rear of this. After tipping the yardmaster (Mr. Ellis) and thanking him heartily for his kindness, a sudden jerk of the train quickly convinced me that I was again on my way. The freight conductor was very sociable, so the ride was quite a pleasant one. I satisfied myself with the thought that all my troubles for that night at least were over. A few minutes' ride in the passenger train would take me from Inverkeithing to my destination.

Imagine my surprise and disappointment when just as we entered the station the train from Aberdeen pulled out! The conductor expressed his condolence and showed it beneficially by calling the yardmaster and asking him to see if a freight train would be going down. (It was now near midnight, and the wind [was] blowing fiercely.) He said an engine was going that way and perhaps he could get me on that! I tipped the conductor from Burntisland passenger-fare, shook his hand warmly, and boarded the engine. I saw the engineer and fireman smiling and throwing significant glances as they saw my Prince Albert [suit] and silk hat. But they did not need to suppress their laughter for I soon joined in with them. As the engine steamed along the track, the wind seemed to have risen to a gale, and it was with some difficulty that I kept my "lum" hat[185] from sailing out into the darkness. Yes, my situation was ludicrous! But I had reached Dunfermline, anyhow. Late, it is true, Sunday morning, but that was all right.

After some little trouble I found High Street, and then with the aid of a policeman succeeded in waking the landlady, with whom the elders were stopping. I was four hours and a half getting to Dunfermline! The experience of the last three hours will never be forgotten—neither will the kindness of Mr. Ellis and the other gentleman who helped me out of one of the most ludicrous blunders I have yet made. The next time I go to Dunfermline or any other place, I shall ask if we change cars.

Sunday, 28 August 1898

A cold, wet morning. At 11 A.M., in company with Elders McKinlay and Wickens, went to the hall and met with a few saints in meeting capacity. A good spirit prevailed. Went with Sister Herrin for dinner. Meeting again at 2 P.M. Another good meeting, at least I thought so by the spirit which seemed to prevail and the attention given to what was said. A short council meeting was held at 4 P.M.

Visited [and] had tea with Brother Spowart and wife; she is not in the Church. I then went to Brother and Sister Anderson's, where the elders and several of the saints were. Had two or three hours pleasant talk, singing, etc. We then went to Townhill with Sister Hutchinson. Stayed with her parents

---

[185]The Scottish term *lum* means a chimney and here refers to a tall-crowned silk hat.

(Brother and Sister Neilsen) all night; the brethren went back to their lodgings.

Monday, 29 August 1898

Arose about 8 A.M. Sister Neilsen had a nice ham and egg breakfast prepared. Lizzie (Mrs. Hutchinson) had gone to work at 5 A.M. Administered to Brother Neilsen, who has been ailing for two or three days. He is quite old [and] has had quite a long experience in and out of the Church. Called on Mrs. Claighton, Brother Archibald's relative. Entertained very cordially and invited back. She is very kind, it seems, to the elders. Left Dunfermline at 11:05 A.M. Bid the elders good-bye at the station.

Found things in Glasgow all right. At 6:30 P.M. attended baptismal ceremonies at the Townhead Baths. Mr. Whyte, Mr. [George] Taylor, and Miss [Katie] Faulds were baptized. Brother Edward officiated. A good crowd of saints and one or two others were present.

Received a box of beautiful heather from Elders Mitchell and Nisbet[186] for elders in "LDS Office."

Tuesday, 30 August 1898

Raining. (Do not remember what I did specially during the day—this is September seventh.)

At night, as it was too stormy to hold an open-air meeting, we went to a Mr. Richardson's and spent the evening very pleasantly, singing hymns and playing Scotch airs and other selections on the organ. Cordial invitation to hasten back. The family are English—very entertaining. Contrast.

Wednesday, 31 August 1898

Brother Stewart,[187] a new Elder, arrived. We need him. He will be kept in Glasgow for the present. Miss Sharp called. Open-air meeting at Anderston Cross. Brother William Leggat and Brother Calder were the speakers. An excellent meeting. It is surprising how attentively the people listen, yet how few give heed!

---

[186]William P. Nisbet (1869-1940) was born in Claythorne, Renfrewshire, Scotland, and emigrated to America in 1890. He joined the LDS Church the next year and was set apart for a mission to Great Britain on 18 March 1898, arriving in Liverpool on 7 April 1898. In the Scottish Conference Nisbet labored in the areas of Ayrshire, Dundee, and Paisley. He was released in May 1900 and returned to Utah the following month. Later, Nisbet became Salt Lake County deputy sheriff and the chief gardener at the Utah State Capitol. See the William P. Nisbet Collection, Accession 1754, located in the Manuscripts Division, J. Willard Marriott Library, University of Utah, Salt Lake City.

[187]Niel M. Stewart (1855-1935) was a baby pioneer and survivor of the ill-fated 1856 Martin Handcart Company, having been born in Peoria, Illinois, on 15 April 1855. In Salt Lake City he was set apart on 12 August 1898 for a mission to Great Britain, arriving in Liverpool on 29 August 1898. Stewart was assigned to serve in the Scottish Conference and labored in the areas of Aberdeen, Dunfermline, Edinburgh, Fifeshire, and Lochgelly. He returned to his home in Meadow, Utah, in October 1900, and three months later Stewart was set apart as the bishop of the Meadow Ward in the Millard Stake, Utah, which position he held for nine years.

Thursday, 1 September 1898

Attended to duties pertaining to the conference. When Brother Pender returned from Newarthill, he reported a case out there of a young lady possessed of evil spirits. Spent several hours with Miss Sharp at her friend's, Miss Lewis. She has been undergoing an examination for her health. I hope there is nothing serious. Testimony meeting at night at Buchanan Street Station.

Friday, 2 September 1898

Raining. Went to the tailor's with Brother Stewart. At 2 P.M. according to previous arrangement Miss Oliver, a charming young lady from Newcastle (whom I met last Wednesday by letter of introduction from Walton), called and together we visited [the] Art Gallery on Sauchiehall Street and the Municipal Buildings. She ate tea with us at six. Very jolly. She left for Dennistoun at 7 P.M. Open-air meeting at Bridgeton Cross—Brother Edward, Brother Calder, and I. Brother Edward was the first speaker. I followed. Shortly after I began, it started to rain. We were invited inside the clock canopy, built in the center of the cross. The crowd followed us and the meeting continued. Brother Calder followed in his usual convincing style.

Saturday, 3 September 1898

Went to Newarthill to see the young girl [Charlotte Duncan] who is sick. Found her in a nervous or spasmodic fit. Brother Orr said she was possessed of evil spirits, and indeed it did appear that such was the case. She would laugh and talk [and] tell the priesthood to go home and not torment her, ask their name, etc. Sometimes she would try to rise out of bed, and although she was but a lassie weighing less than 100 pounds, it was all I could do to hold her and put her again in a quiet position. She seemed to be entirely unconscious when in this state. Her eyes were closed, and when she spoke, the sound came from her throat—not a lip moved. Just before regaining consciousness, her body became rigid, her hands clenched so tightly that the nails penetrated the skin, and her whole body—every muscle it seemed—became as stiff as a board. She would lie in this state for a moment and then awaken, weak and limp, entirely exhausted. These attacks came on every few minutes, each one lasting about five minutes or more. We administered to her and she obtained peace for about an hour and a half, during which time she sat up and talked as intelligently as anyone. She had another spell before we left. (We were then fasting for her relief.)

Went to Airdrie with the brethren and stopped all night with them at Mrs. Clark's.

Sunday, 4 September 1898

Met with the Airdrie saints at 11 A.M.

After meeting we walked five miles back to Newarthill where, after a forty-eight-hour fast, we were going to rebuke the evil power—whatever it was—afflicting the girl. The fast meeting was held in Sister Major's house. As we entered, Charlotte was suffering from another attack. She had walked from Brother Orr's—about a quarter or half a mile. As the meeting commenced, the attacks became more frequent. One elder had to hold her all the time. These spells continued until after she partook of the sacrament. She then had peace during the meeting until we were about to unite in prayer before administering to her. Just as we began to consecrate the oil, she went into one of these fits—or had another attack. This was a long one. I told the saints (the house was full) that we would all kneel around her and unite with the one who was mouth in prayer.

Taking her in my arms, I took a seat in the center of the room. When she regained consciousness, I told her we were all going to pray for her and asked her to unite with us. She feebly answered that she would. Brother Leatham[188] was mouth. At the conclusion she said, "I can walk now," but she was told to sit in the chair until we administered to her. After the ordinance, she walked back to her chair and participated in the rest of the meeting, joining in the last song with as much spirit as though nothing had ever been the matter.

After the dismissal, she joined in lively conversation and, after shaking hands with those remaining, walked back to Brother Orr's. When we passed the house about one hour later, she sat by the window, hailing us as [we] went down the road toward Motherwell. We all felt thankful to the Lord for this plain manifestation of his power. (I was told a few days later that the attacks had not returned.) Bidding the brethren good-bye, I walked the rest of the way to Motherwell and there boarded the train for Glasgow.

Meeting in the hall at 6 P.M., after which we held an open-air meeting on Miller Street. This was truly a busy day and one long to be remembered.

Monday, 5 September 1898

Attended to usual office duties. Brother Pender has learned that a Mrs. Greer, who emigrated to Utah about one year ago, is coming back. She is detained in New York. Has a fine (?) story about the treatment she received in Utah. We anticipate trouble when she arrives.

The elders from Newarthill came in to baptize Miss [Nellie] Jack for her health[189] and one of Sister [Margaret] Graham's little boys. I confirmed the latter a member of the Church.

---

[188]John S. Leatham (1856-1920) was set apart for a mission to Great Britain on 3 December 1897, arriving in Liverpool on 23 December 1897. He was assigned to the Scottish Conference and labored in the areas of Airdrie, Burnbank, Dumbarton, and Hawick. Leatham was released in November 1899 and returned to Utah the next month. He worked most of his life as a rancher.

[189]Carl S. Hawkins, "Baptism," in *Encyclopedia of Mormonism*, ed. Daniel H. Ludlow (New York: Macmillan Publishing Co., 1992), 1:94, stated that the nineteenth-century "practice of rebaptism . . . for a restoration of health in time of sickness is no longer practiced in the Church."

Tuesday, 6 September 1898
Called on the U.S. consul, Mr. Taylor, to see if he knew anything about this Greer affair; some of the officials here have been asked to investigate it. He was not in. Went to Bridgeton to get records for Brother Pender. Later went to Shettleston to get a recipe for curing [a] cataract from an old lady whom I had met sometime before. She told me about her being cured. Sometime after, I met Mrs. Lewis, who is now blind in one eye from cataract. I promised her to get the recipe and it was to fulfil the promise that I went today.

> *RECIPE*: Take dandelion roots, wash and scrape them. Put in a pot and boil to a pulp; strain, put liquid in a bottle; cork and let stand for a fortnight. Bathe the eye twice a day.

At night the Glasgow saints gave a social in honor of Brother Pender. We had an enjoyable time. Returning elders arriving. Received word from Liverpool of President Woodruff's[190] death, September 2nd.

Wednesday, 7 September 1898
Arranging for sailing of boat. Conference house full of emigrants and three elders. Open-air meeting at Anderston Cross. Elders Edward and [Frederick J. A.] Jaques were the speakers. A good meeting.

Thursday, 8 September 1898
Twenty-fifth birthday! Received two kind, loving letters from home— from Mamma and Nettie. Twenty-dollar present from Mamma. Their loving words and good wishes brought tears. O, if the world would have peace and happiness, let them make every home one where love abounds. The loving confidence expressed today would keep a man from every sin. God bless my parents and loved ones.

Went to Anchor Line office. Dinner down to the docks at 3 P.M. A large crowd present. Many friends came down to see Brother Pender away. Boat sailed at 4 P.M. Went to Greenock. Pleasant sail. Parted with Brother Pender—my true friend and sturdy brother. Boarded the tender back to Princes Pier, Greenock. Took train to Glasgow, where I arrived at 8:15 P.M. Sent letter to Liverpool.

Friday, 9 September 1898
Visited Sister Gain, Brother Leggat and family, Sister Neilson and fami-

---

[190]Wilford Woodruff (1807-1898) joined the Church in 1833 and was ordained an apostle five years later. He married eight women, though two of his plural wives divorced him. In April 1889 he became president of the Church and the next year he issued the Manifesto ending public support for new plural marriages. See Thomas G. Alexander, *Things in Heaven and Earth: The Life and Times of Wilford Woodruff, a Mormon Prophet* (Salt Lake City: Signature Books, 1998).

ly, [and] Mrs. Harrison. At night called on Mrs. Lewis and daughter. Decided to go to Aberdeen and meet with the saints next Sunday. Writing.

Saturday, 10 September 1898

Left Glasgow at 9:15 A.M. Just before I said good-morning to the boys, Brother Calder received his release. He will be missed. He will stay in Glasgow until after my return from the north; I intend to go to Wick. Spent the day in Stirling, visiting the brethren and acquaintances. Persuaded to stay over night. The evening was spent very pleasantly at Mrs. Sharp's. Miss Sharp is quite unwell.

Sunday, 11 September 1898

Mrs. Sharp and Annie were up in good time and prepared a nice, warm breakfast for me before train time. After enjoying which, I took my leave and at 7:45 boarded the train for Aberdeen. The ride was a pleasant one. The morning was clear. The cool, refreshing breeze coming through the window was exhilarating, and the green rolling hills dotted with grazing cattle and sheep, together with the fields of ripening grain on either side of the track, made a charming landscape scene, pleasant to look upon.

Arrived in Aberdeen at 11:30 and was met by Brothers Kenley and [William J.] Mortimer. They took me through the principal streets to Mrs. Park's, the lady with whom I stayed. Saw Lord Byron's[191] birthplace, 68 Broadgate Street. Passed the house in which my father stayed seventeen years ago, 15 Windy Wynd (now Spring Garden) Street. Aberdeen is a pretty city, clean and well-located. It is truly "the Granite City."[192]

At three o'clock met with saints and held memorial services in honor of President Woodruff. Several strangers were present. They (the saints) have given up their hall, and I was told that two quarter's rent is yet due. Called a special meeting at night to consider means of liquidating the debt. After laying the matter before them, I asked them what they would do. All voted to contribute freely and have the debt cleared before two weeks. There is jealousy existing among some, so I called a special priesthood meeting for Monday night to consider the organization and other matters. It seems that some think that rent money and other donations have been used for individual benefits. Blessed a baby, George S. Kenley.

Monday, 12 September 1898

After a good night's rest, felt refreshed. Spent the morning hours play-

---

[191]George Gordon Byron or Lord Byron (1788-1824) at the age of ten became the 6th Baron Byron of Rochdale. He was a leading figure of the Romantic movement and famous for his poetry and satires, such as *Don Juan*. Byron died while campaigning for Greek independence from the Turks.

[192]The locally quarried granite, which has been used in the city's buildings and even the paving stones for the streets, literally sparkles in the sunshine.

ing and singing hymns, etc. (Brother Kenley has a psalmody and Mrs. Park, a piano). Brother Kenley called at ten and together we visited the old Bridge of Don, the King's College, the old cathedral (Fig. 36), and church yard. On one tombstone was the following inscription:

Pain was my portion, physick was my food,
 Sighs was my devotion, drugs did me no good,
Til Christ my Redeemer who knoweth what is best,
 To ease me of my pain, has taken me to rest.

In the afternoon Brother Mortimer accompanied us. We visited the Rubislaw Granite Quarry, Duthie Park, Bridge of Dee. Beautiful black and white swans were in the ponds in the park. The black swans were very trim and stately.

I was told during the day that there would be *war* in the meeting at night. I acquainted myself with the trouble, inquired into the financial trouble, and decided upon a definite course. The man who was going to cause the trouble proved to be the best supporter of the proposition advanced; in fact, he made most of the motions, every one of which was unanimously adopted. We had an excellent meeting, after which several saints and friends came in from the adjoining room (where they had been gathering while the meeting was going on), and we held a fine social—singing, reciting, music, etc. Among the strangers present were Mrs. Forkehenson, the Misses Knowles, Mrs. Park, and the brethren.

I was sorry when 10:30 came and I had to leave to catch the eleven o'clock boat for Wick, where I intended to visit old friends of my father's. Brother Kenley went with me. It was a long way to the wharf and as usual I had to hurry. Got there just as the boat was ready to start. The gangway was taken down, but they put it up again. Secured cabin passage. The night

Fig. 36 *St. Machar's Cathedral, Aberdeen.*

was pleasant. Retired about twelve midnight. The boat was the S.S. *St. Claire*. My rest was a disturbed one.

Tuesday, 13 September 1898

About five o'clock, I began to feel *funny* (?) and I knew from past experiences that I would soon be following the example of Jonah's whale. However, I escaped with a few strains and groans and the loss of my supper. Arrived in Wick at 8 A.M. Walked four miles to Tannach, where I surprised all my friends. (I was surprised, too.) They gave me a cordial welcome. The heathery moors surround them here and the peat bogs are numerous. Spent the day with them.

Wednesday, 14 September 1898

At 9 A.M. after a good breakfast of porridge and rich milk, I left Tannach and walked back to Wick, where at 10:50 I boarded a train for Thurso. My object in going there was to visit my father's birthplace. At twelve o'clock I was asking a policeman the way to the "Brig o' Mas" (I asked for the "Brig o' *Saw*") in Janetstown and, being shown the road, began my walk towards my father's native town. At the "brig"[193] stands a "wee shoppy" kept by a William McKay. I went in to buy sweeties (?) and to see if they remembered anything about my father or grandparents. The lady remembered hearing about "the black minister"[194] and directed me down the "burn"[195] to a wee cottage kept by Angus McKay and wife.

An old lady answered the knock. As soon as she learned who I was, she said: "Ye'll com' right in the hoose and ye'll sit right doon! An' ye're David's son! Weel, I'm right glad to see ye! An' I mind yer gran'father weel!" So she continued. I have never enjoyed a visit anywhere as I enjoyed that one. To hear her tell about the time when Grandfather and his family joined the Church was more interesting than a good theatre. "O, what times they used to have," she would say. "Lots o' folk aboot here were awfu' ill aboot it! Awfu' ill aboot it!! O, I canna tell ye what times we used to have. Ochanee![196] Ochanee!! Deed, I'm the one wishin' to have yer granmother's memory. She could talk like a minister. When she was workin', she wadna' halt all the day!" She prepared a nice lunch. When I told her I do not use tea, she exclaimed: "Do ye no? Weel, neither did your father. I mind when he was *hame* here aboot sixteen year ago. I was awfu' put aboot about it. I didna' ken what to gie him; but ye'll tak' milk." She remembered this little circumstance sixteen years!

---

[193]The Scottish *brig* refers to a bridge.

[194]According to David Lawrence McKay, *My Father, David O. McKay*, ed. Lavina Fielding Anderson (Salt Lake City: Deseret Book Co., 1989), 27, David O. McKay's grandfather, William McKay, had received this nickname due to his black hair and beard.

[195]The Scottish *burn* refers to a brook or stream.

[196]*Ochanee* is a Scottish interjection expressing sorrow or regret.

Fig. 37 *The Home of William McKay, Thurso.*

Spent about two hours—two interesting hours—with her and then went to another little cottage nearby, in which my father was born (Fig. 37). As I bid her good-bye, she kissed my hand and cried and said, "I wish ye weel; I wish ye' weel!" The house to the right is kept by a Mrs. McKiver. She made me welcome, for Father stayed with her when he was here on his mission. How I enjoyed the thought of sitting in the same room in which my father first saw the light of day and spent his boyhood hours!!! Saw the old chest upon which he sat as he preached to the family and friends who came into the little room. The kitchen (in which these events happened) is very small with stone floor, boarded roof, and whitewashed walls. The old fireplace is small and ancient looking. To the right of it is an indentation in the wall containing two shelves upon which the dishes are kept. An old mantle is above it. The furniture consisted of a cupboard, two small tables, five chairs, the old chest, and one stool. An old-fashioned bed, covered, was also in the room.

It is a farming district and the *corn*[197] was just ripening. I enjoyed my visit very, very much, indeed.

At Thurso called on a Rev. Mr. Miller, with whom one of Uncle Hugh's sisters lived. She was away, but he received me kindly. Left Thurso (a neat, clean town) at 6 P.M. After dark, crossing moor—lost. Home at 9 P.M.

Thursday, 15 September 1898
Spent the entire day writing. Wrote letters to conference friends (about duties) and two to home—one to Mamma and one to Claire.

---

[197]In Scottish, the word *corn* refers to oats.

Friday, 16 September 1898

David and I went to Wick. Visited Staxigoe School, in which Bella is a teacher. I was introduced to the principal, Mr. Sutherland, as "a cousin from America." In answer to his questions "from Canada or U.S.," I said, "I come from Utah." "Ah, that's where the Mormons live." "Yes," I answered. "I'm a Mormon." "You don't mean that," he said quite surprised. "Yes, I am a Mormon, was born one." "Are you in earnest?" "Yes, I'm in earnest. Why are you so surprised?" "O," said he, "you know we up here haven't very exalted opinions about the Mormons."

Then followed an interesting conversation. His son, a bright young man attending college, became a very interested participant in it. Soon it was time for school. I shall only give space for notes: Whistled for a bell; roll for both rooms called by headmaster, "Charles Denny." "Here, sir." "Tommy Hooly." "Absent, sir." "Go fetch him." (A little girl left to hunt him.) Class called, "Four or five take front seat, bring geographical readers." At this point Tommy Hooly came in. "Where have you been?" "Couldn't get here in time." "That is not true!" etc. Little girl making a noise was called up, told to put her hand on back of book, and then received three hard strokes on the palm with a stick two-feet long, an inch and a half wide, and split at the end!! "That's the way we treat girls who simper!" he roared as she walked back to her seat. Whipped three others during one recitation. Schoolroom small, no convenience. Dismissed without any order. System of *grants* paid so much for attendance and efficiency. He was very willing to explain; in fact, occupied nearly the entire hour after recess.

Invited to tea. Met Mrs. Sutherland, a real nice woman. Mr. Sutherland and I had a lively discussion on the gospel. As we parted, Mr. Sutherland (the son) said, "Well, I have a much better opinion of the Mormons than before I met you." This was a pleasant afternoon. We walked back to Tannach as Uncle had got tired of waiting with the cart. At night several neighbors came in and the evening was spent in music and social chat.

Saturday, 17 September 1898

Bid Collin, Tena, and James[198] good-bye and, in company with the mother, David and Bella started in the cart for Wick. Waited at the boat for two hours and then found out that it would not sail until 8:30 P.M.! Went back to Tannach. (Miss Sinclair and father were at the boat also.) After eating a good lunch, David, Bella, Tena, and I walked to Wick. The boat did not sail until 9:35 P.M., but my companions stayed with me. As the boat left the harbor, they walked back home.

Before we were half an hour at sea, I was seasick. Helped a young girl to her berth and then had to get to mine as quick as possible. Did not rise until the boat stopped in Aberdeen next morning.

---

[198]McKay accidentally repeated the name *Collin*.

Sunday, 18 September 1898

Brother Kenley was at the docks at 4 A.M. and waited until the boat arrived at 7 A.M. He had a nice lunch for me in his pocket. Soon Brother [William J.] Mortimer came down. We spent two hours together, and as the tugboat came to tow us out to sea, they boarded her and bid me good-bye in the midst of the waves. An hour or less of rocking soon turned my stomach and, after losing my morning lunch, went to bed and lay there until 4:30 P.M.—just before we landed in Leith. The steward was kind.

Walked to the elders' lodgings [in Edinburgh], left my bag and coat, and then went to the hall. Surprised the saints. Occupied all the time. Went home with Brother and Sister George White, then went to Sister Whyte's and stayed all night.

Monday, 19 September 1898

In company with Elders Miller and Faddies[199] visited Brother Henderson and Brother Gracie. I then visited John and Donald McKay. At 3 P.M. Brother Miller and I visited Brother [Alexander] Rhynd.

At four left Edinburgh for Glasgow. Found the brethren well and everything all right. Spent the evening writing letters pertaining to conference matters.

Tuesday, 20 September 1898

Office and conference duties occupied my attention nearly all day, except the pleasant hour spent with Miss Oliver, sister to the one who called sometime ago. This night was spent in the office. Returning elders were here: Brother [William H.] Pitt, Salt Lake City, and Brother [William D.] Turner, Murray.

Wednesday, 21 September 1898

Brother Steven and Brother Douglas from Burnbank came in, and also Brother Orr from Newarthill. He asked forgiveness for any offense he might have given in a letter he wrote sometime ago, in which he practically refused to carry out my counsel in regard to taking Charlotte [Duncan] home after the administration. She has gone to her sister's and is again suffering from the attacks. I am afraid [that] Brother Orr is working the saints up to an apostate heat. Advised him to take her home and write to her parents. Open-air meeting at night.

---

[199]Alexander Faddies (1876-1962) of Coalville, Summit County, Utah, was set apart for a mission to Great Britain on 1 May 1896, arriving in Liverpool on 20 May 1896. Initially he was assigned to labor in the Irish Conference and served almost two years there. Then in May 1898 Faddies was released from laboring among the Irish and transferred to serve another six months in the Scottish Conference. He was released in October 1898, arriving back in Utah the following month. Faddies married Eliza Jane Faddies on 27 June 1906. See the Alexander Faddies Collection, Accession 1757, located in the Manuscripts Division, J. Willard Marriott Library, University of Utah, Salt Lake City.

Thursday, 22 September 1898

In the morning went to Anchor Line office with tickets to exchange. Had a little trouble finding some passengers who did not report at the office. Boat sailed at 3:15 P.M. with nine of our passengers aboard. Wrote to Liverpool. Testimony meeting at night—a cold feeling was present.

Friday, 23 September 1898

Visited Neilson's, Alexander Hoggan's, and David Cairney's. The afternoon was occupied in writing. Besides conference correspondence, wrote to Brother Pender. Open-air meeting at night on Cathedral Square. Brothers Edward, Stewart, Muir,[200] and I were the participants. Our singing (?) failed to bring anyone around; in fact, it drove them away. Brother Edward spoke first. He had two men, a lamppost, and the wind as an audience! He stopped once, but again continued, only to give up. I followed and spoke for about half an hour. A few gathered around, but the weather was cold and so were the people. Brother Stewart bore his testimony and Brother Edward dismissed.

Saturday, 24 September 1898

Wrote to parents.

Attended to sundry duties in office. Received an interesting letter from the elders in Ayr.[201] Sent a communication to President Wells and the *Star*. Brother McKinlay in Dunfermline is sick; he will probably have to be released. At 4 P.M. held a meeting with Brothers Neilson and Leggat; considered branch matters. Later Brother Cook from Burnbank came in.

At 7 P.M. attended a meeting of the officers and teachers of the Sunday School to consider methods of procedure in that organization. One of the assistants was under the influence of whiskey! Not much accomplished. Old Satan's influence is beginning to be manifested in the branch again. Petty jealousies, backbiting, [and] lack of confidence in each other are making certain members miserable.

Sunday, 25 September 1898

Priesthood meeting at 11 A.M. Brother Neilson absent. The teachers' reports were favorable. Sunday School at 12:30; only two young ladies present but nearly all the young men. The school lacks system. I shall be glad when a sufficient number of leaflets come. Meetings at 2 and 6 P.M. A very

---

[200]David M. Muir (1862-1898), the son of John W. Muir and Grace Muir of Beaver, Utah, was set apart on 3 May 1887 for a mission to New Zealand, returning in May 1890. He became engaged but left his sweetheart to go on another mission, being set apart for a mission to Great Britain on 26 August 1898. He was only able to serve his mission for one month in Scotland, for he was struck down with a severe illness and died on 19 October 1898.

[201]The letter from the elders laboring in Ayr related a few experiences that led a Mrs. Wilson to being converted to the gospel. McKay copied their letter and had it printed as "A Testimony," *The Latter-day Saints' Millennial Star* 60 (24 November 1898): 747.

good spirit prevailed. Open-air meeting on Miller and Argyle Streets at 8 P.M. A good attendance of the saints (especially the younger ones) but not many others,[202] although hundreds were passing. Brothers Clark and Leggat were the speakers. After this meeting we (elders) went down to Neilson's and administered to him. He is not very sick in body, but his mind is troubled—he borrows trouble.

Monday, 26 September 1898
    Wrote letters to Ayr, Dunfermline, Aberdeen, and to Liverpool, also personal letter to Thomas Gilchrist, Newcastle-on-Tyne. Visited Sister Mc-Donald, Springburn. We did not stay long, as a Mrs. Lang, Miss [Mary] Mc-Donald, and her two companions were there visiting. This is Glasgow's "Autumn Holiday." Later I went to Eastmuir by Shettleston and visited a Mrs. McKinnon. Her son promised to come to meeting.
    It being a holiday, we did not deem it wise to hold an open-air meeting, so spent most of the evening talking and studying. About nine o'clock we took a stroll first through the slums and then through the fashionable streets of the city. While passing through the former, we saw sights most disgusting. Drunken women reveling in sin, ready to sell themselves for a paltry nothing. We passed through a group of them, two of whom were quarreling. Such low, degrading language as they used was disgusting to listen to. Their quarrel ended in a fight, and to see the scratching and hair-pulling indulged in was something awful! Their companions soon separated them and the quarrel continued, others joining in. The vile accusations hurled at each other gave us a good insight to their miserable life and manner of existing. Leaving this place, we walked up to Sauchiehall Street, the fashionable part of town. Here you see the most attractive women—if dress and fine feathers might be called attractive—that one can see. They seem to be far, far ahead of their companions in sin in the slums, yet they sacrifice their honor and purity upon the same altar.

Tuesday, 27 September 1898
    Brother Muir went to Dunfermline, where he has been appointed to labor. Copied the minutes of priesthood meeting held August third. Sundry duties. The afternoon was spent in writing letters to Uncle Morgan and David R.
    At night Brother Edward and I visited Mr. Campbell Wallace,[203] 416 Crown Street. His daughters have attended some of our meetings. They are acquaintances of Brother Edward, who met them while he was tracting. They treated us very well; the evening passed quickly and pleasantly. Mr.

---

[202]McKay originally wrote "listeners," but this was crossed out and the word "others" written above it.
[203]McKay incorrectly wrote "Wallace Campbell."

Campbell [Wallace] is a Burns[204] man. He has a toddy divider and six toddy ladles used by Burns, also the Bible the poet presented to Alison,[205] his first sweetheart. Saw chairs three hundred years old. All invited us back as soon as possible. "Haste ye back soon."

Wednesday, 28 September 1898

Wrote to T. Allen and sent reports to some of the elders. Visited Sister Hunter and daughter. Open-air meeting at night on Anderston Cross. A good crowd of the young folks in the branch were there. The Misses [Jane and Nancy] Wallace, daughters of Campbell Wallace, were also there. Brothers Stewart, Edward, and Leggat were the speakers. Several *drunks* were in the crowd and caused considerable annoyance. One persisted in crying out: "That's the truth! Give it to 'em! Don't be 'fraid, mister!" It was impossible to keep him quiet. Once he said, "We're not dumb." I was standing by him at the time and replied, "Well, I wish you were; perhaps we could get peace!" Quite cold and showery.

Thursday, 29 September 1898

Brother Stewart and I visited Sister Anderson. In the afternoon I visited Sister Leggat and Sister Hamilton.

At 5 P.M. called in to see Sister Gain; she was feeling very much discouraged over the ill will manifested by the Neilson girls toward her daughter. She cried while telling me about unpleasant things which have happened. Ate supper with them, after which we all went to testimony meeting. It was a very wet, stormy night.

Friday, 30 September 1898

Visited Sister Good and family, also Brother Hamilton's family—in fact, the day was occupied in visiting saints. Brother Stirling[206] and David C. Eccles,[207] new missionaries, arrived at 4:30 P.M. I was pleased to talk of home with Brother Eccles.

---

[204]Robert Burns (1759-1796), the foremost Scottish poet, was born in Alloway, Ayrshire, Scotland, and wrote in the Scottish dialect. See James Mackay, *A Biography of Robert Burns* (Edinburgh: Mainstream Publishing, 1992). Throughout his life David O. McKay often quoted from Robert Burns.

[205]According to Maurice Lindsay, *The Burns Encyclopedia* (New York: St. Martin's Press, 1980), 24-25, this probably refers to Alison Begbie.

[206]William Stirling (1841-1915) was born in Forfar, Angus, Scotland. He was set apart for a mission to Great Britain on 9 September 1898, arriving in Liverpool on 29 September 1898. Within the Scottish Conference Stirling labored in the areas of Dundee and Edinburgh. In May 1900 he left four months early due to the sickness of his wife.

[207]David C. Eccles (1877-1941), the son of David Eccles and Bertha Marie Jensen, was set apart for a mission to Great Britain on 1 September 1898, arriving in Liverpool on 29 September 1898. He labored in the Scottish Conference in the areas of Ayrshire and Glasgow and was released in November 1900. Eccles lived in Ogden until 1920, when he moved to Oregon. He became a prominent lumber, railroad, and banking executive there.

Saturday, 1 October 1898

The entire day was spent in making out reports, addressing *Stars*, and sending out quarterly statements of accounts. Brother Edward made out most of the accounts. He is a very useful, energetic elder.

At night we took Brother Eccles and Brother Stirling to see Glasgow on Saturday night.

Sunday, 2 October 1898

Sunday School and meetings (including open-air meeting) as usual. An excellent spirit prevailed throughout the entire day. Brother Campbell,[208] Ayrshire, was in; he is a jolly man. After the open-air meeting at night, we administered to Sister James Clark. There is trouble brewing there; her illness is caused through nervousness.

A "hunt" before retiring. Two captures!![209]

Monday, 3 October 1898

Monthly reports. Correspondence with elders. Brother Stirling will spend a week with relatives. Received a communication from President Wells, with enclosed letter from Brother Eccles[210] (David's father), which showed his anxiety about his boy's success! I am bothered about making some appointments to fields of labor. I hardly know what to do until more elders come. The saints in Aberdeen are calling for an elder, but all are needed in other fields. Brother McKinlay is released on account of failing health. Brother Faddies is also released. Brother Leishman soon will be.

At 6:30 attended the baptismal ceremony of Katie, Thomas, and Grace Leggat; Brother Calder officiated. The confirmations took place at the baths. At 8 P.M. Brother Calder's farewell party or concert was begun. It was held in Breadalbane Hall, thirteen [in attendance]. We had an excellent time. Returning elders were present, beside the elders here and many saints, all of whom appreciate Brother Calder's labors. He is loved and respected by all.

At the conclusion Mr. [William] Reid and Agnes Cooke spoke to me about their wedding, which will take place on November fourth. They desire me to officiate at the ceremony! I have never even *seen* a couple married, not to mention *marrying* them! However, we shall see what can be done; it may be other arrangements will be made.

---

[208]George G. Campbell (1844-1929) lived in Darvel, Ayrshire, Scotland. The George G. Campbell Collection, Accession 851, Box 1, located in the Manuscripts Division, J. Willard Marriott Library, University of Utah, Salt Lake City, includes some diary entries for 1899.

[209]McKay evidently found two bedbugs.

[210]David Eccles (1849-1912) was born in Paisley, Renfrewshire, Scotland, and emigrated to Utah in 1863. His success in business made him Utah's first multimillionaire. Twice Eccles came to the financial aid of the Church by loaning it large sums of money at no interest. See Leonard J. Arrington, *David Eccles: Pioneer Western Industrialist* (Logan, UT: Utah State University, 1975).

Tuesday, 4 October 1898

Arranged for Bella Neilson's passage and fare to Utah. Spent about an hour at Neilson's. Conference house full of returning elders. Brother J. H. Paul, J[oseph J. L.] Paul, Brother [John] Norris, Elijah Larkin, Brother and Sister Sears (Salt Lake City), Brother Faddies, and home elders. Brother Calder, Brother Edward, Brother Eccles, and I spent the evening at Sister McDonald's. The house was full of saints and three others, Sister Lang's sons and wives. Spent a pleasant evening.

Wednesday, 5 October 1898

Wrote a short letter home. Secured rooms in Argyle. With the 6:45 A.M. train from England came Brother and Sister Spokes and family—all emigrating to Utah. They are a very fine family. Kept busy all day with sundry duties. Open-air meeting on Cathedral Square. A nice crowd present. Janet [Lang], Mary [McDonald], Maggie [Gain], the Spokes' girls, and returning elders, besides several young men in the branch and elders, were in attendance.

Thursday, 6 October 1898

House full of luggage and persons. At Anchor Line office in the morning changed tickets and made arrangements for some going saloon. Called at Argyle Hotel and found all saints there happy as larks. The boat, S.S. *Anchoria*, sailed at 3 P.M. with forty-five of our company on board. Went to Greenock; Lizzie Neilson and Janet Lang accompanied Bella that far, also. Came back by train, arriving in Glasgow at 7:15 P.M. Sent letters to Liverpool and then attended testimony meeting.

Friday, 7 October 1898

Writing and attending to a few duties around the office. Nothing of interest. Open-air meeting at Bridgeton Cross. Elders Edward, Stewart, Eccles, and I opened it. Brother Mitchell came later. We had a good meeting.

Saturday, 8 October 1898

Wrote a letter to Claire. Visited, in company with Brother Edward, the Gain girls, also Brother and Sister Leggat, and Brother and Sister Hoggan. As we were coming home about 10:30 P.M., we examined and enjoyed some views as shown in the mutoscope.[211] They were shown in real life; we enjoyed the "Theatre Hats" especially.

Sunday, 9 October 1898

All fasted. Brother Edward and Brother Stewart went to Blantyre. Sun-

---

[211]A *mutoscope* was an instrument for the exhibition of a series of photographs in rapid succession to give the optical effect of a moving picture.

day School as usual—not much interest shown. Meeting at 2 and 6:30 P.M., both of which were well-attended. On account of the stormy weather, no open-air meeting was held. Brothers Johnston, Faddies, Nisbet, and Mitchell, also Brother Eccles, were in attendance at all the meetings. Brother Johnston is released.

Monday, 10 October 1898

The morning hours were spent in fixing up two trolley lines in the kitchen for hanging clothes. After noon Brother Stewart and I visited some acquaintances of his living at 7 Viewfield Street, Denniston—Mr. and Mrs. Hood. They treated us with as cordial a welcome as our best friends could have done. A very pleasant afternoon was this. Conditions in Utah were touched upon; but, when straight reference to doctrine was made, the subject changed. We received a pressing invitation to "call again at any time." Mrs. Hood promised to accompany us to Grangemouth to visit her son, if we choose to go.

I believe more good is done by such visiting than can be done at several open-air meetings; and they are certainly more enjoyable. At 6:45 Brother Stewart, Brother Eccles, and I (Brother Edward not having returned from visiting relatives) went to the Royalty Theatre to see Miss Ellen Terry in *Nance Oldfield*, a comedy in one act, and Henry Irving in *The Bells* from *The Polish Jew*.[212] Both were excellent, especially the latter. The dream of Mathias the Burgomaster, as acted out by Irving, was simply grand. I enjoyed the play while it lasted; but somehow there is something that seems to prick one's conscience after having attended a theatre, when perhaps he could have been doing missionary work—the feeling experienced after the play is over is not the one, by any means, that follows the performance of *duty*; and yet should not a missionary *not* participate in such recreation? I wish I could explain just why I feel as I do tonight—while writing this "after the play is over."

Tuesday, 11 October 1898

After breakfast Brother Edward, Brother Eccles, and I went to [William] Bow's Emporium and purchased linoleum for the lobby and a wool mattress. By the time the conference house is furnished, we shall have had quite an experience in shopping and buying furnishings.

In the afternoon Brother Edward and I went to Neilson's to assist James in writing his essay for Sunday School, and then we visited Sister Gain and gave Lizzie and Jeanie the *Era* to assist them with their papers on "The Sabbath Day."

At night, according to previous appointment, we visited the Wallace

---

[212]Leopold Lewis's play, *The Bells*, was a translation and adaptation of the French *Le Juif Polonais* (The Polish Jew) by Émile Erckmann and Alexandre Chatrian.

family on Crown Street. Received a cordial welcome and spent an entertaining evening. Religion was the main topic of conversation. We met another son, a school teacher, a very bright young man. Said good-night at 11 P.M.

Wednesday, 12 October 1898

Received list of passengers sailing from Glasgow tomorrow—thirty-eight in all. Went to the Argyle Hotel, from there to the temperance hotel on York Street where the emigrants are, and then back to Anchor Line office. Everything and everybody seems to be all right. A Brother Neilsen, well-acquainted with Joseph L. Peterson, is appointed to preside over the company.

Wrote a letter to Nettie. Visited Mrs. [Duncan] Thomson and Sister Robertson on 18 Comelypark Street. I always feel fine while visiting here: they are kind, intelligent, homelike people.

Open-air meeting at 8 P.M. on Cathedral Square. Sister Cairney, Janet, Maggie, and Jeanie were the ladies present. We had a good meeting. Brother Edward was the first speaker, followed by Brother Leggat. A debate going on a few rods from us took many of our crowd. There were two or three interruptions, but each was hushed by the listeners.

Thursday, 13 October 1898

Letters from Tommy and Nettie.

After breakfast I went to Anchor Line office and to Argyle Hotel. Named Neilsen and [John L.] Cherling for saloon passage. A very nice company sails today. In the afternoon Brother Edward and I visited Sister Harkins, 21 Cathcart Street. She has been complaining about elders not visiting her. We spent about two pleasant hours with her and then hastened to Stobcross Quay to see that all the passengers on our list were on board the vessel, S.S. *Furnessia*. She sailed at 5:15 P.M. Testimony meeting at night. A good spirit prevailed, and all present felt well and encouraged.

Friday, 14 October 1898

A very quiet day, except going to [Samuel R.] McCall's to buy curtains and to see him about a suit of clothes ordered by a returned elder and not yet paid. I did nothing but write. Fixed up the house a bit. "The auld cheer wunna' haud ye, mon!" (Exclamation of Sister Noble as I mounted chair and table to lower curtains.)

At 6 P.M. Brother Johnston came in from Edinburgh and, this being our last opportunity for a few months at least, he desired us to accompany him to see *The Merchant of Venice* [with] Sir Henry Irving as Shylock and Miss Ellen Terry as Portia. Brothers Edward, Eccles, Johnston, and I secured seats in the pit, which was filled by the early door. Irving did not appear; his part was played by [blank]. Portia was fine. It was all very good, but we were a little disappointed.

Saturday, 15 October 1898

Another letter from Dunfermline, stating that Brother Muir is still very sick. Wrote immediately to Stirling, requesting the brethren there to go out and attend him as Brother Wickins is, no doubt, worn out. An appointment in Ayrshire prevents my going. Called on Martha Leggat.

At 6:20 left St. Enoch's Station, bound for Darvel, at which place I arrived two and a half hours later. Elders Mitchell and Nisbet met me at the station and conducted me to Brother [George G.] Campbell's home, where I met his family,[213] Sister Graham from Galston and Brothers Charles Burns and William Hawthorne from Maybole. The evening was spent in singing, reciting, violin music, and "cracking"! Brothers Mitchell and Nisbet went to Galston with Sister Graham. The rest of us sat until 1:30 and retired.

Sunday, 16 October 1898

Brother Burns is an early riser, and notwithstanding the late hour of retiring, he was awake at five o'clock. I wanted about three more hours sleep. At twelve o'clock Brother Campbell, a real staunch, energetic Latter-day Saint—the "Invincible George"—had everything arranged for a cottage meeting. A good spirit prevailed. After this we walked to Galston (five miles) and held another meeting in Brother Graham's house. Sister Graham treated us *royally*. She had an excellent dinner prepared, besides pie and cake for refreshment after meeting. Two young women not of our faith were present. One has applied for baptism.

The weather was too cold for the holding of an open-air meeting, so we spent the evening in social conversation. At 9 P.M. we bid them good-bye, and those of us staying with Brother Campbell began our walk to Darvel, accompanied by the elders and Miss Graham, who did not say good-night until the first mile or more had been walked.

The effects of the cold wind were overcome by the exercise in walking; the sky was clear and *starry*; the roads were smooth; our hearts were light; and our tongues merry, so the distance to Darvel seemed short. The surrounding scenes were beautiful and quite romantic. "Loudon's bonny woods and braes"[214] with the magnificent castle of the same name stood on our left; the road was lined with luxuriant woods; the hill or brae on the right was covered with tall stately forests, surrounding small green openings

---

[213]James S. Campbell, *Biography of George Gordon Campbell* (n.p., 1957), 7, which is located in the Campbell Collection, Accession 851, Box 2, related the following story about the first meeting of his father and David O. McKay: "'Can you tell me where George Gordon Campbell lives?' inquired a tall handsome young man. Wee Davie Campbell looked up from his play in the street. 'Aye,' he replied, 'That's my Father.' He then took the stranger to No. 1, Edith Street—our Darvel home. That was the beginning of many visits and a true and everlasting friendship. This impressive young stranger was David O. McKay on his first mission to Great Britain."

[214]Robert Tannahill (1774-1810), a Scottish poet, published the song entitled "Loudon's Bonnie Woods and Braes" in an 1807 issue of *Scots Magazine*. See *The Songs and Poems of Robert Tannahill* (Paisley, Scotland: J. & R. Parlane, 1911), 24.

upon which during the day small herds of sheep and cattle were grazing—as we passed then, no doubt, these were quietly chewing their cud, lazily rolling on their green, grassy beds.

An occasional light from the farmhouses on the hillside made one think of contentment and peace, while the somewhat doleful cry of the "hoolet" awakened the feeling of romance. What a beautiful evening for a stroll for the swain and the farmer's daughter! The wind through the trees would be music to their souls, while the noise from the nocturnal *crier* would seem but a pleasing accompaniment. As they looked at the lighted mansion in the distance toward the town, they would build their own future mansion and comfortable home, furnished as elegantly as the one belonging to the rich man of Darvel. They would dream of—but here we are again at Brother Campbell's, and as we were up late last night, let us say good-night and retire.

Monday, 17 October 1898

The brethren from Maybole left on the 7:05 A.M. train to get to their work at ten; Brother Campbell and his daughters were at work at 6:30 but returned for breakfast at nine. I left Darvel at 11:30, met the elders at Galston, and went to Kilmarnock. Here we visited the Kay Park, the chief attraction of which is Burns's Monument. Visited the historical museum inside. Saw letters written by the poet, shoes made by "Souter Johnny,"[215] and other interesting relics.

After a short walk around the town, we bid each other good-bye, the elders going to Ayr and I to Glasgow, where I arrived forty minutes later —3:05 P.M.—a much quicker ride than when I went down. All at the conference house well.

Called on Mrs. Harrison. Mr. Harrison will be down tomorrow night to fix gasoliers.[216] Later Brother E[dward] and I and Maggie and Jeanie Gain visited a Brother Easton and wife. He has been away from the Church for years.

Tuesday, 18 October 1898

A letter from Brother McKnight, Dunfermline, states that he found Brother Muir very sick. Sent a telegram, asking if it is possible to remove him here to conference house; answer, No. As I have an appointment tonight with Mr. Harrison, Brother Edward will go to Dunfermline and see what can be done.

Brother Eccles and I visited Mrs. Greer and daughter. They treated us very well. Poor Sister Greer! She has had a hard time of it. Mr. Harrison called at night. Brother William Leggat, also.

---

[215]A *souter* is a shoemaker or cobbler and Souter Johnny is a character in Burns's poem, "Tam o' Shanter," which many feel is based upon a man named John Davidson.

[216]A *gasolier* was a chandelier in which gas was used.

Wednesday, 19 October 1898

Letter from Brother Edward, stating that he found Elder Muir "a very sick man, indeed," but after the administrations yesterday, there was a marked improvement. Met Mr. Harrison at 2 P.M. and bought gasolier and globes. Open-air meeting at night. After coming from which, read a letter from the brethren—Brother Edward stating that Elder Muir's condition is very critical. Offered up another special prayer and retired, feeling very uneasy and sad.

Thursday, 20 October 1898

The first news this morning is a telegram announcing Elder Muir's death![217] He died last night at 1:35 A.M. Cast a dark cloud of sorrow over all. Sent word immediately to Liverpool and spent several hours communicating with President Wells about clothes,[218] home address, date of funeral, etc. At 4:07 left for Lochgelly, arriving there at 7 P.M.

The brethren then told me about the intense suffering of our deceased brother. Brother Wickens did not close his eyes for eight days and nights but was constantly by Elder Muir's side. His constancy and devotion has brought forth the approval and commendation of all. Elders Edward and McKnight did all in their power—both were worn out. Mr. and Mrs. Raeburn were faithful as they could be. The doctor [Frank Dendle] and his assistant attended him regularly but all to no purpose. God wanted him home and took him from us to fill a more glorious mission.

The brethren washed and dressed him and had [a] coffin ordered. The body was wasted and worn. Only one short month among us! O, it is the saddest affair that ever I have experienced! Telegram from President Wells, requesting the funeral to be postponed until Tuesday next. This is almost impossible. Ans[wered] to this effect and asked to send clothes immediately. Mr. and Mrs. Raeburn, with Elders McKnight and Wickens, slept in his parents' home and gave us their entire home. Better-hearted people never lived.

Friday, 21 October 1898

Communicated with President Wells concerning time of funeral. It was sometime in the afternoon before a suitable time was decided upon—

---

[217]John T. Edward, Diary, 18 October 1898, related firsthand details about Muir's last hours: "Elder Wickens had sat up eight nights with Elder Muir, and Elder McKnight had stayed with him one night. So we let Bro. Wickens go to bed and Elder McKnight and I sat up with him. Elder Muir did not rest over five minutes at a time all night. All three of us stayed with him on Wednesday. In the morning I sent Pres. McKay another letter, stating just how Bro. Muir was, as near as I could. We administered [to him] and prayed to our Heavenly Father, without ceasing almost, in Elder Muir's behalf. He did not rest any all day Wednesday, until about three in the afternoon [when] he began to get drowsy. But it did not seem to be a natural sleep, until about nine in the evening when he began to lose consciousness and never regained it again and passed away at 1:45 A.M."

[218]*Clothes* here refers to LDS temple garments and robes for Elder Muir's burial.

12:30 tomorrow. This necessitated the hiring of a special bus from Dunfermline to Lochgelly. This was done. Elder Edward, who had left in the morning for Glasgow, sent a telegram stating the clothes had been sent from Liverpool and that the boat would not sail until 8 P.M. tomorrow. At 6 P.M. the clothes did not arrive; so he was placed in his coffin, quite a number of friends and neighbors being present. Elder Wickens and I stayed together in the house, the family and Brother McKnight going to Mrs. Raeburn's mother's.

Saturday, 22 October 1898

The next morning there was still no word about the clothes but all arrangements were made for the services. The bus arrived at twelve o'clock with the European presidency and all the elders but two. They had the clothes. We had a painful experience in dressing him, as the body was in a bad state owing to inflammation. The particulars of funeral are given attached.[219] Left Lochgelly at 3 P.M., leaving four elders to make necessary settlement, and arrived in Glasgow at 7 P.M. Down to the boat at 8. President Wells and President McMurrin also. All arrangements made. Presidency left for London at 10:55 P.M. Thus ended a day long to be remembered!

Sunday, 23 October 1898

Before Sunday School I called on the Thomson family and Sister Robertson. Sunday School and meetings as usual. The afternoon services were held in memory of Elder Muir. I occupied the time. After the evening meeting, Elders Mitchell, Nisbet, and Stewart went to Rutherglen to administer to a sick woman, and Brother Eccles and I went to Sister Gain's to administer to Flora. Brother and Sister Easton were there.

Monday, 24 October 1898

Arranged financial account of the late funeral and wrote a letter for the *Star.* Elder Stewart appointed to Dunfermline and Elder Eccles to Ayrshire.

Tuesday, 25 October 1898

Elder Edward and I went around the city, trying to secure a suitable hall for conference.

Wednesday, 26 October 1898

Wrote a long letter home, several local letters, and visited one or two halls. At 4:07 left Glasgow for Newarthill, where I met with the elders and saints in that district. Sister Orr and her husband acknowledged wherein

---

[219]This refers to a clipping of the tribute written by McKay and entitled "Death of Elder David M. Muir," *The Latter-day Saints' Millennial Star* 60 (27 October 1898): 682-84.

they had done wrong in disobeying counsel. Sister Major was not feeling well. Returned at 10:20 P.M.

Thursday, 27 October 1898

Elders Leishman, Edward, and I, according to a request in a letter received last night, went to Blantyre to administer to Sister Irvine, who is quite ill of jaundice and other troubles. Doctor has no hopes. She felt much better after our administration. The doctor came before we left, and he was quite surprised to see the change. Left my umbrella in train. Testimony meeting at night. Letters from parents and others.

Friday, 28 October 1898

Elder Edward and I spent the day with office work and selecting a hall. Decided that the saloon hall in the city halls is the most suitable—price and all considered. It seats about 450 persons, and the rental for three meeting[s] is £2/0/0. The afternoon was occupied with visitors: Sister Clunie and Nellie Jack came in. At 7 P.M. we went to Springburn and visited the saints there; one or two of them feel gloomy. Sister Lang, Janet's mother, did not treat us very well.

Saturday, 29 October 1898

Wrote to Tommy.

[In the] afternoon attended to correspondence. At 6:30 P.M. William Reid was baptized by Elder Edward. Quite a number of saints were present. I confirmed him a member of the Church. At the confirmation meeting held in the conference house there were present Brother J. Neilson, Joseph Leggat, David and William Cooke, Brother Reid, Maggie and Jeanie Gain, Katie Faulds, Elder Edward, and I. At 8 P.M. Brother Edward and I visited Mr. Wallace on Crown Street. Spent a very pleasant evening. Had an excellent conversation on the gospel. It was midnight before we finally left them, Mr. Wallace accompanying us on our way home.

Sunday, 30 October 1898

Priesthood meeting at 11 A.M. Every officer late. A little division was manifest in the latter part of the proceedings when a motion was made to have a plate at the hall door for voluntary contributions. Sunday School at 12:30—one of the best we have held. Meeting at 2 P.M.; another at six. Between last two meetings Elder Edward and I went home with Brother and Sister William Leggat. She had prepared a dinner good enough for the queen. Everything clean, too.

Monday, 31 October 1898

All day occupied with monthly reports. It being Halloween and the three of us (Elder Leishman, Edward, and I) having been invited to spend the evening at Neilson's, we accordingly accepted the invitation. A very pleasant evening was spent. "Champit tatties,"[220] in which were articles of luck and ill luck, were eaten until each article had been obtained. The ring was mine; the button, James Neilson's; the doll, Martha's; and the three-penny bit, Tucker's; and the [bell], Lizzie's. Fruit and nuts were in abundance.

Tuesday, 1 November 1898

Finished reports. Wrote letters. Entertained saints who called. Spent the day and evening at the office.

Wednesday, 2 November 1898

Wrote letter to Salt Lake City.

Nothing much accomplished. A Mr. Alexander called. He was at the Talmage lecture and seems to have become quite interested in Utah. Gave him some tracts and made another appointment with him.

Brother Neilson called in the evening and poured forth his "tale of woe" about his losing influence in the branch. He wants more authority. Men here cannot stand positions. They become too arbitrary. Told him to do his duty and never mind influence and authority.

At 8 P.M. we were in Springburn, enjoying another Halloween. I tell you we had a pleasant time! Apples, pears, bananas, grapes, candy, and nuts were placed at our disposal. Songs, speeches, jokes, and verses made the hours pass quickly. We missed the last car, so had to walk all the way to the conference house in a pouring rain. My umbrella lies in some station.

Thursday, 3 November 1898

Just as I was washing the bell rang, and as I opened the door, there stood Lawn [Alonzo] Hyde and Nephi Taylor just from London, returning home from their German mission. Went to Central Station and obtained my lost umbrella. It had been taken from carriage and sent back according to my request. Every station had been notified. It cost me two pence. Honest people over here. Went to several bookstores with Brother Leishman, trying to secure certain books.

Testimony meeting at night. Neilson had another dream. Spoke to him about taking too much time in meetings.

Friday, 4 November 1898

Arose at 6:45 to meet company from London. Elder Edward and I met them at 8 A.M. There were in the company Elder Mark Austin and wife, Elder W. J. Panter and wife, Miss Anna Hughes, [the] Misses Hurley; George Jackson and wife, Mrs. R. T. Johnson and Miss Lucy Johnson of Ogden, and Miss Amy Johnson [of] Salt Lake. Took them to the Argyle.

---

[220]In Scottish, *champit tatties* refers to mashed potatoes.

Fig. 38 *Mitchell Library, Glasgow.*

The day was occupied with emigration duties and in studying a marriage ceremony for the night.

At 6 P.M. William Cooke called to conduct us to Maryhill, where the wedding of William Reid and Agnes Cooke was to take place. Elder Thomas Leishman, Brother Edward, Alonzo Hyde, Nephi Taylor, and the Misses Johnson went as invited guests. When we reached the hall, I felt rather shaky. The tables were spread, the chairs set around, and everything in readiness. I was to marry them—I who had never even seen a couple married! However, everything I [could] think of or could read about in books at my disposal—I frequented the Mitchell Library[221] (Fig. 38)—was prepared. Soon all were ready; the hall was full. The bride entered, leaning upon her father's arm. The bridegroom rose and met them and received his bride from her parent. Then all were silent and the ceremony began. It lasted about ten minutes—ceremony, advice, prayer, and all. Those present pronounced it well done and satisfaction seemed to have been given. After congratulations, tea was served. Then the hall was cleared and the fun began. Dancing, singing, reciting, and social talks were the pleasure of the evening.

At 2 A.M. we bid the company "guid nicht" and went to Glasgow. They

---

[221]The Mitchell Library was established in 1877 with a £67,000 bequest from Stephen Mitchell, who died in 1874. It had two earlier locations before opening on its present site in 1911. In one of his missionary notebooks, McKay noted that it contained 126,000 volumes of which more than 1,000 related to Robert Burns. This library continues to be the major reference library in Glasgow, currently with about 1,500,000 volumes.

"would not go home 'til morning," probably. We got wet and were ready for a morning's rest when we reached home.

Saturday, 5 November 1898

Up at 8:30. "O, what a difference in the morning!" Went to the Argyle Hotel and met all the saints, announcing a meeting at 11 A.M. At this time (11:00) all were in the conference house and received the usual instructions about the voyage. Brother Austin was president. At 2:45 we were at the boat. Went to Greenock with the company. They all felt jolly and gay. I wished I were going with them.

Bid all good-bye at 5:30 P.M. and came back to Glasgow by train, arriving at St. Enoch's at 7:30. Jeanie and Maggie Gain, Janet Lang, Elders Leatham and Smith were at the conference house. We spent the night in singing. Elder Leatham told me that more trouble is anticipated in Newarthill.

Sunday, 6 November 1898

At 10 A.M. boarded a bus at Queen Street and rode to Bothwell. Then walked to Blantyre to meet with the saints in that branch. Sister Irvine was very sick. After testimony meeting, we administered to her. Met a Sister McPherson, who was a member of the Church when a child. She lost track of the Latter-day Saints but ever felt warm towards us; she is married now and hopes to bring her husband in.

Ate dinner at Mrs. Cook's. Visited an old lady, Sister Dunn, who lives all alone in a cold, damp hovel. She is in her eighty-fifth year and has been put in that place—alone—receiving a bare pittance from her only son, who is living in ease on her money, which he took from her! She offered 2/0, but I could not take it.[222] The Lord will bless her for her willingness.

Meeting at 6:30 P.M. in Brother Steven's house, after which I walked back to Irvine's to see how Sister Irvine felt. Found her much better. Remained all night.

Monday, 7 November 1898

Left Blantyre at 6:45 A.M., arriving in Glasgow at 7:30. Brother Edward, who was the only elder in Glasgow[223] yesterday, said he got along fine—good meetings being held. Sent letter and reports to Liverpool, also letters to Utah and Germany about lost trunks.

Relief Society meeting at night. Mrs. Harkins tendered her resignation as first counselor; it was accepted. Brother Edward was sick of a severe at-

---

[222]John T. Edward, Diary, 18 May 1898, related another instance of the generosity of poor members: "She [Sis. McAulay] wanted me to take 2/6 to help me out in my missionary labors, but I told her, no, I did not need it, that she needed it much worse than I did."

[223]McKay originally wrote "was alone in Glasgow."

tack of cold. Applied hot cloths, Herbaline, etc., on his chest, soaking his feet and giving him warm drinks. I am a clumsy nurse.[224]

Tuesday, 8 November 1898

Remained in the house all day with Brother Edward, who is still very unwell. The cold is right on his lungs and his head aches severely. Administered to him and applied such remedies as we thought best. Sister Noble is unwell, too. Fasted.

At 7:30 P.M. as I was sitting all alone by the fire, a telegram came requesting me to "come at once, call at Sister Irvine's—Sneddon." 8:28 found me at the Central [Station] on the train for Blantyre. My head was full of imaginary afflictions concerning Sister Irvine. Arriving twenty-five minutes later, I found her sitting up, looking fine; they wanted me to call there to be directed to Brother Sneddon's, whose little girl was sick. On our way to Sneddon's we met Alex Sneddon and his pretty wife, who told us the baby was much better. As it was impossible to walk over and catch the last train, I did not go. They promised to explain and send word if the child turned badly.

Wednesday, 9 November 1898

When I returned last night—very dark and foggy—I found Brother Edward a little better. His head was easier. This morning he feels fine and is going to get up and sup his porridge as usual. Wrote a letter home to Annie and answered conference correspondence. Brother Joseph Leggat called. In the afternoon went to Mrs. Wallace's and postponed an appointment with Mr. Wallace on account of Brother Edward's health.

At 7:30 Mr. Wallace and his brother called and spent the evening. As I was just going to Mr. Harrison's as they came in, I excused myself, hurried up there, and called on Mr. and Mrs. Harrison, delivered my message concerning gasolier, etc., and was back at 8:30. Brother Edward and Mr. Wallace were debating the principles of Mormonism. The night was spent very profitably. Mr. Wallace seems interested. Invited us to attend the opening exercises of a school next Monday. He left at 11 P.M.

Thursday, 10 November 1898

Still dull and foggy. Brother Edward's health is still improving, although his cough bothers him still. Wrote to Frank L. Layton; to Liverpool office; Janet McKay, Tannach; and Elder William Stirling. Tried to secure a small hall, in which to hold a few choir practices before conference.

---

[224]John T. Edward Diary, 7 November 1898, recorded the following about McKay's assistance: "Went to bed with a bad cold on my lungs and no Prince could do any more for me than Bro. McKay did that night. He was up and down the whole night in my behalf, fixing the fire and giving me medicine and one thing and another."

At 7 P.M. met Elder William Gould,[225] just from Utah. It was pleasing and comforting to hear from home and friends. Testimony meeting at which there was a large attendance and a good spirit prevailed. Neilson went on the warpath after dismissal—James Leggat has said something about his (Neilson's) profit off the soirées. Goodness, it is awful! There is trouble all the time.

Friday, 11 November 1898

Received a fine letter from Tommy. Spent the forenoon in the office. Maggie Gain and "wee Johnny" called. At 1:20 boarded a train for Beith where, according to appointment, I met Elder Nisbet and together we walked to Gateside and visited Brother and Sister [Robert] Gray and family. They welcomed us warmly. We spent the evening and night "debating" and eating.

Retired at midnight.

Saturday, 12 November 1898

At 5 A.M. Brother Gray came in our room to bid me good-bye—Brother Nisbet had decided to stay with them over Sunday. As we shook hands, he dropped two shillings in mine, at the same time expressing his pleasure at our calling to see him and extending a hearty invitation to return.

He is an Irishman—a real typical one, too. He is a keen debater and delights in argument. His earnestness of speech and manner makes one interested and amused. When Sister Gray would try to say a word—try to get one in edgewise, as we say—he would turn impatiently in his chair and cry, "Hauld yer tongue wooman, ye'll no let me speak; I'll give a half hour when I'm through!" Once he desired our opinion on a subject upon which he had his own thoughts, and he half wished ours would coincide yet felt doubtful about it, for he started by saying, "Now, gentlemen, d'ye think this is right —*I know ye'll say it's wrong!*" Then he wondered why we laughed. Well, we had a good time.

Left them at 11:10 A.M., arriving in Glasgow an hour later, where I met Miss [Jennie] Brimhall, Elder [Jesse W.] Knight, and Elder [Edward C.] Rich—all homeward bound. [They had] visited the panorama of the Battle of Bannockburn. A telegram from Stirling stated that Miss Sharp is seriously ill.

Special priesthood meeting at night—eight o'clock. Considered the advisability of putting a plate at the hall door for voluntary contributions. Af-

---

[225]William S. Gould (1866-1946) was married with five children (ranging from eight years to two months) when he was called on his mission. He was set apart for a mission to Great Britain on 14 October 1898, arriving in Liverpool on 6 November 1898. Gould was assigned to the Scottish Conference, laboring in the areas of Airdrie, Burnbank, Edinburgh, Galashiels, Glasgow, Hamilton, Hawick, and Motherwell. He was released in July 1900. See the William S. Gould Diaries, Accession 1674, located in the Manuscripts Division, J. Willard Marriott Library, University of Utah, Salt Lake City.

ter considerable debate, it was unanimously agreed upon.[226] The meeting closed at 9:45. At ten I was at Buchanan Street Station, ready for Stirling.

Found Annie very sick, indeed. Her mother, thinking her on her death-bed, insisted on sending for the minister; but she preferred an elder of our Church. I had an excellent opportunity to comfort her by words of hope regarding our future state. Her mind was upon it; she felt that her time had come. "I'm not afraid to die," she said, "because I have done nothing that I need be ashamed of." She regretted that she had not given religion more thought and wondered if her not joining the Established Church would affect her salvation. She did not think it would when she thought of what the elders had said. She believes the gospel to be true. The others having gone out, I knelt by her side and prayed. "O, that's nice," she said, as I arose from my knees. She felt somewhat easier and chatted very sociably. She had a short sleep—the first for ten days and nights! Retired about 2 A.M.

Sunday, 13 November 1898

Awoke at six, intending to catch train for Glasgow. No train left. Thinking my going back might disturb Miss Sharp, I walked to Cambus-barron and spent the forenoon with Elders [Robert] Gilchrist and McK-night and Brother Thomson. Called on Mr. and Mrs. McKenzie.

When we again entered Mrs. Sharp's, we learned that Annie was no better. When we bid her good-bye, she broke down and sobbed. My, it touched my heart! To see her suffering there and so desirous of living was heartrending, indeed! I was gloomy and sad.

The brethren went with me to the station, and at 5:14 I left for Glasgow, where I arrived in time to attend the evening meeting. A large number were present. After meeting Brother Neilson had a tale of woe to tell—so did Brother Hamilton. Things will soon reach a crisis in the organization of the branch. Jealousy is causing no end of trouble.

Monday, 14 November 1898

Letter from Father. Busy with office duties and conference correspondence. Wrote a letter to Tommy. Theodore Nystrom came from Germany, one or two others from England.

Tuesday, 15 November 1898

Letter came from Stirling, stating that Miss Sharp is no better. Called at Anchor Line office and arranged for saloon passage for seven. House full of returning elders. Relief Society meeting at night. Sister Martha Officer Leggat was chosen and set apart as second counselor to fill the vacancy made by Sister Harkins's resignation. All the officers were re-sustained and

---

[226]McKay originally wrote "it was unanimously agreed upon to put one," and then the last three words were crossed out. The contribution plate was to gather money to pay for the rental of the meeting hall.

the society started out once more. I wonder how long they will keep harmony and goodwill among them.

Wednesday, 16 November 1898
    Letter from the elders in Stirling, stating that they were called in to administer to Miss Sharp yesterday. As I had promised to visit her again this week, I took the ten o'clock train and arrived in Stirling at 11 A.M. She was not much better, but she testified to having obtained relief from the prayers and administration. Her mind wandered occasionally. The doctor is killing her. I do not believe he understands her trouble. Came back to Glasgow at 3 P.M. Committee meeting at night to arrange for the New Year soirée.

Thursday, 17 November 1898
    A busy day, indeed, from 7:30 A.M. to 3 P.M. Forty-nine of a company sailing! Changed tickets and settled grievance at the office. Meeting at 53 [Holmhead Street] at 10:30 to give necessary instruction to be heeded during the voyage. At the boat at 12:30; all on board at 1:30. The second-class passengers were dissatisfied with their accommodations. (Note: Hunting [for] "55 Port Dundas Road." Strange woman! Wrong address, etc.) Testimony meeting at night.

Friday, 18 November 1898
    Office correspondence. Went to *Evening News* office to settle bill for printing six memorandum books and 2,000 letterheads. Mr. McConochie very sociable, so are the young ladies. Letters from Stirling state that Annie is better. The elders administered to her again yesterday. In the evening members of the soirée committee called and plans were adopted for the successful arranging for the coming event. The Albion Hall is secured and tickets ordered [to be] printed. Wrote to Tommy.[227]

Saturday, 19 November 1898
    At 11:20 A.M. boarded the train going to Dunfermline, thence to Lochgelly. Welcomed by Mrs. Raeburn and husband and also by the elders, with whom I spent the afternoon and evening. Met all the acquaintances made when here before. Dr. Dendle was not at home, but Mrs. Nelson treated us courteously when we called. Left Lochgelly for Edinburgh via Thornton at 7:20 P.M. Met the elders and Brother Gracie at 7 Edina Place. We spent the evening at George White's. He and Mrs. White are true, open-hearted Latter-day Saints and they have a hearty welcome for every elder.

Sunday, 20 November 1898
    The morning hours were spent discussing the advisability of perform-

---

[227]McKay originally wrote the word "Father" and then wrote the word "Tommy" over it.

ing certain ordinations.[228]   It was agreed to ordain Brothers Gracie and Henderson (teachers) priests, also George White; and Brothers James White, Alex Rhynd, and Thomas Dahlgleish, teachers. Priesthood meeting at 1:30 P.M. and regular meeting at two, after which the priesthood meeting was continued and the above-named brethren ordained to the priesthood named.

Dined at Sister George White's. Evening meeting at 6:30, several strangers were present, besides nearly all the saints. A good spirit prevailed. The branch is in a good condition. After the evening meeting Brother Miller visited an investigator, and Brother Stirling, Sister White, David, and I went home with Brother and Sister Rhynd. We spent a pleasant evening, bidding our host and hostess good-night about 10 P.M.

Monday, 21 November 1898

Visited Brother George White, Sister M. Whyte, Brother Gracie and wife, and Brother Henderson and wife. Sister Henderson was unwell. Left Edinburgh at 5 P.M., arriving in Glasgow at 6:15. Elders Edward and Gould were all right. Mrs. [Duncan] Thomson called and spent an hour or so with us.[229] I accompanied her home and had a "bit crack" with her and Sister Robertson at their home on Comelypark Street. Later sent conference notice to Liverpool.

Tuesday, 22 November 1898

This being the week appointed to settle disputes between jealous members, I accordingly called on two, asking them or rather leaving word for them to come to the office tonight if they have any grievances. In the afternoon David and James Neilson came with horse and "machine"[230] to help remove the harmonium[231] hired from Robert Mauer to the hall, 9 Oxford Street. This will help us in our practice tomorrow night.

At 8 P.M. Brother Neilson and James[232] Leggat came in to make reconciliation one with another. After one hour and a half of explanation, accusation, and condemnation, they forgave each other, shook hands, and walked home together feeling all right. Brothers Halliday and Sneddon from Blantyre, and Brother Carney and [Sister] McDonald were waiting in another room; so as soon as the meeting was over they came in the room. A few minutes later Brother Hoggan came in hurriedly and requested us to

---

[228]McKay originally wrote "making certain ordinations."

[229]In his diary Gould added that Mrs. Thomson brought a bottle of olive oil to be consecrated. All three elders (McKay, Edward, and Gould) blessed the oil, with Edward being mouth. See William S. Gould, Diary, 21 November 1898.

[230]A *machine* refers to a horse-drawn passenger vehicle or small carriage.

[231]A *harmonium* or reed organ was a keyboard wind instrument in which a current of air from bellows acts on a set of free metal reeds or vibrators.

[232]This relates to the conflict mentioned at 10 November 1898, p. 154, above.

Fig. 39 *Sauchiehall Street, Glasgow.*

hasten to administer to his wife. Elder Edward and I accompanied him. She felt much relieved after the administration. Later [I walked] on Sauchiehall Street (Fig. 39).

Wednesday, 23 November 1898

Ground—or rather stones—covered with snow. Weather keen and piercing. Stayed in the office all day. Wrote to Claire and Cousin Josie. Brother Joseph Leggat called; he is feeling better. Singing practice at night. The harmonium hired is quite a help. After dismissal, listened to a long, monotonous, disagreeable recital of wrongs from Neilson. He thinks he is the most oppressed of men. O, it is disgusting to hear all the stories that are told!

Thursday, 24 November 1898

Four letters from Utah. Visited Sister Gain and enjoyed a nice, long talk with her. In the afternoon Brother Edward and I visited Brother and Sister Hoggan and Sister Anderson; the latter was rather *cold*. "Thanksgiving at home." Wondered where we shall be one year from tonight.[233] Testimony meeting.

Friday, 25 November 1898

Arranged for printing 250 bills for conference announcement. Bought linoleum for large room and attended to sundry duties. At night Brother Edward, Brother Gould, and I went to the Royalty to see the Royal Carl

---

[233]John T. Edward, Diary, 24 November 1898, explained: "In the evening Bro. McKay and I were sitting in front of the fire talking over the duties of missionaries, and as it was Thanksgiving day at home, we were wondering what we would be doing one year from that time and where we would be."

Rosa Company in the opera, *Tannhäuser*.[234] It was grand—inspiring! The theme is a very good one, showing Tannhäuser's faithfulness to his promise to Venus, although to remain "her doughty knight" cost him untold misery and finally death. The singing was fine.

Saturday, 26 November 1898

Wrote to Brother Pender. Put ad in *News*. Accepted proof of bill and had a pleasant conversation with Miss McGhie and Miss [blank]. They promised to attend conference.

At 2 P.M. had dinner with William and Martha Leggat, one of the nicest couples in the branch. At 4 P.M. at Sister Gain's, helping Maggie with her song for conference.

At seven back to conference house. Sunday School teachers meeting at eight. Brother Leggat, Brother Neilson, and Brother Hoggan have made restitution and will perhaps settle their difficulty without much more trouble.

Sunday, 27 November 1898

Priesthood meeting at 11 A.M. A little jealousy was manifest. Some of the local elders feel jealous because the saints call the traveling elders to administer to them. They were told to live their religion and honor their priesthood; the saints would then get confidence in them. Sunday School at 12:30; meetings at 2:00 and 6:30. Good attendance.

After the night meeting Brother Gould and I with Brother Carney went to Auchinairn and administered to a nonmember at his request—five miles![235]

Monday, 28 November 1898

Preparing for conference. Bought articles for conference house. Went to Maryhill and spent a fine, interesting afternoon with Brother and Sister Reid. Practiced song for conference. Went to Springburn; in doing so, rode past twelve stations for two pence! Practiced songs with Janet and Mary.

Tuesday, 29 November 1898

Busy with general preparations. Company sails next Thursday. Nellie Jack spent the evening.

Brother Gould, Brother Eccles, and I went to Springburn and administered to Sister [Jesse Ferguson] Mills. Teachers meeting in Sister McDonald's.

---

[234]Richard Wagner (1813-1883), a German composer, made fundamental and revolutionary changes in the structure of opera. He composed *Tannhäuser* in 1845.

[235]Gould anointed with oil and McKay sealed the anointing. See William S. Gould, Diary, 27 November 1898.

Wednesday, 30 November 1898
    Continued conference preparations. Bought a table from J. Neilson. Sister Neilson donated a carpet for the little room. The saints have contributed freely. Every room now is quite respectable. It is pronounced the best conference house in the mission. A few months ago we had the worst and no means with which to get a better one. Our way has been opened in a manner that exceeds our most sanguine expectations.
    Singing practice at night succeeded nicely. At the conference Sunday next Maggie Gain will sing "Kind Words Are Sweet Tones of the Heart"; Agnes Cooke Reid, "Beautiful Day of Rest"; and eight others, "When Shall We Meet Thee." The choir will join in the choruses of the first two mentioned.

Thursday, 1 December 1898
    At Anchor Line office, arranging tickets for passengers sailing today in S.S. *Ethiopia*. There are twelve adults and eight children, mostly Scandinavians and Germans. Testimony meeting at night.

Friday, 2 December 1898
    Put in a new grate—or better, had one put in—and finished furnishing conference house. Singing practice at night. At 10:30 P.M. four of us met President Wells, McMurrin, and Lyman[236] at the Central Station.

Saturday, 3 December 1898
    At 5:45 A.M. Elders [Walter J.] Knell and Allen[237] of the Irish Conference came in, sleepy and tired after their night's voyage. It being the presidency's wish to have the priesthood meeting tonight instead of Monday, I visited several of the local brethren, notifying them of the change.
    After dinner I accompanied Brother McMurrin. He visited his relatives, Mr. [Archie] Bell and family, 315 London Road; and Mr. George Williamson, Bothwell Park Villa, Cambuslang. At both places the people were courteous and sociable and extended an invitation to visit them again, which I promised Brother McMurrin I would accept.

---

[236]Platte De Alton Lyman (1848-1901) was the son of Apostle Amasa M. Lyman and Eliza Partridge. He was called on a two-year mission to England in April 1867, but the next month before leaving Salt Lake City he married Adelia Robison. From October 1875 to October 1876 he served a second mission to England. In 1879 he married Annie Maud Clark. From 1882 to 1884 he served as president of the San Juan Mission. From 1898 to 1901 he was president of the European Mission. As a compliment to McKay's efforts in refurbishing the headquarters at 53 Holmhead Street in June 1898, Lyman wrote in his diary that he "found good comfortable quarters" at the conference house. See the Platte De Alton Lyman Collection, Manuscript 65, Diary, 2 December 1898, located in the Manuscripts Division, J. Willard Marriott Library, University of Utah, Salt Lake City.
    [237]Thomas Lonsdale Allen, Jr. (1872-1965) was set apart on 4 May 1898 for a mission to Great Britain, arriving in Liverpool on 26 May 1898. He was assigned to the Irish Conference, and in December 1898 he was appointed as president of that conference. Allen was released in July 1900.

At 7 P.M. we were back to the conference house, which was then full of elders and saints. The priesthood meeting, held in the large room, was one of the best I have ever attended. An excellent spirit of unity prevailed and the reports of the elders were gratifying. The presidency was highly pleased with it. At 11 P.M. accompanied some of the elders and saints to the Argyle, Brother Gould having gone before to tell Mr. Doogan not to close the door until we reached there. Ten elders, including the presidency, stayed in the conference house. Slept with President Lyman.[238]

Sunday, 4 December 1898
Fast Day. Dull and stormy. Not very encouraging for an attendance at conference, yet—notwithstanding the rain—at 11 A.M. a good congregation was assembled in the north saloon of the [Glasgow] City Hall. Quite a number of strangers was present, among whom was a *Daily Record* reporter. After the opening exercises I made a few opening remarks and read the statistical report for the last seven months. The authorities of the Church and of the European Mission and Scottish Conference were presented and sustained unanimously. The speakers in the morning were Elders Robert Gilchrist, Thomas Gilchrist (president [of the] Newcastle Conference), and Joseph McKnight. "Beautiful Day of Rest," sung by Sister Reid and the choir, was well rendered.

The afternoon services were attended by a larger number of strangers than was the morning meeting. The hall was well-filled. The speakers were Walter J. Knell of the Irish Conference, Joseph Mitchell, and President McMurrin. The double quartet [sang] "When Shall We Meet Thee," [which] was quite well rendered. At the evening meeting Presidents Lyman and Wells (followed by a few closing remarks from Brother McMurrin) occupied the time. All spoke well and gave us a rare, spiritual feast. "Kind Words Are Sweet Tones of the Heart" by Maggie Gain and the choir was well sung and appreciated by the audience. After singing "The Spirit of God Like a Fire Is Burning" and benediction, the conference adjourned *sine die*.[239] It was pronounced a success.

Monday, 5 December 1898
President McMurrin and I visited Sister Hunter. Found her sick in bed. She had been praying for the elders to come administer to her. The satisfaction she expressed at our calling and the good it seemed to do her made us happy indeed. From here we went to the Anchor Line office where

---

[238]Because of a lack of sufficient sleeping accommodations, it was common for two elders to sleep in one bed. In fact, sometimes it was necessary to have three in one bed. For example, Joseph Mitchell, Diary, 13 September 1897, explained: "Bros. McKay, Bailey, and I slept in one bed—it was a tight squeeze."

[239]The Latin phrase *sine die*, literally "without a day," means that the conference was concluded without any specific date being designated for the next conference.

we were to meet Presidents Wells and Lyman. They had concluded to visit Ayr and in order to do so and make connection with afternoon train to Liverpool had to catch the 11:15 train from St. Enoch's. Thirty minutes only to go to "53" [Holmhead Street] and back to station! Hired a cab and made connections all right; but, just as the train was about to leave, President Wells dropped his ticket in the platform by the side of train! As it could not be reached, he had to go without it, the inspector promising to forward it to Ayr. Excitement!

President McMurrin returned to Liverpool by way of Edinburgh, leaving on the 1 P.M. train. He, too, went off in a hurry, being compelled to run a few hundred yards to catch train. He being so fat, the run fairly exhausted him; and his "Good-bye!—God bless you!—Thank you for many kindnesses!—Whose watch is right now?" were said between efforts to catch his breath.

The rest of the day was spent settling accounts. Miss Graham from Ayrshire was baptized and confirmed a member of the Church, [with] the confirmation meeting being held in the conference house. Several of the elders left for their fields of labor. A few changes were made at conference.

Tuesday, 6 December 1898

Visited places of interest in Glasgow with the brethren from Ireland. The cathedral, Kelvingrove Park (Fig. 40), Industrial Museum, and the Fossil Grove at Whiteinch were the most interesting.

Just as we were sitting down to tea, a telegram came, stating that Brother Orr, Newarthill, was very ill and requesting us to come at once. Brother [John S.] Smith and I accordingly boarded the 7:08 train and a little more than one hour later were at the bedside of Brother and Sister Orr, both of whom were ill. We administered to them, Brother Orr obtaining instant relief; his wife, however, felt about the same.

Came back to Glasgow at 9:35 from Holytown, two miles from Newarthill, a distance we had to walk both ways. Retired after midnight.

Fig. 40 *Kelvingrove Park, Glasgow.*

Wednesday, 7 December 1898

Visited the [Royal] Asylum for the Blind and while doing so spent about two of the most interesting and instructive hours of my life. (For particulars see circular back of book.)[240] After dinner, the party—Elders Knell, Allen, Gould, and I (McKnight and Smith stayed at home)—went to the Botanical Gardens. Brothers Knell and Allen returned to Ireland at night, accompanied by Elders McKnight and Smith.

Thursday, 8 December 1898

Busy all day making out financial and missionary reports for the month of November. Elder Edward assisted. Testimony meeting at night.

Friday, 9 December 1898

Spent the morning hours writing. In the afternoon Elders Edward, Gould, and I ransacked a Xmas card shop, selecting suitable presents for the folks at home—suitable for them and our purses as well. Spent my last six pence. Sent gloves to Mamma and a nice handkerchief to Father. The evening was occupied in writing verses and preparing the cards for posting. Elder [John] Houston, now released, came in from Newcastle.

Saturday, 10 December 1898

In the morning continued the work of last night. Attended to conference correspondence.

About 3 P.M. went with Brother Houston to visit a friend of his, who holds some position in connection with the Barnhill Poorhouse. He was "off duty," so we were informed. During the few moments talk with the gateman, we learned that there are 1,800 inmates and only 800 of these working! The others are supported by the city. There is another besides this one.

At night Maggie, Jeanie, Brother and Sister Graham spent an hour or so. The rest of the time before retiring was occupied in studying. Brother [Neil L.] Gardner also, released, came in from Nottingham.[241]

Sunday, 11 December 1898

Attended the usual Sunday services: Sunday School and two meetings. There is a fine class of young men in the school; the young women were absent this morning. A good spirit prevailed throughout the day. Several of the young men spoke during the day.

---

[240]The leaflet about the Royal Asylum for the Blind that McKay placed at the back of his diary has not survived. However, John T. Edward, Diary, 29 December 1898, pointed out that the 250 blind people there made door mats, willow baskets, and wool and straw mattresses.

[241]John T. Edward, Diary, 10 December 1898, took Gardner on a stroll through the streets of Glasgow, saying: "In the evening I took him out to see Glasgow and I don't think I ever saw so many drunken men and women on the street in my life at one time before."

Monday, 12 December 1898

While walking down to the office of the *Daily Mail*, Brother Edward was seized with a severe pain just to the right and below the pit of the stomach. It seems to be an attack of the same nature as the one that confined him to his room once before. The object of our going to the *Mail* was to get the editor to insert a refutation of some charges which appeared in the columns of the *Weekly Mail* last week (December fifth), in which it was asserted that the Mormons are decoying young girls to Utah. The article was copied from a Welsh paper.[242] Elder Edward wrote to Wales and received the contradiction, which also appeared in the papers there. The editor of the *Mail* promised to print it in tomorrow's issue.

Later Brother Edward had to go to bed. We (Brother Gould and I) administered to him,[243] applied a hot bag of water to the painful part, and [he] seemed to get immediate relief.

In the afternoon I visited Sister McDonald to see how her children are, as we heard yesterday that the little ones were unwell. They are suffering from colds. Spent a pleasant two-hour chat with her and Sister Carney. They have had to meet some taunts regarding the libelous article which appeared in the *Mail*. I read them Dr. Parry's testimony or statement, told them the character of the author of the article in the *Mail*, and then asked them to judge for themselves.

Had a few minutes private talk with Sister Carney, during which she expressed herself too freely for her own happiness. I told her I took the expressions as coming from a sisterly feeling and nothing more. Surprised! (Thankful as I walked home that all went well!) (Goodness! "What might have been!")

When I reached the conference house, Brother Edward was resting easily. Relief Society meeting at night, seven members present. A good spirit prevailed. Two women who absented themselves are working mischief with their stories and sarcastic remarks.

Tuesday, 13 December 1898

Wrote letter to Elder Muir's father [John W. Muir]. Wrote to Brother Johnston also.

Elder Edward is better this morning. I have been bothered today in regard to what should be done in his case. The conditions are unfavorable to his health, and yet he begs me not to write for his release. He is anxious to fulfil his mission and, if God will help him, he will do it. The refutation article appears in today's *Mail*, but it is *condensed*.

At night attended a surprise party at Sister Harkins. It was arranged

---

[242]Alfred W. Trenchard of Cardiff made the allegations in "Mormon Decoys in Wales," which was printed in the *Western Mail*, 30 November 1898.

[243]William S. Gould, Diary, 12 December 1898, added the information that "Pres. D. O. McKay desired that I should anoint with oil, while he was mouth in sealing the anointment."

by Sister Greer. The evening was spent very pleasantly, although several remarks dropped during the early part of the evening showed the feeling these two women have toward us elders.

Wednesday, 14 December 1898

Wrote to Brother Johnston. Sent card to Tommy. Visited some of the saints and one nonmember from whom I learned all about the disgraceful actions of one of our drunken members. He has been before the priesthood once, and it seems he will be again before long. Goodness! If one would judge our Church by the actions of some of the members in Glasgow, he would shun it as he would the hottest corner of H--l! Thank heaven, some others are doing their duty.

At 7 P.M., in company with Brother Houston, visited his cousin, Mr. Houston, assistant governor of the Barnhill Poorhouse. He received us kindly and seemed to enjoy the evening's chat. He offered to spend an afternoon explaining to us all the "in's and out's" of the institution wherein he works. I anticipate a pleasant and instructive day in the near future.

As the boat sails tomorrow, the conference house is full of elders. We retired about 10:15 intending to get a good night's rest; but just as I was dozing, a cab stopped outside and a knock at the door caused me to get up. Two more missionaries had just arrived. They sent no word of their coming. The beds were all full, so there was nothing else but dress and lead them to the hotel. As we do this often, it caused little annoyance.

An unusual experience, however, followed. A young man, not a member of the Church [but who] was intending to emigrate with this company of elders, had not been seen by any of us since noon. As the elder whom he was accompanying had gone to Edinburgh about that time, we concluded that he had changed his mind and gone with the elder. Either this or he was lost. This was our conclusion when we retired. He had neither gone to Edinburgh nor was he lost; but being homesick, sad, or whatnot, he had sought comfort in the "fiery dram."[244] When I returned from the hotel, he was sitting by the door quite intoxicated! With some little difficulty, I got him into bed. The poor fellow seemed to realize his condition and he cried like a child. Before leaving his mother's side, he promised her that he would not taste liquor. He signed the "pledge,"[245] and now on the first night after leaving home, he yields to temptation and breaks his word!

Thursday, 15 December 1898

Our friend who imbibed too freely last night seems to be very downhearted this morning. Not a word is said about last night's proceedings.

---

[244]A *dram* was a small portion of something to drink. In this case, *fiery dram* refers to an alcoholic beverage.

[245]A *pledge* was a contract binding oneself to total abstinence from intoxicating drink.

We shall do our best to show him that we are his friends.

The boat sails at 1:15 P.M.; seven passengers comprise our company. Met Brother Houston's relatives—two young men from Paisley. Invited us to call on them. Wrote to Liverpool. Testimony meeting at night.

Fine encouraging letters from Papa and Tommy this morning.

Friday, 16 December 1898

Sent out letters to branches, thanking the members for conference contributions. At night went with Brother Edward to visit his relatives—Mrs. [Mary] McMinn[246] and family. Mr. and Mrs. Gray were there, also. Mrs. McMinn had prepared an excellent tea, which was followed by fruit and refreshments. The evening was spent in general conversation and in singing.

They would not approach the subject of religion. The views of Utah were shown them, and after singing several of Sankey[247] and Moody's[248] hymns, we concluded with "O My Father, Thou That Dwellest." The words we had with us and I played it on the organ without the music. The girls sang it well and had an interest awakened. Besides this, nothing in regard to religion was said or done. As we bid them good-night, they extended a cordial invitation to return.

Saturday, 17 December 1898

Wrote to Bishop [Walter J.] Beatie concerning the actions and standing of Mrs. Greer. Attended to general conference duties. At 5:30 P.M. Brother Edward and I visited Brother and Sister Alex Hoggan, taking "tea" (warm water and milk) with them. Brother Hoggan has been yielding to temptation. I believe our visit did him good. We advised them to save their money and not live up to every cent that is earned, as they have been doing all along and as the working class in Scotland usually do. Brother McKnight stayed in the conference house.

At 8:15 we were again at the conference house where, according to promise, Brother and Sister Reid were waiting for us. They had been waiting for an hour or so. Spent the evening singing. They are a fine couple. Received letter from Claire—one of the best yet—and another from my old friend, John Hall, with a *five*[-dollar bill] enclosed.

Sunday, 18 December 1898

Sunday School at twelve. Meetings as usual. Brother McKnight occupied most of the time in the afternoon and D. O. [David O. McKay] at night. We ate dinner with Brother and Sister Reid in Maryhill, Agnes having

---

[246]In both cases in this entry, McKay incorrectly wrote "McMurrin" for Elder Edward's Aunt Mary McMinn. The text has been corrected.

[247]Ira D. Sankey (1840-1908) was an American evangelistic singer, organist, and song-leader.

[248]Dwight L. Moody (1837-1899) was an American charismatic evangelist.

prepared a meal—enticing, tasty, and substantial. Maryhill is four miles from our meeting place. We were five minutes late for the evening meeting. Two applications for baptisms after the meeting: one, Brother Cairney's little girl [Susan] and a Mr. [David] Bell, a young man sixteen years old.

Monday, 19 December 1898

Had another photo taken. Wrote article for a daily paper. Received a communication from President Lyman that we are to prepare for the coming lectures on Utah to be delivered here by an Elder Palmer[249] during the month of February.

At night visited Sister Robertson and Mrs. [Duncan] Thomson. Mrs. [Thomas] Thomson from Shettleston was there, also. There is no place in Scotland that I visit that makes me feel better than I do while visiting here. They are really fine women. We cannot get an opportunity to talk to the men.

Tuesday, 20 December 1898

Copied two letters of the article written yesterday for the press. Elder McKnight took one to the editor of the *Daily Mail* and I took the other to *Daily Record*. I do not know whether the entire article will be printed or not. Part of it will. Brother McKnight and I visited Brother Neilson and Mrs. Good.

At 7 P.M. Elder Edward and I went to visit a Mr. [George] Sawers, captain of the S.S. *City of Rome*. Brother Edward had a letter of introduction to him from Mr. Brixen, who sent money to purchase books for the captain.[250] He received us kindly and seemed to be very sociable. He was surprised when we told him we neither indulged in tobacco nor strong drink. "O," said he, "that debars me from joining your church." He promised to attend our meetings. One hour's conversation with an intelligent man like Mr. Sawers is worth a week's association with some of these narrow-minded, orthodox Christians.

After reaching home, commenced a letter to Claire. I have not written to her for some time. She writes encouragingly to me, too.

Wednesday, 21 December 1898

Received a letter from David R. Finished Claire's letter. Wrote to John Hall and Mamma.

The daily papers have printed our letter in its entirety. I hope it will do

---

[249]George W. Palmer (1867-1948) was set apart for a mission to Great Britain on 19 April 1897, arriving in Liverpool on 12 May 1897. He was assigned to the London Conference, but during the last months of his mission he traveled and lectured on "Utah and the Mormons." Palmer was released in April 1899 and returned to Utah the following month.

[250]John T. Edward, Diary, 20 December 1898, indicated that they gave the captain a copy of the Book of Mormon and Parley P. Pratt's *Voice of Warning*.

some good. It will tend to counteract the influence of that libelous article from Wales. Singing practice at night at "53" [Holmhead Street]. Quite a number of the young folks were present. S.S. [i.e., Sunday School songs] were practiced.

Thursday, 22 December 1898

Visited one of our would-be pious brethren, who for several months now has been neglecting his duties and reveling in drink. After some conversation, he expressed his determination to renew his attendance at meetings and to again try to take up his duties. I hope he will have stamina and backbone enough to carry his determinations into effect. The afternoon was spent in writing to Brother Calder and attending to conference duties. Testimony meeting at night.

Friday, 23 December 1898

Elder Edward and I called on Sister Gain, who, as we learned last night, is lying sick. She said as we shook hands with her that she was suffering of a severe cold; but there is something worse troubling her—her mind is worried. For some time past she has received no word from her husband in Australia; her rent is past due. These and other circumstances are preying heavily upon her. She cried as though her heart would break.

Later Elder McKnight and I called on Sister Anderson. Spent the evening with her and her husband.

Saturday, 24 December 1898

After posting some Xmas cards, Brother McKnight and I visited Sister Gain and found her feeling somewhat better, although still confined to her bed. Received several Xmas presents—some were given a day or so back:

One white satin necktie and Xmas card, [from] Brother and Sister William Reid.

One pair knit socks and Xmas cards, Sister Maggie Gain.

One necktie and Xmas card, Sister Elizabeth Neilson.

Cake (for all of us) and Xmas card, Sister [Sandy] Steven.

At 4:30 P.M. Brothers Neilson and Leggat came to the conference house, according to appointment, to consider branch matters. All went fine and smoothly at first, but they crossed swords later and Brother Leggat became quite warm. Once he sprang from his chair and stamped his foot apparently in quite a rage. But he sat down again, and although the spirit that was manifested hindered us from accomplishing much, still I learned much of the men's characters, which I believe will be helpful. They were feeling better when we parted. Brother Neilson thinks he has not enough power given him and Brother Leggat thinks Brother Neilson tries to exert too much—acts too independently of him as his counselor. Brother Neilson thinks, too, that he does not get an opportunity to preach often enough! He used to preach the people to death, relating visions and dreams! Now because he is asked to speak no oftener than a presiding officer should do, he thinks he is oppressed. O my! how little do some men understand the true spirit of the gospel! Our meeting lasted three hours! Several of the young folks came up, but I did not speak to them as they left about 8 P.M.

While feeling a little discouraged, the postman brought a fine, loving letter from dear Mamma and a dainty, loving card from Annie. To read Mamma's encouraging words would banish the most gloomy feelings. I thank God for loving parents and affectionate brothers and sisters! Where true love reigns, there heaven is found. The three[251] of us took an evening stroll. Although Christmas eve, nothing unusual was seen. Saturday night drunks were as numerous as ever.

Inquired at a Catholic church if special midnight services were to be held and were told that the first service would not be until 6 A.M. The priest to whom we spoke was under the influence of liquor! A professing servant of Christ, officiating in a house built to worship God in, was steeped in whiskey, his face was debauched, his eyes red and watery! "The mystery of iniquity doth already work: only he who now letteth will let, until the son of perdition be revealed" [2 Thes. 2:3, 7].

12:30 P.M. Christmas Eve! Two years ago at about this hour I was with my brother and sisters going from a pleasant party!

> When I was playing with my brother,
>   Happy was I,
> O, take me to my loving mother,
>   There let me live and die.

This just about expressed my feelings tonight. I would like to peep into the dear old home and see the little ones preparing for Santa Claus! Perhaps one year from tonight will find us all in the happy home. Heaven grant that this be so!

Sunday, 25 December 1898

As Elders Edward, McKnight, and I arose from our beds, we greeted each other with a "I wish you a Merry Xmas," but the half-hearted manner in which it was expressed showed that there was a doubt that the wish would be realized. Priesthood meeting, Sunday School, and meetings as usual. The stormy scene and bad feeling manifested last night in our meeting made me fear today's meetings would feel the effects. But earnest prayers were answered and a better day throughout is seldom enjoyed. Our Xmas dinner was eaten at Sister Neilson's. While we were eating, Lizzie succeeded in catching Brother McKnight "under the mistletoe." Christmas night found us feeling in better spirits than Xmas morning. We were somewhat tired—Sunday's *strain* usually leaves us feeling so—but as we knelt to have our evening prayers, each one felt thankful for Xmas of 1898.

---

[251]This refers to John T. Edward, Joseph McKnight, and David O. McKay.

Monday, 26 December 1898

The postman's ring—or rather what we received when we answered his ring—made us all feel that Xmas is still here. Cards came from local friends (Miss R[ennie] and Miss Sh[arp]. Claire's photo, an excellent one, and Winnifred's also was received; but the *neatest* present was a beautifully bound volume of Tennyson's *Poems*[252] sent with "Xmas wishes" from Claire.

Visited Sister Gain and tried to cheer her up a bit. She has not heard from her husband for some time and she is worrying. Found her feeling better. At noon enjoyed a Xmas dinner prepared by Mrs. Noble and Georgina.[253] Mrs. Clunie and Miss [Nellie] Jack called in the evening. At 7:30 P.M. attended a Free Church Sunday School concert. Singing *fair*.

Tuesday, 27 December 1898

At the conference house most of the day, except an hour or so spent at Brother Cairney's. The afternoon and evening were stormy; a fierce gale was blowing and every little while the rain came down in torrents! Telegraph wires were demolished—or so broken that communication was stopped, chimney tops were blown down, and a sort of "besom of destruction" [Isa. 14:23] seemed to reign!

Notwithstanding the storm, according to previous arrangements, three baptisms were attended to: Georgina Ferguson, Susan M. Cairney (eleven years old), and David Bell (seventeen) were the persons baptized. I officiated for the first time in my life. The ordinance was performed in the Townhead Baths—the large pond.

There were two applications for rebaptisms.[254] But after talking the matter over, it was thought best not to attend to their request until other steps were first taken. One of the persons is a young man, twenty-four years of age, who made a confession to me that was truly sad. He has transgressed and by so doing has burdened himself for life! He has made another unhappy, also.

> To temptation the young man yielded,
>   By the influence of passion, he became unshielded;
> Out of season partook of "forbidden fruit,"
>   And now henceforth will forever rue it.

Wednesday, 28 December 1898

Wrote to Mamma and I[saac] W. McKay.

---

[252]*The Poetic and Dramatic Works of Alfred, Lord Tennyson* (Boston: Houghton Mifflin and Co., 1898).

[253]Georgina Ferguson was Mrs. Noble's daughter by her first husband.

[254]H. Dean Garrett, "Rebaptism," in *Encyclopedia of Mormonism*, ed. Daniel H. Ludlow (New York: Macmillan Publishing Co., 1992), 3:1194, stated that in the nineteenth century "many members were rebaptized as an act of rededication."

In the conference house all day. At 6 P.M. Brother Edward's aunt[255] came from Aberdeen. She will stop with us in the conference house, although, I dare say, she will be timid—or suspicious—of so many Mormons.

Singing practice at 8 P.M. The young folks came out in force and result was an excellent practice. Charles Stevenson, on his way home, came in from London about 9 P.M. It seemed good to meet him. Returning elders are arriving. About one third of the company sailing next Friday are women —young women, too! Miss Edward will think they are "Mormon decoys" [for] sure!

Thursday, 29 December 1898

Visited several of the saints. Attended to office duties and conference correspondence. Testimony meeting at night.

Friday, 30 December 1898

Exchanged tickets, held a short meeting with the company, and at 11:30 went to the quay. The boat sailed at 12:45 P.M. The passengers (LDS) were well-satisfied. Wrote to Liverpool. Before coming to the conference house, Brother Edward and his aunt, Miss [Libbie] Edward, Elders McKnight, Mc-Quarrie, a Brother Walker from Wales, and I went aboard the S.S. *Ethiopia*, lying at anchor, and had an excellent opportunity to see the state rooms, dining rooms, etc. The *Ethiopia* is not so nicely fitted up as some of the others. Pantomime at night, *'Mid Summer Night's Dream*.

Saturday, 31 December 1898

Wrote to Claire and Winnifred. Sent off a few New Year cards to friends who sent me Xmas greetings or presents.

At 5 P.M. the elders from Airdrie and Hamilton came in. Brother Leatham is not looking well. He is a man that says but little, and since conference time, I fancy he has not been feeling well in spirit. A talk with Brother Mitchell, his companion, revealed the fact that Brother Leatham is very unwell, being subject to weak spells caused by a weakness of the heart. Other things unpleasant in their nature regarding the feeling in Airdrie are quite discouraging! I often feel that the responsibility is too much!

Brother and Sister Reid, Maggie and Jeanie Gain, Janet Graham, and others called about 6:30 P.M. Mrs. Graham, Janet's mother, donated to the conference house two pairs [of] curtains and sent two large cakes, oranges, grapes, apples, and "sweeties" to the elders.

At 8 P.M. I managed to leave to fill an appointment at Martha Leggat's, where we promised sometime ago to spend "Hogmanay."[256] Brother Mc-

---

[255]McKay incorrectly wrote "cousin" here and at 30 December 1898; both have been corrected to "aunt." At 31 December 1898 McKay gave the correct "aunt." John T. Edward's diary gave her name as "Aunt Libbie."

[256]*Hogmanay* refers to the last day of the year, and it also refers to the gift of an oatcake

Quarrie and Brother McKnight went down first to fill the appointment on time. Brother Edward and his aunt followed after me. We spent a very pleasant social evening, chatting jovially and eating cake and fruit until the Old Year breathed his last. "Mistletoe." Old "Hogmanay" tales were told. Customs now dying out were spoken about. One was the custom children had of running from house to house, crying:

> Rise up, guid wife, an' shake yer fithers!
>   Dinna think that we are beggars.
> We're but bairns come to play;
>   Rise and gie us our "Hogmanay."
> Our feet's cauld; our sheen's thin—
>   Give us a piece[257] an' let us rin!"

As the clock struck twelve, the whistles began to blow and the bells began to ring. We watched the Old Friend die; with a feeling of mingled joy and sorrows, we welcomed the New Year gladly, wishing each other "Many, many returns of the day!" Bid Martha and Willie good-morning and took our first New Year walk and New Year ride for 1899 to the conference house. A beautiful New Year present was awaiting me. It came from Annie [Sharp], and the neatness of the present, a lovely white necktie, showed an excellent taste in choosing!

---

or biscuit which was given to or asked for by children. For adults Hogmanay referred to any form of hospitality but especially a drink (such as ginger cordial) given to a guest to celebrate the New Year.

[257] A *piece* refers to a snack, especially a slice of bread or scone with butter and jam, which was given as a Hogmanay present to children.

DAVID O. McKAY
MISSIONARY DIARY THREE
"A FEW HAPPENINGS OF
MY DAILY LIFE"
(CONTINUED)

Sunday, 1 January 1899

O NE YEAR AGO I sat in silent meditation, wondering where I would be and how I would be feeling one year hence! Well, here I am about the same lad as of old. The experiences of the last year have been many and varied—and I hope *profitable*. They have taught me to appreciate the truths of the gospel and to feel thankful that I was born of kind, loving parents in the valleys of the mountains among a people who in *morals*, *freedom* of *thought*, and *true religion* lead the world.

This day was spent about the same as an ordinary Sunday in Glasgow. Sunday School at twelve noon, meeting at 2 P.M., after which three of us— Elders McKnight, McQuarrie, and I—went to Springburn and enjoyed an excellent New Year's dinner with Sister McDonald. This was according to arrangements made two weeks ago. Brother Edward stayed with his aunt [Libbie Edward] in the conference house.

Meeting again at 6:30 P.M. When we reached the conference house at night, we were all quite happy and felt to say that New Year's Day had been well spent. An excellent spirit prevailed throughout all the meetings and our associations were as pleasant as one could wish. New Year greetings were exchanged with a hearty good cheer, manifesting the warmest of true brotherly feeling.

Glasgow, Monday, 2 January 1899
In the conference house during the day. Some of the young saints and elders came in, prepared for the Airdrie soirée at night.

At 5 P.M. Elders McKnight and McQuarrie, Brother Peter Tucker, Lizzie Gain, Jeanie Gain, Janet Graham, and I left Queen Street Station for Airdrie. We first went to the elders' lodgings, and some remaining there, two or three of us accompanied by Elder Leatham called on Sister [Margaret] Graham. She gave us "oor Nair-Day"[258] and before leaving presented me with a beautiful, silk handkerchief and New Year's cards.

She accompanied us to the party, which was held in the Socialists' Hall, Chapel Street. As we entered, we were greeted by many we knew and by some we did not know. The little hall was quite filled. Tea was served—lemonade and milk to the elders—and an impromptu program was rendered. Each one tried to do his best to make every other one happy; so, of course, a real enjoyable time was the result.

At the conclusion of the program Brother McKnight and I excused ourselves and hastened to Coatbridge (three miles) to catch the 12:45 train to Glasgow. The other elders remained in the hall all night, dancing, playing games, singing, eating, etc. After about three-fourths of an hour of splashing through mud, we arrived at Coatbridge and had the pleasure (?) of waiting thirty minutes for the train. It was 2 A.M. before our heads touched the pillows.

Glasgow, Tuesday, 3 January 1899

About 5:30 A.M. we were aroused from dreamy slumber by the ring of the doorbell. An elder and two girls from the Irish Conference stood at the door when I opened it. They have come over to attend the annual soirée to be held tomorrow night. At 3 P.M. Elders Edward and McQuarrie, Miss Edward, Miss [Maggie] Kelly, Miss Kerr, and I, according to previous appointment, went to Maryhill and spent the afternoon with Brother and Sister Reid. Later we went to the Glen and spent an hour with Mr. and Mrs. McCairns. The conference house is full to overflowing with elders and saints from surrounding districts. Four will secure beds in the Argyle.

Wednesday, 4 January 1899

During the morning hours Elder Edward and I called to see Sister Harkins who, we learned yesterday, is ill. Found her feeling better. At twelve M. [meridian] I was at the Albion Halls with the committee on arrangements for the soirée tonight. They have secured the large hall and prospects for a good time are bright. Spent the afternoon with the company at "53" [Holmhead Street].

At 7 P.M. we were at the hall ready for our "tea." The committee had a side-room prepared for us and told us to remain there until all the others were seated around the tables in the main body of the hall. The elders were to occupy seats on the platform, where two nice tables were spread for them.

---

[258]The term *oor Nair-Day* means "our New Year's Day present" and traditionally was a drink along with some shortbread or cake.

As chairman of the evening, I was presented with a beautiful badge—a present from the members of the committee. I shall keep it as a souvenir of the pleasant evening spent and as a token of respect from the *givers*. After all present had partaken of the lunch set before them, the concert began. It consisted mostly of songs from the young boys and girls in the Glasgow Branch. Each one did his or her part in a manner that was commendable.

At 10:15 the room was prepared for dancing, but the musician was not present; so everyone gave way to the children who played "Wee Ba' Baberty" to their hearts' content and to the *discontent* of all who appreciate good order. The people's patience was about abating when the musician finally arrived. The music was an English concertina.[259] The grand march, though too slow, was nevertheless very good. The dances following were just as enjoyable as any I ever had at home. About twelve midnight refreshments were served and a few more songs sung. Then dancing was again indulged in. Four o'clock in the morning found the dancers enjoying the last dance. When the music stopped, there was even a look of regret in some of the faces because the dance was closing so early!

One reason—the principal one—for keeping the entertainment up until the morning hours is this. The saints from surrounding districts have no place to go except to the hotel and this would incur unnecessary expense; so in order to make the evening pleasant and the morning hours short until *train time* (five, six, or seven, as the case might be), the singing and dancing, etc. is continued. It would be better to commence it earlier in the afternoon and dismiss in time to catch the last train.

Accompanied the Steven family to the station. When I got to the conference house, elders were dozing in every corner. Some were in bed, others on the couch, while others were on the floor or in chairs! (I afterward learned that they had been very rude and noisy upon entering.) "O, what a difference in the morning!"

Thursday, 5 January 1899

At 8:30, while we were still napping, the postman brought American mail. Some of the elders were too sleepy to even read their letters. I received one from Father and another from Tommy. Some of us ate our breakfast at the usual hour—nine o'clock, while others preferred to sleep. Miss [Maggie] Scott, Brother Edward's cousin, and Miss [Libbie] Edward occupied the "little bedroom," it being too *early* for Miss Scott to go home. They joined the sleepy company about 10 A.M. and spent the day with us. The girls from Ireland—Miss Kelly and Miss Kerr—were here also.

Nothing was done during the day. I felt as though it would have been better to have come home at a reasonable hour. Elders Stewart, Wickens,

---

[259] A *concertina* was an accordion-like musical instrument, composed of a bellows with two faces or ends, on which are placed the various stops or studs by the action of which air is admitted to the metallic reeds that produce the sounds.

Miller, Nisbet, and Eccles left for their fields of labor. The feelings today prove the truth of the poet's words:

> Pleasures are like poppies spread,
>   You seize the flower—its bloom is shed;
> Or like the snow falls on the river,
>   A moment white, then gone forever.[260]

Note: Brother Leggat came up about 11 A.M. What for? Question. Talking with Brother Miller at the time. Asked him to stop in room. Left in about two minutes. Reason solved.

Testimony meeting at night. Significant hymn given out by Brother Neilson. His remarks afterward showed that he feels that he was not sufficiently honored last night. "Puir buddy!" He has a hard time of it! Some of the elders could hardly keep awake—much to the chagrin of the others. We had a very good meeting all the same.

Friday, 6 January 1899

In the conference house most of the day. Miss Edward went home to Aberdeen. She seemed to have a much warmer feeling toward the Mormons than she had when she first came. The Misses [Bessie, Jessie, and Maggie] Scott were at the station.

Began to make out monthly reports. Elder [Louis C.] Duncan and Miss Kerr left for Ireland at 11 P.M. Miss Kelly will stop in Glasgow. Received word of the death of Brother [John] Napier's little boy.

Saturday, 7 January 1899

At 12:15 Elders McKnight, Gould, and I went to the Hamilton Palace Colliery and conducted the funeral services over the remains of the little son of John Napier. He has been excommunicated, but his wife is still a member of the Church.

About fifteen strangers were present, most of them being her relatives. We sang "Weep Not for Him That's Dead and Gone." Prayer by Brother Gould. Singing, "Your Sweet Little Rosebud Has Left You." Brother McKnight then spoke a few minutes upon the atonement of Christ, making his remarks very appropriate. I followed him, speaking such words of comfort and counsel as I thought fit, concluding by reading the hymn "Farewell, All Earthly Honors" and pronouncing the benediction. The child was buried in Hamilton.[261]

It was 5:13 P.M. before we again reached Napier's. After tea and a short talk with those present, we bid them good-bye and walked to Bothwell (Fig. 41), accompanied by Brothers [John and Alexander] Sneddon. Brother

---

[260]Robert Burns, "Tam o' Shanter," in *The Complete Illustrated Poems, Songs and Ballads of Robert Burns* (Secaucus, NJ: Chartwell Books, 1990), 243. Burns wrote "then *melts* for ever."

[261]William S. Gould, Diary, 7 January 1899, added that McKay offered the prayer for the dedication of the grave.

Fig. 41 *A Street in Bothwell, Lanarkshire.*

Gould stopped in Hamilton. Arrived in Glasgow at 7:30. Sunday School meeting in the large room.

Sunday, 8 January 1899

At 10 A.M. left Queen Street in a bus for Airdrie. At Coatbridge Sister Gates came in. So I had company to the meeting, which convened at twelve noon. There was a good attendance. We (Elder Mitchell and I) accepted Sister Graham's invitation to dinner, after enjoying which we walked to Newarthill, where an evening meeting was held in Brother Orr's house.[262] Brother Leatham had met with the saints here in the afternoon. The good spirit which characterized the Airdrie meeting prevailed here also. After dismissal, I had an hour's talk with Sister Jack. Her "testimony is not weakened, but her spirits are dampened" by the foolish actions and thoughtless words of some of the injudicious members.

Walked back to Airdrie—twenty miles. Stayed with the elders.

Airdrie, Monday, 9 January 1899

Got an opportunity to inquire about Brother Leatham's health. I have been informed that his heart is affected and that occasionally he is suddenly seized with fainting spells. He told me his health has been good all during his mission and that he is feeling well now. Left Airdrie at 10:15 A.M.

At the conference house found a letter waiting [for] me from Brother Kesler,[263] president of Eastern States Mission, stating that he would arrive

---

[262]Joseph H. Mitchell, Diary, 8 January 1899, added that "at both meetings [McKay] gave some excellent instructions."

[263]Alonzo P. Kesler (1868-1918) was set apart in January 1894 for a mission to Great Britain and returned in February 1896. He served as president of the Eastern States Mission from 1897 to 1899. Kesler worked as postmaster in Salt Lake City from 1904 until his death.

in Glasgow about the tenth. Spent the day making out monthly reports. Relief Society meeting at night. Only seven sisters were present.

Tuesday, 10 January 1899
   Still at reports, [with] Brother Edward assisting. He is the best hand around the office that can be found anywhere. The yearly reports show that there have been seventy-one baptisms as compared to fifty-five last year and that the amount of tithing paid this year is £12/7/0 more than the corresponding amount last year. £58/1/7 is the total amount this year. There are forty-one tithe payers this year (1898), thirty-seven last (1897).
   The statistical report for the Scottish Conference for the year ending December 31, 1898, is as follows: missionaries, 14; local priesthood: elders, 30; priests, 12; teachers, 16; deacons, 10; members, 270; total officers and members, 325; children under eight years, 109; total number souls, 434; baptisms, 71; emigrated: over eight years old, 13; under eight, 2; excommunicated, 4; died, 8; received, 8; removed, 9; strangers' houses visited: in tracting, 33,112; by invitation, 1,511; gospel conversations, 2,488; tracts distributed, 90,229; books distributed, 384; meetings held: 2,760 indoor and 764 outdoor.
   Note: Janet [Lang]'s letter. Proposal—advice sought.

Wednesday, 11 January 1899
   Brother Kesler arrived here about 10 A.M. Went with him to see Mr. Aitchison, agent, Anchor Line. Most of the day was occupied by general conference duties and copying reports. The three elders went to the pantomime in the Royalty. Singing practice kept me in. We had a good practice.
   About 6 P.M. Sister Cairney was here and in private conversation told me some facts regarding the condition and feelings of the woman connected with the case of the young man referred to in December.[264]

Thursday, 12 January 1899
   Brother Kesler left for London on the 8:45 train. The day was spent in the office.
   At night Brother McKnight and I visited Mr. McColl according to his letter of invitation. Mrs. McColl met us at the door and by her cordial welcome and pleasant manner made us feel at home at once. The object of our visit was to discuss the subject of religion. So after tea served at 6:30, the conversation began in real earnest. Mr. McMinn, also an invited guest and an intimate friend of Mr. McColl, did most of the talking on our host's side of the question. They are spiritualists;[265] they reject the Bible as being the

---

[264]See David O. McKay, Diary, 27 December 1898, p. 170, above.
   [265]Spiritualists believe that the spirit component of a person survives bodily death and that one can communicate with spirits of the dead through a "medium."

word of God and will not accept Christ as being the savior of mankind. The arguments advanced against Christianity were different from any I have before heard. Confucius, they said, preached practically the same doctrine. We worship the "Pauline conception of Christ." "No man hath seen God at any time" [John 1:18]. "Bible contradictions." "The Jews' idea of Christ." These were some of their points; and the manner in which they were put made their refutation quite difficult. However, the evening was truly a pleasant one and, I believe, very profitable.

Note: Bro. Mitchell came in. Relating to Janet's case, etc., etc.

Miss McMinn is a medium, but she did not feel inclined to give any manifestations that night, although we asked her to do so. She did not like it when we said that her manifestations were from an evil source. "Will you tell me," said she emphatically, "how it is, if these spirits are evil, that I see a halo of light around them." "Do you really see this?" I asked. "Yes," she replied unhesitatingly. After being told that "His Satanic Majesty can 'appear as an angel of light'" [D&C 128:20; 129:8], she made no answer. It was eleven o'clock before we bid them good-night, promising to spend another such evening in the near future.

As far as the argument on the divine authenticity of the Bible is concerned, we got badly worsted for we did not successfully meet their points, but in regard to the Godhead, our object here on earth, and "good and bad spirits," I believe we held our own.

Note: Ran against iron fence running for car—stiff hat! cape, etc., etc.

Friday, 13 January 1899

Brother Mitchell's errand has been on the whole quite successful, though not by any means what I would like. The old lady [Sis. Lang] whom he was asked to influence is very *set* in her ways and will not yield, even though by so doing she would confer a lasting benefit on and gain the eternal gratitude of an *anxious* daughter [Janet Lang].

At twelve Elders Edward, McKnight, and I started for Cambuslang. They went to Brother [James] Robertson's and I to Mr. [George] Williamson's, Brother McMurrin's relatives. Mr. and Mrs. Williamson were both in —so were three of their daughters and one lady friend. Spent three pleasant hours with them, then joined the brethren at Robertson's. After an hour or so at social conversation during which the object of our visit was freely discussed, we went to Westburn and called on the Cook family. We are desirous of securing a little hall in that district and hold a meeting every Sunday. The families there are willing to assist, so on Sunday, January 22—if all goes well—we shall hold our first meeting.

Fish supper[266] (?) and then retired.

---

[266] A *fish supper* consisted of deep-fried, battered fish (usually haddock) with fried potato chips.

Saturday, 14 January 1899
> Wrote a letter to Nettie.
> Took a stroll around part of the city, looking for a cheap parlor grate. At night several of the young folks of the branch came in and spent the evening singing songs and preparing the Sunday School lesson for tomorrow.

Sunday, 15 January 1899
> Sunday School and meetings as usual. At 4 P.M. Elder McQuarrie and I, with Peter Tucker, took dinner with the latter's brother-in-law and sister, Mr. and Mrs. Barrie, 5 Tillie Street, Westend. We were made very welcome and treated fine. They are not in the Church, yet appear to be very favorable. Invited back as soon as convenient.
> At 9 P.M. Elder Edward and I went to Springburn and administered to a Mr. Ferguson, a young man who appears to have faith, yet whose life does not correspond to his profession. Blessed a little baby, Peter Ferguson Mills, son of William Mills and Jesse Ferguson, born 15 December 1898.

Monday, 16 January 1899
> No letter from home—disappointed.
> Visited Sister Harkins. During our conversation, she told about a woman belonging to the Church who deserted her husband and went to Utah. She told her husband she was going to Ireland for her health. She wrote a letter on board the ship, telling him of her intention to go to Utah. Many queer circumstances happened in the early part of this Church!
> At 7 P.M. Janet Lang and Sister McDonald came in. This was the appointed time for Janet to send her answer to her *affiancer*.[267] Rendered some assistance! Peculiar position!
> Later a messenger came from Rutherglen, requesting us to go and administer to Mrs. Faulds. It seems to us that this woman is trifling with the ordinances. She is to be pitied, anyway. Gave her a little money. If more is not received from home this week, I shall be *left*.
> I feel tonight as though there would be much more happiness for me at home. Many little *knotty* questions are arising that almost rack a person's mind.

Tuesday, 17 January 1899
> (Wednesday. Just began to write when Brother McKnight suggested "Ludo."[268] So here goes! Elder Hector McQuarrie, Elder Joseph McKnight, and I are the competitors. *Shake for luck!*)
> Brother M[cKnight] and I took a bath; had a good swim. In the afternoon we called on several secretaries of literary associations, endeavoring to

---

[267] An *affiancer* was one who betroths or binds himself by promise of marriage to another.
[268] *Ludo* was a game played with dice and counters on a special board.

get one to give the coming lecture on "Utah and the Mormons" under the auspices of the association. Their courses of lecture were complete.

At the Crown Halls. Secured a grate.

At night the young woman connected with the unpleasant affair mentioned under date of December 27th, 1898, called in company with her brother-in-law and Sister Cairney, and stated her feelings about the young man's marrying her. Had a long talk with her and them. She is about twelve years older than he.

Wednesday, 18 January 1899

Wrote to Edinburgh, Airdrie, Ayr, and Liverpool concerning the proposed lecture. Secured the Albion Hall. Wrote a letter home.

At 6:30 Mr. C., the young man in the difficulty mentioned in yesterday's account, called according to my request. He states that there was no promise of marriage—no mention of it at all. He says he cannot marry her. "It would be through *pity*," if he did, and this would make both lives unhappy. He promised to see her and try to come to an understanding.

Mr. Houston called. Promised to visit him next Monday. Singing practice at 7:45 P.M. Played Ludo (mentioned on top of other page),[269] got beaten once, and came second the next time. Brother Edward, who came in later, beat. Wrote this and retired. Twelve midnight! Elders' hours!!

Thursday, 19 January 1899

In the house during the morning hours. Called on Sister Gain, also Sister Neilson. Testimony meeting at night. The testimonies borne were excellent and the spirit manifested was indeed encouraging and instructive.

The Glasgow Branch is in a good condition; so is the one in Edinburgh and the one in Airdrie; the Burnbank Branch is not flourishing. Their hall has been taken from them. The Newarthill Branch is fair; likewise, the one in Dunfermline; while the saints in Ayrshire, though quite scattered, are feeling well and manifesting a lively interest. The elders are all feeling well. These facts are quite encouraging.

Friday, 20 January 1899

This is visiting day. Elder McKnight and Elder Edward will visit some of the saints and I shall visit others. Called on Sister Hunter and daughter; Sister William Hamilton and Miss Hamilton; Sister Joseph Leggat; and Mr. and Mrs. Anderson.

It was 6:40 P.M. when I reached the conference house. Elders Edward and McKnight were just about to get ready for the theatre, not having anything special to do. I joined them, although conscience told me to make an-

---

[269]McKay refers to his mention of the game *Ludo* at the beginning of the entry for 17 January 1899, which was written at the top of the previous page in his diary.

other visit to a family who really need and solicit our visits. The pantomime was *Cinderella*. The house was crowded! Some of the saints were also present. The scenery was beautiful; the costumes dazzling; the girls were pretty, and some of them good singers; but the ridiculous parts were disgusting.[270] We left before it was over.

Saturday, 21 January 1899

Wrote a long letter to Nettie. Elders Smith and Gould came in from their field of labor. The latter and I visited Sister Gain and family.

At conference house later. Brother Leatham called; he reports trouble in the Newarthill Branch. As the elders left for their fields, Maggie [Gain], Jeanie [Gain], and Maggie Kelly called. The evening was spent in singing songs and studying tomorrow's Sunday School lesson. Sister Noble left us today. This means [we] do our own cooking! She is coming back to see us next week.

Sunday, 22 January 1899

Elder Joseph McKnight and I walked to Cambuslang and at twelve noon held a meeting with a few of the saints in that district. Elder Edward met with the saints in Glasgow. This is the commencement of a series of meetings—it was a good one, too. Sister [James] Robertson had prepared an excellent dinner.

After visiting the Russell family, we called to see Mrs. Crosby. Our intention was to be in Glasgow at 5 P.M. to fill an appointment with Sister Neilson, but we had not long been in Mrs. Crosby's before a warm religious discussion was in full sway. She is "saved," so are her two sons. Another Mr. Crosby and wife were present, also. The discussion lasted until 4:45, the time we intended to be in Glasgow! Elder McKnight is an excellent debater: he brings forth solid argument with power and decision. He has all needful quotations right on the "end of his tongue." We were invited back. Every such argument establishes more firmly in my mind the weakness of the prevailing religions and the superiority of the Church of Christ over them all. Joseph Smith was a prophet of God or else religion is a hoax, there was no redeemer, and mankind is deceived!

Meeting in Glasgow at 6:30 P.M. The hall was crowded. Elder McKnight and I occupied the time. After meeting the three of us went to Neilson's and partook of Sister Neilson's hospitality.

Monday, 23 January 1899

Wrote a letter to elders in Airdrie. Visited (in company with Brother McKnight) Sister Hamilton, who is the mother of another fine baby girl.

---

[270]Many nineteenth-century Scottish pantomimes were biting farces, noted for their extravagances.

Note: Fell down steps—running to catch ferry boat!

Sister Noble came in and prepared our porridge for us, swept the close,[271] cleaned the windows, and helped us out fine. She will "no' see us ill aff 'til we get somebudy to come an' keep the hoose." She "does na' like tae leave," but her husband wants her to. Brother Edward cooked dinner.

At 2:30 P.M. he and I filled our appointment with Mr. Houston, assistant governor of the Barnhill Poorhouse. He met us at the door of his office and, after a few words of greeting, began to explain to us things concerning the institution. The certificates for entrance, given to the applicants by a doctor or some responsible official certifying to the eligibility of the holder, are made out on paper of two different colors—the red certificate signifying to the officials that the applicant is not only poor but lazy also; the white one showing that the person holding it is willing to work.

After the applicant's credentials have been accepted, he is ushered into the bathroom, where all his clothing is changed and he gets a good cleaning —something most of them are not accustomed to. Mr. Houston informed us that some of the clothing thrown off are literally *alive* and must be destroyed! Other articles, upon which the "Scots Gray"[272] and little black hoppers[273] are not so numerous, are thrown into the fumigator for one hour, where a heat of 260 degrees Fahrenheit kills all forms of life, thus making the clothing safe to be handled.

There are about 1,300 inmates in the poorhouse, nearly one third of whom are sick and infirm, lying in hospital wards and attended to by the doctor.[274] It is a pitiful sight to walk through these wards and see sick persons—including aged men, little children, and old women—lying helpless! The men, women, and children are in separate wards.

It is interesting to enter the children's ward and see the little cherubs, sitting around in their cribs. Poor little things! Many have never known what a mother is; some have parents in the poorhouse; while others have been picked up in the street, having been deserted by their mothers![275] Wives and children are in this institution, who have been deserted by their husbands and fathers. Aged women by the hundreds are eking out an existence and fanning the dying flame of life in the poorhouse, after having raised a family of sons and daughters!

Husbands and wives, ruined by drink and devoid of natural affection, live here as total strangers to each other! Instead of nourishing their love for

---

[271] A *close* was an entryway to an apartment house.

[272] The term *Scotch Gray*, in the plural, refers to lice.

[273] The term *hoppers*, i.e., insects or insect larvae that hop, here refers to fleas.

[274] According to John McKenzie, *Barnhill: A Scottish Poorhouse*, 47, during the 1890s the Barnhill Poorhouse had a high death rate of nine percent to ten percent each year. The attendant physician was Dr. William Core.

[275] John T. Edward, Diary, 23 January 1899, indicated that there were 130 children in the poorhouse, with the youngest being only six months old.

one another, they centered it upon drink—that soul-destroying, hellish liquid that fires so many minds and consumes their souls in hell! One old man, eighty-one years of age, and his aged wife, both in the poorhouse because of drink, never speak to each other—pass each other in the yard without saying a word. The warm love of their youth seems to have turned to wormwood, and its bitter dregs must now be drained in misery instead of the sweet nectar of ripened love!

There is one aged woman, Mrs. J. O'Donald, who is over a century old; she is in her one hundred and second year! She has a daughter in America seventy years old! Her mind is still bright and active. She talks intelligently and, true to her Irish nature, still enjoys a good joke. She was sorry that Brother Edward is married because she is "still looking for a chance"! She has outlived two husbands *already*! She came to Glasgow before there were any railroads here. She remembers the Battle of Waterloo. "I was quite a lass," said she, "when that took place." She had never heard of Mormons but remembered something about "Brigham Young and his forty wives." "Ye dinna belong tae him, d'ye?" She was quite surprised to learn that the Mormons are a religious body. Her life seems to be a proof in favor of tobacco using, for she used it all her days; but I think she is 102 years old *in spite* of the effect of tobacco and not *because* of it. She seemed pleased that we called on her and said "God bless ye" as we shook her frail hand and said good-bye.

There is another woman whose life has been an interesting one because of its sadness. For nineteen years she has been an inmate of the poorhouse, during which time she has been constantly in her bed helpless! She is paralyzed and can use only one arm—[and only] her forefinger and thumb! Her time is occupied in picking and counting stamps that have been used. Last year up to May or June she had collected 53,000 and has now 23,000 on hand! These are sent to her from offices and other places and she cleans and counts them and sends them to London. She was very thankful for some American stamps I gave her.

As we passed through the different hospital wards, our attention was drawn to the different colored paper at the head of the beds. At the head of one was a white paper, while perhaps at the next there would be a purple one. This distinction, Mr. Houston informed us, was made on account of the patient's religion. The white signified a Protestant, and the purple a Catholic. This is simply a guide to the priests and ministers and makes no difference in the care or treatment of the individual. In answer to the question what color he would adopt for a Mormon, Mr. Houston replied, "Oh, we should have to get a special one for them."

In the children's ward is a little boy, twelve years old, still unable to walk. He was all right at birth; but through sheer neglect of the mother, he has been dwarfed, his limbs are undeveloped, and his life practically lost. This is a crying sin! Such creatures, professing to be men and women, should be prohibited from bringing children into the world! Most of the little ones in this ward have been taken from their parents because of the latter's cruelty or neglect!

In the adult departments the able men and women are put to work. The men break stones, cut and saw kindling wood, or work at the joiner's trade, or carve wood, work in brass, make wire picture frames, etc.; while the women do laundry work, knit, and sew.

The inmates—and especially the men—are, generally speaking, shirks. Their principal object, it seems, is to deceive. When this propensity is carried too far, the lazy rascal is shut up in a "stone cell," in which is put a certain amount of work which must be done before he gets anything to eat. The less they work, the less they get to eat. Besides this, there is a "prison cell" where the rebellious ones are securely locked until they manifest a humble spirit. Then there is the "observation room," where men (or women either, I suppose) brought in suffering of "delirium tremens" are shut up until the fire in their brains dies out and their natures become quiet.

The large dining room, having a seating capacity of 700, is used also for services held twice a day and on Sunday as well.

The class of people in here is, of course, among the lowest, although some intelligent features are seen among them. The experience of seeing them is not a pleasant one—it makes one feel too gloomy; but I am glad we had the opportunity and that our esteemed guide made our visit so interesting.[276] He expressed a desire to continue the acquaintance, promising to call on us as soon as possible. He accompanied us to the outer gate and at 5 P.M., thanking him for his kindness, we took our leave, feeling that the afternoon had been well-spent.

Tuesday, 24 January 1899

Wrote five or six letters pertaining to conference and lecture matters.

Elder McKnight and I called on [James] Clark. He is almost a wreck! He seems to have lost all faith in the gospel. We also called on Mrs. Harrison—no one home. At 7 P.M. I visited Mr. Duncan Thomson and family. Thomas Thomson and his wife were in from Shettleston. Sister Robertson was there, also. The evening was spent very pleasantly. I felt, however, that I stayed too late; but the conversation, which ended in a sort of discussion, seemed to be hard to "break off."

Later joined the brethren in a game of Ludo—beaten. Retired. The city enveloped in a dense fog all day.

Wednesday, 25 January 1899

Wrote letters to Annie, Claire, Elsie, and sent a photo to each; also one to Nettie and John Hammond.

---

[276]John T. Edward, Diary, 23 January 1899, summed up this experience: "Take it all in all, it was the greatest sight of the kind I ever saw in my life."

Brother Kesler returned from England. Called at Anchor Line Office. Singing practice at night. An excellent attendance. A good practice. Dainty present for Fay from Sister Reid. Maggie Gain commenced her E[migration] deposits. Brother Edward went to a party with his cousins.

Thursday, 26 January 1899

Went through the Municipal Building with Elders Kesler and [John G.] Teuscher. Had a two-hour conversation on the Fall, which was instructive and interesting. Visited the Queen's Park and Art Gallery. Testimony meeting at night.

Friday, 27 January 1899

A dense fog prevails this morning—the thickest I have ever seen! Went to Anchor Line office. Elders left St. Enoch's at 1 P.M., the boat having gone to Greenock yesterday. There were only four of our company, including Brother Kesler. At 4:30 Brother Eccles came in from Ayrshire to see about the lecture to be delivered there.

At five o'clock Elder Edward and I groped our way through the blackness to Queen Street and boarded the train for Shettleston (about three and a half or four miles out), where we arrived one hour and ten minutes later! The train was hindered by the fog! When we got off the train, we could scarcely see our hand[s] before us. Brother Edward wanted us to go right back and not try to find Mr. [Thomas] Thomson's; but as we had promised to visit him and his wife, I thought it best to launch out and try to find their home at least. The darkness was thick and black; but after much inquiry, we succeeded in finding our friends, who made us right welcome. The evening was a pleasant one after that.

We left about 9:15 P.M. and walked to Glasgow, preferring this to an hour's ride in a cold car.[277] Mr. Thomson accompanied us quite a distance; so we had no difficulty in finding our way.

Saturday, 28 January 1899

The fog still continues. Several fatal accidents happened yesterday. Attended to conference duties. Sunday School meeting at night. Quite a number of young folks were present, waiting in another room.

Sunday, 29 January 1899

Elders McQuarrie and Edward went to Cambuslang; Elder McKnight and I remained here in Glasgow. Priesthood meeting at 11 A.M., Sunday School at 12:30, and regular meeting at 2 P.M. Brother McKnight went out

---

[277]John T. Edward, Diary, 27 January 1899, added: "We walked back in less time than it took the train to run out."

to Mr. Barrie's for dinner and I went to Brother Hamilton's; the others were to be here to accompany us but failed. Miss Hamilton had everything arranged nicely. Spent an enjoyable dinner hour. Evening services at 6:30 P.M.

Monday, 30 January 1899

Word has come from President Lyman that it is the desire of President Snow[278] that the late Elder Muir's body be exhumed and taken home. This is a task I almost dread. Attended to office correspondence. At 1 P.M. met Brother Neilson and Brother Joseph Leggat and tried to secure a more suitable hall for our public meeting. Failed. Called on a "writer"[279] and asked his advice in regard to the legal steps to be taken in order to uncover and exhume the remains of Elder Muir. Learned that it will be a difficult, as well as an expensive, undertaking. Interview [cost] 5/0.

At 6 P.M. Elder McKnight, James Neilson, and I, according to a previous appointment, visited a Neilson family on Cambridge Street. Besides the two daughters and parents, there were present two young lady friends— Miss Walker and Miss Bridges. The evening was spent in singing, reciting, enjoying music, and in playing games. A *forfeit* game was introduced but, of course, we had to refrain.[280] A good time was had. Good-nights [were said] at 11 P.M.

Tuesday, 31 January 1899

Brother J. Leggat called in the morning. Spent about two hours conversation with him. Attended to general duties.

At night the Misses [Maggie and Bessie] Scott, Brother Edward's cousins, called and made the evening hours pass very pleasantly indeed. They are very good singers. Their memory of Scotch and familiar home songs was good and their rendition of the same, sweet and entertaining.

Wednesday, 1 February 1899

Wrote letters in the morning. Brother Smith came in from Hamilton, and at 2:20 P.M. we went to Newarthill to adjust a difficulty that has arisen between the elders and Brother Orr. Elder Smith went as a witness, as he is acquainted with all the affairs.

The following is the minutes as recorded by Elder Joseph Mitchell:

Minutes of special meeting held in Newarthill, February 1st, 1899. Called by president of branch, Elder Robert Orr, to consider some misunder-

---

[278]Lorenzo Snow (1814-1901) joined the LDS Church in 1836, was ordained an apostle in 1849, and served a nine-month sentence in the Utah Territorial Penitentiary for polygamy during the 1880s. He became president of the Church in 1898, being noted for his emphasis on tithing and reducing the Church's indebtedness. See Richard S. Van Wagoner and Steven C. Walker, *A Book of Mormons* (Salt Lake City: Signature Books, 1982), 333-38.

[279]In Scotland, a *writer* was a law agent, an attorney, or a solicitor.

[280]The *forfeit* game probably included having to kiss someone as the forfeit.

standings that had arisen between him and the traveling elders who had been appointed to, and were laboring in, that district.

There were present: president of Scottish Conference, David O. Mc-Kay; John S. Leatham, John S. Smith, and Joseph Mitchell, traveling elders; Robert Orr, president [of the] branch; and Brother Alex McKie of the Newarthill Branch. President D. O. McKay presided.

Meeting opened by singing hymn, page 108. Prayer was offered by President McKay. Singing, page 148.

The question of which held precedence in the conducting of the affairs of the branch was first introduced. Brother Orr claimed that he had the right to act independently of the traveling elders, while the traveling elders claimed that it was their duty to control all the affairs of the branch and that Brother Orr should preside under their direction.

Brother Orr gave as a reason for the position he assumed that he thought that a branch was a part of the church and was separate from the conference.

Brother McKay explained the order of church government briefly as follows: The European Presidency under the First Presidency of the Church has control of, and are responsible to, the latter for all things connected with the Church in Europe; that President McKay, under the direction of the European Presidency, had charge of all the affairs of the Church in Scotland—branches included; and that the traveling elders in the districts where they were appointed had charge of all the affairs of the church under his [their] direction. Brother Orr said that he had in the past been taught that he as president of the branch was only responsible to the president of the conference and that the traveling elders in his district were subject to him! He understood this was right and acted accordingly.

After further explanation by President McKay, he (Orr) said he was willing to work in the future under the direction of the traveling elders. Other misunderstandings that had arisen through the above conduction of affairs were explained, and Brother Orr promised to make all necessary explanations to the saints in meeting, in order to remove from their minds false impressions he had made at different times when he was of the opinion that he was not under the direction of the traveling elders.

After further instructions from President McKay, all parties interested expressed themselves as being satisfied with the rulings made by Brother McKay; also that they had no bitter feelings toward any individual. Meeting then adjourned, Elder John S. Leatham offering the benediction.

Joseph Mitchell, secretary.

After this meeting we retired to Sister Major's, where the saints were waiting to hold their regular meeting. Brother Orr made the necessary explanations. After meeting we ate a *bite* prepared by Sister Major and then hastened to catch the train.

I went to Airdrie with the brethren, arranging for the lecture, and then came to Glasgow. Tired and worried.

Thursday, 2 February 1899

Office work. Visited Sister Hunter. Our bachelor's life is not very agreeable. Brother McQuarrie and Brother Edward do very well with the cooking, but *dishwashing* is not pleasant.

Testimony meeting at night.

Friday, 3 February 1899

Went with Brother Neilson to see a hall which seems to be suitable for a meeting place. It is on the banks of the Clyde in a respectable locality. It is the Carlton Hall and seems to be just the hall we have been looking for. Asked for lowest rates, etc.

Brother Edward and I visited Sister McDonald. Later several of the elders have come in from their fields to attend the special priesthood meeting tomorrow. A good attendance is anticipated. Six baptisms from Burnbank District.

Saturday, 4 February 1899

At 10:15 A.M. all the elders but one were here ready for meeting. After singing and prayer, the reports of the condition of, and prospects for, the work in the different fields were given. On the whole they were quite encouraging. The elders are feeling well in their labors and toward each other. An excellent spirit prevailed, and everyone seemed to be well-pleased and much encouraged in the work.

After meeting my time was spent in settling accounts, conversing with the elders, and giving such advice as seemed necessary. At night two or three young folks from Glasgow Branch came in to study the Sunday School lesson.

Sunday, 5 February 1899

At 10 A.M. started for Blantyre on the bus. Met with the saints there at 12:30. The six persons baptized last Friday were confirmed and two children blessed. The testimony meeting was good. After dinner (3:30 P.M.), I started on foot for Cambuslang where I was to meet Elders McKnight and Stewart, who had been holding a meeting there. Brother Halliday accompanied me about one and a half miles.

Overtook the brethren at Rutherglen Bridge and together we continued our walk to Glasgow, arriving at the hall at 6:30, just in time for the evening meeting. The hall was crowded—several strangers being present. Brother Stewart and I were the speakers. After meeting administered to Sister Hoggan and Sister [Leggat].

Monday, 6 February 1899

Called at printing office and ordered 500 printed posters, 5,000 handbills, and several hundred tickets for the coming lecture to be delivered in Edinburgh, Glasgow, Ayrshire, and Coatbridge.

Visited Sister William Leggat and Sister Hoggan. Found them much better. After attending to some conference correspondence, I went to Dunfermline with Brother Stewart, boarding the 8:15 P.M. train at Queen Street and arriving in Dunfermline about ten. Brother Wickens was feeling all right. Their lodgings are not very good. Some of our elders are not cautious enough in securing suitable lodgings. These elders are *putting up* with conditions which I think are very unfavorable. They will change soon.

Dunfermline, Tuesday, 7 February 1899

Breakfast at 8:30.

Elder Wickens and I called on Dr. Dendle and ascertained from him what "writer" would take the case in hand through the sheriff's court. Elder Muir's body is to be disinterred and before anything can be done in the matter a warrant must be obtained from the court. Mr. John S. Soutar, solicitor, was employed. Found that it will be necessary for me to have an affidavit from the father of Elder Muir, authorizing me to act in the matter.

After calling on some of the saints, left Dunfermline for Glasgow, where I arrived at 6:30 P.M. Maggie [Gain], Lizzie [Gain], and Maggie Kelly were cleaning [the] conference house. Later four returning elders and one young woman came from England. They sail Thursday.

Wrote to J. W. Muir.

Wednesday, 8 February 1899

Arose at 6:15 A.M. At 6:45 A.M. met Miss Lucy Birchall at Central Station. She comes from Preston and is on her way to Utah. Spent the day in attending to emigration and conference duties.

Elder McKnight and I visited Sister Noble. Georgina was in and expressed her determination to marry James Leggat, stating that she understands full well the responsibility she is taking upon herself. She knows, too, what his financial condition is. So, all we say to her now is may God prosper you and overrule the marriage for the good of you both.

Telegram from Liverpool to meet President Lyman at 11:05 P.M. At the stated hour quite a number [of] us, including returning elders, met him at Central Station. President Loutensock[281] and LeRoi Snow[282] of the German Mission were with him. Took them to the Argyle, where we had a pleasant half-hour's chat. President Lyman has come up on business connected with the transportation of German emigrants.

---

[281]Peter Loutensock (1848-1925) on 20 July 1896 had a farewell party in Eureka for his call to the Swiss and German Mission. On 1 August 1896 he left Salt Lake City, heading for Liverpool and then Bern, Switzerland. Loutensock was called to the mission headquarters in Bern to translate for the church publication, *Der Stern*, in October 1896, and then he was appointed president of the Swiss and German Mission in November 1896. Three months later, when the mission was divided into the Swiss Mission and the German Mission, Loutensock was appointed over the latter mission. See his reminiscence and diary, Manuscript 226, located in the LDS Church Archives, Historical Department, The Church of Jesus Christ of Latter-day Saints, Salt Lake City.

[282]LeRoi C. Snow (1876-1962) was the son of Lorenzo Snow and Minnie Jensen. He was set apart on 20 March 1896 for a mission to Great Britain and when he arrived in Liverpool was assigned to the Swiss-German Mission. Because of his missionary activity, he was arrested in Bavaria, imprisoned, and then banished from the country for life. He was released from his mission in February 1899 and arrived in Utah the next month. He became private secretary to his father and tithing clerk of the Church.

Thursday, 9 February 1899

After breakfast went with President Lyman (who came from the hotel quite early) to the Argyle, where we were joined by President Loutensock, and the three of us called on Mr. Aitchison. An agreement was soon arrived at. Mr. Aitchison soon dispatches business. Changed tickets.

At 11:30 all the company of elders and emigrating saints met in the conference house and received instructions concerning the voyage. Brother Loutensock was placed in charge. The passengers went aboard at 4:30 P.M. It was a jolly company—seventeen in all. Among them were Mr. and Mrs. Neal, Miss Twissel, Miss Birchall, Elders Snow, [Frank W.] Penrose, [Henry C.] Brown, and others. Left the boat *Furnessia* at 6:30 P.M.

Testimony meeting at eight. President Lyman spoke fine. His text was "whosoever drinketh of the water I shall give him shall never thirst," John 4:14. Letters from Nettie, Claire, and Bishop Beatie.

At 10:45 President Lyman left Central Station for Liverpool. His visit here was very pleasant and profitable to us. He gave me much satisfaction, in commending our efforts and paying a fine compliment. I hope I merited it. Tired at night. Busy, though a successful, day.

Friday, 10 February 1899

Sent posters and bills to Edinburgh. Called at *News* office and at Argyle Hotel. Finished financial report.

At 6:43 Elders McKnight, Nisbet, Eccles, McQuarrie, several of the young saints, and I left Queen Street Station for Burnbank, where we attended the soirée given by the branch there. The concert began at 7:45. The program was good [with] several talented strangers taking part, among whom was a Mr. Bowie, pianist. Tea served at 9:15. Dancing at ten, continuing until 5:45 A.M., interspersed occasionally with songs[283] and refreshments. We had a very enjoyable time and met several strangers who seemed to be pleased to meet us. Received an invitation to a grand ball to be given in Hamilton on the third Friday in March.

Left Burnbank at 6 A.M., arriving in Glasgow at 6:45!

Saturday, 11 February 1899

After starting the fires and *attempting* to write—I say attempting because I fell asleep while doing so—I lay down to rest. Brother Edward, who stayed at the conference house, feels fine this morning, while the rest of us are paying for the "fiddler." Arose at twelve noon. Tried to study, but it was only a *trial.*[284]

---

[283]William P. Nisbet, Diary, 10 February 1899, added: "Bro. Eccles and myself sang 'There'll Be a Hot Time in the Old Town Tonight,' most of the words being our own composition, reference being made to all the elders in the Scottish Conference. The song was very much appreciated by the elders and many of the saints."

[284]William P. Nisbet, Diary, 11 February 1899, explained that in the conference house that

Sunday, 12 February 1899

Went to Cambuslang and held meeting at twelve noon. Went to Brother Russell's daughter's (Mrs. Mack) home for dinner. After calling on Brother and Sister [James] Robertson, then on Brother and Sister Russell, boarded the five o'clock bus and came to Glasgow. Brother and Sister Reid and Willie Cooke came in also.

Meeting at 6:30, after which went to Brother Neilson's. Brother Edward is suffering from a very bad cold. He is discouraged.

Monday, 13 February 1899

Arranged for the posting of bills for the lecture. Ordered more handbills. Called on Mrs. Stewart and Sister Gain. Flora [Gain] cleaned house for us.

At night Elder Edward and I called on Mr. [Archie] Bell and family, 315 London Road. We had a lively conversation on the essentiality of baptism. Miss Bell is as bright as a sunbeam and sees through a question quickly and clearly. Mr. Bell said he would look up the question and be prepared for us when we called again. They invited us back, and we promised to accept their invitation with thanks.

Tuesday, 14 February 1899

Letter from President Lyman, containing a copy of one from President [Lorenzo] Snow, stating that there is no definite period for a missionary to remain in his field. The presidents of missions are to give releases as they feel impressed.

Attended to office duties. At night Brother Edward and I went to a Bible class conducted by Rev. [J. Williams] Butcher. The class was studying Drummond's *Natural Law in the Spiritual World*,[285] subject "Death." (1) Natural death, separation from environment. (2) Spiritual death, a separation from communication with divine influences. (3) Another death, being dead to sin. See Romans 8:5-17, Colossians 3:1-10.

"Three ways by which we can become dead to sin: *suicide, mortification*, and *limitation*." By suicide is meant the stopping of a certain sin at once and doing it no more. "He that steals, let him steal no more." *Drunkenness* is another example. Mortification is the overcoming of evil habits or traits of character such as jealousy, evil temper, etc. *Limitation* is applied to habits in life "that are right when carried to a certain point; but beyond this they are wrong." An example of such habits is the desire to save money. This is a right desire when not carried to an extreme. Such is an outline of the minister's subject.

---

evening Nisbet delivered a recitation of Burns's "Tam o' Shanter" at the request of John T. Edward.

[285]Henry Drummond, *Natural Law in the Spiritual World* (London: Hodder and Houghton, 1896).

As he was in a hurry, we had no time to make ourselves known to him; but he invited us back, and we shall no doubt accept his invitation.

Wednesday, 15 February 1899

Wrote to Nettie and Claire. Mailed bills, made arrangements to have more posted, and attended to conference duties. Singing practice at night. Spoke to Brother and Sister Reid about coming to keep the conference house. They are both willing to come. This will put an end to our bachelor's life. Thank goodness!

Thursday, 16 February 1899

Brother Edward's cold still continues. A harsh cough is racking his system. Busy with preparations for lectures. Called on Sister Clark.

Brother Mitchell came in from Newarthill, quite discouraged. The affairs out there are no better. A fresh outburst has occurred, and the condition of some of the members is certainly precarious so far as their standing in the Church is concerned. One told Brother Mitchell right in the presence of nearly all the members of the branch that he had no business to mention a principle which he did mention while preaching; adding as he left the room in anger that Brother Mitchell had the spirit of the Devil! O, it is awful! They are in the dark and cannot see who their true friends are! However, we know that the actions taken have been right, so we shall not worry unnecessarily. Decided to continue in a course of kindness, yet using a firm hand.

Testimony meeting at night.

Friday, 17 February 1899

Sundry duties attended to during the day.

At night Brother McKnight and I went to the wedding reception of "Jimmy" Leggat and Georgina Ferguson, held in a side-room at the Breadalbane Hall. I have been opposed to the wedding on the grounds that (1) he is unprepared and that (2) she is worthy of a better man than he has proved himself to be in the past. The company gave us a nice round of applause as we entered and took our seats at the table nicely spread with cakes, buns, and cups of tea—also two glasses of milk for us.

After tea was served and while all were still seated around the table, each one as his turn came either sang a song (or tried to), gave a reading, or "begged to be excused." The ones that were excused were the most appreciated! After the concert (?) the table was cleared, the violinist [was] brought in, and dancing commenced, interspersed with refreshments. Some of the actions of one or two were disgraceful for Latter-day Saints. However, it was only one or two; otherwise, everything went off smoothly. Dismissed at 1 A.M.

About one hour before dismissal, the bridal couple quietly disappeared! They had no home of their own to go to; but I afterward learned that they went to her mother's and took possession until she (the mother) and her husband came home. The latter, having become intoxicated, when he saw his bed occupied, flew into a passion! Then a scene was enacted that can easily be imagined. The bride sprang out of her bed and settled things by finally striking her mother's husband and making things in general quite warm!

Oh, it is a discouraging fact that many of the members of our Church are very uncouth and uncultured, showing no refinement whatever. Think of a marriage under such circumstances as above! If the bride had any love for her husband, the saying that "love is blind" is truly verified; if she married him simply to "get a man," she will be sadly disappointed for she has not a *man* at all! His actions have been anything but *manly*.

Saturday, 18 February 1899

The American mail brought no letter from home, and I am out of money! Financial prospects are beginning to look gloomy!

Immediately after dinner boarded the train for Edinburgh to attend the lecture on "Utah and the Mormons." Went to Sister George White's, left my coat and satchel, and then, after promising to return for tea, walked over to the elders' lodgings, thence to the hall in Picardy Place, where Elder Robert Anderson and the Edinburgh elders were preparing the screen and stereopticon. The prospects for the lecture were fair, and the brethren seemed quite hopeful. At 7:30 we were again at the hall, in which had gathered about one hundred persons.

After a few introductory remarks by the chairman, Elder George W. Palmer delivered his lecture illustrated with 100 views of mountain scenery, railroad bridges, life in Salt Lake City, etc.[286] He was frequently interrupted by applause. The name and photograph of President Brigham Young was applauded vigorously and, even when polygamy was mentioned, there was only one expression of dissatisfaction, and that came from an old woman noted for the misery she has caused by her actions toward some of our elders. The lecture was a success! The receipts will equal the expenditures, and the prejudice that will be removed can be estimated only by results yet future. After the audience dispersed, we went to Mrs. Watson's, ate a light supper, and then, bidding Elders Palmer and Anderson good-night, I went to Sister White's. Brother White was very sociable, so was Sister White; so the wee sma' hours crept on us unawares.

Retired about 2 A.M., well-satisfied with the result of our first lecture, yet dubious, though hopeful, of the ones to come.

Edinburgh, Sunday, 19 February 1899

It was ten o'clock before I arose from bed. After breakfast and a good

---

[286]See "Palmer and Anderson Lecture," *The Latter-day Saints' Millennial Star* 61 (9 March 1899): 154-55.

morning talk, called on the elders at Mrs. Watson's and together we went to meeting.

Elder Anderson was the speaker. Dinner at Mrs. White's. Meeting at 6:30. Elder Palmer occupied the time. Sunday night spent at Sister Watson's. The associations and services during the day were pleasant and gratifying. Slept at Sister White's.

Monday, 20 February 1899

Before eating breakfast, called on Elders Stirling and Miller and straightened accounts for lecture.

Also visited Brother and Sister Rhynd, Montgomery Street. It was my intention to stay only a few minutes, but Brother Rhynd began to ask questions and an hour passed before we knew it. One of his questions was: "Does the spirit of man return directly to God after it leaves the body?" Read the fortieth chapter of Alma. Left them feeling well.

It was after eleven o'clock when I reached Sister White's for breakfast. Called on Sister Whyte, Bothwell Street, Brother and Sister [David] Henderson, and Sister [Isabella] Gracie, the latter laying sick of fever.

Left Edinburgh at 1 P.M., arriving in Glasgow about 2:15. Found the brethren well. Went to Maryhill to see Agnes Reid about coming to keep house for us. She was out. At 5:15 met Elders Palmer and Anderson at Queen Street Station, hired a cab, and drove to Albion Hall, where we left luggage and retired to conference house. Spent the night writing and doing several little things preparatory to the lecture tomorrow night.

Tuesday, 21 February 1899

Helped Brother Anderson put up screen and lantern. In the afternoon called on Sister Anderson, the Neilson family, and Sister Good.

At 7 P.M. we were at the hall ready to meet and seat the people coming to the lecture. Brother McQuarrie was chairman. The attendance was small, only about one hundred and fifty being present. The lecture was good and the views of Salt Lake City and scenes in Utah were excellent. Among those in the audience, I was particularly pleased to see Mr. and Mrs. McColl and Mr. McMinn. Our receipts were £2/2/0.

After lecture went to restaurant.

Wednesday, 22 February 1899

Spent the morning hours in and about the conference house. Took dinner at Sister Neilson's. With all the faults and failings of Brother and Sister Neilson, this much can be truthfully said: a more welcome home for the elders cannot be found. They treat us to their very best and that, too, with an *open* heart. Called on Sister Gain and family.

Lecture at 7:45 P.M. The audience was smaller than the one last night! Mrs. Crosby, Lesmahagow, was there. She has been *bitter* against us. I hope her opinion was changed—so does her husband. Well, we shall no doubt go

Fig. 42   *The Birthplace of Robert Burns, Alloway.*

behind financially. I hope a letter comes from home tomorrow, containing a little cash.

Thursday, 23 February 1899

No mail! American mail has not yet arrived. I still have hopes.

At eleven o'clock Elder[s] Edward, Palmer, and Anderson, and I left Glasgow for Ayr. Elders Eccles and Nisbet and Smith met us at the station and took us to their lodgings, 94 High Street.

After dinner we visited the home—birthplace—of Scotland's favorite poet, "Robby" Burns. As we were walking out through Ayr, we were shown the inn where Tam o' Shanter and Souter Johnny "sat bousin' at the nappy, and gettin fou an' unco happy."[287] A half hour's walk brought us to the birthplace of Burns, the long, low, old-fashioned house (Fig. 42):

> Stands by the roadside, not far frae the town,
>   An tho' it is aged an' worn.
> It is dearer tae *some* than the mansions in town—
>   The cottage where Burns was born.

By paying two pence each, we were admitted to the rooms. The bed in which he was born was pointed to with pride by the old lady who keeps the house, so also was the old chest, and fireplace, and other old relics of the poet (Fig. 43). The roof is just a little over six feet from the floor; and the rooms show that Burns's early life was indeed a humble one, and as one thinks of the poet's humble circumstances and considers what gems of thought he was given to the world, one is reminded of the saying of Longfellow:[288]

---

[287]Robert Burns, "Tam o' Shanter," in *The Complete Illustrated Poems, Songs, and Ballads of Robert Burns* (Secaucus, NJ: Chartwell Books, 1990), 242.

[288]Henry Wadsworth Longfellow (1807-1882) was the most famous American poet of the nineteenth century, writing such popular works as *Evangeline*, *The Song of Hiawatha*, and *The*

Fig. 43   *The Interior of Burns Cottage, Alloway.*

> Lives of great men all remind us,
> We can make *our* lives sublime,
> And, departing, leave behind us
> Footprints in the sands of time.[289]

A few minutes walk from Burns's cottage brings us to the auld Alloway Kirk (Fig. 44), where:

> Tam saw an unco sight!
> Warlocks and witches in a dance:
> Nae cotillon, brent new frae France,
> But hornpipes, jigs, strathspeys, and reels,
> Put life and mettle in their heels.[290]

But there are no signs of ghosts around the old ruins now. The ivy-covered walls are crumbling, and the only thing that makes it interesting is its age and Tam o' Shanter. The supposed grave of Souter Johnny is near the northwest corner of the kirk. After securing a few ivy leaves as a memento of our visit, we walked a short distance to the Brig o' Doon, where:

> The carlin claught her by the rump,
> And left poor Maggie scarce a stump![291]

After gazing a while on the banks and braes o' bonny Doon and listening to Brother Nisbet recite "Tam o' Shanter," we retraced our steps, coming back to Ayr by another road. It was a beautiful drive —a real boulevard; and as one looked at the beautiful cottages on either side and met the charming lassies out riding their bicycles, one thought of the poet's remark about:

---

[289]Henry Wadsworth Longfellow, "A Psalm of Life," in *The Complete Poetical Works of Henry Wadsworth Longfellow* (Cutchogue, NY: Buccaneer Books, 1993), 3.

[290]Burns, "Tam o' Shanter," 245.

[291]Ibid., 248.

Fig. 44 *Alloway Kirk, Alloway.*

> Auld Ayr, wham ne'er a toun surpasses,
> For honest men and bonie lasses.[292]

The lecture was poorly attended,[293] although we have gone to quite an expense advertising it, yet it seems that the [hand]bills have done no good.[294] About seventy-five or one hundred persons listened attentively to the history and condition of the Latter-day Saints. The photo of Brigham Young was greeted with applause. Expressions of surprise at his intelligence were heard from several persons, who evidently had pictured him in their minds as a dissipated monster! Many little incidents happened while preparing for and after the lecture, but I shall keep those in memory.

Left Ayr at 10:20 P.M. for Glasgow. I am afraid that the cold ride home at such a late hour will not do Brother Edward much good. He has a severe cold already and his system is racked with a dry, harsh cough. I hope he will not catch an extra dose of cold. Retired about 1 A.M.

Friday, 24 February 1899

Morning hours spent in the conference house—correspondence, etc. ·No mail from home yet!

At 4 P.M. Elders McKnight and Anderson went to Coatbridge to ar-

---

[292]Ibid., 242.

[293]John T. Edward, Diary, 23 February 1899, explained: "The lecture in Ayr, as in Glasgow, was a success in every way but financially and in getting people in the hall."

[294]William P. Nisbet, Diary, 22 February 1899, indicated that the elders in Ayr had spent nearly the whole day distributing handbills about the lecture.

range the stereopticon and put up screen. Brother Palmer and I followed at 5:45. Got in wrong part of train and were taken several miles off our road. Changed cars at Bothwell and arrived at Coatbridge about 7 P.M.

Lecture at eight. Audience about as usual. This is the last in our conference and I am glad of it! It does not seem that the attendance has repaid us for all our worry and expense! The elders in Airdrie feel well, so do most of the saints. McKie of Newarthill still manifests an apostate spirit.

Left Coatbridge about 10:30, arriving at Queen Street about 11 P.M. We are a *discouraged* crowd tonight!

Saturday, 25 February 1899

No letters from home! Made out statement of lecture expense, which is as follows:

			Expense			*Receipts*		
Feb.	8	Edinburgh	3	0	8½	3	2	0
Feb.	21 22	Glasgow two lectures	5	5	9½	3	12	12½
Feb.	23	Ayr	15	15	11½	1	3	0
Feb.	24	Coatbridge	2	7	8½	1	4	1
			16	10	2	9	1	3½
		Donation from elders				3	10	0
Feb.	27	Fares to Ireland, cab	1	6	6			
		By balance				5	5	4½
			17	16	8	17	16	8
Mar.	1	To balance	5	5	4½			

Spent the day in writing and settling accounts.

At 8 P.M. held a short Sunday School officers' and teachers' meeting. There were only a few present, yet I have never before felt such a manifestation of the Holy Spirit. Everyone present experienced it, and peace and unity reigned.

While we were holding our meeting, the U.S. mail was delivered, and to my comfort and satisfaction I received letters from home, stating that all is well. The letter was twenty-one days on the way! Besides the ones from Father and Tommy, I received five others—one from each of the following:

Claire, Ray, Elsie, Brother Johnston, and Robert Gilchrist.

Later saw Glasgow "Saturday night"!

Sunday, 26 February 1899

Elders McKnight and McQuarrie went to Cambuslang. Attended priesthood meeting at 11 A.M., Sunday School at 12:30, meeting at 2:00, and evening services at 6:30 P.M. Elder Palmer spoke during the afternoon services, and Elder[s] Anderson and McQuarrie at night. We had an excellent day; every meeting was well-attended.

Monday, 27 February 1899

Visited Sister Cairney—baby boy!

Went to Whiteinch with the brethren to visit the "fossil gardens" (Fig. 45). The fossilized [tree] stumps brought on a conversation on the creation, which lasted one hour! The time passed before we knew, so interested did we become in our topic. Rode back on [a] clutha.

At 11 P.M. Palmer and Anderson left Central Station for Ardrossan, thence to Belfast. They expressed themselves as having had an enjoyable time in Glasgow.

Tuesday, 28 February 1899

Brother Edward spent a bad night last night. The cough simply *racked* his body, and it seemed almost continuous. Wrote to Liverpool concerning lectures, etc., and recommended Brother Edward's release. Brother McQuarrie went to Wales. After prayer and administration, Brother Edward felt better.

Wednesday, 1 March 1899

A beautiful day. March comes in "like a lamb."

After hearing that I had sent to Liverpool for his release, Brother Edward (feeling much better this morning) begged of me to send a telegram to

Fig. 45 *Fossil Grove, Whiteinch, Glasgow.*

stop it. He said he did not want to go home and would risk all consequences. In accordance with his urgent request, I asked President Lyman to write to Brother Edward before sending release. Wrote to Mrs. [Lizzie] Edward concerning her husband's health, intimating to her that unless his health improves, he will be released.

At night called on Maggie Gain and assisted her with her essay for next Sunday. Elders Eccles and Nisbet came in.

Thursday, 2 March 1899

Brother Edward is much better. He received a letter from President Lyman, stating that he could receive an honorable release at any time and that he must not risk his health for a few months' service in the mission field. Brother Edward answered this, stating that he "does not feel that he'll be running any risk by remaining in Scotland."

Friday, 3 March 1899

Last night was the worst night Brother Edward has yet spent. He did not rest five minutes scarcely without coughing; his breathing was quite short. About five o'clock he went to sleep and rested for about an hour and a half. Wrote to President Lyman. Called in Dr. [Robert] Grieve, who, after examining Brother Edward, said that there was nothing dangerous about his cough. Thought he had bronchitis. He prescribed a mixture to be taken every four hours. Bought a bottle of Herbaline and rubbed his chest, applying hot cloths afterward. This gave him relief.

Stayed in the house all day. Wrote a letter to the Y.M.M.I.A., Huntsville. Retired about 1 A.M.

Saturday, 4 March 1899

Letter from Isaac W. [McKay.]

Brother Edward feels a little better this morning. He is up and able to write a letter to his wife. Wrote to Claire.

About 11 A.M. Brother Orr of Newarthill came in. About two hours were then spent in listening to and suggesting ways out of the difficulties and misunderstandings that have occurred recently in that branch. After dinner I attempted to devote an hour or so to study, but elders and saints coming in, settling accounts, etc., prevented me from doing so.

About six o'clock Brother and Sister McKie, Newarthill, called; and shortly after, Sister Major and daughter, Newarthill, came in. These were followed by Sister Taylor and son from Rutherglen. In a private interview with Sister Taylor, the sad fact was revealed that she had been forced to leave her home! The particulars in brief are these. On Thursday night last Mr. Taylor and a friend came home under the influence of liquor. He had been drinking freely for some time past. Thursday night Sister Taylor's patience having become exhausted, she told him plainly and emphatically (I suppose) what she thought of his conduct! She evidently made some threats. Taylor became enraged and in the fire of his passion ordered her out of the house, threatening to throw her if she did not go. It was eleven o'clock at night and she had no where to go! The little ones were left in the house. She found shelter with a neighbor until morning, then went to Springburn to her mother and sister, with whom her eldest son is now living. She sent George, her son, back to Rutherglen to get her baby boy. The three of them were here to tell the story—and a sad one it is.

Well, I promised her to call, according to her request, and speak to Taylor and do what I can to bring about repentance and reconciliation. She felt better after confiding her troubles and said good-night with quite a hopeful spirit. Brother McKie's troubles came next. They were nothing compared with those I had just listened to; his were all caused by himself.

Maggie [Gain], Sister Kelly, Janet [Lang], and Mary [McDonald] were also here enquiring about Brother Edward. Brother Eccles and Brother [Robert P.] Herrick (who came from Liverpool on a visit last Friday) returned from Ayr. Retired about twelve.

Sunday, 5 March 1899

Brother Edward, about the same. Fast Day. Walked to Cambuslang and held meeting with the saints there at twelve noon. Brother Reid went with me. This was his first attempt at fasting. Ate dinner at Sister Russell's. The saints take turn[s] about in taking the elders home [to give them a meal], and we must be careful not to make too many visits to any one house or offense is given to others.

On our way to Glasgow, stopped at Taylor's in Rutherglen. (Brother Reid and Willie Cooke walked leisurely along, waiting until I came out.) A little, bright-eyed, eight-year-old lassie answered the bell. "Why, it's Brother McKay!" she said joyfully. Around the kitchen fire, half-burning on top of old ashes, sat the father, two little sons, and the little girl. He was in his stocking feet, his coat and vest were off, his hair uncombed, and his appearance generally showed that he was feeling as dejected as he looked. The little ones, too, showed the absence of a mother's care. Their earnest sober countenances brought forth a feeling of pity! The room was untidy; the bed was unmade; the fireplace uncleaned; and on the table stood unwashed dishes! The husband's gloomy feelings could not be hid, although he tried to do so. The little ones manifested a longing for one not there. In fact, everything seemed to throw gloom and sadness all around; and as I sensed the sad feelings manifested, I fully realized that a home can be either a heaven or a hell—and this one at present [was] a bitter hell!

We were not long in bringing our conversation direct to the point. He expressed his regret for having acted so hastily, acknowledged that he had done wrong, and promised to welcome Mrs. Taylor back at any time. The primary cause of all his trouble he acknowledged to be drink—the accursed, hellish drink! He felt grateful for my visit.

Joined the brethren, who were cold and tired waiting so long, and continued our walk to Glasgow, riding on the car, however, from Dalmarnock.

Meeting at 6:30 P.M. Brother Eccles and D. O. [David O. McKay] speakers.

At 8:30 P.M. in company with Brothers Neilson, William Leggat, and Cairney, called on [John] Currie and sons, who were deprived by death of their wife and mother.[295] Found them feeling quite badly. The mother died from the effects of a burn. What she suffered during her married life perhaps few will ever know. I say this, judging from some remarks the old man made while explaining how one of his sons "was born deaf." The father came home under the influence of liquor. During the night the wife, lying by his side, said she was unwell and that a little baby would soon be born. He in his drunken stupor, inhumanly replied, "Ah, haud yer tongue wooman; ye'll be alright til mornin!" They were lying in one of these old-fashioned beds, to get in which steps were used. When the reprobate by her side refused to get the necessary assistance, the woman arose to get it herself; and as she was going down the steps from the bed to the floor, her infant came into this world, striking its head against the step! The effects of the blow are felt by him to this day! Had I not listened to the above as it was spoken by the mouth of the man who acknowledged to being that inhuman wretch, I would not have believed that a person could become so vile and contemptible! I record this as another awful lesson against the use of that hellish fire and soul-destroying liquid drink!

Reached the conference house at 10:15 P.M. Sister Reid prepared a nice tea, which was very tasty. She is doing fine. The conference house is more like a home now. Brother Reid, too, does all he can to make things pleasant and comfortable. Had they been here ten months ago, the elders and the conference would be *better off* than we are.

Monday, 6 March 1899

Wrote local letters. Made out monthly financial report. Brother Joseph Leggat called.

At 2:30 conducted the funeral services over the remains of Sister Currie. They were held in the morgue, Royal Infirmary, while the body in another room was being coffined and prepared for burial. The services were short. Brother Neilson spoke, Brother McKnight and I respectively offered the opening and benedictory prayers. Went to the cemetery. It is a cold manner they (the Scotch people) have of laying away their dead! At conference house for tea, after which went to Mrs. [Mary] McMinn's and informed her of Brother Edward's illness. Relief Society meeting at 8 P.M.

Before Brother Edward retired, I rubbed him well on the back and chest

---

[295]Elizabeth McGallan Currie (1838-1899) was born in Prestwick, Ayrshire, Scotland. She was baptized into the church in August 1883 and had three sons and two daughters. See *The Latter-day Saints' Millennial Star* 61 (16 March 1899): 176.

with a mixture of turpentine, camphorated gum, and hartshorn. Brother McKnight returned from visiting one of his investigators, and Brother Eccles and Brother Herrick returned from Edinburgh about 10:30. After they retired, Brother Edward went to sleep and has slept undisturbed since, and at this hour, 1 A.M., he is resting quietly and peacefully as can be. I sincerely hope and pray that he will soon regain his usual health, for if anything serious would happen to him, I believe it would make me the most miserable person on earth.

(1:20) The pain seems to have extended from Brother Edward's side to his stomach. He has awakened and his pain is worse. At 3:30 he is resting a little easier. Retired and slept until 8:15 A.M.

Tuesday, 7 March 1899
Brother Edward is very sick. Whenever he moves, the pain in his side fairly brings distortions to his face. Brother McKnight went for Sister Gain. Meanwhile Agnes [Reid] prepared hot poultices. When Sister Gain came, she poulticed his back and chest, and several applications soon brought relief. There is no one [who] can attend a sick person as a mother can. Sister Gain's kind and effectual attendance proved this.

Brother [Edwin T.] Wood, returning elder, came from Bristol. Brother [George M.] Smoot is already here.

Before Sister Gain left at night, she rubbed Brother Edward well with a penetrating mixture, which in about half an hour made him suffer on intense heat; it helped him. Mr. Wallace spent the evening. Mrs. McMinn called.

Wednesday, 8 March 1899
Brother Edward slept very little. He is very weak this morning. Miss Morrison, upstairs, has manifested much kindness, although we are practically strangers to her. She has lent us several very convenient articles. Sister Gain continued the poulticing. Sent a telegram to Liverpool, stating Brother Edward's condition. Answer: "Sail tomorrow." [Reply:] "Impossible." Brother McKnight and I are fasting and praying. About 2 P.M. Brother Edward began to be himself again. From that hour he has continued to improve and tonight he feels better than he has for several weeks. We acknowledge the answer to our prayers and administrations.

At 6 P.M. Miss Sauer[296] came from Liverpool. She comes from Germany and is on her way to New York, thence to Utah. Her history is truly an interesting one, especially since she heard of Mormonism. Born and raised a Catholic, she was being educated for the convent. The first time she heard about the Mormons, she was in a Catholic hospital in Kiel, Germany, practicing as a trained nurse. One of her girl companions told her about the

---

[296]Louise M. F. Sauer had a good education and could speak five languages.

Mormons, and together they stole away and attended the LDS meetings. At her first meeting she was handed a tract, "Is Belief Alone Sufficient?" This she studied. She bought a Bible and hunted for the passages quoted. The Bible, she secreted in a pocket sewed in her *petticoat!* Desiring to know if the same doctrine was taught in the Catholic Bible, she crept into the priest's room one day and took a Catholic Bible and to her surprise found that the teaching was the same. She attended the Mormon meetings and became convinced that the Latter-day Saints teach the gospel of Jesus Christ.

When the "Virgin Sister" found out that Miss Sauer was attending Mormon meetings, she prohibited her from going out and began preparations to send Miss Sauer to the convent. But Louise said she would not go to the convent! Whereupon the matron gave her a choice: to leave the hospital or the Mormons. Miss Sauer was given one hour to give her answer. This hour was occupied in packing her trunk to leave the hospital.

But the matron, surmising the course the girl would take, telegraphed to the girl's father, who came immediately to the hospital and threatened to take Miss Sauer direct to the convent. Seeing the girl's obstinacy, he took her home, locked her in a bathroom for eleven days, and whipped her every day,[297] trying to get her to deny Mormonism and go to the convent. Although her body was black and blue, she absolutely refused, saying she would be killed before she would be a Catholic. The father said he would rather kill her than see her join the Mormons!

The effects of this punishment caused illness. After her recovery, still refusing to give up her desire to join the Church of Christ, she was taken to a "rescue home." This is a place for immoral women. When it was learned that she was a moral girl with no other charge against her than her desire to be a "Mormon," the father was not permitted to put her in. He then took her back home, whipped her again, and then took her to Berlin to put her in an institution there.

Upon his application, the countess sent the father to a magistrate to fill out some necessary papers. When the government official saw the girl, he asked her what was the matter; and she told him unhesitatingly, showing the bleeding wounds on her head as proof. Hearing her sad story, the magistrate imprisoned the father for six weeks, sent the girl to a hospital [for] eighteen weeks, [where she] lost her long black hair,[298] and forbade the father to interfere with her.

She lived at her aunt's in Berlin, and while she was there, the father thought she would be all right. But it happened that the Mormons held

---

[297]John T. Edward, Diary, 12 March 1899, copied notes made by McKay four days earlier, and these notes add the information that Louise's father "would allow her nothing but bread and water."

[298]John T. Edward, Diary, 12 March 1899, added from McKay's notes information about Louise's hair: "While in this hospital, the doctor had to cut all of her hair off so that the wounds on her head would heal. Prior to this her hair was so nice and long that when she stood up straight on her feet she could stand on her hair."

meetings just near the aunt's, and as soon as the girl found this out, she attended, and after the first meeting was handed the same tract, "Is Belief Alone Sufficient." "Oh, I've had that one," she said. "Give me another one." Well, she had to leave her aunt's and was left penniless and without a change of clothing and had to seek a situation! As soon as her father and brothers heard where she was, they would send word to the mistress, blackening Miss Sauer's character. Coming from the father, of course, the reports or accusations were believed and she would lose her situation. So determined were her folks to make her give in, that they even hired boys to stone her as she walked in the street! At length in her desperation she advertised in a foreign paper for a situation as a trained nurse. She secured a situation in London as a housemaid! Her passage money was borrowed from friends, and when she landed in London, she was penniless.

Her new mistress, seeing her destitution, paid her £1/0/0 in advance for the purpose of getting the necessary change of clothing. Instead of buying clothing, she sent 18/0 to her friend in Germany as part payment on what she borrowed, paid 1/6 for a chemise, and kept six pence as spending money for the month!

Six months after landing in London, she found the Mormons at an open-air meeting. Elder B. J. Stewart[299] was distributing "Is Belief Alone Sufficient." He offered her one but was, no doubt, surprised to hear her answer, "I've had that twice. Give me another!" She was delighted and soon told her story. On the following Sunday she was baptized by Brother Stewart and confirmed by Apostle Lund.[300]

Sometime after this she received a letter from her brother, stating that her father was dead and that she was to come home to get her share of the property. She had not sufficient means but pawned her watch and ring, both presents from her mistress, sold her bracelets, and went back to Germany, buying a return ticket.

The letter was simply a scheme to get her back home. For as she entered the house, there sat her father, smoking his long pipe! "Why," she exclaimed, "are you risen again!" Then to use her own words, "They laughed shustht [just] like the very Debbil was in 'em, saying, 'we have the bird in the cage again!'" Although she only had about 1/6 in her pocket, yet she replied, "Oh, no you haven't. I'll go back to London." She stayed that night with a Protestant clergyman's family and, as soon as possible, returned to London, landing in that city with 1½ penny!

She was sick when she landed and was taken to a hospital, where she

---

[299]Barnard J. Stewart (1873-1931) was set apart for a mission to Great Britain on 1 May 1896, arriving in Liverpool on 20 May 1896. He was assigned to the London Conference and returned to Utah in February 1898.

[300]Anthon H. Lund (1844-1921) was ordained an apostle on 7 October 1889. He was a counselor to Joseph F. Smith from 1901 to 1918 and then to Heber J. Grant from 1918 until his death in 1921.

was visited by the elders in London. As she began to recover her strength, she lent books and tracts to other patients, until prohibited from doing so by the priest and ministers.

When she left the hospital, having been away from her situation about six weeks, she went back to her mistress only to find that another girl was in her place, the mistress saying that she could not wait so long. She was now homeless and penniless. Too proud to make known her distress to any of the elders or saints and being determined to be independent, she started out to find another situation. For five days and five nights she was on the streets of London without food and shelter![301] One night a policeman, seeing her so drenched with rain, being wet through and shivering of cold, invited her into the police office, but she refused even that, for fear people would think she had been taken there for some other cause.

After wandering about from place to place, vainly trying to get a respectable situation, she was about to despair and in her misery knelt down in the street and asked God to pity her and open up her way. She remembers rising and walking somewhere, but she knows not how far or where she went. She evidently fainted in the street, for when she regained consciousness, she was lying in a hospital, having been found (they told her afterward) near Kent Road.

After her recovery here, she secured a situation; but five days' experience in the house showed her that the inmates were immoral; so she left immediately, being advised to do so by one of the sisters as well. She then engaged herself to a lady in London for a situation in Brussels. Her debts not having been all paid, she had to leave her trunk and belongings and sail back to the continent without much necessary or extra clothing. In two months, however, she received her trunk.

While in Brussels she first met her "young man"—and the meeting was rather singular. One day while waiting for her mistress just opposite a hall where some persons were singing hymns, a young man, a total stranger to her, was attracted, as she was, to the door to listen. "Go in," she said, "you'll get salvation," and she half pushed him inside.

She heard no more about him until one day they were introduced to each other by one of the elders. She then learned that he was the person whom she pushed into that meeting, which, by the way, was a meeting of Latter-day Saints. He became converted, joined the Church, and was then an active member in the branch where they had met.

Five months' acquaintance resulted in an engagement. Meanwhile her mistress had died and the daughter desired Miss Sauer to go to New York to service to one of [the] mistress's relatives. She accepted the situation, made arrangements to meet her lover and his mother in New York during

---

[301]John T. Edward, Diary, 12 March 1899, added from McKay's notes: "One day she saw a little boy on his way to school throw a crust of bread away . . . and picked it up and ate it."

the following September, and together they would go to Utah.

Since her determination to join the Mormons was first known, she has been homeless and penniless five times, having to start life anew, as it were, each time relying entirely upon her own resources and ability with the guidance of Providence. She compares her life to a little barge, thrown out upon a stormy sea without sail or rudder. She has been tossed about hither and thither by the storms of persecutions; she has been stranded upon the cold, merciless rocks of *poverty*, the sandbars of difficulty and temptations have been struck many times. Yet her eye has been fixed on her guiding star— truth. And the power obtained when she embraced the gospel has given her strength to overcome all difficulties and row safely into the peaceful harbor of, it is to be hoped, a contented and happy home.

Brother Edward was much better at night. We feel that our prayers in his behalf are answered. Broke fast at 5:30 P.M.

Thursday, 9 March 1899

A letter from Father.

Brother Edward continues to improve. After breakfast went to Anchor Line office, accompanied by Miss Sauer. Secured her a nice berth in a good part of the ship and then visited the Art Gallery on Sauchiehall Street. Heard from her of the disgraceful actions of Fred Pieper. As a result of his hypocrisy and sin, one girl has tried to commit suicide and now lies in a hospital, another is broken-hearted, and a third he married. He sent all three to Utah while he was president of the Holland Mission. One had a child to him before she went. He has been excommunicated. Boat S.S. *Anchoria* sailed at 7 P.M. As I bid her good bye, she gave me a nice pocketbook, insisting that I should keep it as a token of remembrance and an expression of her appreciation of the kindness she said she received in Glasgow.

Sister Gain, Nellie [Jack], Miss Steven, Miss [Mary] Major, and Peter Tucker were at the office when I returned. We all went to testimony meeting. A spirit of opposition and discord was manifested, or rather only *felt*. Wrote to Liverpool.

Friday, 10 March 1899

Brother Edward insisted on rising. He sat up awhile but had to lie down again; he is very weak. Wrote diary to date. Brother Miller and Brother White came in from Edinburgh. Visited Sister William Leggat and had a talk with her in regard to the Relief Society. Chatted with the brethren and retired.

Saturday, 11 March 1899

Brother Edward feels fine, excepting a slight headache; he wrote a letter to his wife.

Assisted Brother McKnight in sending out the *Stars*.

Elder Leatham came in from Newarthill and reported affairs there in a worse condition than ever. Orr has misrepresented some of the counsel given him last Saturday and in so doing has made Brother Mitchell feel very discouraged. Wrote a letter to Brother Mitchell and one to Sister Jack, declining to *assist* "her husband's minister" in marrying her daughter Jeanie. The elders and some of the saints in the Burnbank District came in to attend the baptism of one Mr. [David L.] Miller.[302] Brother Smith baptized him at 5:30 P.M. and Brother Gould confirmed him a member of the Church. John Cook, president of the Burnbank Branch, called later. I have reason to believe that everything is not just right with the branch out there.

Brother Cairney, James Neilson, Willie Cooke, Maggie Gain, Maggie Kelly, and one or two others called. Very tired at twelve, when we retired.

Sunday, 12 March 1899

Brother McKnight went to Cambuslang. I attended Sunday School at twelve, afternoon service at two, and evening service at 6:30. An excellent spirit prevailed throughout the day. Mrs. Jack accompanied me from the hall to conference house during the dinner hour and explained the condition and cause of the trouble in Newarthill.

Brother Edward is still improving, but I fear he is too careless in going from one room to another. Should he catch cold and take a relapse, it will certainly go hard with him.

Monday, 13 March 1899

Brother Edward, feeling fine, takes his meals as usual.

Attended to office correspondence, including a letter to Mr. Soutar, solicitor, Dunfermline; sending him the *form* properly signed by Mr. Muir, Beaver, authorizing me to act in the matter of disinterring the late Elder Muir's body. Wrote to Liverpool.

In the afternoon visited Sister Hunter and heard the history of some of the "goody-goody" members of the branch. Meeting at night with Brothers Neilson and Leggat. Discussed branch matters and chose a finance committee. Mr. McMinn called to see Brother Edward; Mr. Smith also called. After Brothers Neilson and Leggat left, I chatted a while with the two gentleman and convoyed Mr. Smith a short distance home. He is going to Washington. Promised to come to our meeting next Sunday night. When I returned, Brother Edward was suffering intensely from the pain in his side. Brother McKnight and I administered to him, and we all retired.

We had scarcely laid down before Brother Edward began to cough and his pain became almost unendurable. He wanted a plaster. Went to the doctor's after one, but he had none. He advised us to apply poultices. The linseed meal was gone, so I made a poultice out of oatmeal and mustard.

---

[302]William S. Gould, Diary, 11 March 1899, indicated that the baptism was held at the Townhead Baths.

Fig. 46 *Charing Cross, Glasgow.*

Brother McKnight was then called, and he stayed with Brother Edward, while I went to Charing Cross (Fig. 46) after linseed meal. It was then 2:30 A.M. Returning, Brother McKnight retired and I made a poultice, applying it to the afflicted part. Brother Edward then slept until 5:30 A.M.

Tuesday, 14 March 1899

About nine Brother McKnight went for Sister Gain, who came and applied poultices to his back and chest and side. He is a very sick man. At 3 P.M. when the poultices were removed, he could hardly speak. At this hour —6 P.M.—he is sleeping. At 10 P.M. he was feeling a little easier and, if he gets a good night's rest, he will be better. Wrote for his release. Sent out letters to the elders appointing a general fast from tomorrow (Wednesday) 10 A.M. until Thursday morning. Sister Gain remained all night. Arrival of Elder Elwell.[303]

Wednesday, 15 March 1899

Brother Edward did not cough once during the night. The pain in his side is no worse, but he is still very weak. Letter from President Lyman. Receipts, etc. Remained with Brother Edward all day. Wrote to Mrs. [Lizzie] Edward, Father, and Ray. Some of the saints called to see Brother Edward, bringing him flowers and delicious fruit.

At 6 P.M., the hour appointed for all the elders to offer a special prayer, Elders McKnight, Elwell, and I administered to Brother Edward. Brother Elwell offered prayer, I anointed, and Brother McKnight sealed the anoint-

---

[303]Isaac Elwell, Jr. (1880-1928) was born in Birmingham, England. His parents joined the Church and emigrated to Utah in 1881. He was set apart on 17 February 1899 for a mission to Great Britain, arriving in Liverpool on 13 March 1899. However, he returned on S.S. *Anchoria,* which left Glasgow on 25 March 1899. He arrived back in Utah on 10 April 1899.

ing.[304] Later Sister Gain rubbed his back and chest well with a mixture of turpentine and something, and after all had left or retired, he fell asleep.

Thursday, 16 March 1899

Last night Brother Edward slept well and has awakened this morning much improved and strengthened. Yesterday he had to be assisted to sit in bed; this morning he gets up almost without an effort. His pain is nearly gone. He said to me that a more direct answer to prayer and a more effective *administration* he has never before experienced. He feels much encouraged. Broke our fast at 9:30. His honorable release came from Liverpool with an encouraging letter from President Lyman.

Attended to correspondence. Testimony meeting at night. An excellent attendance. A good spirit was manifest.

Brother Edward is suffering of a severe headache.

Friday, 17 March 1899

Trouble and disappointment never come in moderation! Brother Edward must go home on account of his ill health. And this morning Brother McKnight's release has come with a letter from President Snow through President Lyman, stating that Brother McKnight's father is ill and that he (Brother McKnight) must sail on the 25th current! Missionary life is made up of changes and surprises!

Brother Elwell is completely discouraged. He dreamed last night that he was taken home in a coffin, and this has frightened him so that he is determined to return home immediately. All the counsel and entreaties that we can possibly give are of no avail! "I'm going home," he says. "I don't care what follows!"

Brother McKnight left for Edinburgh. Later in the day Brother Elwell and I had a sincere, confidential talk, during which he made a confession that makes his immediate return home necessary. The poor boy is in a serious difficulty, made more serious by his coming on a mission without making reparation for his act at home. He cried bitterly as he told me his story and asked advice in regard to the course of action he should pursue. He is a bright young man, but his early associations have been injurious to his morals. However, if he carries out the determinations he expressed to me, his future life will be a better one than his past. By his manly confession and good desires expressed, he has won my sympathy and regard. Wrote to President Lyman about allowing Brother Elwell to return home with the next boat!

---

[304]It was common during this period for an administration of the sick to consist of three parts: the prayer, the anointing, and the sealing. For example, at 19 October 1897 when McKay simply said "we administered to her," Joseph H. Mitchell, Diary, 19 October 1897, gives the details of this administration: "I was called to offer the prayer, Bro. Johnston anointed her, and Bro. McKay sealed the anointing."

Saturday, 18 March 1899

Brother Elwell and I addressed and sent away *Stars*.

Brother Edward is still improving. Several elders and saints called. A provoking case or difficulty has arisen between Brother Neilson and the Relief Society! O, it is disgusting; they act like children! And yet they mean to do what is right! One is sometime put to his wit's end to know just how best to act.

At 6:45 Elder Thomas Kerr[305] arrived. He comes from Cache Valley and will labor as a traveling elder in this conference.

Sunday, 19 March 1899

Brother McKnight and Brother Elwell went to Cambuslang. Brother Edward, of course, remained in the room, he being unable to go out, and Brother Kerr and I went to Sunday School at 12:00, meeting at 2:00, and evening services at 6:30.

There were seven strangers at the evening meeting—Mr. Smith, his daughter, her two young lady friends, and three others. They expressed themselves as being well pleased with the meeting. They seemed to be favorably impressed, even going so far as to say if she attends any more, she might have to join. She was told to be sure and attend.

All in the conference house felt *fine* at night.

Monday, 20 March 1899

Letter from Counselor Naisbitt[306] regarding Brother Elwell. The latter will be allowed to return home next Saturday.

Called on Brother Neilson. Trouble brewing between him and the Relief Society! Trouble over a paltry ten shillings! Attended to sundry duties.

Tuesday, 21 March 1899

Letter from President Lyman, favoring the course taken with Brother

---

[305]Thomas A. Kerr (1849-1942) was born in Harthill, Lanarkshire, Scotland. He was set apart for a mission to Great Britain on 17 February 1899, arriving in Liverpool on 13 March 1899. Within the Scottish Conference Kerr labored in the areas of Ayrshire, Edinburgh, Glasgow, and Uddingston. He was released in September 1900. See the Thomas A. Kerr Diary, Accession 1751, located in the Manuscripts Division, J. Willard Marriott Library, University of Utah, Salt Lake City.

[306]Henry W. Naisbitt (1825-1908) was set apart in October 1876 for a mission to Great Britain, returning two years later. He had seven wives—marrying Elizabeth Paul in 1853 (eight children), Mary Ann Luff in 1862 (six children), Catherine Hagell in 1867 (eight children), Elizabeth Irvine Hagell in 1870 (five children), Frances Hirst in 1879 (four children), and Rachel Bowes and Alice Ann Clark (dates and children not known). For his practice of polygamy, Naisbitt was twice imprisoned in the Utah Territorial Penitentiary: May to November 1886 and May to October 1890. He was set apart on 4 November 1898 as a counselor in the presidency of the European Mission, returning in June 1901. Naisbitt wrote *Quiet Chats on Mormonism* (Salt Lake City: The Deseret News, 1902) and *Rhymelets in Many Moods* (Salt Lake City: Star Printing Co., 1901).

Elwell.[307] Brother McQuarrie came home this morning about five o'clock. He says he had an enjoyable trip visiting Cardiff, Wales, London, and Belfast.

Made inquiry at undertakers concerning the shipment of Elder Muir's body.

Wednesday, 22 March 1899

Wrote part of a long letter to Annie but was interrupted.

At 1:13 left Glasgow for Airdrie. Joined the elders there and together we went to Newarthill, where serious trouble is still brewing. Called on all the members and found them feeling quite well spiritually, with the exception of Orr, in whom only seems to center all the trouble.

Meeting at 6:30. Excellent feeling prevailed. After meeting Brother Mitchell and Brother Orr[308] made friends, shook hands, and parted in good spirits, the latter promising to make the required public explanation. (Tales of woe from Orr and a long run to catch the train!)

Back to Glasgow at 10:30 P.M.

Thursday, 23 March 1899

In office until after dinner. About 2:30 P.M. took Brother Kerr to a new *tracting street*—St. Vincent. This was his introduction to the pleasant (?) duty of tracting![309] Distributed about twenty, taking one side of the street and he the other.

Testimony meeting at night. Elders Mitchell, Nisbet, Eccles, Smith, Kerr, and Elwell went with Brother McKnight and held an open-air meeting at Bridgeton Cross,[310] returning to testimony meeting before it dismissed.

Several returning elders are here also, so the conference house is well-filled.

Friday, 24 March 1899

Arose at 6:45 A.M. and went to Central Station to meet the Masters family. Secured a van[311] and sent their luggage to the docks. I went down on the clutha.

Broke fast at 10:30 A.M. Preparations are being made for the marriage ceremony tonight. This will be my second experience as *parson*. At 6:30

---

[307]Platte De Alton Lyman, Diary, 20 March 1899, recorded: "Received a letter from Isaac Elwell in Glasgow, who came in the last company of missionaries, stating that he was going home, even though he had to work his passage."

[308]McKay wrote "Bro. Mitchell and Bro. McKay," but the difficulties are between Mitchell and Orr—so the editors have corrected the text.

[309]Thomas A. Kerr, Diary, 23 March 1899, wrote about his first experience at tracting: "Don't think very much of the job. However, I had very good success."

[310]William P. Nisbet, Diary, 23 March 1899, explained that McKnight wanted to hold the open-air meeting (which lasted two hours) because he was leaving in two days.

[311]A *van* was a closed carriage for carrying the luggage of railway passengers.

P.M., the friends of the bride and bridegroom being present and "all necessary requirements having been met and no objections having been offered," the marriage ceremony of Mr. David Cooke, Jr., and Miss Jeanie Major Jack was performed.

Jeanie was quite agitated, but David stood the ordeal *fine*.[312] After the ceremony, all sat around the tables spread with the *delicacies* of *Scotland* and enjoyed the company of the new married couple during the rest of the evening. Songs and recitations were the order. At 10:30 all was over and the happy couple left for their home near Cambuslang, amid the hearty congratulations and best wishes of all present.

Owing to Brother Edward's not feeling so well as usual, everything was kept as quiet as possible. The day has been one of intense anxiety to me, for Brother Edward seems to have taken a slight relapse and the thought that the crowd's coming into the house might make him worse has me really miserable. However, there's no use "crossing the bridge 'til we come to it."

Saturday, 25 March 1899

At 10:15 A.M. met Brother Neilson, according to appointment, and together we called to see the proprietor of the new hall, making final preparations for our first meeting to be held on Sunday, 16th April.

Called at Argyle Hotel, found all the returning elders and saints well, and then went to Anchor Line office and exchanged passengers' tickets. Exchanged £20/0/0 English currency for American coin for Brother Masters and sent £120/0/0 to Liverpool through Henderson Brothers.

Meeting with company at Argyle Hotel at 4 P.M. All went to the boat —S.S. *Furnessia*—and went aboard at 5:30.

Brother Elwell is feeling gloomy, but it is a good thing that he is going home.

Wrote to Liverpool. Found it necessary to go back to docks to get an address from Masters and to give Brother McKnight 5/0. The boat did not sail until 9:30 P.M. Brother Eccles and Brother Nisbet will not go back to their field tonight but [will] wait and assist us tomorrow. Tired.

Sunday, 26 March 1899

Brother Eccles and Brother Stewart went to Cambuslang, while Brothers Kerr, Nisbet (who came in from Elderslie), and I remained in Glasgow.

Priesthood meeting at eleven, Sunday school at 12:30, afternoon meeting at 2:00, and evening services at 6:30 P.M. A special priesthood meeting was called after the night meeting to consider some unfinished business— the excommunicating of some of the members who have for years been "falling away."

---

[312]Joseph H. Mitchell, Diary, 24 March 1899, added: "Bro. McKay tied the knot in a very impressive manner and gave them some excellent advice."

Monday, 27 March 1899

Letter from Father. Wrote to Liverpool, Dundee, and other places. Called on Sister Harkins.

Meeting at 7 P.M. (they did not come until 8:00) with Neilson and Leggat. We got along nicely with all deliberations until they began to manifest a desire to be honored more by the officers of the Relief Society and Sunday School. Then I almost became disgusted. The idea of men asking to be honored more! They ought to always remember that "he that humblest himself shall be exalted and he that exalteth himself shall be abased" [Luke 14:11].

Mr. Wallace called. Retired at 10:30 P.M.

Tuesday, 28 March 1899

Wrote to Annie and Tommy. Spent the day in the office. Raining all day.

Wednesday, 29 March 1899

Prepared to go to Dunfermline. At 1:20 left Queen Street Station and arrived in Dunfermline about 3 P.M. Elder Stewart and Wickens met me at the station and together we went to their lodgings.

Called on Mr. Soutar. Obtained the sheriff's warrant to exhume the remains of the late Elder Muir. Paid him £3/0/0 for his services and then went to find the undertaker, whom I made an appointment to meet at six o'clock. At that hour the contract was made that he should make a substantial, lead-lined coffin and packing case, attend to all the sealing, etc., and bring the remains from Bowhill Cemetery to Dunfermline Station for £12/10/0.

Made a few calls that night and retired.

Thursday, 30 March 1899

At 9:30 A.M. called on Dr. Dendle and obtained his certificate that deceased died of a noninfectious disease. It was left with Soutar, who charged 10/6 for certificate. Called on Lamberton and made final arrangements.

Next interviewed the U.S. consul [McCunn], making an appointment to meet him next Saturday morning and take him to the scene of exhumation, which it is necessary for him to witness. All arrangements now being completed in Dunfermline, my next step was to go to Lochgelly. As there was no train at that hour, 11:30 A.M., I concluded to walk. The brethren decided to accompany me. The weather was fair and the roads comparatively good, so we had but little trouble. We walked the distance (eight miles or more) in exactly two hours.

Called on Mr. [Robert] Wilson, the undertaker, and obtained his certificate as to identity. The registrar was seen next and the necessary papers obtained from him. Then had to see the sexton. This necessitated a walk of four miles, which was made in a hurry, as we desired to go back to Dunfermline on the 5 P.M. train.

Everything was successful. Left Dunfermline at 8:26 P.M., arriving in

Glasgow about one hour and thirty minutes later. Found Brother Edward still improving.

Letters from Claire, David R., and [blank].

Friday, 31 March 1899

Called on Sister Harkins and the Neilson family. Busy with conference correspondence and office duties. Sisters Gain and McDonald, and Jeanie [Gain] called in the evening. About 8 P.M. Miss Sharp came in from Innellan on her way home. She is looking very well and feeling well, also. Accompanied her to the train.

Saturday, 1 April 1899

Boarded the 6:40 A.M. train bound for Dunfermline, where I arrived a few minutes before eight o'clock. Found that the elders had already started on foot to Lochgelly.

After eating a light breakfast at the hotel (porridge, nine pence), met the U.S. consul at his office. At 10 A.M. we took train to Lochgelly. Hired cab from station to Bowhill Cemetery, two miles from Lochgelly. At 10:30, the hour appointed to raise the body, we were on the spot, standing by the open grave containing the coffin. A few minutes later Mr. Lamberton and his men came and action was begun at once. The coffin was raised, placed on two stretchers, and carried to a quiet corner in the cemetery.

Being desirous of knowing beyond the possibility of doubt that the coffin contained the body, I requested the men to remove the lid. They did so. Then we beheld a ghastly sight! I shall not attempt to describe it! The lid was quickly fastened and the coffin containing the body [was] put into a casket lined with lead. The casket was then hermetically sealed and put into a packing case eight feet two and a half inches long and two feet nine inches wide. A policeman, the parish minister, and one or two others moved by idle curiosity had now come on the scene, while in groups across the street stood men and boys watching the proceedings with intense interest. It took more than two hours to complete the packing, and a cold wind was blowing all the while.

After all was finished, Mr. McCunn and I hastened to the station to catch the 1:28 train for Dunfermline. It was 2 P.M. before we arrived in the latter town and only two hours and thirty-six minutes left to draw up papers, find the doctor, and complete all preparations before the body could be shipped! Mr. McCunn went without his dinner and worked diligently to finish all arrangements. After all was over, he expressed himself as being pleased to have met me and hoped the acquaintance would continue. He said he would be pleased to do all he could for our people.

At 4 P.M. I was at the station, met Mr. Lamberton, paid him £12/10/0, and bid him good-bye.

The case containing the remains was put into a special car, conveniently switched to make the transfer from the lorry easy. Paid the railway company £2/4/0 for booking corpse. Arrived in Glasgow at 6:30 P.M. Wylie and Lockhead took remains to their morgue. It took twelve or fourteen men to handle the casket, which weighs 500 pounds or more! After seeing the body at rest in the morgue, took car to conference house.

Tired. Brother Smith, Brother Mitchell, Brother Leggat, Maggie Gain, Maggie Kelly, and the Misses Wallace were in. Leggat wanted money; gave him 3/6. Retired about 11:30!

Sunday, 2 April 1899
Fast Day. Walked to Cambuslang and held meeting at twelve noon. Ate dinner at 3 P.M. at Mrs. Cooke's. Brother Reid accompanied me. After calling on Brother and Sister [James] Robertson and Brother and Sister [Crawford] Russell, where Mr. and Mrs. Mack were waiting to see us, we hastened to Glasgow to fill an appointment at 5 P.M.

Meeting at 6:30 P.M. Brother Edward attended the afternoon meeting, notwithstanding the inclemency of the weather, a Scotch mist[313] having fallen all day. [James] Clark occupied the time at night. A poor sermon. He seemed to be utterly devoid of the spirit. Felt hurt because he had not been called upon more often. Revels in drink Saturday night and then thinks he ought to preach to the saints on Sunday! Not much! The best sermons are preached by acts, not words.

Monday, 3 April 1899
Letter from Miss Sauer, George E. [Ferrin].
Spent the entire day writing to Liverpool and making up accounts. Janet [Lang], Mary [McDonald], the Misses Steven, Mrs. Steven, Mrs. Clunie, and Miss Park called. At night Brother Edward and I visited Mrs. McMinn, S[outh] S[ide].

As we were coming home, he stepped off the car near the post office and in some way tripped over my foot, falling full length upon the hard pavement. A large crowd gathered around and for a moment we thought he was seriously hurt, but besides skinning his knees and hand, he suffered no injury. Retired 10:30. Up at twelve, again at one o'clock, opening the door for Thomson and Brother McQuarrie.

Tuesday, 4 April 1899
General duties. In and around office all day. Marked box containing Elder Muir's body.

At night Elders Edward and McQuarrie and I visited Mr. and Mrs. Barrie's. Spent a very pleasant evening indeed. During a short discussion on

---

[313]The term *Scotch mist* refers to a particularly heavy and wetting mist, which is notably continuous, dense, and penetrating.

religion, the belief of the Swedenborgians[314] concerning the Godhead was brought up. They believe the three personages—Father, Son, and Holy Ghost—to be one in *substance*. Mr. Barrie did not agree with this idea, and he was very much surprised when he discovered that the catechism of his own church teaches the same doctrine. He threw the catechism down, saying, "Well, I didn't know that was in there before." He believed with us that there are three distinct personages.

Stormy.

Wednesday, 5 April 1899

Made a call on Sauchiehall Street. Settled with Wylie and Lockhead and had the remains of Elder Muir put aboard the S.S. *Ethiopia*.[315] Found out that Anchor [Line] Company was charging too much for shipping corpse.

At night while on my way to [Duncan] Thomson's, off Gallowgate, fell in with Mr. McColl and Mr. McMinn. A long discussion on Mormonism and Spiritualism followed. Mr. McMinn is a shrewd debater. We are going to meet again.

It was 10 P.M. when I reached Thomson's. Found all well, but Sister Robertson and the baby have been ill. Retired at 11:30.

Thursday, 6 April 1899

At 7:45 A.M. met Johnson and family at St. Enoch's Station. Made arrangements for taking luggage to boat. Brother Eccles, who has been called into the conference house to take Brother Edward's place, took charge. Conferred with Anchor Line Company and succeeded in getting a reduction of £8/0/0 for transportation of corpse. Exchanged tickets. Wrote instructions for, and gave all necessary papers to, Brother McQuarrie.[316]

Boat sailed at 5:30 P.M., thirty-eight passengers in LDS company. Testimony meeting at night. Wrote to Liverpool.

Friday, 7 April 1899

Secured Townhead Baths for baptism tomorrow. Called on Sister Noble, who is not getting along very well. Visited Georgina [Leggat], also. She says she feels all right and is quite well-satisfied with her lot. Attended to correspondence.

---

[314]Emanuel Swedenborg (1688-1772) was a Swedish philosopher and biblical theologian, whose main interest was cosmology and the nature of the human soul. He wrote an eight-volume compendium on doctrine entitled *Arcana Coelestia*. After his death, various followers established three separate church bodies: the General Conference of the New Church (in England), the General Convention of the New Jerusalem, and the General Church of the New Jerusalem (both in the United States).

[315]Thomas A. Kerr, Diary, 5 April 1899, explained his assignment by McKay: "In the afternoon went to the morgue and looked after the loading [of] the body of Bro. Muir in the ship to be sent to Utah for burial."

[316]John T. Edward, Diary, 6 April 1899, clarified that "the remains of Elder Muir were sent in charge of Elder McQuarrie."

At 7:30 P.M. Brother Edward and I visited the Wallace family and enjoyed a good gospel conversation with the mother and her two daughters, the old gentleman himself "has taken tae beer again." James came in later; but I fancied he seemed a little cold. However, they all gave us a warm invitation to return soon. "Dinna' be lang til yer back again."

Saturday, 8 April 1899

Wrote to Claire and Mr. Muir. At 1 P.M. Brother Edward went to Edinburgh. At 4 P.M. the elders from Airdrie came in. Brother Mitchell will now labor in Glasgow.

At 6 P.M. Elder Leatham performed three baptisms—Peter Selkirk, Jeanie Orr, and Mary McKay. All were afterward confirmed in the conference house.

At 8 P.M. a special priesthood meeting, previously called, was held in the conference house for the purpose of hearing the reasons from members "falling away," why they should not be dealt with. Six summons had been sent and only one answered personally,[317] two by letter, while three sent no answer at all. A good spirit prevailed in the council. No action to excommunicate was taken. All were given another chance. The meeting lasted four hours.

Sunday, 9 April 1899

Thirty-eighth anniversary of Father and Mother's wedding. Brother Mitchell and Brother Eccles went to Cambuslang—I stayed in "Glasga' all my lane"!

Sunday School at 12:00, meetings as usual at 2:00 and 6:30 P.M. Ate dinner at Martha Leggat's. After the night meeting, we all went to Neilson's.

Monday, 10 April 1899

Made out monthly reports.

Letter from Claire.

At night accompanied Brother Edward (who returned from Edinburgh today) to visit his relatives, the Scott family on New City Road. Miss Maggie [Scott] is unwell. However, we spent a very pleasant evening but had no conversation on the gospel.

Tuesday, 11 April 1899

Sent reports, cash, etc., to Liverpool. Secured draft for passage money for Brother [William] Gracie's family.

In and around the office all day.

At night Miss Nellie Jack, Mrs. Clunie, and the Misses Wallace called.

---

[317]John Currie, Sr., came to the meeting, expressed repentance, and asked for forgiveness.

Wednesday, 12 April 1899

Writing in the forenoon. Ordered suit. Called on Miss and Mrs. Hunter.

At night the three of us—Brother Edward, Brother Eccles, and I—went to the Royalty Theatre to see *The Runaway Girl*. Pretty girls and fine costumes were the only commendable features about it. The theatre, though, was crowded and considerable enthusiasm was manifested; but it is not a good play.

Thursday, 13 April 1899

Spent the morning hours writing. In the afternoon attended to sundry duties. Testimony meeting at night.

Friday, 14 April 1899

At 10 A.M. Brother Edward and I boarded the train for Stirling, where we arrived less than one hour later. Went direct to Miss Sharp's, who knew of our coming. She met us at the door and gave us a hearty welcome.

After a few minutes chat, we went out to visit the castle. On our road stepped inside the East and West Churches, the former being noted for its *age* and the latter for the crowning of Queen Mary when she was only eight months old. Our two-pence tickets admitted us into the Guild Hall as well. After looking at old relics—the pulpit of John Knox, old weights and measures, views, etc.—we walked out to the cemetery and climbed the Ladies' Rock, from the top of which a good view of the King's Park is obtained.

But the castle is the best place from which to see everything—best with the exception of the [Wallace] Monument—so to the castle we wended our way, passing Snowdown House and the poor old blind man, who is *always* on this particular walk, greeting the passersby with a "It's a fine day," "There's a cauld wind the day," or "Soft[318] day today," etc. The remark changing with the weather. He never asks for a penny, but he gets them all the same. We soon climbed the steps leading to the esplanade. Just opposite stands the Statue of Bruce, the hero depicted as unsheathing his sword as he gazes on the Field of Bannockburn. I shall not describe the castle here. Suffice it to say we secured a good guide and spent an interesting hour. We came down the steps again and walked around the "back walk," leading to the hill upon which stands the famous Beheading Stone.

It was then time for dinner, and as we did not wish to keep Miss Sharp waiting, we hastened to "No. 9" [Douglas Street]. It is needless to say that the dinner was excellent! After enjoying it and assuring our sweet hostess that we did enjoy it, we walked to Abbey Craig, upon which stands the Wallace Monument (Fig. 47). After climbing 246 steps, we were at the top of the monument from where one beholds one of the most beautiful land-

---

[318]In the Scottish dialect, *soft day* refers to a wet or rainy day in which the soil is kept soft.

Fig. 47 *William Wallace Monument, Stirling.*

scaped scenes on earth![319] Today the wind was blowing a hurricane, as usual, so we did not stay long. By the time we reached the bottom of the hill, Brother Edward was about tired out. In fact, he thought he would have "to roll down," as his ankles seemed to be giving away. However, we managed to the car and were soon comfortably seated in the easy chairs in our "Stirling Home." The rest of the evening was spent here, with the exception of an hour with Mr. McKenzie. James [Sharp] was more sociable than he had ever been before.

Saturday, 15 April 1899

Seven o'clock came too early! But we had to get up as Brother Edward wanted to board the 8 A.M. train for Aberdeen. Annie had breakfast ready as soon as we were ready for it; and after doing it justice, we went to the station and Brother Edward rolled out for the North. I returned to "No. 9" and spent the rest of the day with the Sharp family. I believe Annie will yet join the Church, but I am doubtful about the others—it is difficult to get gospel conversations with them.

Arrived in Glasgow at 5:30 P.M. All were well. Elders Miller, Wickens, Nisbet, Kerr, and Gould, in response to letters sent to them, have come in to attend the opening services in the Carlton Hall tomorrow.

Wrote to Liverpool. Maggie Gain, Maggie Kelly, and Jeanie [Gain] called.

Sunday, 16 April 1899

Brother Eccles and Brother Kerr went to Cambuslang, while the rest of us stayed in Glasgow. Sunday School as usual, after which we went directly to the new hall, 4 Carlton Place—a neat, little, cozy hall, capable of seating comfortably about 200 persons. Opening services at 2 P.M., after which I offered a dedicatory prayer, prefacing the same with a few remarks. Elders Miller, Wickens, and Gould were the speakers.

Dinner at Brother [William] Hamilton's. Evening services at 6:30. Good attendance. Elders Kerr, Eccles, and Nisbet occupied the time. A good spirit prevailed. All seemed well-pleased with the change, and as a result, a bright future is opening for the branch.[320]

---

[319]John E. Edward, Diary, 14 April 1899, added: "The landscape from the Wallace Monument on a clear day is the most beautiful I ever saw in my life. From it we could see the windings of the River Forth, which are very beautiful to look upon."

[320]McKay wrote the following about the Glasgow Branch: "The necessity of securing suitable halls for public worship in respectable localities is apparent to every missionary throughout the British Mission. This fact has been realized by the members of the Glasgow Branch; and yesterday [16 April 1899] they met in a new hall so far superior to the one they are leaving that there is really no comparison. Several elders from surrounding districts attended the opening services, the saints were out *en masse*, and, as all were united and gratified with their new surroundings, a rich outpouring of the Spirit was manifested. All seemed to realize that a new era is dawning for the work in Glasgow. The officers and members are to be congratulated upon the progressive step they have taken." See David O. McKay, letter of 17 April

Fig. 48 *David O. McKay, Joseph H. Mitchell, and John T. Edward.*

Monday, 17 April 1899

Around town making sundry calls. After dinner Brother Eccles and I called on Mrs. Rankin and Mrs. Hildar, and were warmly welcomed by each and cordially invited to visit them some evening in the near future. As we were returning to the conference house, we met C[hristian] Sorensen and Brig Jensen on Union Street. They are returning from their missions in Scandinavia. At 6 P.M. Brother Edward returned from Aberdeen. He, C. Sorensen, Jensen, Elder Eccles, and I went to the Royalty Theatre to see *A Trip to Chinatown*. The company was rather weak. However, we enjoyed it quite well.

Tuesday, 18 April 1899

Office work. Wrote a long letter to Mamma. Went to Sister McDonald's. In the evening several of the young folks, including Christian Sorensen and Brig Jensen, called and spent an hour or so singing.

Wednesday, 19 April 1899

Letter from Fred Schade, giving character of one Peter Neilsen, who has applied for a ticket to Utah. Spent the day in attending to emigration duties. At night Brother Edward's farewell social was given (Fig. 48).[321]

1899, in "Abstract of Correspondence," *The Latter-day Saints' Millennial Star* 61 (20 April 1899): 244.

[321]Elders Edward, Mitchell, and McKay had a group photograph taken this day.

Fig. 49 *Princes Pier, Greenock.*

This was the first of the kind held in the new hall and was a good success. The Misses Scott, Brother Edward's cousins, assisted by their good singing in making the program spicy and interesting. The Misses Wallace applied for baptism.

Thursday, 20 April 1899

It was late last night before we retired, and it seemed that our eyes had scarcely closed when the doorbell rang. It was some passengers for the boat, who had just come from Ireland, 4:45 A.M. After starting a fire and making them as comfortable as possible, I lay down for another hour's rest. Soon the others in the house began to stir and sleep was out of the question. After breakfast changed tickets, money, etc. Meeting with elders and emigrants at 2 P.M.

At 5 P.M. we were at the quay, where a large crowd had gathered to see Brother Edward away. Sister McDonald stood the parting with her little child, Maggie, very well.[322] Miss [Maggie] Scott came aboard and comforted the little one, taking care of her as far as Greenock, where she and I bade good-bye to Brother Edward and the rest of the company and, boarding the tender to Princes Pier (Fig. 49), took train to Glasgow. The German passengers, having been delayed, came aboard at Greenock. After a pleasant hour's ride, we arrived in Glasgow. Accompanied Miss Scott home, 767 New City Road.

Friday, 21 April 1899

At 10:20 A.M. left St. Enoch's Station bound for Kilmarnock. Was met at the station by Elders Nisbet and Kerr. Spent an hour or so in Killie and

---

[322]Because Sister McDonald was a widow with eight children and because Elder Edward and his wife had lost their only child when she was six weeks old, he offered to adopt her five-year-old daughter Margaret and take her home to Utah. Sister McDonald decided to allow this. See John T. Edward, Diary, 17 and 25 March 1899.

then walked about four miles to Galston and visited Brother and Sister Graham. They seemed pleased to see us and made us as welcome as possible.

Desiring to get back to Kilmarnock to catch the 6:15 P.M. train for Ayr, our visit with [the] Grahams was short. When we reached the Kilmarnock Cross, we had only twenty-five minutes to go to the elders' lodgings, get our coats and satchel, and get back to station! O, what a hurry! What a run! And then after all—after rushing into the station, tired and breathless— there was no train at 6:10! Brother Nisbet had made a mistake; the train to Ayr was an hour later! This changed our arrangements.

At 7:15 boarded train for Ayr. Brother Nisbet held the appointed meeting in that town and Brother Kerr and I continued on to Maybole and held a meeting at C. Burns's with the saints there at 10 P.M. Retired at twelve.

Saturday, 22 April 1899

Arose about eight o'clock, ate our ham and eggs prepared by Mrs. Burns, bade our kind hostess good-bye, and walked to the station to board the 9:15 A.M. train for Ayr. Saw all the Burnses and [William] Hawthorne before leaving. The train was on time—something unusual in Scotland—and in about three-fourths an hour we were again in "the auld toon."

Brother Nisbet failed to meet us, so we started out alone, and after no little difficulty, succeeded in finding Sister Thomson. Called on Mrs. Wilson, with whom I had a warm discussion. She is angry at the elders laboring there. Later met Brother Nisbet at a Mr. Frith's. Dinner at Mrs. Thomson's. Left Ayr for Kilmarnock at 2:05 P.M. At the Kilmarnock Station we were met by Brother Campbell from Darvel. All repaired to the elders' lodgings and had a "guid crack."

At 5:30 Brother Kerr and I went to Gateside near Beith to visit Brother and Sister [Robert] Gray, and the other two—Brother Nisbet and Brother Campbell—remained in Kilmarnock to hold an open-air meeting. When Brother Gray was told that I had only one hour to stay with him, he said, "Well, I'm real sorry fer that, ye might ha' stayed 'til Munday—a good room, good fire, good bed, plenty o' *mate*[323]—why can't ye stay?" He and Sister Gray are feeling very well. Brother Kerr remained with them until m[orning], and I came to Glasgow, arriving the latter place at 10 P.M.

Found two new elders at the office—Elders John Young[324] and William Cameron[325]—they supply a long-felt want.

---

[323] A *mate* or mat was a bedcover.

[324] John B. Young (1866-1946) was born in Gorebridge, Midlothian, Scotland. He was set apart for a mission to Great Britain on 31 March 1899, arriving in Liverpool on 21 April 1899. In the Scottish Conference Young labored in the areas of Cambuslang, Edinburgh, and Glasgow. He was released in May 1901 and returned to Utah the following month. See the John B. Young Diaries, Accession 1738, located in the Manuscripts Division, J. Willard Marriott Library, University of Utah, Salt Lake City.

[325] William Cameron (1862-1928) was born in Inkerman, Renfrewshire, Scotland. He was

Sunday, 23 April 1899

Brothers Mitchell and Young went to Cambuslang; the rest of us in the office attended the regular meetings. At night, however, in response to an invitation from Mr. Barrie, I accompanied him and his wife to a lecture on "The Impending Judgments of Christendom," delivered by an evangelist of the Catholic Apostolic Church[326] in the Saint Andrew's Hall. After the meeting was dismissed, accepted the invitation to go home with Mr. and Mrs. Barrie and discuss points of likeness and difference between the doctrine advanced and the Latter-day Saints' belief. Mrs. Barrie said, "It's enough to make us all turn heathen—so many ways being taught!" Spent a very pleasant evening.

Monday, 24 April 1899

Attended to conference correspondence. Called at Anchor Line office to see about some extra charges that were made from Carlisle to Glasgow in railroad fares.

At night visited the Wallace family, thinking they would set a night for baptism; but their baptism was not mentioned. Mr. Wallace though, I believe, was more sociable than ever, as indeed all were, but yet they did not seem very anxious about the gospel.

The other brethren held an open-air meeting at Bridgeton Cross. They said they had a fine time. There are good prospects for lively open-air work this summer.

Tuesday, 25 April 1899

Did nothing much during the day but study. A full company (forty) of Scandinavians arrived. They will sail Friday morning next.

An open-air meeting on Cathedral Square was well-attended, the crowd manifesting a keen interest in what was being said. Some sect took their station a short distance from us and began to sing but, after singing two or three hymns without attracting our crowd, they gave it up and left. A good spirit seemed to prevail. Subjects: atonement and the principles of the gospel.

Wrote to Ray.

Wednesday, 26 April 1899

Elder Eccles and I visited—or rather called at the doors of—Sister Gain, Martha Leggat, Sister Easton (whom we wished specially to see), Sister Cair-

---

set apart on 31 March 1899, arriving in Liverpool on 21 April 1899. He labored in the Scottish Conference in the areas of Ayr, Dundee, Glasgow, and Uddingston. Cameron returned to Utah in May 1901.

[326]The Catholic Apostolic Church was established in England in the 1830s. It was controlled by a group of twelve apostles but also had prophets, evangelists, and pastors. They believed in speaking in tongues, the Second Coming, prophecy, and healing.

ney, Sister Hamilton, and Sister Joseph Leggat. Of course, the brethren were working; that is why I write *Sister*. Nearly everyone was out.

Charles Crisman came up from England. Open-air meeting at night at Anderston Cross. Many of the Scandinavian company were present, as also were Maggie and Jeanie Gain. Elders Young, Eccles, and Crisman were the speakers. We had a good meeting, Brother Eccles speaking exceptionally well. A few drunks made it a little unpleasant.

Thursday, 27 April 1899

Letter from Father, containing good news as usual. He never writes anything else, nor do any of the others either. They do not want me to have any thought of the cares or worries of things at home. Brother Palmer came in. He, too, sails tomorrow.

Meeting with company at 10:30. Changed tickets, securing four saloon passages. This will save jealousy or offense. Meeting at night in which the visiting brethren spoke, the Scandinavians in their native tongue. Very interesting meeting. Branch matters about the same. The Neilson family angry at me for not giving them enough "honor," I suppose. Well, it is hard to say what is the matter.

Friday, 28 April 1899

Boat sailed at twelve noon; the passengers went aboard at 10:30 A.M. After seeing all comfortable, I called on Sister Gain and Hoggan. Singing practice at night. L. N. [Lizzie Neilson?] very "down." Would not shake hands. Poor thing!

Saturday, 29 April 1899

Wrote to Ray.

Brothers Cameron and Leatham came from Dumbarton to spend Sunday with the branch here. Practiced some songs for conference. The weather being cold, no open-air meeting was held. A Sunday School meeting of officers should have been held, but as only two or three came it was decided not to convene.

Letter from Father.

Sunday, 30 April 1899

At 10:30 A.M. left Glasgow on the bus for Burnbank. Met in meeting assembled at Brother [John] Cook's house at 12:30 P.M.[327] A large number of the saints were present and a good meeting was enjoyed. Mr. and Mrs. Hunter, Brother Cook's son-in-law, had given an invitation for the elders to

---

[327]William S. Gould, Diary, 30 April 1899, told of the surprise visit by McKay: "I went to meeting and met a kind, smiling face at the gate or entrance to the house where the meeting was held. It was the face of the president of the Scottish Conference, D. O. McKay."

Fig. 50 *Hamilton Palace in Hamilton Park, Lanarkshire.*

visit him and have dinner with him. He was very sociable and manifested interest in our belief.

Meeting again at 6:30. Stayed all night at Brother Halliday's, being entertained as the guest of Mr. and Mrs. John Halliday, Brother Halliday's newly married brother. Midnight found us still out of bed, and two o'clock heard us still talking as we lay on the pillow. A piano and organ, too, are in the house, so we had plenty of music. Paintings, etching.

Monday, 1 May 1899

Raining. At 10 A.M. bade my friends good-bye and in company with Mr. J. Halliday walked over to the elders' lodgings. Here Mr. Halliday and I parted and I went with the elders to visit the mausoleum in Hamilton Park (Fig. 50). This is a large dome built of solid rock, the floor being laid with colored granite. As the creaking iron door is closed behind, a sound is heard as of distant rolling thunder. Inside is an ancient Egyptian *tomb*, said to have contained the body of the daughter of Pharaoh. It now conceals the remains of the 10th Duke of Hamilton,[328] who built the mausoleum. The park is beautiful and spacious.

Walked to High Blantyre and visited Sister Sneddon.

Visited a coal mine and were shown the workings at the head of the pit. About 1,000 tons of coal are taken from this mine daily. Over 300 men are employed. It is 150 fathoms deep. Forty head of horses down the pit. Seventy-five women are employed sorting and shoveling coal—most of them are young girls—quite pretty, too. They seemed to be happy and contented, notwithstanding their besmeared faces and calloused hands. Formerly women were allowed to work down in the mine but such degradation is now prohibited by law. Their avocation as it is at the head of the pit is unwomanly and altogether too course and dirty for women's employment.

Came to Glasgow at 5 P.M. Open-air meeting at Bridgeton Cross, at the conclusion of which a man evidently well-versed in scripture came to me

---

[328]Douglas Alexander, the 10th Duke of Hamilton (1767-1852), built a mausoleum with a 120-foot dome to house his remains. When the tomb was demolished in 1927, it was found that it belonged to a court jester and not a princess. McKay wrongly wrote "Moslem" for "mausoleum."

and asked some questions about the apostasy of which I had been speaking. He started on polygamy, too. He accepted my invitation to the office, where we could sit unmolested and discuss the principles with the scripture before us. The apostasy was taken up first. Isa. 24; 2 Tim. 4; 2 Thes. 2; 2 Peter 2; and Rev. 13:7 were discussed. But oh, how he did try to spiritualize the plain language, saying it did not mean what it said! Brother Mitchell became disgusted with him and went to bed. The others of us contended with him until 2:30 A.M.! He acknowledged the first principles but thought we were wrong on others. He knew the Bible by heart!

Tuesday, 2 May 1899
Visited saints in Springburn, including Taylor's family. Assisted Brother Eccles with reports. At night visited the Misses Scott, with whom I spent a delightful evening.

Wednesday, 3 May 1899
Father's Birthday. Wrote to Father, Claire, and George E. [Ferrin], sending present to David S. Brother Mitchell went to Newarthill. Open-air meeting at Cathedral Square. The young folks of the branch were nearly all out, so our singing was fine and attracted a large crowd. Brothers Eccles and Young were the speakers. It was a very good meeting.
Letters from Mamma and Brother McKnight.

Thursday, 4 May 1899
Studied. At 6 P.M. Brother Eccles and I had tea at Mrs. Wallace's. Testimony meeting at 8 P.M.

Friday, 5 May 1899
Letter from Mamma and Annie, also from Brother McKnight.
Attended to office correspondence. Visited Mrs. Good, Mrs. Harkins, and Mrs. Greer. Had a long talk with the latter about her recommend. Singing practice at night, after which Brother [Thomas] Halliday gave an entertainment with his gramophone.[329] Some of the selections were excellent. Brother Worthington,[330] a new elder, came in and gave us a pleasant surprise. I hope more follow before conference.

Saturday, 6 May 1899
Wrote two summonses for individuals who have "fallen away." The

---

[329]A *gramophone*, invented by Emile Berliner, was an instrument for permanently recording and reproducing sounds by means of a tracing etched into some solid material.

[330]William M. Worthington (1878-1964) was set apart for a mission to Great Britain on 10 April 1899, arriving in Liverpool on 4 May 1899. Within the Scottish Conference Worthington labored in the areas of Dunfermline, Edinburgh, and Paisley. He returned to Utah in June 1901.

Newarthill "Presidency" came in.

Brother Eccles and I at 1 P.M. went to the Royalty Theatre to see Mr. Wilson Barrett in *The Manxman*. It was excellent. The play teaches moral lessons and right conduct by showing the opposite of these. The play was over at 5 P.M. and at six I was in the train for Edinburgh, where I met the elders at their lodgings and some of the saints at George White's.

After taking a stroll up Princes Street (Fig. 51), we ate supper at Mrs. White's. Sat and chatted until about 1 A.M. and returned.

Edinburgh, Sunday, 7 May 1899

Fast Day. In company with the elders, called on Sister M. Whyte and Brother Wells, both of whom are ill.

Priesthood meeting at 1:15, testimony meeting at 2:30, and evening services at 6:30 P.M. I think I enjoyed the spirit manifested throughout the day better than at any other time in Edinburgh, and this is saying a *good deal*. After the evening meeting, we visited Sister M. Whyte and found her somewhat better. The saints in Edinburgh are all feeling well, and the reports show the branch to be in a prosperous condition.

Stayed all night at George White's.

Edinburgh, Monday, 8 May 1899

It was after nine o'clock before I arose. After breakfast, in company with Elders Miller and Stirling, went down to Portobello. The day was clear and beautiful and an unusual one for Scotland! In fact, I must here mention that we have had fine weather now for five successive days! This is a good record for *misty Britain!*

A walk along the beach on the sands of Portobello was very much enjoyed by each of us; but it was necessarily short as we desired to call on one or two of the saints before noon—Sister Henderson, [Sister] Gracie, and Sister Whyte.

Boarded the 2:35 P.M. train for Dunfermline, where I arrived at 3:05 and walked to the elders' lodgings.

Fig. 51 *Princes Street, Edinburgh.*

Dunfermline

I had not sent word as to the time I would arrive; so when I reached their quarters, I found them out. The landlady informed me that they had been to meet the 1:45 train and were out now to meet the 4 P.M. train. Found them at the station. Through the kindness of Sister [Lizzie] Hutchinson, we were shown through a large linen factory, where about 600 lasses are employed daily. Visited Spowart, Neilsen, and Anderson. The branch here is about dead. The elders, however, are feeling encouraged as several intelligent investigators attended their meeting last Sunday. Even a conversation is encouraging.

Tuesday, 9 May 1899

At 9:53 A.M. left Dunfermline for Alloa. The weather was a little misty, no doubt our week of fine weather is at an end. A few minutes walk from Alloa Station took me to Mrs. Thompson's, where I was greeted with every cordiality. Soon after entering the house, Miss Benzie, knowing of my coming, came in, having come out of school bareheaded and without cape or cloak. In response to her invitation to go and meet her mother, I accompanied her back to the school where she excused herself to her class and principal (her father) and then went to her home—a neat little cottage not far from the schoolhouse. Mrs. Benzie was very amiable and seemed quite pleased with the proposal made to her daughter by a Mormon elder, Brother Gilchrist.[331] Soon Mr. Benzie came in and an appointment was made at 3 P.M. for me to visit his school.

After spending a short but pleasant hour in conversation, singing, and music from the piano, I went back to Mrs. Thompson's.

At 3 P.M. was at the school and was introduced to each teacher and department by Mr. Benzie. There are about 700 pupils and twelve teachers in all. On the whole the school was quite prosperous, the pupils seemed to be bright; but I had no opportunity to hear any recitations as the teachers stopped as we entered and did nothing but talk to us while we were there.

One told us—right before her pupils, too—how convenient her room was for seeing the inspector as he entered the headmaster's room. This gave her an opportunity to set her own room in order and then to inform the other teachers of the inspector's presence. This same one—a lady teacher, of course—said that often the teacher was not allowed to be in her own room while the inspector was examining her pupils. The discipline was fair. The gov[ernment] is more arbitrary than in our schools. My visit was a very pleasant one.

Left Alloa at 4:30 P.M. Arrived in Stirling a few minutes later. Called on Brother Thomson, next at McKenzie's shop, and then at Mrs. Sharp's.

---

[331] It is not known which "Brother Gilchrist" made this proposal to Miss Benzie of Alloa, but neither Robert F. Gilchrist nor Thomas Gilchrist married her.

Felt at home as usual. Stayed all night with them. Notes: "Baptism all right"—minister. [Illegible.] Attack by "Helper," etc.

Wednesday, 10 May 1899

Raining. After breakfast, bade my kind friends good-bye and started for the station. Brother Thomson met me and accompanied me to the train, which left for Glasgow at 9:40 A.M. Found all well at the conference house. The Scandinavian company sailing tomorrow has arrived. Singing practice. Open-air meeting Friday night.

Thursday, 11 May 1899

Letter from Brother Edward. Exchanged tickets at Anchor Line office. Boat sailed at 1:15 P.M. Went to Greenock. The sail down the river in the *Ethiopia* was delightful, as the weather was so fine and the scenery on both sides of the river so green and beautiful. Back to Greenock at 5 P.M. Called on Miss Scott and Mrs. McMinn. Testimony meeting at night. Called on Sister McDonald.

Friday, 12 May 1899

Wrote to Liverpool and attended to office correspondence. Practiced some songs. Open-air meeting at night on Cathedral Square.

Saturday, 13 May 1899

Wrote to Brother Edward and sent a card to Lizzie. In the afternoon went around "shopping" with Brother Thompson,[332] a new elder, who arrived here yesterday. He was with Brother Gibbs and Brother Berry,[333] when they were murdered in Tennessee.

At the [public] baths.

Priesthood meeting at night. A stormy scene. Brother Neilson would not preside, but we managed through fairly well. Not much was accomplished, however. The object of the meeting was to take action against three

---

[332]Henry B. Thompson (1859-1941) served as a missionary in the Southern States Mission from October 1882 to September 1884. Because of his near-tragic experience on that mission (see the next footnote), when he was called on another, he was allowed to pick the place when he wanted to serve. Thompson was set apart for a mission to Great Britain on 21 April 1899, arriving in Liverpool on 10 May 1899. Within the Scottish Conference he labored in the areas of Edinburgh, Galashiels, Glasgow, Govan, and Hawick. Thompson was appointed president of the Scottish Conference in May 1900 and returned to Utah in June 1901. See the Henry B. Thompson Diaries, Accession 1743, located in the Manuscripts Division, J. Willard Marriott Library, University of Utah, Salt Lake City, with the originals being at the LDS Church Archives.

[333]John H. Gibbs (1853-1884) and William S. Berry (1838-1884), two LDS missionaries in the Southern States Mission, were murdered in Tennessee on 20 August 1884. John B. Young, Diary, 12 May 1899, referred to those who killed the missionaries as "an infuriated mob." For an account of the murder of the elders and the rescue of their bodies, see Gary James Bergera, ed., *The Autobiography of B. H. Roberts* (Salt Lake City: Signature Books, 1990), 137-55.

who have "fallen away." It was decided to give them another opportunity. Some of the members here are the worst persons to create complicated questions that I have ever heard of! They are always "wrangling." A change will have to be made in the presidency or the branch will be broken up.

Sunday, 14 May 1899

At 10 A.M. I was in the bus bound for Airdrie. A ride of one hour and forty-five minutes took us to the Airdrie Cross, and a few minutes walk from there brought us to the hall. Brother and Sister Gates joined me at Coatbridge. The saints in Airdrie have secured a fine hall and seem to be feeling well. After meeting went to Rawyards and ate dinner with the Graham family.

While passing through the "park," an instance occurred which well-illustrated the characteristic Scotch wit. The park has been but recently opened and, of course, needs much improvement. One of the company, a young "Scotty," desiring to say something, remarked that "this park is like me; it's in a crude state." The sentence was hardly finished before "Uncle Willie," a real wit, answered: "Weel, there's a difference, for they'll mak' somethin' oot o' the park, but a' doot they'll mak' naething o' you!"

A pleasant afternoon was spent at [the] Grahams. Called on Sister Beggs and Brother and Sister Gates at Coatbridge. Boarded the 5:30 P.M. train for Glasgow, where I arrived in time to attend the evening service. Brother Leggat is at "war" with Brother Neilson. Application for baptism.

Monday, 15 May 1899

Wrote to Liverpool, to Joseph L.[Peterson], R[obert] Gilchrist, Mrs. Thompson, Bro. McMillan, and attended to general duties. About 3 P.M. a very dark thunder storm came on. Had to light the gas.

Open-air meeting on Douglas and Argyle Streets. Stood in a shower of rain but did not dismiss.[334] We had a very good meeting. After dismissal, while we were walking up Argyle Street, a woman touched my arm and said, "I want to speak to you." At first I hesitated, but a second glance showed that she was respectable. "I heard you preaching," she continued. "Yes," said I, half wondering what was coming. "Yes," she went on, "and I want Jesus." "Well, you come to 4 Carlton Place next Sunday and it will be told you there how you can get him. The address is on the tract they gave you and which I see you now hold in your hand." The answer hardly seemed to satisfy her; so I asked, "Will you come?" "Yes," she replied, "but I wanted him now." "When you go home tonight, then," I continued, "just kneel down and pray for Jesus to comfort you until next Sunday. He will give

---

[334]When rain stopped an open-air meeting, Thomas A. Kerr, Diary, 21 June 1899, wrote: "It is quite wet at this writing—4 P.M. Doesn't look like the people of Edinburgh will be blessed by having any Mormon elders speak on their streets tonight."

you light that will keep you until then and will also show you ordinances to be obeyed after accepting which you can keep Jesus forever." This seemed to satisfy her. She promised to do as was counseled and come to meeting. Perhaps she will change her mind though.

Tuesday, 16 May 1899
Wrote a letter to Mamma and attended to other correspondence. Letter from Father. Singing practice at night.

Wednesday, 17 May 1899
The morning hours were spent in the office, attending to sundry duties. At 2:20 Brother Young and I went to Holytown, thence to Newarthill, where we visited all the saints and held meeting at 6:30—a cottage meeting in Sister Major's.

A good feeling seems to prevail. At 9:33 we were aboard the train at Holytown, bound for Glasgow. Arriving here at 10:05 P.M., we walked to Sister Gain's, who was being given a surprise. Spent a pleasant hour or so and came to our rooms.

Thursday, 18 May 1899
Glasgow celebrated the Queen's birthday. Raining all day. Stayed in the house all day.

Baptism at 6:30 P.M., Brother Mitchell officiating. The Misses Wallace were the persons immersed. The baptism was a success. After all were ready, we repaired to the conference house and held a confirmation meeting, Brother Eccles confirming Jane, and I Nancy. Then followed the regular testimony meeting in the hall. Several returning elders being present, we had a large meeting, characterized by a good feeling.

A large company [will] sail next Saturday in the *City of Rome*. Brother [Walter J.] Knell, Brother [Jabez W.] West, and others came in. They sail Saturday.

Friday, 19 May 1899
Changed tickets and money, attended to general emigration duties, and met with the elders and emigrants at York Street Hotel, giving some necessary instructions about going on board, traveling, etc. Accompanied Brother West down to Alex Hoggan's. The weather is disagreeable. A "Scotch mist," sometimes turning to real rain, having been falling all day.

Tomorrow the boat sails from Greenock. I desire to go to Newcastle, so it means moving with dispatch! For further particulars, see book no. [blank].[335]

---

[335]This sentence is unfinished. Also, the next page has some genealogical details of John T. Edward's grandfather and great-grandfather.

Saturday, 20 May 1899

Breakfast at 8 A.M. At 8:45 A.M. we were at St. Enoch's Station with all the elders and emigrants, hurrying to and fro [and] seeking convenient carriages in the train bound for Greenock. About one hour's ride found us at Princes Pier, Greenock; and soon we were aboard the tender, smoothly sailing out to the *City of Rome*, lying at anchor a short distance from the pier. She is a beautiful vessel, having a tonnage of 8,453 tons. Standing forward on her deck and looking aft, one can easily imagine that he is looking along a street. After all were comfortably located in their rooms, the tender coming alongside the vessel, I bid good-bye to the company.

[Then I] came back to Glasgow, arriving here about 1:10 P.M. At 3 P.M. met Mr. Johnston at Queen Street Station and secured a ticket at reduced rates to Newcastle, England, leaving Glasgow at 5 P.M. and arriving in the city on the Tyne at about 9:05 P.M. At the station I was met by Miss Oliver and two elders—Elder [Harris E.] Sutton and [James E.] Meeks. Miss Oliver was the first to accost me in the crowd and her merry "How do you do, Mr. McKay?" seemed very welcome indeed, as I had anticipated meeting only strangers.

A half-hour's walk took us to the conference house, 37 Cavendish Road, Jesmond, where the *whole-souled* Brother [Thomas] Gilchrist gave me a hearty welcome. Here I met for the first time President James L. McMurrin[336] and President Henry W. Naisbitt of the European Mission. Brother [T. Lonsdale] Allen of Ireland [was] also present, besides several elders of Newcastle Conference. The night was spent in social conversation, which was continued even after we retired until the "wee sma' hours o' mornin'" bade our eyelids close and our weary muscles rest.

Sunday, 21 May 1899

The morning opened bright and clear, promising an excellent day for conference. About one hour before the appointed time, we left the rooms and walked leisurely through the Montgomery Park toward the hall. The trees were dressed in their freshest green, the grass made a velvety carpet on either side, and the flowers were blooming all around, filling the air with fragrant perfume, wafted by the gentle morning breeze. As we walked along, enjoying the delightful surroundings, one was forcibly impressed with the fact that Utah is not the only place for beautiful scenes. Utah and Western America has grandeur and sublimity, but Britain has refined beauty!

At 10:30 A.M. President Gilchrist opened the morning service. President McMurrin, Elder James E. Meeks, and President Naisbitt occupied the

---

[336]James L. McMurrin (1864-1902) was a missionary to Great Britain from 1884 to 1886. On 21 April 1899 he was called as first counselor to Platte D. Lyman, president of the European Mission. He got cancer during this mission and had an operation while in England. In June 1901 he returned to Ogden and then moved to Salt Lake City, where he died in 1902.

time. The speakers at the afternoon service were D. O. McKay, President Allen, and President McMurrin. After the adjournment, Elders Sutton, Meeks, and I in company with the Misses Oliver took tea at a Mrs. [blank], who was very kind and sociable. At 6:30 Presidents Naisbitt and McMurrin occupied most of the time. The conference was a success.

Meeks, Allen, and I stayed all night at [the] Olivers.

Monday, 22 May 1899

[The day] opened bright and quite clear, but heavy clouds were seen hanging around, which showed that the sunshine would not last long. Walked to "37" [Cavendish Road] and attended priesthood meeting, which lasted from 10 A.M. until 2:30 P.M.

After dinner the elders all started for Hebburn to attend a social to be given by the branch in that place. We walked to the River Tyne and waited one hour in the cold and rain, for the heavy clouds seen in the morning had been emptying their contents for several hours. However, a boat finally came along and we were soon sailing down the river. The social was quite a success, notwithstanding the absence of good music. A concertina and mouth organ did very well. It was 2 A.M. before we retired at 37 Cavendish Road.

Tuesday, 23 May 1899

Spent the morning hours with the brethren. At 11 A.M. we all assembled in the Montgomery Park and had a photograph of the group taken. The occasion attracted quite a crowd.

Then followed a walk through beautiful Jesmond Dene, which shall be long remembered. President McMurrin, Elders Sutton, [George H.] Toone, and I formed a party of four. As we strolled through the park blooming luxuriantly all around, President McMurrin told us about his experience in first meeting the woman who afterward became his wife. Met at Lime Street Station, Liverpool. He mentioned another similar circumstance in his life and testified to the blessing and guidance of God in his course of action regarding his married life. He was very confidential and wept emotional tears. It was a walk and conversation long to be remembered.

After dinner I began preparations for Glasgow, although the brethren desired me to remain until the following morning; but conference in Glasgow next Sunday required my presence at the office to attend to preparations. At least I felt so, although the elders, no doubt, would get along just as well without me. But I decided to take the 3 P.M. train. President McMurrin, President Gilchrist, and President Allen accompanied me to the station, and after a warm farewell, I was soon looking out of the window of a flying train at green fields, shady woods, lovely glens, quiet hamlets, and thriving towns, at old ruins and ancient cliffs near the sea with frequent glimpses of the waves dashing against the rock-bound coast. The ride was

Fig. 52 *Jamaica Bridge, Glasgow.*

a pleasant one.

At Berwick-on-Tweed sent a telegram to Brother Miller, Edinburgh, asking him to meet me at Waverley Station. We failed to make the connection, and in my eagerness to find him I nearly got left, leaving my grip,[337] umbrella, etc., in the Aberdeen portion of the train. When I found my mistake, there was only one minute before the Aberdeen train left and only four minutes before the Glasgow portion left! The Aberdeen portion was on No. 9 platform; the Glasgow on No. 13. There being no time to run around the trains, I just jumped between cars, found the number of the carriage I was in, opened the door, seized my belongings, and got out again just as the train was pulling away! Hurrying back to No. 13, I took my seat in the carriage and was soon on my way to Glasgow, without having seen Brother Miller, although as I afterward learned he was there looking for me.

Singing practice was going on when I reached the conference house. Everything was all right.

Wednesday, 24 May 1899

Queen's Birthday! Opening of Jamaica Bridge (Fig. 52). Immense crowds!

Busy with conference preparations. Returning elders and emigrants are arriving. The boat sails tomorrow. Mr. Bleckhert, Emil Nelson's father-in-law, is among the number. He is a jolly Dutchman.

Open-air meeting off Paisley Road. The bills announcing our conference when distributed during our meeting seem to attract attention and I believe will prove an effective means of advertising.

---

[337]A *grip* or *gripsack* was a valise or hand-satchel for a traveler.

Thursday, 25 May 1899
Busy with emigration duties. Company left feeling all right. Testimony meeting at night.

Friday, 26 May 1899
Made out reports for last six months and attended to a hundred-and-one little duties preparatory to conference. The elders are coming in from surrounding districts. They divided into fours and held open-air meetings, distributing bills announcing conference.

Saturday, 27 May 1899
Met President McMurrin at Queen Street at 11:15 A.M.[338] The rest of the day was occupied by sundry duties. On account of a card from President Naisbitt stating that he and Brother McFarlane can not be here until late tonight, the priesthood meeting announced for tonight will be postponed until Monday at 10 A.M. Elder Woolfenden,[339] president of Leeds Conference, has come up to visit us.
Met President Naisbitt and Elder J. C. McFarlane at 8:30 P.M. Lodgings for elders and saints have been secured in the Argyle Hotel. Before separating, we all gathered together in the large room at "53" [Holmhead Street] and united with President McMurrin in prayer. All felt well.

Sunday, 28 May 1899
Was the most beautiful morning I have seen in Glasgow! It was just such a day as was prayed for last night. It made everyone happy!
Conference convened in the City Hall (North Saloon) at 10:30 A.M. The saints from surrounding districts were out in large numbers—comparatively speaking—and everyone seemed to be expecting a good time. After the usual opening exercises, Elders T. L. Allen and William Nisbet addressed the audience. A quartet was then rendered, followed by remarks from President H. W. Naisbitt.
During the remarks of the previous brethren, I noticed one or two strangers in the audience showing signs of disapproval. As Brother Naisbitt proceeded, this disapproval grew into an interruption. One fiery-looking individual spoke right out in contradictory terms, saying, "That has been fulfilled, Sir!," referring to the prophecy of Malachi, which says "the Lord

---

[338]James L. McMurrin, Diary, 27 May 1899, as quoted in Gibbons, *David O. McKay*, 53, stated: "On the 27th of May I went to Glasgow where I met President D. O. McKay, one of the finest young men it has ever been my lot and privilege to become acquainted with."

[339]Charles Woolfenden (1863-1924) was born in Manchester, England, and emigrated to Utah in 1884. He served three missions to Great Britain: 1890-1892, 1898-1900, and 1903-1905. For his second mission Woolfenden arrived in Liverpool on 17 March 1898 with his wife Laura and two children, and he was appointed to the Leeds Conference. Later he was sustained as president of the Leeds Conference and released in May 1900.

shall suddenly come to His temple" [Mal. 3:1]. The speaker continued, unheeding the interruption. Soon he cried out again and, rising to his feet, insisted on talking. Brother Leggat tried to put him out! This made him worse. He started for the platform, talking vehemently all the time. As he ascended the steps, two or three of us caught his arm and I escorted him to his seat. Meanwhile, policemen had been called and just at this point entered the door. I assured them that everything was over and I believed he would remain quiet. President Naisbitt continued his sermon uninterrupted. At the conclusion of the meeting just before singing, I made a few remarks upon the feeling manifested, pointed out the difference between the spirit of the world and the spirit of the gospel, and said something about the "truth's cutting like a two-edged sword." It kindled again the flame of opposition. The man jumped up and began to talk. He was warned to sit down[340] but instead of doing so, he walked toward the door, saying, "I shake the dust off my feet," etc. A few more remarks were [made], a quiet subdued feeling prevailed, and conference adjourned until 2 P.M.

At the appointed hour, the hall was full, many strangers being present. The general church authorities and missionary authorities [i.e., the presidency of the European Mission and the President of the Scottish Conference] were presented and unanimously sustained. The speakers were Elders Charles Woolfenden, Joseph C. McFarlane, and President James L. McMurrin. Dinner at conference house at 4:30 P.M. Evening service at 6 P.M. The speakers were Elder Stirling and Presidents Naisbitt and McMurrin. The conference was truly a success and everyone present, especially the saints, felt well repaid for having attended.

Monday, 29 May 1899

A priesthood meeting[341] was held at "53" [Holmhead Street]. The meeting commenced at 10 A.M. All the elders, including visitors and a few of the local brethren, were in attendance. As the elders began to give their reports,[342] it became evident that an excellent spirit of love and unity was amongst us. A peaceful heavenly influence pervaded the room. Some of the elders were so affected by it that they had to express their feelings in tears.[343]

---

[340]John B. Young, Diary, 28 May 1899, added: "President D. O. McKay acted very calm-[ly] and wisely, saying to the enraged gentleman in tones of kindness, yet with a spirit of firmness, that if he did not act like a gentleman he would have to withdraw from the meeting."

[341]For a discussion of this meeting, see the Editors' Introduction, pp. xxxviii-xxxix.

[342]In the official minutes of this meeting, McKay "stated his pleasure in meeting with the brethren . . . [and] requested that all express themselves freely regarding the work of the Lord, and their feelings toward each other and the Priesthood of God." See the Scottish Conference Records, the British Mission, LR17716, ser. 11, vol. 3, located in the LDS Church Archives, Historical Department, The Church of Jesus Christ of Latter-day Saints, Salt Lake City, which is quoted in Gibbons, *David O. McKay*, 49.

[343]In the published account of this meeting, William Leggat, "Scottish Conference," *The Latter-day Saints' Millennial Star* 61 (1 June 1899): 342, said: "The brethren were unanimous

Just as Brother Young sat down after giving his report,[344] Elder Woolfenden[345] said: "Brethren, there are angels in this room! I see two there by Brother Young. One is his guardian angel.[346] The other is a guardian angel, too; but I don't know whose it is." Everyone present, impressed with the spirit of the occasion and sensing the divine influence, could testify to the truth of his (Brother Woolfenden's) remarks.[347] Although he was the only one who saw them, yet we each felt their presence.[348] Elders wept for joy and could not contain themselves. Sobs came from different parts of the room and they seemed fitting, too, for "it seemed manly to weep there." At the conclusion of the reports, all joined with me in a prayer of thanksgiving to the Lord for his blessings and manifestation.[349]

President McMurrin then addressed the meeting, saying among other things[350] that the "Lord has accepted our labors and at this time we stand

---

in their feelings of love for each other, also in sustaining the Priesthood of God."

[344]Henry B. Thompson, Diary, 29 May 1899, added some details: "Before our meeting was ended, there seemed to be a most glorious feeling in the room. Bro. Eccles was unable to express himself, being overcome with joy with the Spirit he enjoyed. Bro. Young was the same and immediately after sitting down, Bro. Woolfenden said: 'Bro. Young, there is an angel just over your head.' Yes, there are two of them: one is yours and I don't know who the other belongs to.'"

[345]In the 1950s William Cooke reminisced about Woolfenden's appearance: "I shall never forget the look on Brother Woolfenden's face when he told of seeing those angels. It was plain that the angels were not visible through ordinary mortal eyes. His eyes had an exalted spiritual expression, which was very moving." See James S. Campbell, *Biography of George Gordon Campbell* (n.p., 1957), 9.

[346]John B. Young, Diary, 29 May 1899, gave his own version: "While I was speaking, the room was filled with the spirit of the Lord. Pres. Woolfenden saw two holy angels, one of them he said was my guardian angel. From the feeling that was in the room, I am sure that the room was full of holy beings." For an explanation of guardian angels, see Joseph Fielding McConkie, *Answers: Straightforward Answers to Tough Gospel Questions* (Salt Lake City: Deseret Book Co., 1998), 113-14.

[347]Thomas A. Kerr, Diary, 29 May 1899, wrote that Brother Woolfenden also "described how they [the angels] were dressed."

[348]William S. Gould, Diary, 29 May 1899, said: "Great was the Spirit of God on that occasion insomuch that some of the elder[s] did bear testimony of seeing the angels with the meeting of the priesthood." William P. Nisbet, Diary, 29 May 1899, recorded: "During the meeting, which lasted nearly five hours, two heavenly being[s] appeared in the room and were seen by some of the brethren, but their holy influence was felt by all."

[349]In the official minutes of this meeting, McKay "said he truly appreciated the esteem and love in which he was held by his brethren of which he felt he was somewhat unworthy. He made reference to the power of God made manifest in the healing of Bro. Edward, also of the rich outpouring of the spirit of God and the presence of holy angels in our midst, and in acknowledgment of the same, desired to offer a humble prayer to our Father in Heaven and asked the brethren to join him. He then offered the sentiments of his heart in solemn prayer to our Creator." See Scottish Conference Records, the British Mission, LR17716, ser. 11, vol. 3. Joseph H. Mitchell, Diary, 29 May 1899, recorded: "President McKay with heart full...asked the brethren to unite with him in offering a short prayer of thanks to our Heavenly Father for the rich outpouring of his spirit that had been manifested in our meeting."

[350]One of the "other things" that President McMurrin said—but which McKay in his modesty did not record in his diary—was the following statement: "'Let me say to you, Brother David, Satan hath desired you that he may sift you as wheat, but God is mindful of you.' Then he added, 'If you will keep the faith, you will yet sit in the leading councils of the Church.'" See David O. McKay, "Two Significant Statements," *The Deseret News*, Church Section, 27 October 1934, 1, 8, with the spelling "counsels," quoted in David O. McKay, *Cherished Experiences*, comp. Clare Middlemiss (Salt Lake City: Deseret Book Co., 1955), 14.

pure before him."[351] President Naisbitt made a few closing remarks and at 2:30 P.M. the meeting was dismissed by singing and prayer. It was the best meeting I have ever attended.[352]

After dinner we all went to Trumbull, the photographers—the result of our going will be seen later.

An impromptu concert and dance were given at night, the entire arrangements being made in about three hours— notifying saints and all! One or two unpleasant features happened, but on the whole everything went smoothly.

Tuesday, 30 May 1899

According to arrangements made yesterday, Presidents McMurrin and Naisbitt, Elders McFarlane, Woolfenden, Allen, Worthington, and McKay at 10 A.M. left Buchanan Street Station bound for Stirling. The morning was beautiful and everyone being happy and contented was in a fit state of mind to enjoy the ride through wooded braes, past green fields, and quiet hamlets, through small stations over *burns* and canal, until we reached the Vale of Leven with the Abbey Craig in the distance. After a ride of forty-five minutes, we were walking out of the Stirling Station toward the arcade. After passing through which, we stood looking at the Statue of Sir William Wallace, the hero of Stirling Bridge. After ordering dinner at the Whitehead Hotel, we wended our way toward the castle.

The East and West Churches, the Guild Hall, the cemetery, and the Ladies' Rock were visited before we ascended the steps leading to the esplanade. A good guide was secured and every interesting and historic place in the castle was pointed out by him. The rebuilt portion of the wall battered by General Monck, the old moat and double portcullis, the dungeon of Roderick Dhu, the King's Royal Palace, the Lion's Den, the view from Point Lookout, the figures on the east side of the old armory, the old house of Parliament, the Douglas Garden, and the views from castle wall, from the Stands of Queens Victoria and Mary were all pointed out and described in detail. After having obtained satisfaction with castle and surroundings, we walked back to the hotel above mentioned and enjoyed a good dinner.

---

[351] According to the official minutes of this meeting, "The heavenly beings remained some length of time, and the Spirit of God pervaded every bosom to an unexpressible degree. President James L. McMurrin bore testimony to the presence of the holy beings, seen by Bro. Woolfenden, one being the guardian angel of Bro. Young, the other the guardian angel of Bro. Eccles. Said those brethren were pure and spotless in the sight of God, and admonished them to continue so. President McMurrin said further: 'Brethren, all your guardian angels are with you. Your labors are accepted by the Lord and you are all clean before him.'" See Scottish Conference Records, the British Mission, LR17716, ser. 11, in LDS Church Archives, but compare Campbell, *Biography of George Gordon Campbell*, 8.

[352] Joseph H. Mitchell, Diary, 29 May 1899, expressed his opinion: "It was the greatest spiritual feast I ever enjoyed." John B. Young, Diary, 29 May 1899, wrote: "This was one of the grandest meetings that ever I had [the] pleasure of attending." Thomas A. Kerr, Diary, 29 May 1899, stated: "This was the grandest meeting I ever witnessed in my life."

Then we visited Bannockburn, where Bruce made his stand against King Edward.[353] The enthusiasm of Brother McMurrin and Brother Mc-Farlane was now at its height, and those of our company who were not real Scotch men wished they were, while one or two others by tracing their genealogy back four or five generations satisfied themselves that Scotch blood was in their veins and joined in the enthusiasm. A ride on the car from St. Ninian's to Causewayhead was a rest and helped us in our climbing to the top of the [Wallace] Monument on Abbey Craig, from whence is obtained one of the most beautiful landscape scenes in the world!

This being the last point of interest and Brother Woolfenden desiring to go to England, we hastened to the train and were met at the station by Miss Sharp, who had heard of our being in town and of our not having time to call. We left the station, comfortably seated in an apartment to ourselves. The first stop was at Larbert. We thought the train was rather long in starting but were busy in conversation and paid little heed to the delay until the ticket collector opened the door to punch the tickets. "Why this ticket is to Glasgow," he said. "That's where we want to go," one replied. "Well, you're in the wrong portion of the train—you ought to be in front; this portion goes to Edinburgh."

Then there was a rush and a run forward, but we were too late. Our train had just left. [Each] one looked at the others, each one laughed, said something about "getting left," etc., and sought consolation in the remark that "they ought to have told us to change." But the hour and eighteen minutes in Larbert was not all lost, and when we secured a first-class compartment in the next train, we were not sorry we did get left. It furnished much amusement, for several little incidents happened that were full of mirth and merriment.

Soon after our arrival in Glasgow, Mr. Barrie called. He and Mrs. Barrie had been here before. She was waiting outside. It being so late they did not stay, but I accompanied them down Sauchiehall Street and made an appointment for next Tuesday night. The night's rest was richly enjoyed.

Wednesday, 31 May 1899

Visited interesting places in Glasgow—Municipal Building, Cathedral, and Necropolis. Called on Anchor Line Company also. President Naisbitt and Brother Worthington left for Edinburgh. Many of the elders have gone to their field, two to Ireland to visit. Returning elders arriving. Boat sails tomorrow. Brother McFarlane will stay with us all week.

Thursday, 1 June 1899

President McMurrin and Brother Allen went to Edinburgh early this

---

[353]Edward II (1284-1327) became King of England in 1307. He misruled for twenty years, was deposed, and murdered in captivity.

morning. Busy changing tickets, money, etc. The S.S. *Furnessia* sailed from Glasgow about 4:30 P.M., Brother McFarlane and I going as far as Greenock. Brother [Christian N.] Lund sailed with this boat. The ride down the River Clyde was a pleasant one, the weather being so clear and favorable and the hills on either side so green and beautiful. Came back to Glasgow by train, arriving about nine o'clock.

The brethren came back from Edinburgh about an hour later and then plans were laid for the morrow. President McMurrin, Brother Allen, and Brother Eccles are going to Ireland, and Brother McFarlane and I are going to the Trossachs by way of Aberfoyle.

Friday, 2 June 1899

At 8 A.M. accompanied the brethren going to Ireland to the station. Returning, prepared for our trip.

At 10:30 Brother McFarlane and I left Queen Street Station for Aberfoyle well-equipped for a pleasant journey, although threatening clouds gave premonitions of rain. Twelve o'clock found us at Aberfoyle, admiring the beautiful surrounding country. But beautiful as it was, it had not sufficient attraction, for our mind was intent upon the Classic Lakes and the Trossachs, from which were still seven miles. This distance was walked for several reasons—we did not want to hurry past beautiful scenes. The walk was really delightful and not in the least fatiguing. At every turn in the road we were met with a new and interesting aspect of the scenery!

The road was excellent, as all the roads are in this country, and tripping cheerfully along leaving mile by mile behind us, we were on the shores of Loch Achray (Fig. 53) almost before we realized it. The first sight of this beautiful, placid lake, surrounded by stately hills covered with green trees and luxuriant foliage, with the Trossachs Hotel standing like a fine mansion in the midst of a garden, is indeed very impressive! As we neared the shore, we saw that the water was ruffled by the breeze, but this only seemed to make the scene more animated. Dark, heavy clouds hung over Ben A'an and almost covered Ben Venue, and lowered occasionally as if to frighten us

Fig. 53 *Loch Achray and Ben Venue, Trossachs.*

Fig. 54 *Loch Katrine with Ellen's Isle, Trossachs.*

away from the peaceful scene! But Loch Achray was not the object of our visit.

A walk along its shores through the "toll gate" charges for vehicles only and across the bridge spanning a typical Utah mountain stream brought us to the "circular path through the old pass and back through the Trossachs."

Following this path we were in the vicinity where James Fitz-James,[354] when in pursuit of the royal stag, lost his "gallant grey" [horse]:

> Woe worth the chase, woe worth the day,
> That costs thy life, my gallant grey![355]

Emerging from the deep glen we came in full view of lovely Loch Katrine (Fig. 54)! Many poets and writers have tried to depict this beautiful scene, [Sir Walter] Scott's description of it is grand—but even it, as all the others, fails to convey to the reader the enchanting beauty of this lake and surroundings! Tranquil beauty, subdued grandeur, enchanting murmurs of a stream, or the voice of a warbling songster seem to charm one to the spot! But we cannot stop long here.

The Silver Strand and Ellen's Isle are to see yet! But first we must eat our lunch for the walk from Aberfoyle and the fresh mountain air have whetted our appetites to the keenest point. A boat tied in a quiet corner of the lake was chosen for the dining room; and there on the peaceful waters of Katrine we enjoyed our bread and cheese, etc., as fully as ever a king enjoyed the richest repast spread before him.

A few minutes walk over a little knoll brought us to the Silver Strand, where:

---

[354]The James Fitz-James in Sir Walter Scott's *Lady of the Lake* is James V (1512-1542), King of Scotland. The severe policy of James V alienated his nobles and he lost to the English at Solway Moss in 1542.

[355]Sir Walter Scott, *The Lady of the Lake*, canto I, ix, in *Scott: Poetical Works*, ed. J. Logie Robertson (London: Oxford University Press, 1971), 209.

In listening mood, she seem'd to stand,
The guardian naiad of the strand.[356]

To look at Ellen's Isle from the distance was not enough, so we retraced our steps, walked to the boathouse, secured a little shallop,[357] and began to ply the oars. After exerting a vast amount of energy—much of which was misspent—we reached the coast of the enchanted isle. Tying our boat securely to a tree, we stepped ashore and explored the rocky, though tree-covered, island. No trace of a hut can be found. After satisfying ourselves and securing a few bunches of Scottish bluebells and leafy ferns as souvenirs of our visit, we stepped once more into our boat and started back. But oh, my! It was hard enough coming over for we were then rowing against the wind; but now it seemed that our boat would go any way and every way but the right way. Once or twice we thought we would not get back, but we did and the blisters on our hands show how. We were told afterward that we sat too far forward, thus tipping the boat so the wind and water caught the helm.

Fully satisfied with our visit to the lake and it being too late to go back to Aberfoyle, we walked back to the Trossachs Hotel and secured comfortable lodgings for the night, 2/6 each, 1/6 attend. After a refreshing wash, we repaired to the reading room and spent several hours writing to friends and loved ones at home. The enjoyment of the scenes around us made us wish for others to share our joys!

Saturday, 3 June 1899

At 7:15, after a splendid night's rest, we awoke to see the sunbeams of a beautiful morning stealing through the blinds. Our morning toilet over, we walked down to the shore of Loch Achray and there saw mirrored in the crystal surface all the trees, foliage, and mountains surrounding the lake. The different and variegated colors reflected were beautiful. Walking back to the hotel, we partook of a light breakfast (2/6 each) and started back to Aberfoyle by way of the Brig o' Turk (Fig. 55), where "the headmost horseman rode alone."[358]

From here we were told to take a "short path" leading to the Aberfoyle road. One little boy said it was much nearer but added, "It's a gay[359] dirty road." The road or route we followed was certainly "gay dirty," but we did not find the "short path." After wandering around seeking in vain for the path (but all the while feeling confident that we were going in the right direction), we suddenly found ourselves on the shores of a mountain lake. Re-

---

[356]Scott, *Lady of the Lake*, I, xvii, 212. A *naiad* is a water nymph or goddess presiding over lakes, rivers, and springs.

[357]A *shallop* was a small boat propelled by oars or by a sail and used chiefly in shallow waters.

[358]Scott, *Lady of the Lake*, I, vi, 209.

[359]In the Scottish dialect, *gay* means "very."

ferring to a small local map, we found that it was peaceful Lake Drunkie. The sight of this repaid us for our wanderings—for we were beginning to seriously realize the fact that we were lost.

However, we saw a landmark in the distance to our right—an old quarry—which set us right. And after half hour or so of trailing through heather and broom, we reached the road and stepped firmly along until we were again in Aberfoyle. A lunch to refreshen the inner man secured, we were soon comfortably seated in the train, which hurled us through many a beautiful vale and glen past quiet towns and thriving farms to auld, busy, bustling, smoking Glasgow. The afternoon was spent in refreshing and resting ourselves and in making preparations for Sunday services.

> Auld Scotland, wham ne'er a toun surpasses
> For beautiful locks and trackless passes!
> Twa exploring youths like a wandering monkey
> Got lost ane day on the banks o' Loch Drunkie.
> —McFarlane

Sunday, 4 June 1899

Priesthood meeting at 10:30 A.M., Sunday School at twelve noon, afternoon meeting at two, and evening service at 6:30 P.M. After the night meeting, Brother McFarlane and I strolled leisurely along Sauchiehall Street, enjoying the pleasures of a summer evening's walk.

All the time in the council meeting this morning was consumed by the reading of minutes of two previous priesthood meetings!!

Monday, 5 June 1899

Letter from Miss C[laire].

At 8:40 A.M. Brother McFarlane and I were at St. Enoch's Station en route for Ayr. An hour later we were in the "auld toun," walking toward the home of "Robbie" Burns. Shall not go into details of our visit here,

Fig. 55 *Brig o' Turk, Trossachs.*

Fig. 56 *Brig o' Doon, Ayr.*

suffice it to say the Alloway Kirk,[360] the [Burns] Monument, the Brig o' Doon (Fig. 56), the "banks and braes o' bonnie Doon"—some of them— were all visited and associated with the man and his poems, who has immortalized them all. Our walk back was by way of the "esplanade" on the seaside. Aside from a short conversation with a pretty lass, our visit here was not interesting. Visited the Twa Brigs[361] also.

At 4 P.M. we were again in Glasgow, and at 5 P.M. at Queen Street Station we bid each other good-bye, after a pleasant week's association among historic and classic scenes. Brother McFarlane went to Edinburgh, thence back to Liverpool. At 5:10 met Brother Neilson and made arrangements about the hall rent up to May 28th. Open-air meeting at 8 P.M. on Cathedral Square.

Tuesday, 6 June 1899

At "53" [Holmhead Street] most of the day. Brother Joseph Leggat called. Talked to him about making a change in the branch presidency. In the evening, Mr. and Mrs. Barrie called and spent several pleasant hours in social conversation upon religious and other subjects. Gave them a "Scotch convoy."[362] Talked until near midnight.

Wednesday, 7 June 1899

Wrote letters to Father, Mother, and Claire.

Open-air meeting on New City Road, at the conclusion of which a man

---

[360]McKay incorrectly wrote "Alloa Kirk."

[361]*Twa Brigs* refers to the two bridges—the Old Bridge and the New Bridge—of Ayr. In Burns's 1786 poem, "The Brigs of Ayr," these bridges speak back and forth to each other.

[362]A *Scotch convoy* refers to accompanying a person part—often half—of the way on his journey home.

opposed our doctrine. Brother Mitchell answered him. This attracted a large crowd and we were soon packed in the center of it. Not being able to refute the doctrine, our opponents began to attack the plural wife system. He was answered in a cool, reasonable manner and his unreasonableness was seen by the crowd, whose sympathy we seemed to have.

"How dare you," he cried, "come over here and teach the word of God when you practice such doctrine at home!" He said something about "*stoning,*" whereupon one in the crowd said to him: "Are you a Christian?" "Thank God, I am," he replied. "Well," continued the other, "that's a fine Christian spirit you're showing. You would be the first one to throw a stone at these men!"

Our opponent answered by referring to Jesus scourging the temple. This was replied to by one of us and Christ's forgiving spirit was shown. "If we are deluded," one said, "why not show us in a spirit of kindness wherein we are wrong. Why become so enraged and condemnatory!" "Yes," he retorted, "but you are not deluded! You are intelligent men, teaching doctrine that will make other men less intelligent than they are now!"

We gave the crowd to understand what our object is, announced our place of public meeting and also our room address, extended an invitation to all to come and learn further, shook hands with one or two, and bade them good-night. Everything passed off smoothly and quietly and decidedly in our favor.

President McMurrin and Elder [Attewall] Wootton came from Belfast. Spent the night chatting and decided to visit Stirling and the Trossachs tomorrow.

Thursday, 8 June 1899

At 10 A.M. President McMurrin, Elder Wootton, Elder Eccles, and I left Buchanan Street Station bound for Stirling, where we visited the interesting places and feasted once again upon the beautiful landscape scenes. To visit the [East and West] Churches, the Guild Hall, Ladies' Rock, the Castle, the Beheading Stone on the Gowan Hill, the [Wallace] Monument on Abbey Craig (Fig. 57), and to catch the 3 P.M. train for Callander compelled us to keep moving. We lost no time, but a good deal of perspiration was wiped from our brows. We had a jolly time, boarded our train all right, and were soon rolling toward Callander.

Here we rested an hour or so at a temperance hotel, ate dinner, and started for the Trossachs. Callander is a beautiful place, having a population of about 1,600. The thickly wooded hills with Ben Ledi in the distance make the surroundings attractive and interesting. The Callander Hydropathic Establishment is situated about one mile southwest of Callander, the grounds extending to thirty acres mostly covered with evergreens.

As we walked from the hotel toward the bridge crossing the river to our right as we go to the Trossachs, we saw the "Stars and Stripes" waving in the breeze above a hotel. The sight put new life into us! We saluted the flag, hummed "The Star-Spangled Banner," and went tripping along the road, whistling patriotic airs. There is no other flag in the world like the *Red, White, and Blue*! Our route to the Trossachs was along the shores of Loch Vennacher, past the Brig o' Turk and Loch Achray. By the time we reached the latter place President McMurrin was rather quiet. His shoes were too tight for him and the long walk over hard roads had blistered his feet. His pain must have been severe, every step adding to his torture, but he would not give up. The walk through the Trossachs was followed and Loch Katrine's beautiful water and shores reached just at sunset. Our lunch was eaten on the Silver Strand.

Before going back to the lodgings secured by the Brig o' Turk, I exchanged shoes with Brother McMurrin and thus gave him a little comfort. It was 11 P.M. when we reached our lodgings, tired, footsore, and sleepy, yet well-satisfied with the day's journey. We had walked about twenty miles and had seen some of the most interesting places in Scotland.

Friday, 9 June 1899
Arose at eight o'clock and prepared for a morning's walk back to Callander. Loch Vennacher was seen in all her beauty. The sun shone brightly and mirrored the trees and shrubbery on the hillside in the placid waters of the lake. Our lunch was eaten by a cool spring, like the mountain springs in Utah. Before we reached Callander, Auld Sol had become hot and brought the perspiration out in large drops. It was my turn now to know what it is to walk ten miles in a pinching shoe! My feet were fairly blistered before we reached the station, but I said nothing because it would only worry Brother McMurrin. I was glad to sit in the train and rest my feet! Left Callander at 11:08 A.M. Once in Glasgow our feet were bathed, our "inner man" replenished, and a few hours of quiet rest taken. Later Brother Wootton went to Edinburgh, and Brother McMurrin and I called on his relative on London Road. We were tired at night but felt that our energy had been well spent.

Fig. 57 *Abbey Craig, Stirling.*

Saturday, 10 June 1899

Went to Rutherglen with Brother McMurrin and visited Mr. and Mrs. [blank], his relatives. They treated us fine and urged us to stay with them; but we could not, as Brother McMurrin had to go to Liverpool and I had to see after the emigration. Brother McMurrin left at 1 P.M.

The S.S. *Ethiopia* sailed at 8 P.M. with quite a number of our people on board. Called at Wallace's to fulfill a promise.

Letter from Father.

Sunday, 11 June 1899

Brother Young and I went to Cambuslang. Affected an organization of that branch, Elder Young being sustained as president. Dinner at [James] Robertson's. Attended evening services at Glasgow at the usual time.[363]

Monday, 12 June 1899

Spent most of the day writing and contemplating the best means of making a change in the presidency of the Glasgow Branch. Open-air meeting at Cathedral Square.

The conditions in the branch presidency are these: (1) division and lack of harmony, (2) refusal to be reconciled as brethren with implicit trust in each other, (3) not sustained by the laboring priesthood, [and] (4) lack of judgment and discretion on the part of the presiding officer. Other reasons for a change besides these.

"To the 'Scots at 42'"

President McMurrin, President Naisbitt, Elder McFarlane, and Elder Wootton: *Scots in spirit and endurance.*

-1-

> Ye Scots! wha' boast o' landscapes green,
> Wha' bonnie braes and glens ha'e seen,
> Tae Classic Lakes and scenes ha'e seen,
>   Come list tae me!
> Ye've been tae Stirling Castle old
> Ha'e heard o' men ne'er bought wi' gold,
> Wha' fought and bled sair lang and bold
>   For liberty!

-2-

> There 're some wha' think Scotch heroes dead,
> That all Scotch bluid wi' Bruce was shed,
> That men are afraid many miles tae tread
>   For Scotland yet!

---

[363]John B. Young, Diary, 11 June 1899, added: "President McKay delivered a powerful discourse upon church organization."

But they dinna ken o' clansmen true
Wha' noo reside at "forty-two"
Wha' visited scenes o' Roderick Dhu
    And wet wi' sweat!

-3-

Wha' went for miles and walked it too,
Endured the heat and a pinching shoe
Talked about Ellen wham Fitz-James first knew
    In mountain wild.
Through Trossachs wild their course they took
And neither one his shoes forsook
'Til all sat down and at lunch partook
    Near Ellen's Isle!

-4-

O James-Fitz-James and Roderick Dhu
Douglas, brave Bruce, and Wallace too!
You've endured great suffering fought brave and true
    Nor ance did fall!
But the heroes now at "forty-two"
Wha' walked for miles in a pinching shoe
Or rowed against wind Ellen's Isle tae view,
    Outshine you all!!

-5-

Scots, wha hae wi' Wallace bled
Scots, wham Bruce hae often led
Receive great praises on their head
    And rightfu' too.
But noo's the day an' noo's the hour
When Bruce an' Wallace maun gie o'er
And share their honor an their power
    Wi' "Scots at 42"!

The above was sent to the brethren at [42 Islington Street] Liverpool in answer to couplets and expressions of Scotch enthusiasm received from them upon their return to the office after their enjoyable visit to Scotland. In answer to the above, I received the following verses, with the heading, "Scots at '42' (continued)."

-6-

There's ane frae Glasca named McKay
Wha' like a hero led the way,
By mountain loch an' ower brae,
    And legends told
Of Douglas brave and Roderick Dhu,
And Ellen fair and Fitz-James, too.
Relieved his friend of torturing shoe,
    Like hero bold.

-7-

Although the shoes made calloused feet,
Ower dusty road in scorching heat,
'Twad mak' a dastard sairly greet.
    But no' McKay.
Old heroes bled for selfish end;
But he, to ease a suffering friend,
Endured until the journey's end
    At close o' day.
                            Signed, Wootton.

Brother Wootton's feet were blistered as well, but he proved himself equal to every task.

Tuesday, 13 June 1899

The weather still continues fine—exceptionally so for this country. Made out monthly reports.

Sister Clark called to see me and related a story that was sad, indeed. Her husband [James Clark] got drunk last Saturday night and in his drunken temper and madness cruelly beat her and then left the city. Her blackened eye and bruised body testified emphatically to the truthfulness of her story.

In the evening visited Sisters Greer, Harkins, and Gain, in company with Brother Eccles and Brother Cairney, the teacher in that district. Mrs. Reid is away visiting her sister [Jeanie Cooke]. We are "batching" it. "It's not good for man to be alone!" [Gen. 2:18].

Wednesday, 14 June 1899

Wrote to Miss Horne and others. Studied. Open-air meeting at night on New City Road. Beautiful flowers from Annie.

Thursday, 15 June 1899

Visited Gain's, Willie Leggat's, and Alex Hoggan's. Testimony meeting at night. Returning elders coming in. Attended to correspondence.

Friday, 16 June 1899

Busy with returning elders and emigrants, changing tickets, money, etc. At night assisted Brother Cairney in his teaching, visiting Easton's and Mrs. Rankin and her daughter[Miriam], [and] Mrs. Hildar.

Saturday, 17 June 1899

Train left St. Enoch's Station for Greenock at 8:45 A.M. There was a hurry and bustle at the station, but all finally reached the boat all right. The S.S. City of Rome was the boat sailing.

After all were away, in the afternoon I visited Joseph Leggat and J. Neilson, conferring with them about the change in the presidency of the branch. Appointed a meeting with them at 8 P.M. They were both on hand at the appointed hour, and after some talk *pro and con*, they forgave each other—or at least said they did. It was then agreed that they both be honorably released from their respective positions and that the president of the conference by virtue of his office act as president of the branch. It was intended that these two brethren would act as assistant presiding officers, but Brother Neilson positively refused to act in that capacity with Brother Leggat. Affairs seemed to be more complicated than ever at the dismissal of our conference together. I assure you, I was worried and had a restless night.

Sunday, 18 June 1899

At 11 A.M. the *special* priesthood meeting convened and the proposition to honorably release the branch presidency was placed before them and unanimously sustained. The president of the conference was also unanimously sustained as president of the branch. The hand-dealing of the Lord was manifested in this action and even in the disturbance last night. Everything went just as I had prayed for it to go!

Sunday School at twelve and meeting at 2 P.M. The saints unanimously sustained the above change. Meeting at 6:30 P.M. Administered to Brother David Cairney's child. At the afternoon meeting the little baby boy of Brother and Sister William Carney, Springburn, was blessed by the writer at the special request of the parents. The little one was named "David Oman McKay Carney."

Monday, 19 June 1899

In and around the conference house, attending to office and conference duties. Open-air meeting at night on Douglas Street.

Tuesday, 20 June 1899

Writing most of the day. At night visited the Misses Scott and spent a very pleasant evening with them. The elders were also visiting: two in Elderslie and two with Brother David Cairney. Brothers Mitchell and Eccles in the former place and Brother Young and Brother Ashby,[364] newly arrived, in the latter place.

Wednesday, 21 June 1899

About the only things worth mentioning today are the open-air meeting held off the New City Road and our meeting sisters from Zion, who came in last night on the S.S. *Anchoria.* They are Miss [Annie] White and

---

[364]William Ashby (1854-1920) was set apart for a mission to Great Britain on 26 May 1899, arriving in Liverpool on 15 June 1899. He was assigned to the Scottish Conference, but because of ill health he was released in September 1899 to return home to Utah.

her sister Mrs. [Maggie] Urie, Mrs. Adin Brown, and Mrs. [Mary] Morris. The first two mentioned will visit their brothers and friends in Edinburgh, and the last two relatives and friends in England.

As soon as our open-air meeting commenced, one of the men who disturbed our meeting one week ago began to interrupt us again. Brother Eccles was the first speaker and held his own well. He was followed by Brother Nisbet, who met our opponent with such indisputable truths that he had to resort to calumny and slander in order to keep up his disturbance. He yelled to the crowd that "these men are Mormons!," thinking that we would think that an insult, I suppose.

At the conclusion of Brother Nisbet's remarks, I stepped into the ring and told the people we are Mormons and are glad of it and think the term no reproach. I stated a few truths as emphatically as I could and announced our place of worship and our room address as well. The meeting dismissed without further interruption. At the conclusion one or two asked a few questions for the purpose of information. The opposition assisted us very much by attracting a large crowd, many of whom condemned the unchristian-like conduct of our opponent.[365]

Mrs. Brown was present at the meeting. The White girls went to Edinburgh this afternoon.

Thursday, 22 June 1899

This day was spent in visiting some of the saints. Testimony meeting at night. A good spirit prevailed, nearly everyone present bearing his or her testimony. The room was full.

Friday, 23 June 1899

The forenoon was occupied by attending to conference correspondence. In the afternoon Brothers Mitchell, Young, and I went to Dumbarton, where we met the three elders laboring there, and all visited the Dumbarton Rock, where an old castle used to stand.

Held an open-air meeting at which there was a large crowd—mostly men—all of whom seemed to listen attentively. No opposition.

Back to Glasgow at 10:45 P.M.

Saturday, 24 June 1899

S.S. *Anchoria* sailed at 11 A.M., only two of our passengers on board. Letter from Father, in which he informed me of my appointment as one of the Sunday School Board in Weber Stake.

At 4:17 P.M. Brother Young and I went to Elderslie and visited Mrs.

---

[365]William P. Nisbet, Diary, 21 June 1899, recorded that the man who interrupted the open-air meeting kept insisting that "water" really meant "word" in the passage "Except a man be born of water and of the Spirit, he cannot enter the kingdom of God" (John 3:5).

[Isabella P.] Nisbet, Elder Nisbet's mother. He and the two sisters from Wyoming, Maggie Kelly, Maggie and Jeanie Gain, and several members of the Nisbet family were present also. We had an enjoyable time and I believe did some good.

To be out of the noisy city was refreshing itself, add to this our cordial treatment and the beautiful country surroundings and one could not help but feel well and happy. Saw a beautiful sight—the large full moon rising and throwing her silver light through the green, leafy trees.

Sunday, 25 June 1899

Priesthood meeting at 10:30 A.M. Much business transacted, harmony prevailing. Clark was released from his positions as teacher in the branch and in the Sabbath School. Meetings at two and 6:30 p.m., as usual. Dinner at William Hamilton's.

Monday, 26 June 1899

Mrs. Brown and Mrs. Morris left for Nottingham. Brother Nisbet goes back to Dundee.

At 8 P.M. held a fine open-air meeting on Cathedral Square. It was really good. The audience was large and attentive and a good spirit prevailed. Many questions were asked after the meeting and one man accompanied us to our rooms.

Experience with a woman—a "Tartar"!

Tuesday, 27 June 1899

Called at Clark's. Visited Sister Gain and Brother Hoggan. Attended to conference correspondence.

Theatre at night—*Kenilworth*, dramatized from Scott's novel of the same name.[366] The staging was excellent, but some of the acting was rather stiff. Brother Young, Brother Eccles, and I [attended].

Wednesday, 28 June 1899

Wrote a letter home.

After dinner called on Mrs. Anderson and found her in a poor condition spiritually. At 5:18 P.M. left Central Station for Newarthill via Holytown. Meeting in Orr's at 6:30 P.M., after which called on Sister Jack and spent some time in social chat with her and Mr. Jack, who is now very friendly. Back to Glasgow at 10:30 P.M.

Thursday, 29 June 1899

After attending to duties in and around the office, went out to some of

[366]Sir Walter Scott, *Kenilworth* (London: Blackie and Son, 1821).

the members. Testimony meeting at night. Mailed an album and picture to J. Sharp as a wedding present.

Friday, 30 June 1899

At 10:30 A.M., in accordance with invitation and previous arrangements, left Glasgow (Queen Street) en route to Balfron to attend the marriage of James Sharp, Stirling, and Miss Trotter, Balfron. Was met at Balfron Station by Jeanie, who took me to the "wagonette"[367] waiting in readiness to convey the company to the town, which lies about two miles from the station. After the salutations and introductions were over, we were hurled along a smooth road, shaded on either side with beautiful trees, to the quiet little village in the glen—Balfron. As we passed the hotel, James came out and hailed us. At Mr. Trotter's we were made acquainted with others of the company. His daughters—four nice young women— were quite sociable and seemed eager to make the guests comfortable. But, as is usually the case, there were only one or two men to a houseful of women and girls, so after partaking of some refreshments—sandwich, etc.—Mr. Trotter and I walked up to the hotel to see James. He had not seen his sweetheart that day at all, having remained in the hotel all the time.

Took a pleasant stroll with him along the banks of a mountain stream near the Ballochinrain estate. Everything in nature seemed to be flourishing. The trees were dressed in their richest green, the ferns were waving along the path, and flowers bloomed on every side. The wild rose, newly born, scented the air with its fragrance, while the little birds in the trees warbled their songs as an accompaniment to the harmony that seemed to prevail.

There are many beautiful walks in Scotland! Many beautiful scenes! It was in this district that Rob Roy[368] is supposed to have stolen his grey mare that he escaped with. His wife was stolen from here also, so it is said.

Retracing our steps we were soon back to the hotel. He would not go down to Trotter's—"it would be bad luck"—to see his bride before the appointed time. Went back to Trotter's and at 3 P.M. amid a shower of rice from women and children congregated at the corner of the house, entered the carriage with four others, and drove back to the hotel. The rest of the company soon followed, the bride and her father coming last. When all were ready (including the minister), the bridegroom, best man, and bridesmaid stood up and the father advanced with the bride and *gave* her to her future husband.

---

[367] A *wagonette* was a pleasure vehicle, with or without a top, holding four or more persons and having at the back two lengthwise seats facing each other and in front one seat running crosswise.

[368] Rob Roy (1671-1734), a famous Scottish outlaw, was immortalized as a romantic hero in Sir Walter Scott's historical novel of the same name. His real name was Robert MacGregor, having received his nickname (Gaelic for "Red Rob") because of his dark red hair.

The ceremony was then performed—a long tedious one it was, too—and here were:

> Two souls with but a single thought,
> Two hearts that beat as one.[369]

Kissing and congratulations were then in order followed by dinner and refreshments. Wine and whiskey were then passed and toasts proposed and responded to. The minister proposed most of them and drank his cup of wine after each. No wonder there is so much drinking in Scotland when the "spiritual advisers" set such an example!

Mr. Trotter had learned that I am a "T.T."[370] soon after I entered Balfron, so he did not insist on my taking any at the marriage. Others near me refused it as well. I believe it had a good effect for so little of the whiskey was drunk that Mr. Trotter said: "When my next daughter marries, I shall not buy any whiskey. See how much is left." Lemonade was brought in instead. The evening was spent in singing and dancing. Several of the young men became quite intoxicated, marring by so doing the enjoyment of the evening. It was not a nice ball at all, although I had one or two very pleasant dances.

Note: I should have mentioned above my introduction to the minister and his wife, both of whom were much surprised to learn that I am a Mormon and that Mormonism is growing.

Slept in another hotel.

Saturday, 1 July 1899

At 7 A.M. I was up and dressed and in a few minutes was out in the morning air. A "Scotch mist" was falling and made it very disagreeable underfoot as well as above. Thinking that none of the Trotter family would be awake, I did not call upon them but went direct to the station in a "machine" with Mr. and Mrs. Trotter and Mr. and Mrs. D. McCallister, all from Glasgow. During our ride on the train to Glasgow, had an excellent conversation on religion. Mr. McCallister gave me his card and extended a cordial invitation for me to visit him. He has investigated nearly every religion, except Mormonism.

Found all well at Glasgow. Boat sails at 5 A.M. tomorrow morning. Passengers go aboard tonight at 8:30.

Sunday, 2 July 1899

Called to see Clark. Mrs. Clark is feeling discouraged again.

---

[369]Eligius Franz Joseph, Freiher von Münch-Bellinghausen, *Ingomar, the Barbarian: A Play in Five Acts*, trans. Maria Lovell (Boston: Walter H. Baker and Co., 1896), 31. He used the pen name of Friedrich Halm.

[370]The abbreviation *T.T.*, that is, the term *teetotaler*, refers to one who pledges and practices total abstinence from alcoholic drinks.

Sunday School at the usual hour. Fast meeting at 2 P.M. Sister William (Martha) Leggat had her baby blessed, Brother Eccles being mouth. The little one was named Joseph Leggat. Dinner at Martha's in honor of the "baby boy."

Usual evening service at 6:30 P.M.

Young and Leatham to Cambuslang.

Monday, 3 July 1899

At 8:45 A.M. Brother Leatham and I left Queen Street Station, bound for Edinburgh to spend five days in the registry office. I promised to do this for Brother Edward, and this is my opportunity to make my promise good. Searched the records from 10:15 to 4 P.M., then visited Brother Miller, and the three of us hunted for lodging. It being holiday week in Edinburgh, this was not an easy task. Mrs. White's rooms were occupied, so were others where we used to stay. Then, too, we desired to secure rooms near the office. After enquiring at about twenty-five places, we secured a room with Mrs. Murray, 2 Leith Street Terrace.

Took supper with Brother Miller. Called on Sister George White and their visitors—Mrs. [Maggie] Urie and Miss [Annie] White. Spent a few moments in social conversation and bid them good-night. Half an hour later we were on a fairway to "dreamy slumber."

Tuesday, 4 July 1899

> The star-spangled banner!
> Oh, long may it wave
> O'er the land of the free
> And the home of the brave!

One of the first sights that caught my eye this morning as I looked out the window was the "Stars and Stripes," our nation's emblem, floating gently in the morning breeze. It was not there because it is the *Fourth*, but it was an easy matter for us to make the association. In fact, Edinburgh is putting on its gala-day attire. The streets are streaming with flags and bunting. The old lion and the Union Jack are seen floating in all directions. Why? Because it's the Fourth. Ah, no, Britain likes America, but she is not so favorable as to celebrate America's natal day. The decorations are for the *Prince*[371] *of Wales*, who makes his royal visit to Scotland this week.

Spent the hours between ten and four in the registry office. Did not have much success.

After four o'clock, according to previous arrangements, a crowd of

---

[371]Edward, Prince of Wales (1841-1910) was the oldest son of Queen Victoria and Prince Albert and was made Prince of Wales by his mother when he was one month old. When his mother died in 1901, he became King Edward VII, with no one in English history serving longer as heir to the throne.

seventeen Americans—some real Americans and others Americans in spirit —climbed Arthur's Seat and, while on the highest eminence overlooking Edinburgh and the surrounding country, we all joined in singing that old patriotic hymn, "The Star-Spangled Banner."[372] Scraps of other national airs were sung, patriotic remarks made, and a general spirit of Yankee enthusiasm aroused. A crowd of people down in the Meadows, a balloon ascension near Leith, the decorations of the streets in the city, and the firing of the soldiers' guns in the Queen's Park seemed appropriate and fitting; and of course, we said all this was going on because it was the *Fourth*!

After eating our oranges and cherries and satisfying our enthusiasm, we descended the hill and walked to Portobello with Nellie Jack. The company consisted of Mrs. Whyte; Miss Lilly Whyte; Miss Annie White; Mrs. Urie; Miss Jack; Elders Leatham, Kerr, Miller, Worthington, and Gardner;[373] Master Joseph White; and the writer. Our walk to Portobello was pleasant, but it was almost too late to be enjoyable.

Boarded the 4:15 P.M. train at Portobello Station and in a few minutes were back again to Edinburgh. Mrs. Murray was waiting for us. Told her we are Mormon elders and had a very pleasant talk with her. She has been acquainted with our people sometime.

Wednesday, 5 July 1899

In registry office from ten till four. Some of the old records are quite a curiosity. Here is a copy of an entry made Feb. 10, 1717:

> Alexander Milne and Isabell Archbald, both in this parish, were contracted. Alex Milne in Mill of Murtle and Alex Archbald cautioners[374] [affirm] that their intended marriage shall be performed under the failure of forty pound Scots. And they were married March 7th, 1717.

Went down to the elders' lodgings. Attended an open-air meeting just off Leith Walk. The Misses White, Mrs. Whyte, Miss Cady, Miss Scott, George White, Mrs. Urie, and all the elders were present. The crowd was quite large and proved to be an attentive audience. Brother Miller called on me to occupy the time. Several promised to come to our meeting next Sunday.

Thursday, 6 July 1899

Edinburgh is now at the height of her celebration. The decorations are all completed, the Prince has already opened the Highland Cattle and Agri-

---

[372]Thomas A. Kerr, Diary, 4 July 1899, wrote: "It was quite a hard pull to get to the top, but when we got there, it was well worth the climb. You caught a splendid view of the surrounding country."

[373]William H. Gardner (1877-1959) was set apart for a mission to Great Britain on 12 May 1899, arriving in Liverpool on 3 June 1899. Within the Scottish Conference he labored in the areas of Dunfermline, Edinburgh, Glasgow, and Paisley. He was released in August 1901.

[374]In the Scottish dialect, a *cautioner* is one who stands as surety for a pledge.

cultural Show, and today he is to be given the freedom of the city. Brother Leatham and I have been granted a holiday and will finish our five days' search on Saturday instead of Friday.

We had made an appointment with the elders and the girls to meet at 10 A.M. at the P. O. [Post Office] Corner, but at the appointed time only Miss Cady and ourselves were there. After waiting about twenty minutes, we followed the immense crowd moving toward the McEwan Hall, where the ceremony of making the Prince a burgess was to take place. We selected a good place near the barricade (which lined either side of the streets through which the Prince was to pass) and waited for His Royal Highness to pass.

We stood for nearly two hours, during which time the streets were packed with people—men, women, and children—all eager to get a glimpse of [the] Heir Apparent. It is said that Carlyle made the statement that, "society is founded on hero worship, that worship of a hero is transcendent admiration of a great man, that great men are [still] admirable, and that at bottom there is nothing else admirable."[375] Edinburgh, today, is certainly indulging in a piece of hero worship, and they are doing it in an excellent manner. But who is this *hero* that they are worshiping? What has he done to merit this expression of goodwill and enthusiasm?

Yesterday's *News* says:

> He is no saintly visitor, no heroic guide to the narrow way that leads to life eternal—rather a frequent pedestrian on the broad path which leads elsewhere; he is no man of great, commanding, intellectual gifts—never in his life was the visitor known to be guilty of an original idea. Intellectual mediocrity marks him for her own. He has never distinguished himself in the battlefield. Although a field marshal in the British Army, he knows nothing of the storm and strife of war. Of all that he is as innocent as the tin soldier of the nursery. The distinguished visitor has had nothing to do with steering the ship of state successfully among political breakers. For what then is this man being honored? What has he done that the dwellers in the most intelligent city in the world should bow the knee in worship before him? If he is not a saintly man, if he is not a thinking man, if he is not a heroic man, if he is not a statesman, why all this adulation? *Because he is the son of his mother!*

The Gordon Highlanders lined each side of the road just inside the barricade. Mounted policeman and policeman on foot were kept busy clearing the roadway and squeezing the people behind the bolted planks. Sometimes they were making an opening in the crowd for some dignitaries going to the hall, again they were making an opening for some pedestrians to get out of the street behind the crowd, or perhaps they would be pulling out of the crowd some poor unfortunate overcome by the pressure and heat. The manner in which these large crowds are controlled and the good order that

---

[375]Thomas Carlyle (1795-1881), a Scottish essayist and historian, wrote *On Heroes, Hero-Worship, and the Heroic in History* in 1841, arguing that social progress is made due to leaders with superior spiritual insight. The quotation is found on p. 19 of the 1892 edition.

prevails is simply admirable!

Well, after waiting about two hours, the Prince passed, and we saw him. He raised his hat—to us, of course—and seemed quite pleased to see us in the crowd (?). He is quite gray. The Duke and Duchess of Buccleuch[376] and Lord Balfour[377] were with him in the carriage, which was drawn by four brown horses and guarded by the Scots Grays. For an account of the procession through the street, see the clipping.[378]

The decorations are beautiful and very extensive. A very pleasing feature about them, and one that adds to their beauty and attractiveness, is the frequent appearance of the "Stars and Stripes." Over the hotels the U.S. flag waves alongside the British ensign and the Union Jack. But not over hotels alone is our flag seen, but hanging right in the midst of the decorations in the street and on houses and large business blocks as well. It shows a friendly feeling—one that America should reciprocate.

After dinner we went down to White's. Held an open-air meeting out at Hay Market. Brother Leatham and Brother Miller were the speakers. Had a very good meeting.

Friday, 7 July 1899

Again in the registry office. At 4:15 P.M. met Mrs. Urie and Miss White and the four of us went out to the show. Although it was the last day and the last hour in the day, still we felt well-paid for going. The horses, cattle, and Shetland ponies were all fine; the seed display was excellent, so also was the machinery.

Our stay here was necessarily short as we had an appointment in the evening at Mrs. Cady's. At 7:30 we were all back at Mrs. Murray's, and about 8:15 P.M. we were at Mrs. Cady's door, being received by Miss Cady, Miss Nellie Jack, and Mrs. Cady. The evening was spent very pleasantly. Strawberries and cream served with lunch. Some of the sorrows (?) of missionary life.

Saturday, 8 July 1899

Spent four hours in office. While eating dinner, received a telegram stating that Dr. [James E.] Talmage was in Glasgow. Attended to some writing. Brother Leatham and I then went down to Edina Place, according to promise, and in company with the other four elders partook of an excel-

---

[376]William Douglas-Scott, the 6th Duke of Buccleuch (1831-1914), had an annual income of £300,000, which was about three times that of the Prince of Wales.

[377]Arthur James Balfour or Lord Balfour (1848-1930) was born at Whittinghame, East Lothian, Scotland, and entered the House of Commons as a Conservative in 1874, becoming first lord of the treasury and leader of the Conservative Party in the Commons in 1891. He served as prime minister from 1902 to 1905. The Balfour Declaration of 1917 expressed official British approval of Zionism.

[378]McKay referred to a newspaper clipping with an article entitled "The Prince of Wales' Visit," which he placed in his diary.

lent *American* dinner, prepared by the Misses White. This was followed by an hour's social chat interspersed with songs, and then at 6:45 P.M. I bade them good-night and went to Glasgow.

The brethren were out visiting. Met Dr. Talmage at the Balmoral Hotel.[379] He will meet with the saints here tomorrow, but I shall return to Edinburgh in the morning to fill appointments there. Everything seems to be going along all right.

Sunday, 9 July 1899

At 8:30 A.M. left Queen Street Station for Edinburgh. Caught the train while it was moving out the station. Had to ride in guard's carriage through the tunnel to Cowlairs. Here was put in a first-class carriage. Arriving in Edinburgh, I went direct to Mrs. Murray's and had a "wee kirk a' tae oorsels."[380] She is much interested in the gospel.

Meeting at 2 P.M. Brother Leatham, Brother Kerr, and I were the speakers. Dinner at Mrs. Whyte's. Evening service was well-attended, the little hall being well-filled. I was asked to occupy the time. A good spirit prevailed, even the strangers present seemed to partake of it. Brother Leatham and I went to Brother and Sister Rhynd's and spent an hour or so with them.

Monday, 10 July 1899

Visited a few of the saints. While we were at Brother Henderson's, word reached us that Brother Mitchell wanted to see me about an important matter. He was released last night by telegram to take charge of company from Holland, sailing from Glasgow next Thursday. He was surprised, though pleased all the same. I regret to see him go, but I suppose it must be. Answered telegram.

Took a sail with Brother Mitchell down to South Queensferry under the famous Forth Bridge (Fig. 58), the most marvelous structure of the kind in the world. The entire time taken in its construction was seven years and the number of workmen employed averaged 4,000. The height of the cantilevers is 360 feet; length of central girders, 350 feet; length of large spans, 1,710 feet; headway above high-water mark at center of spans, 150 feet; depth of bottom of lowest caisson below high-water mark, 89 feet; and the weight of iron and steel used was about 54,000 tons. The total length of the bridge is about one mile and a half, the cost being nearly 3¼ million sterling pounds.

Returning to Leith, we went direct to Sister Whyte's, thence to Sister

---

[379]James E. Talmage, Diary, 8 July 1899, said: "Pleasant call by Bro. David McKay, conference president, who had hastily returned from Edinburgh on hearing of my visit here."

[380]The Scottish phrase *wee kirk a' tae oorsels* means a "small church meeting all to ourselves."

Fig. 58 *The Forth Bridge from North Queensferry.*

White's, remaining there until time to catch the 5 P.M. train, which brought us to Glasgow.

Open-air meeting on Cathedral Square.

Tuesday, 11 July 1899

Attending to duties in Glasgow. Visited Mrs. Rankin and learned to our sorrow that Miriam, her twenty-four-year-old daughter, was dead. We comforted the bereaved as best we could, although our words seemed to furnish but little consolation.[381] The mother is quite heartbroken. She expressed a desire for us to conduct the funeral services next Thursday.

Wednesday, 12 July 1899

In Glasgow. Most of the day spent in writing.

Brother Mitchell's social was held at night in the hall, 4 Carlton Place. We had an excellent time, Brother Mitchell receiving much praise and many words of commendation for his excellent labors as a missionary; and, indeed, he fully merited all that was said. He has been earnest and faithful.

Thursday, 13 July 1899

This is sailing day. On account of the funeral services of Miss Rankin having been appointed for 3 P.M., I cannot attend to the duties at the boat. Brother Mitchell, however, understands all about the company's needs. Bid him good-bye at St. Enoch's Station. Felt somewhat gloomy and worried.

At 3:10 P.M. Elders Eccles and Young reached the Rankin home, and services over the remains of Miriam were begun. They consisted of the

---

[381]John B. Young, Diary, 11 July 1899, added: "Bro. McKay offered a few words of consolation to the bereaved mother. We all knelt down in prayer; Bro. McKay being mouth, he asked the blessings of the Lord to be with the bereaved family."

usual ceremony of the Church—singing, prayer, consoling remarks and admonitions, singing, and benediction. Several strangers were present. At the cemetery, the grave was dedicated before the body was covered. Miriam was a member of the Church. As we bid the bereaved family good-bye, they earnestly asked us to hasten back.

Testimony meeting at night.

Friday, 14 July 1899

Elder Young and I called to see Brother Clark. Cold reception. Stormy argument. He (Clark) felt that he had been unjustly dealt with. Remained with him about two hours, seemingly without influencing him in any way.[382] Shook hands with us, however, upon leaving.

Called on [George] Thomson, apostate, Gallowgate, with Brother Eccles. Had no interview.

About nine or ten o'clock at night Brother and Sister Clark called at our rooms. At first I thought there was more trouble, but the reverse was the case. He asked forgiveness from us, inasmuch as he had injured our feelings. He felt very penitent and desired to do anything possible to become reinstated in the confidence of his brethren. We all parted feeling well and much encouraged.

Saturday, 15 July 1899

Visited Sister Rankin and others.

Special priesthood meeting at night, at which four persons[383] were excommunicated from the Church, our action being sanctioned by the presidency of the European Mission. A good spirit prevailed.

About 10 P.M. took a bicycle ride.

Sunday, 16 July 1899

Usual meetings. At the afternoon meeting the action of the priesthood last night was unanimously sustained by the saints. Dinner at conference house with Mr. and Mrs. Stephenson, Maybole. Supper at Sister Good's.

Monday, 17 July 1899

At the office preparing for a visit to Wales. Called at one or two of the saints' homes. Kindness of Mr. Aitchison—free pass to Liverpool. At 11 P.M. at the Central Station bid good-bye for a time to Brothers Eccles and Young and started for Liverpool. As only two of us were in the compart-

---

[382]John B. Young, Diary, 14 July 1899, added: "Bro. McKay tried to show him his position, reasoned with him very patiently. We stayed with him for nearly two hours. Finally, he calmed down, seemed to feel and realize that we were his brethren."

[383]John Currie, Jr., was excommunicated for adultery and deserting his wife; James Currie for fornication; John Hartley for apostasy; and Elspeth Barnes for adultery.

ment, I took possession of one seat, my unknown friend the other, and each of us was soon lying at full length resting our heads on the pillows rented for night traveling. Stopped at Carlisle about three-fourths hour.

Tuesday, 18 July 1899

At 5:50 A.M., after a somewhat wearisome night's journey, I arrived at Lime Street Station, Liverpool. After a refreshing wash and *brush* at the station toilet rooms, started at once for "42" [Islington Street]. The brethren were all in bed, so I did not disturb them but took a morning stroll.

About 7:30 seeing signs of life at the office, I knocked at the door and received a hearty welcome from President Lyman,[384] President McMurrin, and Brothers McFarlane, [Joseph D.] Holther, and [Attewall] Wootton. Remained at "42," counseling with the presidency until 3:20 P.M., at which hour I left for Cardiff. President McMurrin accompanied me to the station and had he not been so unwell would have gone to Cardiff.

The ride through rural England toward the hills of South Wales was very much enjoyed. Passed through Hereford (from whence come the Hereford cattle), changed at Pontypool, arrived in Cardiff about 8:30. Met Brother [Samuel T.] Clarke at 188 Cathays Terrace, the mission address.

I had come to Wales for the express purpose of attending the Eisteddfod[385] and of visiting relatives whom I supposed lived in Aberdare. The information in my possession as to their whereabouts was very meager, and had I depended upon that alone, subsequent developments proved that I should have left Wales a disappointed boy. But, providentially or otherwise, I met an Elder [David B.] Thomas, who had accidentally met a women who had been inquiring about a "McKay in Scotland." "She had a letter from Jeanette McKay, Huntsville," he said, "and she is expecting you to call on her." This was just the information wanted and, as I found out afterward, had I not obtained it, I might be vainly looking around Aberdare until now (August ninth) for the persons wanted live in Cefn Coed by Merthyr.

Before retiring Tuesday night met many of the elders in the conference.

Wednesday, 19 July 1899

This is a day long to be remembered! At 10 A.M. several of the elders and I went to the Welsh National Eisteddfod, securing at first only an entrance ticket. Brother Clarke pointed out the renowned Dr. Parry[386] and, having a kind letter of introduction to him from Professor Stephens,[387] I

---

[384]Platte D. Lyman, Diary, 18 July 1899, recorded: "Pres. D. O. McKay of the Scottish Conference came in on his way to Wales on business and a visit to relatives."

[385]The *eisteddfod* was a competitive festival of the arts, especially in poetry and singing.

[386]Joseph Parry (1841-1903) was a Welsh composer and music critic and from 1888 until his death was lecturer in music at University College, Cardiff.

[387]Evan Stephens (1854-1930) was a Mormon composer and conductor. Stephens served as director of the Mormon Tabernacle Choir from 1890 to 1916. The current LDS hymnal has

concluded at once that this was my opportunity. He received us heartily, talked very freely, and accompanied us around the park, introducing us to some of his friends whom we chanced to meet. Among these were two young women—[the] Misses Edwards from Scranton, Pennsylvania. They sang at the World's Fair, Chicago, in the choir competing for the first prize with the Salt Lake [Tabernacle] Choir. We spent most of the day with them.

One of the most notable features of the exercises this day was the singing by the Ladies' Choir. Six of them competed. Their singing was grand! We sat for seven hours listening to the competitions and awarding of prizes. Our seats were comfortable and in an excellent part of the pavilion, but they became very hard before five-thirty in the afternoon. In the evening the immense pavilion was crowded with an eager audience assembled to hear *Elijah*[388] performed by 500 choir voices accompanied by 100 instruments!

Our friends from Pennsylvania were near us again, and we had the pleasure of meeting their father—Dr. Edwards,[389] the second presiding officer at the Eisteddfod. During the ten-minute interval, I had a conversation on the gospel with the Edwardses.

There was a scene during the concert that bordered on pandemonium! Miss Davis, a sweet young soprano, had just sung a solo, which the chorus took up before the applause ceased. The audience wanted an encore; the conductor wanted to carry on the theme in the music: so it was audience against conductor and choir.

Thursday, 20 July 1899

About 10 A.M. Elder Thomas and I left Cardiff for Merthyr. The ride through the valleys and over the hills was quite pleasant, made all the more so by the thoughts that every mile passed took me nearer the birthplace of Mother—a spot that seemed dear even before it was seen.

From Merthyr to Cefn Coed we rode in a "machine." A few minutes walk up the High Street and a turn to the left past the old Unitarian Church brought us near to the home of Mrs. Richard Harris, a relative whom Brother Thomas had previously met. She seemed pleased to meet me, and it goes without saying that I was pleased to meet her. A hundred-and-one questions were asked and answered—most of them relating to the early history of the family, the changes made, and of their present condition. While we were eating the lunch prepared by Aunt Janet, her daughter Margaret (now Mrs. [blank]) and a Mrs. Thomas from Dowlais came in. Mar-

---

nineteen pieces that he authored, composed, or adapted.

[388]Felix Mendelssohn (1809-1847), a German Romantic composer, wrote the oratorio *Elijah* in 1846 and it was first performed in Birmingham, England.

[389]Thomas Edwards (1848-1927) was born in Wales and emigrated to America in 1870 to be the Congregational minister of churches in Ohio and Pennsylvania. He won many eisteddfodic poetry prizes, composed hymn tunes, and was a prominent conductor.

garet seemed at once to be a charming, sociable, little cousin, and planned my visits during my stay with a decision and ability that were surprising.

It will occupy too much space and consume more time than I now have to spare to tell about my meeting with Aunt Betsy [390]and her family and the hearty welcome each accorded me. The afternoon was spent in calling on old friends of the family. It was very interesting to note the pleased, surprised expressions.[391]

❖   ❖   ❖   ❖   ❖   ❖   ❖   ❖   ❖   ❖   ❖   ❖   ❖   ❖

Editors' Concluding Note

This marks the end of David O. McKay's missionary diaries. The last entry is for 20 July 1899, which McKay wrote on or soon after 9 August 1899. McKay returned to Glasgow on 26 July 1899 and that same evening spoke at an open-air meeting.[392] McKay did not leave Scotland until a month later. He spent these last weeks in (1) visiting and saying good-bye to members in Glasgow, Edinburgh, Aberdeen, and other areas in Scotland; (2) speaking at various meetings[393] to missionaries, members, and investigators; (3) instructing James K. Miller concerning his duties as the incoming president of the Scottish Conference; and (4) packing his belongings.

David O. McKay's last night in Scotland was an occasion for a farewell celebration. The party, consisting of songs, recitations, readings, and a dance, was held in a rented hall during the evening of Friday, 25 August 1899. The proselyting elders gave McKay a walking cane[394] and the members gave him a dressing case. President James L. McMurrin commented: "It was very gratifying to hear the warm expressions of friendship towards him [McKay] and to note the high esteem in which he was held by all who knew him."[395] The farewell program finally adjourned at 3:00 A.M., but there were a dozen missionaries and only one bed in the conference house.

---

[390]Elizabeth Jane Evans (1856-1890) was born in Cefn Coed, Glamorganshire, Wales, and married Albern Allen in 1882.

[391]Though it is not stated in the diary, McKay located the home where his mother, Jennette Eveline Evans McKay, was born. See David Lawrence McKay, *My Father, David O. McKay,* ed. Lavina Fielding Anderson (Salt Lake City: Deseret Book Co., 1989), 34.

[392]John B. Young, Diary, 26 July 1899, indicated that McKay preached on general and individual salvation.

[393]At the priesthood meeting on 7 August 1899, McKay said that "he had learned to love his brethren and sisters, which had indeed made his missionary labors the happiest time of his life. Referred to his departure, the leave-taking of his friends and brethren causing him pain, even with the prospects in view of a happy reunion with loved ones. Trusted all would continue faithfully in the path of duty." See the Scottish Conference Records, the British Mission, LR17716, ser. 11, located in the LDS Church Archives, Historical Department, The Church of Jesus Christ of Latter-day Saints, Salt Lake City.

[394]John B. Young, Diary, 25 August 1899, indicated that the cane had a gold band with the inscription: "To our Brother David O. McKay, from his co-laborers in the Scottish Conference."

[395]James L. McMurrin, "A Trip to Scotland," *The Latter-day Saints' Millennial Star* 61 (7 September 1899): 574.

Fig. 59 S.S. *City of Rome*.

Most had to sleep on the floor.[396] As it turned out, McKay, Miller, and Gould stayed up all night, talking the whole time.[397]

On 26 August 1899 McKay departed at 10:00 A.M., going by train to Greenock and then boarding S.S. *City of Rome* (Fig. 59) for his voyage home to Utah. With him on the ship were twenty-one other Latter-day Saints—four other missionaries, six tourists, and eleven British immigrants. After five days on the ocean, his ship collided with a huge iceberg near Cape Race in Newfoundland. The following is McKay's account of this frightening experience:

> Last evening [31 August 1899] about six o'clock we were sailing along at a good rate of speed through quite a dense fog, when suddenly all on board were terrified by the violent stoppage of the ship and a terrible crash. The jar threw passengers against the walls or on the floor. Dishes were hurled in a broken heap. My heart seemed to jump to my throat as all the horrors of a shipwreck rushed before me. With a cry, "We're on the rocks," I rushed on deck. We had collided with an iceberg, huge pieces of which we could now see floating in the seething waters around us. Providentially for us, the captain saw the floating obstacle in time to have the engines reversed before the boat ran in collision. Much credit is due Captain [Hugh] Young for his prompt action.
>
> An inspection showed that the vessel was uninjured. She had stood the shock bravely, and in a few hours we were slowly moving along again. But oh, the terror depicted on the countenances of many of the passengers, and not alone among the women either. Strong, robust men turned deathly pale as they sensed the probable peril we were in. The nervous state of the women was pitiful in the extreme; yet, to their credit be it said, under the circumstances they controlled their actions very wisely.
>
> All around, the water was in commotion; and, in its turbulence, seemed to be eager to swallow everything in one angry seething whirlpool. Every movement of the vessel, every noise on board seemed to produce an ominous feeling confirming one's fears of disaster. It is at such critical moments as these that one fully appreciates the comforting prophetic assurance, "You shall go in peace, and return in safety," spoken by [Seymour B. Young] a servant of God. The experience was truly a dreadful one and one never to be forgotten.[398]

---

[396]Thomas A. Kerr, Diary, 25 August 1899, explained his good fortune: "Three got the bed and the rest the floor—I happened to be one of the three."

[397]William S. Gould, Diary, 25-26 August 1899.

[398]David O. McKay, letter of 1 September 1899, in "Abstract of Correspondence," *Millennial Star* 61 (21 September 1899): 604. For two other accounts of this collision with an iceberg, see the Editors' Introduction, p. xl, above. McKay arrived back in Utah on 10 September 1899.

APPENDIX A

THE PATRIARCHAL BLESSING
OF DAVID O. McKAY[399]

BROTHER DAVID Oman McKay, thou art in thy youth and need instruction. Therefore, I say unto thee, be taught of thy parents the way of life and salvation, that at an early day you may be prepared for a responsible position, for the eye of the Lord is upon thee. He has a work for thee to do in which thou shalt see much of the world, assist in gathering scattered Israel, and also to labor in the ministry. It shall be thy lot to sit in counsel with thy brethren and to preside among the people and exhort the saints to faithfulness.

Therefore, again I say unto thee, remember to honor thy parents and hold sacred their counsel and prepare thyself for events to come, and thou shalt go forth wheresoever thou art sent by the Priesthood, like a roaring lion in the forest, none to stay thee, for the power of God shall rest upon thee, and give thee strength, wisdom, and understanding so long as thou art in the discharge of thy duty, and thou shalt bring many to a knowledge of the truth, for thou shalt confound the wisdom of the wicked and set at naught the counsels of the unjust.

Study the law of nature and follow the promptings of the still small voice of the Comforter, and thou shalt be healthy and strong in body and mind, and thy days and years shall be many, and in due time thou shalt have a companion who shall be a helpmeet unto thee; thy posterity shall be numerous, and bear thy name in honorable remembrance from generation to generation. Therefore, put thy trust in the Lord. Thou shalt also be mighty in healing the sick by the laying on of hands, for this shall be thy gift

---

[399]David O. McKay's patriarchal blessing was given by Patriarch John Smith on 27 July 1887 at Huntsville, Weber County, Utah Territory, and is printed from a copy in the possession of his son, Robert R. McKay. The first paragraph of this blessing is found in Jeanette McKay Morrell, *Highlights in the Life of President David O. McKay* (Salt Lake City: Deseret Book Co., 1966), 26.

through prayer and faith; thou shalt also, if necessary, perform miracles in the name of the Lord Jesus Christ.

Thou art of Ephraim and entitled to the blessings of Abraham, Isaac, and Jacob, with the gifts of the Priesthood. It shall be thy province, also, to feed many with both spiritual and temporal food. Therefore, look forward to the future with a prayerful heart and an inquiring mind and all shall be well with thee, both here and hereafter. This blessing I seal upon thee in the name of Jesus Christ and I seal thee up unto eternal life, to come forth in the morning of the first resurrection a savior among thy kindred. Even so, amen.

APPENDIX B

GLOSSARY OF SCOTTISH TERMS

aboot: *adv.*, about.
aff: *adv.*, off.
ain: *adj.*, own.
ance: *adv.*, once.
ane: *adj.*, one.
auld: *adj.*, old.
awa: *adv.*, away.
awfu: *adj.*, awful.
bairn: *n.*, child, offspring.
bit: *adj.*, small, short.
bluid: *n.*, blood.
bonnie, bonny, bonie, bony: *adj.*, beautiful, attractive, or pleasant to look at.
bousin: *pres.part.*, drink heavily.
brae: *n.*, a hillside, especially along a river.
brent: *adj.*, smooth, unwrinkled.
brig: *n.*, bridge.
buddy: *n.*, a person, a human being; a puny or little person.
burn: *n.*, a brook or stream.
canna: *v.*, can not.
carlin: *n.*, a witch.
cauld: *n.*, cold.
cautioner: *n.*, one who stands as surety for a pledge.
champit tatties: *n.*, mashed potatoes.
cheer: *n.*, chair.
claught: *v.*, claw, tear, scratch.
close: *n.*, entryway to an apartment house, passageway giving access to the common stair.
corn: *n.*, oats; a single grain.
cousie: *n.*, a self-acting incline on which one or more filled, descending coal-boxes pull up a corresponding number of empty boxes.
crack: *v.*, chat, talk, or gossip.
deed: *adv.*, indeed.
didna: *v.*, did not.
dinna: *v.*, do not.
doon: *adv.*, down.
doot: *v.*, doubt.
eyne: *n.pl.*, eyes.
fithers: *n.pl.*, feathers.
flit: *v.*, leave a place, move house.
fou: *adj.*, full; drunk, intoxicated.
frae: *prep.*, from.
gay: *adv.*, very, rather, considerably.
gie: *v.*, give.
gloaming: *n.*, evening twilight, dusk.
guid: *adj.*, good.
gray or **Scotch gray:** *n.*, a louse.
hame: *n.*, home.
haud: *v.*, hold.
Hogmanay: *n.*, the last day of the year; a New Year's Eve gift.
hoolet: *n.* owl, owlet.
hoose: *n.*, house.
ken: *v.*, know.
kirk: *n.*, church.

lane: *adj.*, lone, solitary.

lang: *adj.*, long.

lass or **lassie:** *n.*, young girl.

linn: *n.*, waterfall, cataract.

loch: *n.*, a lake, pond.

lum: *n.*, chimney; a tall silk hat, a top hat.

mate: *n.*, a mat; an underlay for a bed; a bedcover.

maun: *aux v.*, must.

mind: *v.*, remember.

mon: *n.*, man.

na, nae: *adv.*, not.

naething: *pron.*, nothing.

Nair-Day: *n.*, New Year's Day; a gift, or a drink or food given in hospitality on New Year's Day.

nappy: *n.*, a drinking vessel.

nicht: *n.*, night.

noo: *adv.*, now.

oor: *pron.*, our.

oorsels: *pron.*, ourselves.

ochanee: *interj.*, expressing sorrow or regret.

oot: *adv.*, out.

ower: *prep.*, over.

piece: *n.*, a piece of food, a snack, usually a piece of bread or scone with butter and jam.

puir: *adj.*, poor.

rin: *v.*, run.

sair: *adj.*, sore, severe.

sheen: *n.*, shoes.

soft: *adj.*, mild, not frosty; wet, rainy, damp.

souter: *n.*, a shoemaker or cobbler.

strathspey: *n.*, a Highland dance, performed by four persons.

tatties: *n.*, potatoes.

tak: *v.*, take.

tae: *prep.*, to.

toun, toon: *n.*, a village, town.

traveler: *n.*, a head-louse.

twa: *numeral*, two.

twad: *v.*, it would.

unco: *adj.*, strange, awful, remarkable, extraordinary.

wadna: *v.*, would not.

water: *n.*, a stream, brook, or river, esp. a small one.

wee: *adj.*, small or little.

weel: *adv.*, well.

wham: *pron.*, whom.

wi: *prep.*, with.

writer: *n.*, a law agent, an attorney, a solicitor.

wunna: *v.*, will not.

ye: *pron.*, you.

yer: *adj.*, your.

APPENDIX C

"WHAT E'ER THOU ART, ACT WELL THY PART"[400]

David O. McKay

IN MY STUDY I have a little book that contains what I call "literary nuggets," taken from Church works, from poets, writers such as Scott, Burns, Longfellow, and others. May I share several of them with you?

"The greatest battle of life is fought within the silent chambers of the soul."

I ask you fellow workers of the Church to do again what undoubtedly you have done frequently—sit down and commune with yourself. Life is a battle for you and for me each day. Fight this battle with yourself and decide upon your course of action regarding what your duty is to your family, to your Church, and to your fellow men.

Associated on that page was this comment found in *The Simple Life*:

> First, be of your own country, your own city, your own home . . . your own workshop. Then, if you can, set out from this to go beyond it. That is the plain and natural order, and a man must fortify himself with very valid reasons to arrive at reversing it. Each one is occupied with something else too often than what concerns him. He is absent from his post. He ignores his trade. That is what complicates life, and it would be so simple for each one to be about his own matters.

Decide what your duty is, ever remembering that the greatest battle of life is fought within the silent chambers of your own soul.

The second that I picked out is this: "What e'er thou art, act well thy

---

[400]This essay is reprinted from David O. McKay, "What E'er Thou Art, Act Well Thy Part," *The Improvement Era* 62 (October 1959): 726-27, 770-71, with the permission of the Church of Jesus Christ of Latter-day Saints.

part." That, of course, applies to moral and lawful endeavors and not to harmful or villainous actions. That influenced me more than fifty-nine years ago when, as I have told some of you before, Peter G. Johnston and I were walking around Stirling Castle in Scotland. I was discouraged. I was just starting my first mission. I had been snubbed that day in tracting. I was homesick, and we walked around the Stirling Castle, really not doing our duty. As we reentered the town I saw a building, half-finished, and from the sidewalk to my surprise I saw an inscription carved in stone on [over] the lintel of the front door. I said to Brother Johnston, "I want to go over there and see what that inscription says." I was not more than halfway up the pathway leading to it when this message struck me: "What e'er thou art, act well thy part."

As I rejoined my companion and told him what I had read, do you know what came to my mind first? The custodian at the University of Utah, from which school I had just graduated. I realized then that I had just as great a respect for that man as I had for any professor in whose class I had sat. He acted well his part. I recalled how he helped us with the football suits, how he helped us with some of our lessons. He was unassuming, unostentatious, but did his duty well. To this day I hold respect for him.

When an ordinary man is set apart in his community as a sheriff, there is something added to him. When a policeman holds up his hand, you stop. There is something more about him than just an individual; there is the power that is given him.

And so it is throughout life. No man can be given a position without being enhanced. It is a reality. So, too, is the power of the priesthood. It was so real in the days of Peter that Simon the sorcerer, who was making money by his tricks, wanted to buy that which Peter had, and offered the apostles money: "Give me also this power, that on whomsoever I lay hands, he may receive the Holy Ghost."

Oh, what a denunciation Peter gave him! "Thy money perish with thee, because thou has thought that the gift of God may be purchased with money. . . . For I perceive that thou art in the gall of bitterness, and in the bond of iniquity. . . . Repent therefore of this thy wickedness, and pray God, if perhaps the thought of thine heart may be forgiven thee."

And so strong was the denunciation given by Peter that Simon the Sorcerer said, "Pray ye to the Lord for me that none of these things which ye have spoken come upon me" (Acts 8:19-24).

There was no doubt in Peter's mind about the reality of the power of the Holy Ghost. "What e'er thou art, act well thy part."

The third: ". . . there is none other name under heaven given among men, whereby we must be saved" (Ibid., 4:12). It was a most dramatic scene when that sentence was uttered, and so you have this thought expressed as follows: The world's hope and destiny are centered in the Man of Galilee, our Lord and Savior, Jesus Christ.

In the moment when you are fighting the battle of the day, will you look introspectively and see whether you really believe that? Paul Kane once asked this question:

> Is Jesus only a legendary figure in history, a saint to be painted in the stained glass of church windows, a sort of sacred fairy not to be approached and hardly to be mentioned by name, or is he still what he was when he was in the flesh, a reality, a man of like passions with ourselves, an elder brother, a guide, a counselor, a comforter, a great voice calling to us out of the past to live nobly, to guide bravely, and keep up our courage to the last.

What is he to you, my fellow laborers? When you kneel down to pray [at night, do you feel his nearness,][401] his personality, that he hears you; do you feel a power that operates perhaps as the radio or a greater power so that you feel that you are communing with him? You are not just saying your prayers, you are praying. Do you know that he is real, our Savior, the Head of the Church? I know that he is!

He is a weak man who flies into a passion, whether he is working a machine, plowing, writing, or whatever he may be doing. A man of the priesthood should not fly into a passion. Learn to be dignified. You cannot picture Christ flying into a passion. Indignant with sin? Yes. He drove out the moneychangers when they insulted God and defiled the temple. Yes, but he was so dignified and noble that when he stood before Pilate that ruler was impelled to say: "Behold, the man" [John 19:5].

"What e'er thou art, act well thy part."

---

[401]The *Improvement Era* article accidentally skipped one line and the words in brackets are added from the version of McKay's talk in *Conference Reports*, October 1954, 82-85.

Fig. 60 *Apostle David O. McKay.*

SELECTED BIBLIOGRAPHY

Manuscripts

Anderson, Archibald R. Collection, Accession 1735, located in the Manuscripts Division, J. Willard Marriott Library, University of Utah, Salt Lake City.

Calder, Hyrum B. Collection, Accession 1730, located in the Manuscripts Division, J. Willard Marriott Library, University of Utah, SLC.

Edward, John T. Collection, Accession 1710, located in the Manuscripts Division, J. Willard Marriott Library, University of Utah, SLC.

Faddies, Alexander. Collection, Accession 1757, located in the Manuscripts Division, J. Willard Marriott Library, University of Utah, SLC.

Gould, William S. Collection, Accession 1674, located in the Manuscripts Division, J. Willard Marriott Library, University of Utah, SLC.

Johnston, Peter G. Collection, Accession 1755, located in the Manuscripts Division, J. Willard Marriott Library, University of Utah, SLC.

Kerr, Thomas A. Collection, Accession 1751, located in the Manuscripts Division, J. Willard Marriott Library, University of Utah, SLC.

Leishman, Thomas A. Collection, Accession 1740, located in the Manuscripts Division, J. Willard Marriott Library, University of Utah, SLC.

McKay, David O. Collection, Manuscript 668, located in the Manuscripts Division, J. Willard Marriott Library, University of Utah, SLC.

Mitchell, Joseph H. Collection, Accession 1770, located in the Manuscripts Division, J. Willard Marriott Library, University of Utah, Salt Lake City, with the original diaries being at the LDS Church Archives.

Nisbet, William P. Collection, Accession 1754, located in the Manuscripts Division, J. Willard Marriott Library, University of Utah, SLC.

Thompson, Henry B. Collection, Accession 1743, located in the Manuscripts Division, J. Willard Marriott Library, University of Utah, Salt Lake City, with the original diaries being at the LDS Church Archives.

Young, John B. Collection, Accession 1738, located in the Manuscripts Division, J. Willard Marriott Library, University of Utah, SLC.

Books and Articles

Allen, James B. "David O. McKay." In *The Presidents of the Church: Biographcal Essays*, ed. Leonard J. Arrington, 275-313. Salt Lake City: Deseret Book, 1986.

Anderson, Joseph. *Prophets I Have Known: Joseph Anderson Shares Life's Experiences*. Salt Lake City: Deseret Book Co., 1973.

"Apostle David Oman McKay." *The Juvenile Instructor* 41 (15 June 1906): 353-54.

"Apostle David Oman McKay." *The Latter-day Saints' Millennial Star* 68 (9 August 1906): 498-99.

Armstrong, Richard N. *The Rhetoric of David O. McKay, Mormon Prophet*. New York: P. Lang, 1993.

Brown, Hugh B. "President David O. McKay." *The Improvement Era* 65 (September 1962): 639-41, 665-66.

_____. "God Makes a Giant among Men." *The Improvement Era* 73 (February 1970): 88-91.

Clark, J. Reuben, Jr. "Our Tribute to President McKay." *The Improvement Era* 56 (September 1953): 641.

"David O. McKay Becomes Ninth President of the Church." *The Improvement Era* 54 (May 1951); 324-25, 363.

"David O. McKay: Highlights of His Life and Works." *The Improvement Era* 66 (September 1963): 736-45.

Evans, Richard L. "David O. McKay: Portrait of a President." *The Improvement Era* 54 (June 1951): 400-403, 458.

Gibbons, Francis M. *David O. McKay: Apostle to the World, Prophet of God*. Salt Lake City: Deseret Book Co., 1986.

Hanks, Marion D. "The Soul of a Prophet." *The Improvement Era* 71 (September 1968): 3-5.

"Inspirational Stories from the Life of David O. McKay." *The Improvement Era* 69 (September 1966): 768-72, 816.

Josephson, Marba C. "At Home with the McKays." *The Improvement Era* 56 (September 1953): 644-45, 680, 683.

McKay, David Lawrence. "Keeping a Promise." *The Instructor* 105 (August 1970): 275.

_____. "Remembering Father and Mother, President David O. McKay and Sister Emma Ray Riggs McKay." *Ensign* 14 (August 1984): 34-40.

_____. *My Father, David O. McKay*. Ed. Lavina Fielding Anderson. Salt Lake City: Deseret Book Co., 1989.

McKay, David O. "Lime-light Views: Scottish." *The Latter-day Saints' Millennial Star* 60 (11 August 1898): 509.

_____. "Death of Elder David M. Muir." *The Latter-day Saints' Millennial Star* 60 (27 October 1898): 682-84.

_____. "A Testimony." *The Latter-day Saints' Millennial Star* 60 (24 November 1898): 747; reprinted in *The Improvement Era* 68 (September 1965): 799.

_____. "Abstract of Correspondence." *The Latter-day Saints' Millennial Star* 61 (20 April 1899): 244.

_____. "Abstract of Correspondence." *The Latter-day Saints' Millennial Star* 61 (21 September 1899): 604.

_____. "The Glory of All Creation." *The Latter-day Saints' Millennial Star* 68 (28 June 1906): 416.

_____. "True Beauty." *Young Woman's Journal* 17 (August 1906): 360-62.

_____. "How to Teach." *Improvement Era* 20 (December 1916): 179-80.

_____. "Disobedience to God's Laws: The Cause of World's Misery." *The Latter-day Saints' Millennial Star* 79 (20 September 1917): 593-98.

_____. "Jesus Christ, the Son of God and the Redeemer." *The Latter-day Saints' Millennial Star* 80 (17 October 1918): 657-61.

_____. "Exhortation to Youth of Israel." *Young Woman's Journal* 29 (December 1918): 659-64.

_____. *Ancient Apostles*. Salt Lake City: Deseret Sunday School, 1918.

_____. "Teacher Training Classes." *Young Woman's Journal* 30 (July 1919): 371-78.

_____. "Reaching the Souls of Men." *Improvement Era* 23 (November 1919): 18-22.

_____. "The Effect of Revelation on Man's Creed." *Improvement Era* 23 (April 1920): 506-13.

_____. "What the World Needs Today." *Young Woman's Journal* 31 (July 1920): 386-88.

_____. "Testimony of the Gospel." *The Latter-day Saints' Millennial Star* 83 (24 March 1921): 177-79.

_____. "Our Lady Missionaries." *Young Woman's Journal* 32 (September 1921): 503-507.

_____. "Jerusalem—Then and Now!" *The Latter-day Saints' Millennial Star* 83 (22 December 1921): 801-805.

_____. "The Church and Missionary Work." *Improvement Era* 26 (December 1922): 185-89.

_____. "Two Significant Statements." *The Deseret News*, Church Section, 27 October 1934, 1, 8.

_____. "President Grant Still Young at Eighty." *The Improvement Era* 39 (November 1936): 661.

_____. "President Grant: The Benefactor." *The Improvement Era* 44 (November 1941): 655.

_____. "Joseph Smith—Prophet, Seer, and Revelator." *The Improvement Era* 45 (January 1942): 12-13, 54-56.

_____. "The Church and the Present War." *The Improvement Era* 45 (May 1942): 276, 340-42.

_____. "Nobility of Character Essential to a Great Nation." *The Improvement Era* 46 (May 1943): 270-71, 313-14.

_____. "Sylvester Q. Cannon." *The Improvement Era* 46 (August 1943): 465, 509-510.

_____. "The Prophet Joseph: On Doctrine and Organization." *The Improvement Era* 48 (January 1945): 14-15, 45-47.

_____. "President Heber J. Grant." *The Improvement Era* 48 (June 1945): 334, 361.

_____. "Honoring the Utah Pioneers—and Lasting Values." *The Improvement Era* 50 (May 1947): 270-71, 345-48.

_____. "Faith Triumphant." *The Improvement Era* 50 (August 1947): 507, 562-63.

_____. "An Exemplar to All Men: A Birthday Greeting to President George Albert Smith." *The Improvement Era* 53 (April 1950): 267.

_____. "The Greatest Responsibility—The Greatest Honor." *The Improvement Era* 54 (June 1951): 406-407.

_____. "The Transforming Power of Faith in Jesus Christ." *The Improvement Era* 54 (June 1951): 406-409, 478.

_____. "President McKay Explains Policy in Choosing Aides." *The Improvement Era* 54 (June 1951): 464.

_____. "This Christmastide." *The Improvement Era* 54 (December 1951): 861.

_____. "Counteracting Pernicious Ideas and Subversive Teachings." *Improvement Era* 54 (December 1951): 874-76.

_____. "The Nearness of Our Father." *The Improvement Era* 55 (September 1952): 629-30.

_____. *Gospel Ideals*. Salt Lake City: Improvement Era, 1953.

_____. "Some Characteristics of 'The Kingdom.'" *The Improvement Era* 57 (August 1954): 557-58.

_____. "Righteousness: Key to World Peace." *The Improvement Era* 58 (June 1955): 395-97.

_____. *Cherished Experiences from the Writings of President David O. McKay*. Comp. Clare Middlemiss. Salt Lake City: Deseret Book Co., 1955.

_____. *Pathways to Happiness*. Comp. Llewelyn R. McKay. Salt Lake City: Bookcraft, 1957.

_____. "My Mother." *The Improvement Era* 61 (May 1958): 303.

_____. "The Two Waifs." In *Christmas Silhouettes: Two Christmas Stories*, by President David O. McKay and Llewelyn R. McKay, 1-13. Salt Lake City: Bookcraft, 1958.

_____. "What E'er Thou Art, Act Well Thy Part." *The Improvement Era* 62 (October 1959): 726-27, 770-71.

_____. *Secrets of a Happy Life*. Comp. Llewelyn R. McKay. Englewood Cliffs, NJ: Prentice-Hall, Inc., 1960.

_____. "A Personal Testimony." *The Improvement Era* 65 (September 1962): 628-29.

_____. *Treasures of Life*. Comp. Clare Middlemiss. Salt Lake City: Deseret Book Co., 1962.

_____. "Over the Years." *The Improvement Era* 67 (September 1964): 716-17.

_____. *True to the Faith*. Comp. Llewelyn R. McKay. Salt Lake City: Bookcraft, 1966.

_____. *Man May Know for Himself: Teachings of President David O. Mc-*

Kay. Comp. Clare Middlemiss. Salt Lake City: Deseret Book Co.,
1967.

_____. "Priesthood Holders to Be Examples in Daily Life as Representa-
tives of the Most High." *The Improvement Era* 71 (December 1968):
84-86.

_____. *Stepping Stones to an Abundant Life.* Comp. Llewelyn R. McKay.
Salt Lake City: Deseret Book Co., 1971.

_____. *Choose You This Day.* [Compiled from the writings of David O.
McKay.] Salt Lake City: Deseret Sunday School Union of the Church
of Jesus Christ of Latter-day Saints, 1971.

_____. *"My Young Friends . . ." President McKay Speaks to Youth.* Comp.
Llewelyn R. McKay. Salt Lake City: Bookcraft, 1973.

McKay, Llewelyn R. *Home Memories of President David O. McKay.* Salt
Lake City: Deseret Book Co., 1956.

McKay, Robert R. "A Son's Tribute to the Prophet." *The Improvement Era*
70 (June 1967): 79-80.

Middlemiss, Clare. "With the President in Europe." *The Improvement Era*
58 (November 1955): 799-800.

Morrell, Jeanette McKay. "Ancestry of President David O. McKay." *The
Relief Society Magazine* 40 (September 1953): 574-81.

_____. "Boyhood of President David O. McKay." *The Relief Society Mag-
azine* 40 (October 1953): 656-62.

_____. "Life of President David O. McKay." *The Relief Society Magazine*
40 (November-December 1953): 730-37, 813-20.

_____. *Highlights in the Life of President David O. McKay.* Salt Lake City:
Deseret Book Co., 1966.

Moyle, Henry D. "President McKay—Exemplar of Missionary Service."
The Improvement Era 64 (July 1961): 511-12, 520.

Peale, Norman Vincent. "A Man with a Secret." *The Improvement Era* 68
(September 1965): 767-69.

Richards, Stephen L. "On the Eightieth Birthday of Our President." *The
Improvement Era* 56 (September 1953): 640.

Schluter, Fredric E. *A Convert's Tribute to President David O. McKay.* Salt
Lake City: Deseret Book Co., 1964.

Stewart, John J. *Remembering the McKays: A Biographical Sketch with Pictures of David O. and Emma Ray McKay.* Salt Lake City: Deseret
Book Co., 1970.

Tanner, N. Eldon. "True Exemplar of the Life of Christ." *The Improvement Era* 73 (February 1970): 91-93.

Terry, Keith. *David O. McKay: Prophet of Love.* Santa Barbara, CA: But-
terfly Publishing Inc., 1980.

West, Emerson Roy. *Latter-day Prophets: Their Lives, Teachings, and Testimonies.* American Fork, UT: Covenant Communications, Inc., 1997.

Woodger, Mary Jane. "Educational Ideas and Practices of David O. McKay,
1880-1940." Ed.D. diss., Brigham Young University, 1997.

Fig. 61 *President David O. McKay.*

INDEX

Words are added in parentheses to help identify or geographically locate the entries. Numbers in **bold** indicate an illustration on that page.

ABOUT THE EDITORS

STAN LARSON has a B.A., M.A., and M.L.S. from Brigham Young University and a Ph.D. from the University of Birmingham in England. He is the author of *Quest for the Gold Plates: Thomas Stuart Ferguson's Archaeological Search for the Book of Mormon* and has edited nine other books, including B. H. Roberts's *The Truth, The Way, The Life*.

PATRICIA LARSON was born and raised in Bristol, England. She is the illustrator for *Modern Echoes from Ancient Hills: Our Greek Heritage*. The Larsons are members of the Jordan Oaks Fourth Ward in West Jordan, Utah, and have five children—Tim, James, Dan, Debbie, and Melissa—and six lovely grandchildren—Andrew, Brittany, Caitlin, Samantha, Mitchell, and Emma.